Spenser and the Discourses of Reformation England is a wide-ranging exploration of the relationships among literature, religion, and politics in Renaissance England. Richard Mallette demonstrates how one of the great masterpieces of English literature, Edmund Spenser's *The Faerie Queene*, reproduces, criticizes, parodies, and transforms the discourses of England during that remarkable political and literary era.

According to Mallette, *The Faerie Queene* not only represents Reformation values but also challenges, questions, and frequently undermines Protestant assumptions. Building upon recent scholarship, particularly new historicism, Protestant poetics, feminism, and gender theory, this ambitious study traces *The Faerie Queene*'s linkage of religion to political and social realms. Mallette's study expands traditional theological conceptions of Renaissance England, showing how the poem incorporates and transmutes religious discourses and thereby tests, appraises, and questions their avowals and assurances. The book's focus on religious discourses leads Mallette to examine how such matters as marriage, gender, the body, revenge, sexuality, and foreign policy were represented—in both traditional and subversive ways—in Spenser's influential masterpiece.

A bold and finely argued contribution to our understanding of Spenser, Reformation thought, and Renaissance literature and society, Mallette's study will add to the ongoing reassessment of England during this important period.

Richard Mallette is a professor of English at Lake Forest College. He is the author of *Spenser, Milton and Renaissance Pastoral*.

Richard Mallette

Spenser
and the
Discourses of
Reformation
England

University of Nebraska Press
Lincoln and London

© 1997 by the
University of
Nebraska Press
All rights reserved
Manufactured in the
United States of America
⊖The paper in this book
meets the minimum requirements
of American National Standard
for Information Sciences—
Permanence of Paper for
Printed Library Materials,
ANSI Z39.48-1984.
Library of Congress
Cataloging-in-
Publication Data
Mallette, Richard, 1949–
Spenser and the discourses of
Reformation England / Richard Mallette.
p.   cm.
Includes bibliographical references and index.
ISBN 0-8032-3195-4 (cl: alk. paper)
1. Spenser, Edmund, 1552?–1599.
Faerie queene.   2. Christianity
and literature—England—History—
16th century.   3. Protestantism
and literature—History—16th century.
4. Epic poetry, English—History and criticism.
5. Spenser, Edmund, 1552?–1599—Religion.
6. Reformation—England.   I. Title.
PR2358.M34   1997
821'.3—dc21
96-52793   CIP

SECOND PRINTING: 1999

For Paul Elledge

Contents

Acknowledgments

My debts are many, my thanks inadequate. I began this project years ago under a fellowship from the National Endowment for the Humanities at the Newberry Library at a stage—the beginning of mid-career—when a scholar can most benefit from renewal. At this Chicago haven of learning and civility, I came afresh to value scholarship and the people who pursue it. A subsequent Travel-to-Collections grant from the NEH allowed me, while still teaching at Millsaps College in Mississippi, to continue research at the Folger Shakespeare Library in Washington DC and at the libraries of Harvard University in Cambridge, Massachusetts. The incomparable resources of the Newberry, as well as a carrel from which to inspect them, have remained available to me upon my relocation to Lake Forest College. I am indebted, perhaps more than to anyone, to Mary Beth Rose, director of the Newberry Center for Renaissance Studies, for constant encouragement, for friendship, and for uncannily good advice about various features of this book when I needed it most, even though I didn't know it. Two institutions, Millsaps College and Lake Forest College, have provided me with not only sabbatical leaves and other forms of assistance but also a liberal arts environment conducive to faculty scholarship. In this regard I am especially grateful to Robert H. King and David Spadafora for decanal encouragement of more profound benefit to me than doubtless either realizes. Numerous colleagues and friends have read and commented on portions of the book-in-progress, immeasurably improving it. I can only list their names, with gratitude: J. A. Appleyard, S.J., Kenneth Bennett, Patrick Cullen, Anne Ferry, Nona Fienberg, Paul Gehl, Clark Hulse, Anne Lake Prescott, Thomas P. Roche Jr., Diane Ross, Philip Simmons, William Sessions, and Harold L. Weatherby. Chapters 1 and 5 originally appeared, in modified form, in *Spenser Studies* 7 (1987) and 11 (1994), and I am grateful to AMS Press for permission to reprint. I owe special thanks to Gayle Swanson for expert copyediting.

Finally, I must thank my Cambridge friends Noreen Reilly, James Herman, and David Mason, whose patient hospitality over several summers made it possible for me to work. The dedication to Paul Elledge merely acknowledges what he best embodies: "zeale of friends combynd with vertues meet."

Spenser
and the
Discourses of
Reformation
England

Introduction

This book locates *The Faerie Queene* within the considerable corpus of English Reformation discourses and shows how the poem reproduces, transforms, criticizes, and parodies those discourses. The study expands the conception of theology beyond doctrine and judges the reconciliation of religious and literary texts. It focuses as much on the sociopolitical, ethical, and psychological dimensions of Reformed religion as on theological belief. Each of the following chapters accentuates how religion intermingles with other discursive spheres. Whereas much past Spenser scholarship has treated Reformation texts as sources in traditional ways, this work centers on the overlapping of discourses. The book, then, dilates traditional conceptions of the Reformation and redefines the relations of religious texts to other texts and discourses. It demonstrates how the Reformation helped to redraw the boundaries of previously segregated domains: theological, rhetorical, ethical, sexual, political, literary. To glimpse how this book will proceed, let us examine one of those boundaries, where Spenser's poem converges with a provocative set piece of Reformation polemic.

In his treatise "A Reformed Catholike" (1598), William Perkins sets forth the differences between "the Church of Rome" and "us" by comparing the state of a sinner to the condition of a prisoner. Catholics suppose the prisoner bound hand and foot with chains, enfeebled by sickness,

> yet not wholly dead, but liuing in part: it [i.e., Rome] supposeth also, that being in this case, he stirreth not himselfe for any helpe, and yet hath the abilitie and power to stirre. Hereupon, if the keeper come and take away his bolts and fetters, and hold him by the hand, and helpe him vp, hee can and will of himselfe stand and walke, and go out of prison: euen so (say they) . . . if the holy Ghost come and doe but vntie

his bandes, and reach him his hand of grace, then can he stand of himselfe, and will his owne saluation, or anything else that is good.

What most offends Perkins in this comparison is spelled out in the
last clause: the sinner is able to "will his owne salvation." The comparison overexalts humanity by implying a semi-Pelagian self-re-
liance that contradicts the Reformed core belief that the will's bondage has sunk the sinner too deep in depravity for him even to assist in
unfettering himself. So Perkins proposes another way of thinking
analogously about the human condition, the Reformed understanding of the prisoner's iniquitous state. The captive is not merely sick
but "starke dead": he

> cannot stirre though the keeper vntie his bolts and chaines, nor heare
> though hee sound a trumpet in his eare; and if the said keeper would
> haue him to moue and stirre, hee must giue him not onely his hand to
> helpe him, but euen soule and life also . . . [the prisoner] cannot so mu-
> che as desire or doe any thing that is truely good of himselfe. But God
> must first come and put a new soule into him, euen the spirit of grace
> to quicken and reuiue him: and then being thus reuiued, the will begin-
> neth to will good things.

"This," concludes Perkins, "is the true difference between vs and the
Church of Rome in this point of Free Will."[1]

His comparison is not original or even eccentrically developed. Its
roots are both Pauline and Platonic, and it pervades Christian discourse.[2] The very comparison of the human subject to a prisoner re-
born, to one revived and reshaped, captures the essence of self-description that the coinages "Renaissance" and "Reformation" have
been intended to convey. Characteristically Reformist, Perkins ties
the trope to the will and human vileness. The commonplaceness of
the comparison typifies the English Reformers, who carve out no
new theological niche.[3] Moreover, the comparison raises questions,
some answered (or at least addressed) by Reformed theology, some
posed by a more skeptical age: how did the prisoner become imprisoned; why has the keeper not liberated him earlier; can the freed
prisoner relapse or be reimprisoned; what will assure him of the
keeper's ongoing sustenance?

Leaving aside these questions for the moment, I want to focus on
Perkins's tropological method because it bears closely on an intertextual study of how the matter of the Reformation, as a discursive system, intersects with at least one major early modern text. The con-

cept of the sinner-as-prisoner invites attention *qua* trope to the conventions of romance allegory, specifically of an allegory that compulsively revisits prisons as sites of its characters' woes. Each book of *The Faerie Queene* represents characters as incarcerated, usually literally, always figuratively. The poem gradually sets forth a carceral economy.[4] This is, of course, a stock romance motif: the hero(ine) takes risks, often fails, languishes in prison, awaits freedom. The first book of Spenser's poem, for example, describes the hero's imprisonment in language that seems indebted to Reformation concerns. Redcrosse has been willfully "carelesse of his health, and of his fame" (I.7.7) and is thrown as "eternall bondslaue" (7.14) into Orgoglio's dungeon.[5] Only the might of Arthur, bent "To wreake the guilt of mortall sins" (8.9), seems able to penetrate the dungeon, a liberation the text renders with such (ambiguous) theological markers as "euery dore of freewill open flew" (8.5). There he finds the knight's "vitall powres /Decay'd, and all his flesh shronk vp" (8.41), a condition for which Redcrosse himself may be blameworthy: "of your selfe ye thus berobbed arre" (8.42). The text invites a theological reading, as it does everywhere in Book I, even if, unlike Perkins, it supplies multiple interpretive options. Redcrosse's subsequent brush with Despaire may suggest that even Arthur's deliverance is insufficient to effect the knight's rehabilitation. Like the condition of the "wretched thralles" in Lucifera's dungeon, who have "thrown themselues into these heauy stowres" (5.51), Redcrosse's enfeeblement is so self-originating and thorough that he seems unable, without something akin to new life, to execute his own recovery. The text fairly demands that we read it with theological assistance, even if, *pace* Perkins's comparison, it does not mark a single theological path to its nucleus.

We cannot stop here. *The Faerie Queene* invites, indeed it requires, that we interpret cognate episodes correspondingly. Hence the prisoners of Book II, for example, are also depicted in terms of free will. Acrasia has her victims "thralled to her will, / In chaines of lust and lewd desires ybound." Amavia describes her husband's subjugation similarly; her liberation of Mortdant is accomplished when she "recured [him] to a better will" (II.1.54). Is this a theological condition, betokening spiritual regeneration? Perhaps not, but the text is tapping the linguistic resources of the Reformation to express a problem about the fleshly condition (itself a primary preoccupation of Reformation discourse). Indeed most other unfortunate intemperates in this book of the poem are portrayed with the aid of contemporary debates over the will. To take only the final duo, Verdant and Grill, Acrasia's prisoners: after Verdant is "vntyde" (II.12.82), he is counseled in the ways of temperance and seems regenerated; but Grill, a representative of the "donghill kind," willfully "chooseth" his degradation "with vile difference [i.e., preference]" (II.12.87). How fully, how deeply does this construction of temperance, with its sharp dichotomy between the saved and the damned, draw from Reformation controversies about the will? Are the characters imprisoned by their corruptions and structurally unable to liberate themselves? If we inlay Spenserian temperance within contemporary religious discourses, as its lexical peculiarities invite, how may we re-envision Book II? If intemperance is inscribed in the flesh by virtue of a sinful a priori condition, what will unshackle the prisoner from fleshly iniquity?

And so with other imprisonments in the poem. As it moves from book to book, and prison to prison, the poem seems to migrate ever more distantly from its Reformation grounding in disputes about the will. But that discourse has been sedimented in the text from the outset. We might say the text is enthralled to that discourse and must resist it, even as (or perhaps because) the text is willfully bound to it. As the poem's later books grow seemingly farther from the substratum of the Reformation, their problematic relation to Reformation concerns becomes ever more interpretively interesting. That is the subject of this study: how *The Faerie Queene* engages the resources of the Reformation, interrogates those resources, transmutes them, resists them, and remains in thrall to them.

To continue our prison visits, Book III presents an array of jailed characters. Timias is captivated by Belphoebe ("Thus warreid he long time against his will" [III.5.48]); Florimell is alternately imprisoned by and fleeing from her would-be captors; Amoret is chained at the waist in Busirane's house: all unwilling victims and yet accomplices in their enslavements. Do they also assist, like Perkins's Catholic prisoner, in their own emancipation, or do they need, like his Protestant corpse, to be structurally reconstituted if they are to flourish? Book III and Book IV draw on the holdings of Protestantism to reconfigure eros, that most imprisoning of human attributes, and thereby suggest the troublesome relation of desire and volition. Book IV—the most nontheological unit in the poem and seemingly remote from Reformation circumstances—presents an assortment of characters locked up, some clearly by their own will. How different, as a prisoner of desire, is Scudamour, trapped in that stronghold of jealous insecurity, the house of Care, from Amoret and Æmylia in the cave of Lust? Once freed from its confines, Scudamour, "With fleshly weaknesse, which no creature may / Long time resist" (IV.5.43), imposes himself on Amoret, whom he plunders from the Temple of Venus (never, he says, "Could she her wished freedome fro me wooe" [10.57]). Placidas honestly admits that he deliberately has himself imprisoned in order to be with his friend and look-alike, Amyas, "For whose sole libertie I loue and life did stake" (8.60). These and other tortured characters in the central books are constructed in the lineaments of the Reformation controversy that seeks to understand the role of individual agency in the travails of the human condition. In the international domain of Book V, Belge colludes in her surrender to Geryoneo ("Him entertayn'd, and did her champion chose" and "did at last commit / All to his hands, and gaue him soueraine powre" [V.10.12,13]). After she is "restor'd to life againe" (11.16) by the "wondrous grace" (11.18) of Arthur, he must complete his apocalyptic reformation of her lands by destroying the monster beneath the idol of Geryone. Finally, in Book VI, Calidore anguishes over how he might "saue [Pastorella's] life" (VI.11.34) in the Brigants' cave. Once freed, she is "reuiued . . . / And wondrous ioy felt in her spirits thrall" (11.44). Her mother later does not know whether to interpret her restoration as "fortunes spoile" (12.16) or the benefaction to one "whom high God did saue" (12.17). Here the issues of free will, so distant from their theological origins in Book I, are reexamined under a nontheological aegis.

As this synecdochic excursion through some of the poem's prisons suggests, the Reformation is deeply structured into the allegory and plays a dialectical role in its formation. This study tracks *The Faerie Queene* through the intertextual maze of the Reformation with the aim of demonstrating how the poem has kidnapped those discourses (to use Harry Berger's term) and is in turn captivated by them at every stage of its labyrinthine unfolding, even when it appears most distant from theology.[6] The poem not only represents and refracts Reformation texts and values, many of these competing and even self-contradictory, but also challenges and frequently undermines Reformation certainties and assumptions. The study establishes how

Spenser's poem absorbs theological discourse into other domains—
as diverse as marriage, politics, and rhetoric—where it is re-
scrutinized and redefined.

Examining literary texts for the presence of other texts and discourses has lately come to the forefront of criticism and has greatly
enhanced, if not supplanted, the search for sources and influences
that had preoccupied literary scholarship for generations.[7] Because
of its enormous scope and syncretic diversity, *The Faerie Queene*
proves a model site for us to address the distinctions, and overlaps,
between influence and intertextuality. The poem's relation to the materials of the Reformation is neither outside the sphere of "influence"
nor entirely relegated to "unconscious, socially prompted types of
text formation."[8] *The Faerie Queene*'s engagement with the Reformation cannot be exactly attributed to more or less conscious authorial intention, but as Book I demonstrates most readily, it cannot
be entirely segregated from what "Spenser" endorses or disowns.
This study treats *The Faerie Queene* as inhabiting an impersonal
sphere of crossing texts, but the poem often seems self-consciously to
evoke texts, issues, and especially idioms of the Reformation as a
means of engaging its controversies. *The Faerie Queene*, as much as
any work in English, insists on its intertextual structures, ranging
from the explicit to the implicit, as one may readily discern from
scanning Greenlaw's *Variorum* or *The Spenser Encyclopedia* (even
when entries are concerned with locating the poem's "sources").
Thanks to recent reconceptualizings of how literary texts relate to
other texts and discourses, we need not fret as much as scholars once
did about how to distinguish "genuine" influences from commonplace images, techniques, or ideas on the one hand, and on the other,
the presence of earlier texts and discourses "unconsciously" placed
there. Instead we have learned how to judge more astutely the results
of a perceived transmutation of materials. The present work explores how one spacious text adapts, elaborates, and often parodies
Reformation materials.

Because this study treats literary history as a reticulation of discourses, we may assume the existence, ignored in influence and
source studies, of an already-read discourse of the social text. To do
so provides some degree of certainty to the act of interpretation, as
Jonathan Culler has noted, provided by the reader's awareness of
conventions.[9] One of the purposes here is to foreground insuffi-

ciently appreciated discourses in *The Faerie Queene*, discourses that constitute the subjects of subsequent chapters: Reformation representations of preaching, for example, or the body, sexuality, revenge, marriage, the will, apocalypse. Indeed, in some respects, they constitute the text, and of course the text frequently contests and even repudiates these discourses. The text both represents and is constricted by discursive structures, transactions this book identifies, isolates, and judges interpretively. *The Faerie Queene* critiques, rather than mirrors, Reformation concerns, recasting and refurbishing religious discourses in each of its books.

The early Reformation in England, as historians have emphasized for more than a generation, was comprised of strenuous and subtle controversies not readily reducible to competing camps of belief, such as the anachronistic dichotomy of "Puritan" and "Anglican."[10] Profiting from prolific research over the past three decades by political historians and historians of religion, literary studies have recently begun to regard the English Reformation of the sixteenth century as a collection of discourses, an array of voices and currents of thought.[11] The term "Reformation" encompasses events, productions of texts, and changes in institution, practice, and belief as diverse as the eradication of papal supremacy, the reformulation of relations between church and state, the employment of the vernacular Bible, a reconceptualizing of the clergy, and redefinitions of theology. In England these changes stretched over several decades and, far from being the outcome of a preconceived theological program, grew out of a series of provisional historical phenomena as well as ongoing and complicated theological strife.[12] The Protestantization of Elizabethan England was not a foregone conclusion in 1558, but rather a process contingent upon political circumstances and theological uncertainty. Over the past fifteen years scholarship has been seriously engaged in redefining, both revising and counter-revising, the English Reformation—a vital project far from complete, but one that has already allowed us to see this revolution in more depth and detail than before. To help formulate an interpretive model of how *The Faerie Queene* confronts the materials of the Reformation—and to judge the osmotic effects of the Reformation on that synthesizing text—it will be useful to glance at recent historiographic developments in English Reformation studies. These innovations in understanding the English Reformation can help us to reenvision how Spenser's poem transfigures its discursive formations. We can appreciate these conceptual innovations by temporarily segregating recent historiography into two groups of practitioners, recognizing the artificiality of the division and the overlapping of their projects: scholars focusing mainly on Reformation political history and those investigating the history of Reformation theology.

Although they have strenuously asserted the Reformed character of sixteenth-century England, its Calvinist consensus, religious historians have come generally to recognize what Patrick Collinson calls a series of corrugations over the theological landscape.[13] During the reign of Elizabeth, the Reformed Protestantization of the English became widespread, but it was not yet complete. This second phase of the Reformation was to begin with acceptance of earlier Reformed theology, reflected in formularies and official texts such as the Thirty-nine Articles, *The Book of Homilies*, *The Book of Common Prayer*, and such unofficial texts as Nowell's catechism and the Geneva glosses.[14] The dominant group of religious historians has continued to argue that Elizabethan theology was principally predestinarian, as evidenced, say, by the published sermons at St. Paul's Cross after 1570, or the glosses to the Geneva Bible of 1560, or, most important, the preponderance of published doctrinal controversialists.[15] Dewey Wallace's survey of these works has made clear that Reformed theology ruled the religious culture and sought to quell opposition. Those on either end of the spectrum who differed from the official Reformed theology of the Elizabethan Settlement in the intensity of their views, and who came to be known as "Puritans" and "Arminians," were restrained until late in the period and into the next century.[16] Historians of religion continue to investigate the prevalence and popularity of such fundamental beliefs as predestination and free will, but most have concluded that Reformed doctrine held sway, with its emphasis on total human depravity, the powerlessness of the will to assist in salvation by means of "works-righteousness," and the absolute might of God to elect some for salvation and to hurl the majority to their deserved reprobation.

Another group of religious historians, sometimes labeled "revisionist," has argued that the Elizabethan church included a spectrum of more or less admissible doctrinal positions and that the church was not as steeped in Calvinism, particularly in the Reformed theology of grace and its concomitant predestinarianism, as had been previously thought.[17] The revisionist project has stressed, on the one hand, the peaceful, if uneasy, acceptance of subterranean Catholicism within the culture and, on the other, the minority view within Reformed orthodoxy that works are an aid to salvation. Revisionism has been especially keen to account for the variety of religious belief outside London and the universities and to demonstrate wide geographical variations in orthodoxy. In short, revisionist historians have asserted, first, the vitality of theological pluralism; second, the confinement of theological disputes to elite and academic circles; third, ongoing residual loyalty to doctrines of free will and faith embracing merit.[18]

Despite their disagreements, all religious historians recognize that the various theological articulations are deeply embedded in political circumstances. One need only examine the formularies and the introductions to the major public documents of the Reformation to sense that the faith had to be imposed on recalcitrant believers. The penalties and fines threatened in the Act of Uniformity in 1559 against parishes reluctant to adopt *The Book of Common Prayer* or against those parishioners unwilling to attend church on Sundays and holy days suggest how forcibly the Elizabethan Settlement achieved its famed via media and how competing or subversive ideologies endangered that fragile settlement and its uniformity.[19] The glosses and other annotations to the Geneva Bible (and, less prominently, to the official Bishops' Bible) are uncompromisingly Reformist and must have had a similar conforming, and deeply evangelizing, effect. Reformed theology as well as antipapal propaganda were thus dispersed in the culture. This via media—while firmly Protestant in theology, as reflected in the Thirty-nine Articles—was deliberately ambiguous about issues that divided Protestants from one another. Article 17 is notorious in this respect, incorporating the Reformed doctrine of predestination but vague on the role of the will, assurance for the elect, and reprobation.[20] No historian has denied the Reformed hegemony of Elizabethan Protestantism, but as Peter Lake has noted, hegemony is not monopoly.[21] Historians differ on how to account for competing bodies of belief and whether to accord minority or recessive doctrines weightier voices in the theological disputes of the era. Although revisionist historians have perhaps overstated the view that the Elizabethan church held under its umbrella incompatible theological convictions, even anti-revisionists are no longer willing to see this phase of the Reformation solely as the triumph of a cartel-like "Calvinism."[22]

In the same fashion, revisionist political history stresses the ongoing prestige of Catholicism and other forms of resistance to the Reformation. Political historians such as Christopher Haigh, J. J. Scarisbrick, and others since the 1980s have challenged previous explanations of the Reformation as a response to institutional decline. They have instead highlighted such historical features as the liveliness of late medieval Catholicism or the previously neglected opposition of committed conservatives to Protestant policies.[23] Haigh points out that the Reformation in England was not an inexorable process, carried forward by irresistible ideological force, but a succession of provisional steps. The Settlement of 1559 succeeded not because it was popular but because Elizabeth made it less unpopular; Protestantism remained weak until late in the century.[24] Revisionist historians, then, have challenged A. G. Dickens's view, which dominated Protestant historiography for two decades, that there was popular, deep-seated demand for change among a laity disaffected by the formalism and corruption of late medieval Catholicism.[25] Revisionist history also contests the position, associated with the work of Geoffrey Elton, that the Reformation was entirely the result of official coercion.[26] In short, revisionist history depicts the English Reformation not as an inevitable development leading to a predetermined conclusion but as a contingent series of conflicts and crises, varying from region to region.[27] These historians describe the English Reformation as double-barreled, part official, part unofficial, reformation from below and from above. That is to say, recent historiographic views have called into question the distinction between a Reformation by statutory religious regulation and the ability of the new religion to make its own headway, by dint, as it were, of doctrine alone.[28] Thanks to these scholarly labors we now know that even during the second half of the century, committed Protestant ministers encountered great resistance to the evangelical faith. Historians continue to debate the depth of attachment to the new religion among the majority, but there is no reason to believe that a religion as intellectually exacting and as morally demanding as Reformed Protestantism, with its text-centered emphases, had a broad appeal.[29]

How does this historiographic climate help us to reenvision literary history or one major literary text? Most importantly, recent historiography has demonstrated that an atmosphere of greater religious diversity prevailed than had been acknowledged before. Competing views of the Reformation have impelled scholarship to reevaluate the entrenchment of Calvinism in the second half of the century and to grant that Reformed orthodoxy was moderated under the pressure of opposition to the new faith as well as of other, internal challenges.[30] Such a reevaluation is paralleled by the current reestimation in Renaissance literary studies of the relation between dominant ideologies and voices of subversive or marginalized parties. Debora Shuger, for one, has investigated the interpenetration of the orthodox and the subversive within the confines of dominant religious ideology and has shown that "it is not always clear what precisely is subversive with respect to the dominant ideology, nor does orthodox ideology seem quite as monolithic and hegemonic" as scholarship has thought.[31] Literary criticism, when restrained by epistemological models of "sources" and "influence," has often felt the need to demonstrate how a given text conforms to one or another of the dominant (or minor) positions in its cultural matrix, to the exclusion of other voices and positions. Recent developments in Reformation historiography as well as in Renaissance literary scholarship encourage suspension of such judgments and urge us to abandon the critical posture that predisposes us to identify the author's "position" with one or another partisan conviction swirling through the currents of the culture. We might instead profit, as Darryl Gless has illustrated in his balanced treatment of Book I of *The Faerie Queene*, from observing how the text voices more than one body of belief.[32] We can also demonstrate how the text draws from different discursive resources, adapts various discourses, remodels them, questions them—without being constrained to divine which particular theological position the text endorses. We can observe, in short, the overlapping and interpenetration of discursive domains as well as the cultural codes realized and challenged in the text. Most important, we are freer to read Spenser's poem not as allegorized theology (or any other single discourse) but as *allegory*, with all the richness and inclusiveness the term has come to signify in the current efflorescence of Spenser studies.

Recent scholarly developments, then, encourage us to watch Spenser's poem give play to a multiplicity of identifiable discourses. Such encouragement guides this study, and it allows us to situate the poem among other discourses of the Reformation. Recognizing *The Faerie Queene* as a literary text produced among other modes of discourse helps us to see it as part of a common culture using shared languages.[33] To take an historical observation as an example: much of the earlier Reformation prevailed only in the limited circles of urban or university centers, where new ideas generally met a ready reception. Recent historiography has shown forcefully that the Elizabethan propagation of the Reformation was both various and uneven. After the Elizabethan Settlement, Protestant teaching was disseminated widely and deeply, among the ignorant as well as the learned. Preaching ministers of the Elizabethan church circulated through England. Reformed doctrine was not merely an academic exercise or even an officially sanctioned body of belief to combat the Roman Catholic enemy but a system of practical instruction, transmitted by sermons and spiritual direction, that reached virtually every member of the realm. A small army of popular preachers and devotional writers mediated the theology by means of sermons, treatises, and individual counsel. These preachers aimed not merely at uprooting popery but at providing spiritual tutelage for increasing and ardent numbers. Published sermons and other books detailing the spiritual life, with special attention to predestination, assurance, and the Reformed order of salvation, poured from English presses.[34]

Their instruction suggests the practical nature of the new religion, a pragmatism that helps to account for the rise of preaching. This rhetorical form, codified as a specifically Reformation *ars praedicandi,* was not merely the means of instruction but an integral feature of salvation itself. The preacher is both the mediator of the gospel and an inspired impersonator of God. The Word, in Pauline terms, becomes the instrument of faith, the very source of salvation: "how shal they heare without a preacher? . . . Then faith is by hearing, & hearing by the worde of God."[35] The English Reformation, even more than its Continental counterparts, is above all a religion of words. The Word itself, of course, is read and heard in an English Bible. Its chief medium is the sermon. There are also prayers and a communal liturgy uttered in English from a state-sanctioned and finely crafted Prayer Book; officially prescribed homilies; and, by the late Elizabethan period, an array of books of religious edification, including cheaply printed catechisms, providing basic and condensed religious education.[36] Awareness of the cultural privileging of the Word, and Reformation words that promulgate it, helps to contextualize Spenser's poem in contemporary religious discourses. *The Faerie Queene* avails itself of a religion suffused with a sense of how the Word, and words about the Word, can pierce the heart (to use a popular Pauline metaphor: Heb. 4:12, Eph. 6:17). In its initial chapters, this study considers how Spenser's poem appropriates and remodels sermons and sermon theory, often to parody them. More generally, this work examines how *The Faerie Queene* becomes a part of a word-saturated religious culture by drawing on a linguistic fund that expresses the breadth of discursive possibilities in that culture. Examining each book of the poem serially, later chapters show how the Reformation is embedded in sociopolitical, rhetorical, and ethical discourses, and how Spenser's poem is structured by engaging those discourses.

It may be helpful to distinguish this study from recent books that address religion in both Renaissance and Spenser studies. First, as the foregoing discussion has stressed, this book does not try to show how Spenser's poem exemplifies or defends theological views. I will not assume that religious doctrine can "explain" the poem, even when the poem responds to concepts found in theological texts. Spenser scholarship has produced a variety of valuable studies that identify *The Faerie Queene* with, and differentiate it from, one or another partisan position of the Reformation. Anthea Hume's *Edmund Spenser: Protestant Poet* is a notable example in a venerable line of scholarship that argues Spenser's conformity to the tenets of English Calvinism.[37] Others have argued the poet's allegiance to other doctrinal positions available during the period.[38]

Second, this is not a study in Protestant poetics, as that term has been used by Barbara Lewalski: "Calvinism provided a detailed chart of the spiritual life for Elizabethan and seventeenth-century English Protestants, and this map also afforded fundamental direction to the major religious poets."[39] Nor will this book examine the allegiances of *The Faerie Queene* to a literary tradition specifically "Reformation" in character. John N. King's ground-breaking book, *Spenser's Poetry and the Reformation Tradition*, contextualizes the allegory in the particular genres and conventions of other Reformation writers and demonstrates how Spenser's work can be seen as "generic hybridization and mutation that entails a 'fruitful question-

ing' of received literary models."[40] Nor do I study idolatry, iconoclasm, or iconophilia—subjects that have recently engaged such diverse commentators as Linda Gregerson, Kenneth Gross, and Ernest
B. Gilman.[41] Unlike John N. Wall Jr., I do not suggest that "formal
theological discourse and religious poetic discourse [are] mutually
informing."[42] Nor is this, like Darryl Gless's *Interpretation and Theology in Spenser,* a study primarily of Book I of *The Faerie Queene*
and its relation to theology.[43]

Unlike many recent studies of Spenser's ties to the Reformation,
the present work shifts attention from theology to religious discourses, which, for the Reformation, encircle a wide assortment of
human endeavors. The language of these discourses is, of course, informed by theological assumptions, whether or not the discourses
actively defend or dispute theology. In its central books, for example,
the poem foregrounds discourses of marriage and sexuality that may
at first seem remote from Reformed religion. Drawing upon post-
structuralist feminist approaches that have played a revolutionary
role in contemporary Renaissance studies, later chapters will demonstrate how Books III and IV reconfigure Reformation discourses
about marriage and the family, gender and sexuality, in nontheological ways. Other chapters rely on more traditional historically based
methodologies to show how the poem employs Reformation rhetorical and political preoccupations in the construction of the allegory.
This study, in short, demonstrates how religious discourse is assimilated into other discursive spheres, such as Spenserian allegory,
where it is reformulated and reenvisioned.

Finally, this is not an examination of the entire text of *The Faerie
Queene.* While it attends to most cantos, it barely touches upon a
number of cardinal episodes, such as the battle of the Dragon, Briton
moniments, the Garden of Adonis, the marriage of the Thames and
the Medway, much of the first half of Book V, and the Mutabilitie
Cantos. These episodes may seem glaring in their absence. Such la-
cunae in a comprehensive treatment of *The Faerie Queene* can be understood by noting that this study identifies the intertext of Reformation discourses. Into episodes of the poem that I do not find central to
such an investigation I do not tread.[44]

In their elegant study of the "mind" of the English Reformation,
Charles and Katherine George note that a body of thought is never

granitic but is attached to a sea of tensions and contradictions. Hence the notion—which they see at the heart of Christianity and intensified in English Protestantism—that humanity is exalted, loved by God, and worthy of life, on the one hand, and on the other, that humans are base sinners and worthy only of destruction.[45] One may revise the Georges' insight by suggesting that the distinctive force of the Reformation is felt in rechronologizing this dichotomy: Reformation discourse *first* emphasizes that humanity is worthy only of destruction; only *then* that God has graciously and mysteriously saved some. The opening of the second selection in *The Book of Homilies,* "The Miserie of Al Mankynd," avers that "S. Paule in many places painteth us out in our colours . . . that we cannot thinke a good thought of our selfes, muche lesse we can saye wel, or do wel of our selfes" (72). Like most Reformers, the homilist seems never to tire of reminding his hearers "how of our selfes, and by our selfes, we have no goodnes, helpe, nor salvacion, but contrariwise, synne, dampnacion and death everlastynge" (74). But the next homily, "Of the Salvacion of Mankynd," brings the good news of justification by faith, so efficacious (for the saved) "that there remaineth not any spotte of synne that shalbe imputed to [our] dampnacion" (79). In a similar fashion, the opening of *The Book of Common Prayer* announces that "the Scripture moveth us in sundry places, to acknowledge and confess our manifold sins and wickedness." This sobering admonition is at once followed by tidings that "we may obtain forgiveness . . . by his infinite goodness and mercy" (50). No branch of Christianity thinks humanity can achieve salvation on its own—although (as we saw in Perkins's prisoners) this form of Pelagianism is what Catholics came to be accused of, especially later in the Elizabethan era.[46] Reformed Protestantism has a powerful fealty to sin. At the heart of the Reformation is a story of depthless human wickedness from which the believer has been redeemed without any merit or effort of "works" but only by a God-given faith. Because salvation is entirely by grace, and not the product of human worth or exertion, God alone is the guarantor of salvation for the faithful made just. The Reformed development of this core belief into an order, the *ordo salutis,* provides a formulaic program for the believer to chart his or her progress in salvation: a spiritual sequence starting with predestination and proceeding to calling, justification, sanctification, and—finally and hereafter—glorification.[47] As Perkins's prisoner analogies make vivid, the particular quarrel with Catholicism is with an alleged overconfidence about human nature's ability to assist in its own salvation. Hence the centrality of the will to the Reformation.

The issue of free will, then, inaugurates this book's investigation of *The Faerie Queene*'s bond to the Reformation, but it is only a starting point. The poem responds to primary motifs of Reformed Protestantism, and they form an important intellectual reservoir from which the poem draws sustenance. Reformation discourse presents humanity in its widest array, mired in corruption and yearning for salvation or life. These are, of course, also the polarities that structure Spenser's poem: fierce wars and faithful loves. From this point we may begin to explore how the poem transmutes these resources. For the discourses of the Reformation provide the poem with more than a map or a conceptual foundation. They provide the allegory with a dimension of what Thomas M. Greene calls a *mundus significans,* a rhetorical and symbolic vocabulary, "a vast, untidy, changeful collection of techniques of meaning, expressive devices feasible for communication, a vocabulary grounded in the spoken and written language but deriving its special distinctness from the secondary codes and conventions foregrounded at its given moment. Only through them, and within the limits they allow, reflecting as they do the epistemological and other shared assumptions of their community, can a subject express himself into existence and individuate a moral style." The relation of Spenser's poem to the collection we call the Reformation is, as Greene demonstrates about the relation of Renaissance texts to antiquity, a matter of both extending and violating the historically given signifying universe. As Greene concludes, "To read in terms of a mundus is not to close off the polyvalence of a text, but to seek its potency within the richness of the writer's play with his own codes."[48] *The Faerie Queene* asks us to learn its codes and the historicity of its words and tropes in endless permutation. Its relation to the Reformation, as subsequent chapters show, both extends and violates, stabilizes and disjoins, those tropes and codes. The poem's attachment to the Reformation is not always systematic, and its allegiances are continually changing. The purpose of this study is to construct interpretive order and stability from that changing and untidy corpus.

Discourses of
Preaching in Book I

At a pivotal point in the Legend of Holinesse, with Redcrosse cast into Orgoglio's dungeon and Una's spirits languishing, Arthur makes his ceremonious entrance into the poem. The scene in which he consoles Una and volunteers as her champion deserves closer attention than it has received, because the method Arthur employs "in saving Una from despair," to quote A. C. Hamilton, is firmly bound to the role of the preacher in the Reformed *ordo salutis*.[1] The scene can serve as the gateway to wider implications of the art of preaching in Book I, for it highlights how that book's preoccupation with "words of wondrous might" (10.24) merges with Reformation mindfulness of "how we heare Gods word, that it may be effectual to our salvation."[2]

The episode expands the traditional romance duty of succoring a maiden in distress. Arthur's wordless arrival, iconographically premodern, contrasts markedly with the lively conversation he and Una conduct, one largely devoted to what we would now call analyzing emotional states.[3] With the panoptic vision of a later era, the episode looks disconcertingly therapeutic, especially when they try to find "feeling words" (7.38) for the heart's "anguish" (7.40). After Arthur approaches Una decorously, he learns of her "secret sorrow" and resolves to "allay, and calme her storming paine" by encouraging her with "Faire feeling words" to vent her misery. She responds with "bleeding words" (7.38) but resists his offer: "My last left comfort," she says, is "my woes to weepe and waile" (7.39). Arthur patiently entreats again, urging her to "vnfold the anguish of your hart," because, he says,

> Mishaps are maistred by aduice discrete,
> And counsell mittigates the greatest smart;
> Found neuer helpe, who neuer would his hurts impart.
>
> (7.40)

Psychological asseverations (sharing anguish eases it; "counsell" relieves misery) mingle with homespun wisdom (advice masters mishaps). In his capacity as counselor, Arthur distinguishes Una's emotional condition, her "greatest smart," which he hopes to relieve with words, from such external adversities as Redcrosse's imprisonment, her abandonment, and so forth, which may require material assistance. The distinction underlines Arthur's particular duty as the primary emotional, as well as martial, champion of Book I. His attentiveness, sonorous of both theological commonplace and analysis of "grief," has a distinctly pastoral component, which centers on his quelling her despair with "faith":

> O but (quoth she) great griefe will not be tould,
>> And can more easily be thought, then said.
>> Right so; (quoth he) but he, that neuer would,
>> Could neuer: will to might giues greatest aid.
>> But griefe (quoth she) does greater grow displaid,
>> If then it find not helpe, and breedes despaire.
>> Despaire breedes not (quoth he) where faith is staid.
>> No faith so fast (quoth she) but flesh does paire.
> Flesh may empaire (quoth he) but reason can repaire.

(7.41)

The stichomythy transcends repartee or even intellectual exchange: Arthur *corrects* Una's feeling. His verbal prowesse—sympathetic, proverbial, in fact homiletic—not only consoles but also induces "faith," perhaps the key word of the book:

> His goodly reason, and well guided speach
>> So deepe did settle in her gratious thought,
>> The her perswaded to disclose the breach,
>> Which loue and fortune in her heart had wrought.

(7.42)

Healed of this much of her anguish, Una can now recount her story in full. Arthur's response allows the canto to end hopefully:

> But be of cheare, and comfort to you take:
>> For till I have acquit your captiue knight,
>> Assure your selfe, I will you not forsake.
>> His chearefull words reuiu'd her chearelesse spright,
> So forth they went, the Dwarfe them guiding euer right.

(7.52)

Two of Arthur's words compel special attention: "comfort" (repeated three times in the scene) and "assure." The episode dramatizes a version of sixteenth-century emotional therapy. The scene reproduces the age's chief medium of that curative process, Protestant spiritual counseling, which often consists in comforting and assuring the listener's "chearlesse spright" of the hope of salvation. Both words, "comfort" and "assure," open on vistas of the Reformed theology of grace. Assurance, the belief that the promise of salvation applies to the elect individual in particular, and perseverance, the belief that the elect cannot easily waver or lapse into sin, are doctrines much debated and subjected to fine theological discriminations, particularly among Reformed commentators. But preoccupation with the assurance of salvation pervades the spectrum of Reformation writers. Show diligence, says Richard Hooker, to "this blessed assurance of faith unto the end." "Our dutie," says William Perkins, "is, to labour to bee setled and assured in our conscience that God is our God: for first in this assurance is the foundation of all true comfort."[4] The doctrines of assurance and perseverance also comprise distinctive features of Reformed psychology.[5] Proceeding from the Lutheran conviction that the doctrine of *sola fide* is "comfortable" because it liberates fallen beings from either the ability or the need to contribute to their salvation by dint of good works originating in the sin-enslaved will, the Reformed doctrines of assurance and perseverance give the believer wellsprings of security and certainty. The redeemed are to be solaced that their salvation is sure, that their good works follow inevitably from their election, that a sanctified life is indication of election, a source of comfort, and assurance of salvation.

The contours of the doctrine of assurance bear closely on the Reformed conception of the preacher and his practical duty to tend the flock. Citing as prooftext Paul's pronouncement that the preacher "speaketh unto men to edifying, and to exhortation, and to comfort" (1 Cor. 14.3), Reformation pastors asked with John Downame "what peace can wee have, if wee be not assured of our election, but have our minds racked between faith and doubting, hope and despaire?"[6] This problem dominated the Reformed practical ministry and much "affectionate" writing: how can the elect be assisted to enjoy the security of their salvation and be comforted in their inevitable and recurrent doubt or in their commission of sins?[7] It was a problem, then, not only to be thrashed out by theologians but also to be faced in everyday concerns of practical instruction and guidance.[8] Hence Richard Greenham's noteworthy work as a soother of the distraught: "his masterpiece," declares H. C. Porter, "was in comforting wounded consciences. For although Heaven's hand can only set a broken heart yet God used him herein as an instrument of good to many, who came to him with weeping eyes and went from him with cheerful souls."[9] The description, amply borne out in Greenham's own account of his ministrant duties, bears on Arthur's solacing words to Una. While Una's conscience has, of course, no cause for recrimination, she takes comfort and assurance from her new champion, a figure the text associates with heavenly grace.[10] Such ministration Una will find herself extending to Redcrosse, first when she advises the newly liberated knight to "maister these mishaps with patient might" (8.45) and later when she rescues him from Despaire and assures him of his part in "heauenlie mercies" (9.53).

The preacher's words of assurance comprise only one aspect of his duties, words reflecting a more powerful Word he is obliged to promulgate. "He that is oppressed with misery in this world," says the first sermon of *The Book of Homilies*, shall find in Scripture "relief in the promises of eternal life, to his great consolacion and comfort" (62). Preaching these promises, of course, has a powerful affective component. The Reformation diviner of Scripture aims to kindle his hearers to a passionate grasp of dogma. As Perkins sums it up: "the word preached must pearce into the heart" (cf. Heb. 4:12; Eph. 6:17), to arouse feeling and hence to inspire devotion.[11] The emotional might of "the word preached" preoccupies Reformation writing and is professed, especially by English Reformers, as the means of illuminating the darkened mind, softening the hardened heart, quelling doubt, and saving souls. Paul's prooftext is quoted tirelessly: "How shal they heare without a preacher? And how shal they preache except they be sent? . . . For faith is by hearing, and hearing by the worde of God" (Rom. 10.14–17). The affirmation of preaching is heard not only among Calvin's many English followers but also across the spectrum.[12] Hooker, for example, calls sermons the "blessed ordinance of God" that serve "unto the sound and healthie as food, as physicke unto diseased mindes."[13] Preaching becomes, by this turn of phrase, the source of life. Greenham states the matter baldly: "So it is that preaching brings hearing, hearing breedes beleeving, and by beleeving we are saued."[14] Such a formula of cause-and-effect makes preaching integral to every Reformed version of the *ordo salutis*, as Perkins's categorical pronouncement emphasizes:

"The preaching of the Gospell is the key of the kingdome of heauen: so that look how necessary it is for a man to haue his soule saued and to enter into Heauen, so behoouefull it is for him to heare Sermons: for that is the turning of the key whereby we enter into this king-dome. . . . He that is of God, heareth Gods word: and hee that heareth it not, is not of God" (3:305).

A revolution so imbued with belief in the power of its texts must rely on a wealth of essential utterances, both public and private, writ-ten and heard, for accomplishing its mission. The project of saving souls also involves the reformation of a culture and demands evan-gelizing and counseling on an unprecedented scale. For Reformation culture, it is a small step from reading the Word to hearing words about the Word. Calvin's notion resounds across Reformation writ-ing: "Because among so manie excellent gifts wherewith God hath garnished mankinde: This is a singular prerogatiue, that he vouch-saueth to consecrate the mouthes and tongues of men to himselfe, that his owne voice shoulde sounde in them." The "Church is not otherwise builded but by outwarde preaching," for "with God re-maineth his power to saue, but (as the same Paul witnesseth) he vt-tereth and displayeth the same in the preaching of the Gospell" (1.4.5; fols. 338ᵛ–339ʳ). Calvin's careful phrasing insures that the work of salvation remains the property of grace, but he finds within its operations ample room for the skill of the gospel's proclaimers. Preaching, then, answers the question, how shall Reformed religion be instituted? How shall its doctrines find acceptance and give com-fort? A Reformation adage sums up the answer: *praedicatio verbi Dei est verbum Dei.*[15]

Or, to ask the question more globally, how shall the Reformation, as a historical enterprise, gain a beachhead on English shores? The task falls largely to homilies and sermons.[16] In reforming the work of centuries of Christianity, powerful forensic weapons would have to be devised. None were to prove more effective than homily, partic-ularly in radically moving congregations of hearers to accept the new doctrines. *The Book of Homilies* is an excellent case in point. The purpose of the collection is inescapably political. The homilies are of-ficially enjoined, in the monarch's name, to be uniformly read in al-most every parish in the realm. They constitute official certification of the Reformation avowal of preaching to insure conformity and quell dissension.[17] By the admission of its own evangelists, the success of the Reformation depended upon rhetorical efficacy. Its triumph is evidenced by not just the enormous outpouring of sermons, but even in the concomitant and paradoxical laments over the dearth of preaching; clearly, some could not hear enough.[18] What William Haller has termed a "vital rage for utterance" underlines the preeminence of preaching among the discourses of the era.[19] Historians of the English Reformation have investigated the social, political, ecclesiological, and liturgical impact of preaching.[20] In literary studies, however, preaching remains neglected—a condition only moderately improved over the one about which Haller was complaining some fifty years ago when he noted that "preachers exercised an incalculable influence on the development of popular literary taste and expression, an influence no less great for having been ignored by critics and historians."[21]

This "influence"—or intertextual structure—is represented in *The Faerie Queene* in the Legend of Holinesse, and it would be a surprise if it were not, given the tasks of Book I and the primacy of preaching in the age. Arthur's remedying of Una's distress would find a home, for example, in the roster of the preacher's duties. When she asks that Arthur's "wisedome will direct my thought" (7.42), she seeks the guiding power reserved in sermon discourse for the skill of the homilist. It is worth looking more closely at how sermon theorists formulate the role of the preacher in the drama of his listener's life, because their conception of that duty bears closely on the remarkable amount of advice-giving in Book I. The various pieces of counsel offered throughout, mostly directed at Redcrosse, find their *fons et origo* in the era's homiletic discourse, a "source" drawn upon and reconfigured throughout this book of the poem.

The function of the sermon changes radically in the Reformation.[22] The medieval homily, which customarily teaches by anecdote and exemplum, gives way to a sermon whose scope is greatly expanded to include the newly configured doctrines of faith, good works, and grace—in fact, the entire *ordo salutis*. Furthermore, the sermon occupies a new prominence in the Reformation service and helps displace and dethrone the Roman Catholic emphasis on sacraments in the life of the faithful.[23] Greenham itemizes these changes in his summary of how the preacher is to "apply" Reformed theology in homily: "All application of doctrine must be referred to one of these heads: 1. To teach and establish true opinions; 2. Or to confute false opinion; 3. Or to correct evil manners; 4. Or to frame good manners; 5. Or to comfort the will."[24] Each category speaks to matters either of faith ("opinions," i.e., doctrine) or works ("manners"), with the fifth category touching comfortably on both. Greenham's thumbnail sketch of the complex interrelation of faith and works is duplicated with even greater compression when Richard Rogers says that the "Word is the first and principall" means to "strengthen the beleever and settle him in a good life."[25] *The Book of Homilies* encompasses the chief homiletic purposes of instruction in faith and admonition of behavior.[26] The goal of *The Book of Homilies,* like that of Reformation homily generally, is to effect change in the hearer: to induce faith, to assist sanctity, to assure and comfort.

"Assure your selfe," says Arthur to Una, "comfort to you take" (I.7.52). "Mishaps," he tells her, "are maistered by aduice discrete" (7.40); "Despaire breedes not (quoth he) where faith is staid" (7.41). His comforting apothegms echo throughout this book of the poem, resonating to some of its most vexing issues, such as the role of the will and its relation to "mishaps," or the relation of faith to "errors." Serving as one of the primary preacherly authorities in Book I, Arthur suggests that "aduice" can overcome misfortune, begging the question of *how* individual agency might overcome evil. Mishaps can be "maistered," curbed and controlled, by good advice: can errors and wandering—allegorically originating in the wandering wood and the cave of Errour—then be righted? Arthur employs a common figure in Reformed homiletics to express how preaching profits the hearer. It curbs wayward human nature and masters mishaps. Preaching demands submission from its hearer. As Perkins puts it: "In the right hearing of the word, two things are required. The first, that we yeeld ourselues in subiection to the word we heare: The second that we fixe our hearts vpon it . . . Subiection to God must be yeelded in giuing subiection to his word: and our cleauing vnto God must be by fixing our hearts vpon his word" (3:710). Hearers master their mishaps with discreet advice by subjecting themselves to the preacher's words. Edwin Sandys states the matter in another way: "To stand before the Preacher is to stand before God."[27] While such an isolated formulation risks privileging the preacher above the priesthood of all believers, it is intended instead to exalt the Word preached and God's power to give grace by means of the hearer's "subiection to the word."

The power of that preached Word bears indirectly on the opening stanza of Book I of *The Faerie Queene* and its initial emblem of Redcrosse's condition: "His angry steede did chide his foming bitt, / As much disdayning to the curbe to yield" (1.1). Redcrosse, too, has not learned to yield to the curb of moral instruction, variously encoded in the proliferation of advice he will be given. Unlike the lion, who later "yeeld[s] pride and proud submission" (3.6) before Una, Redcrosse resists beneficial advice at every turn, sometimes relying on himself—his own advice—sometimes following bad advice. "Good" advice, the text quickly makes plain, must be external to the hearer. Redcrosse will be called upon to trust more privileged forms of interpretation, officially sanctioned wisdom, and to quash his self-sufficiency. This is no easy or straightforward task. When confronted with the seductive spright in Archimago's hermitage, his first angry reaction is to slay her—but "He stayde his hand, and gan himselfe aduise / To proue his sense, and tempt her faigned truth" (1.50). On the one hand, testing his senses must surely be prudent; on the other, advising himself clearly proves unwise. His story will dramatize how he must submit to more authoritative forms of counsel—most of which he will first reject—if he is to triumph.

The initial episode inaugurates the ironies of advice-giving developed throughout. The first words of dialogue are Una's, admonishing Redcrosse as he stands before the cave of Errour:

Be well aware, quoth then that Ladie milde,
    Least suddaine mischiefe ye too rash prouoke:
    The danger hid, the place vnknowne and wilde,
    Breedes dreadfull doubts: Oft fire is without smoke,
    And perill without show: therefore your stroke
    Sir knight with-hold, till further triall made.
                                                (1.12)

The proverbial formulation of this common sense may disguise the nature of Una's authority. Certainly Redcrosse easily dismisses it, with perhaps foolhardy self-righteousness: "Vertue giues her selfe light," he says, "through darkenesse for to wade" (1.12). And so Una advances a higher form of interpretation and attempts on his behalf to "read" the language of the wood, which has been obscured for the knight in the pun of Errour's cave (Latin: *cave*). This language Una translates for him when she calls out that "wisedome warnes" caution: "Therefore I read beware" (1.13). Playing on multiple meanings of the verb *to read* current in the sixteenth century, including its original Old English meaning of "to advise" or "to explain,"[28] the incident shows that Una's reading powers comprehend more than the knight's and more profoundly penetrate the signs of the environment they wander in. Because he disdains to yield to the curb of Una's advice, to interpret those signs as she reads them and advises him, the knight is nearly bested by his adversary. Redcrosse's failure to heed Una's authority compels her to demonstrate it more directly a perilous moment later. Her famous and perplexing counsel—"Add faith vnto your force, and be not faint /Strangle her, else she sure will strangle thee" (1.19)—rallies the knight, but neither this nor subsequent episodes provide evidence that he responds to, or even hears, the first of Una's two lines of admonition.

One way of approaching this scene and others that deepen Redcrosse's errors and mishaps is to suggest, with a figurative turn readily borne out in the text, that Redcrosse knows neither how to hear nor how to read properly. He is spiritually illiterate and hard of hearing. In this episode, as later adventures will show only too clearly, he hears only the second half of Una's warning. As Greenham puts it, "we must know that there are two hearings. There is a hearing of the eare, and there is a hearing of the heart: there is a speaking to the eare and there is a speaking to the heart."[29] While Redcrosse is saved in Errour's cave, thanks to advice he can but half interpret, he does so only physically ("of the ear") and not more profoundly ("of the heart"). Greenham states the matter as though reading this episode: "We oft heare the Word, but not as the word of the Lorde, and therefore wee heare it but in part . . . If we heare it not as the word of God, but as the word of man, it will neuer doe vs good, it may breed some little purpose in vs, but it will neuer breede in vs any great practice to our comfort."[30] The Word of God—"faith," the first and final word of the Reformation—here clearly belongs to Una, but Redcrosse hears it only in part. The first sermon in *The Book of Homilies*, "The Readyng and Knowledge of Holy Scripture," claims that "ignoraunce of Gods Worde is the cause of al error. . . . How should thei then escheue error that will be still ignoraunt? And how should they come out of ignoraunce that wil not read, nor hear that thyng whiche should geve them knowledge?" (64).[31] Perkins cautions that "the hearers ought not to ascribe their faith to the gifts of men but to the power of Gods word" (2:670). Redcrosse's "faith," of indeterminate referent in his adventure in the cave, certainly has no certain causal relation to "Gods word," but we sense, at least in retrospect, that he would have been spared much inconvenience had he but heard Una's complete Word, had he fully read both text and subtexts in Una's salvific advice: "a man maie prospere," says the homilist, "with onely hearyng, but he maie muche more prospere with both hearyng and readyng" (65).[32] Readers of the Geneva Bible are instructed in a frontispiece that they may take profit from Scripture if they both "Reade interpreters" and "Heare preaching."[33]

Another way to approach this scene is to suggest that Redcrosse's will needs to be curbed to the words of "aduice discrete." That his will is enslaved to sin is almost as much debated by Spenser's critics today as the issue of free will is disputed in the sixteenth century—and with similar consensus. The first adventure is far from conclusive on whether or how Redcrosse has lapsed. But because he cannot read the (often obscure and punning) texts of Errour's cave, the wandering wood, or Una's words, he remains critically detached from them and vulnerable. He gives no evidence of having submitted himself "of the heart" to the discourse of faith that opens up for the knowledgeable reader of contemporary Reformed Protestantism. His biography will show that he will find freedom only with submission to "words" that for now remain illegible and inaudible. As Bishop Hooper puts it, "it is not ynough for a man to hearken or heare, reade or learne Gods word, but he must be ruled by Gods word, frame his whole life after Gods word."[34] Or as Perkins says, "In the right hearing of the word, two things are required. The first, that we yeeld ourselues in subiection to the word we heare: The second that we fixe our hearts vpon it. . . . Subiection to God must be yeelded in giuing subiection to his word: and our cleauing vnto God must be by fixing our hearts vpon his word" (3:710). The text implies Redcrosse's will has to be tamed like Una's lamb: "by her in a line a milke white lambe she lad" (1.4). Until he learns how to hear with the heart, he will wander as errantly as his pagan adversaries and yet be as immobile, as "vnmoued as a rocke" (2.16), as he and Sansfoy are at their encounter, or as "enclosd in wooden wals full faste" (2.42) as Fradubio. The narrator, like so many characters who attempt to advise Redcrosse, points to the inherent nuisances Redcrosse faces as a fallen creature, the freedom of whose will is problematic at best. In one of his instructive, if baffling, introductory stanzas, the narrator admonishes the knight to "beware of ficklenesse, / In choice" (4.1). Events do not, however, demonstrate whether he is even capable of "choice," other than to make the wrong choice. In the first episode, for example, Redcrosse has perhaps only seemed to act freely. "Enforst to seek some couert nigh at hand" (1.7), he finds himself in the emblematic wood with its "Eugh obedient to the benders will" (1.9). His will may be more constrained than it appears, even to him. The dwarf urges him to "fly," but Una tells him "To stay the steppe, ere forced to retrate" (1.13). Which is he to do? Since he is spiritually hard of hearing and illiterate, his choices are limited. Indeed, if we adhere to Reformed understandings of the fallen will, he may have no (healthy) choices at all.[35] In any event, the "youthfull knight could not for ought be staide" (1.14)—again, his will needs curbing so that it may ultimately be "free." This is no easy paradox. Hence he finds himself enthralled, "wrapt in *Errours* endlesse traine" (1.18), a state Una describes as his "sore constraint" (1.19). His release from Errour's grip proves temporary, of course, for his will, however potentially liberated by hearing Una's words, remains in bondage.

Or so Spenser's commentators usually think.[36] The problem of Redcrosse's will—is it free or enslaved?—has vexed criticism of this book of the poem for over a century. Nobody doubts that Redcrosse acts as a Christian Everyman. His wandering and degeneration enact paradigms much larger than himself, and so it is often deemed legitimate to extrapolate from his story Spenser's views about the fundamental controversy of the Reformation, the nature of the will and its relation to grace and good works. Many commentators have seized on the narrator's isolated statements, most notably 10.1, to demonstrate Spenser's "position" about free will and the poem's relation to one or another doctrinal stance on the subject. To take the famous example, most critics deduce from the statement "all the good is Gods, power and eke will" (10.1) that Redcrosse's will is enslaved to sin and awaiting grace for regeneration. Most commentators presume from this and other exhortative passages that Spenser can be said to "endorse" one or another "position" circulating through the rapids of the Reformation. One may phrase the question of free will in the era's starkest alternatives: does the fallen will, however impaired by its corruptions, retain at least some ability to cooperate with divine assistance in the form of grace, as the Roman Catholic and some moderate Protestants would have it? Or is the fallen will, as per Reformed theology, hopelessly depraved and dependent totally on salvation through faith alone, a faith that God infuses by grace with no cooperation from the human agent, a grace responsible for any good the creature accomplishes, including the initiation of faith? Spenser scholarship has found evidence throughout Book I for most "positions" about this nuclear Reformation controversy—the free versus the enslaved will—although most commentators find, usually by means of selective quotation, confirmation of the Reformed doctrine of the will in bondage.

The text, however, is not arguing or even allegorizing a theological position.[37] The text dramatizes a conflict—Redcrosse's wandering, his errors and mishaps—that certainly has theological dimensions. The issue of the will that has proved so contentious in the commentary on this book of *The Faerie Queene* is more definitively and authoritatively interrogated, as we shall see, in Book VI. Meanwhile, as the scholarship surrounding Book I testifies in its very abundance, the questions of free will have no conclusive, monolithic answers in the Legend of Holinesse. Furthermore, the hero's is a public as well as a personal spiritual crisis. Critics have tended to separate the two quests, and usually ignore issues of free will in analyzing the book's public dimension as a saga of the national church.[38] But, as we shall see, the public and private domains overlap in the book's representation of apocalyptic preaching, especially in later episodes, to suggest how Redcrosse's resuscitation is consonant with the nation's.

If we embed the text in contemporary religious discourses, we will not find the "answer," the monocular right way to understand the theological positions putatively offered by the poet. We will hear instead how the text gives play to those discourses. Rather than advancing a sustained "position" to be revealed by a "reading," the text manipulates features of various discourses—for present purposes, the Protestant *artes praedicandi*—to allegorize the hero's suffering and renewal.

Reformation sermon theory itself is vitally, if indirectly, implicated in the discourse of free will—indeed, matters of free will and faith and sin animate hermeneutic representations of preaching as a speech act. For example, Perkins itemizes one "impediment to hearing": "when a man will heare no other doctrine, but that which is sutable to his corrupt nature, not being willing to frame his heart to the word, but to have the word framed to his heart" (2:70). On the one hand, human "corrupt nature" prevents the will from doing good; on the other, the very phrase "not being willing" implies potential cooperation the hearer might bring to the preached Word. Perkins, like other Reformed sermon theorists, resolves (some would say *finesses*) the danger of incipient Pelagianism, which grants to the will the capability of contributing to salvation through works, by maintaining that the will can do good only when "prevented" by grace. Hence Perkins's statement that "the hearers ought not to ascribe their faith to the gifts of men but to the power of Gods word" (2:670); in other words, grace initiates good.

In either event, whether hearers cooperate with the Word or grace initiates and "prevents" their cooperation, the formulation carries with it a set of ethical and psychological assumptions that bear upon the individual hearer's disposition to preaching and that person's behavior as a result of what he or she hears: "euery hearer must receiue the word with meeknesse, that is, with quietnesse subiect himselfe to the word of God in all things. . . . This hearing eare, is a gift of God, enabling the heart, when it heareth, to conceiue and vnderstand the doctrine taught, and to yeeld obedience thereunto." One has duties to perform after hearing, Perkins says: "he must be obedient vnto it, and testifie to his obedience" (2:70–71). Sermon discourse often implies, if it does not explicitly articulate, a freedom of will or, at the very least, a cooperation, as suggested in the insistence on what the hearer "must" (but clearly need not) do ("yeeld obedience"). The point is crucial. Recent scholarship has determined that although Reformed theology denies the freedom of the will, Calvin and other Reformers speak as though the will is free. Pronouncements on the utter enslavement of the will to sin and its absolute inability to initiate good or even cooperate with grace are often set forth in language that is decidedly voluntaristic.[39] "Lette us," says *The Book of Homilies*, "apply our selfes, as farforth as we can have tyme and leasure, to knowe Gods Worde by diligent hearyng and readyng therof."[40] Most sermon theorists seem to adhere to the strict Reformed position that good is accomplished only through God's grace, not the creature's will. Yet hearers are usually presupposed to have enough freedom both to apply themselves and frame their hearts to the Word and to "yeeld obedience" to its precepts. In the opening episode of *The*

Faerie Queene, Redcrosse parodies the hearer of the preached Word. He yields obedience, not to the "faith" offered in Una's first line of advice, which is cryptic in any event but instead to the merely physical imperatives of the second half of her advice ("strangle her").

The second half of canto 1 presents another scene of advice-giving and complicates the motifs of the first episode. Chancing to meet Archimago—disguised as an "aged Sire," soberly clad, carrying a book, and knocking his breast "as one that did repent" (1.29)—Una and Redcrosse might well anticipate from this "sagely sad" figure some sort of higher counsel. In fact, however, everything about him suggests the antithesis of the godly preacher. His self-description, offered when Redcrosse asks him for direction(s), would immediately suggest—to the reader if not to a deafened auditor—the stereotypical portrait of a Roman Catholic monk, withdrawn silently from the world:

> how should, alas,
> Silly old man, that liues in hidden cell,
> Bidding his beades all day for his trespas,
> Tydings of warre and worldly trouble tell?
> With holy father sits not with such things to mell.
>   (1.30)

Far from replicating the popular image of the "Preachers of Gods Gospell, as messengers, as seruants, as Ministers of Christ"—in Bishop Jewel's words, "Gods messengers appointed to lead and guide"[41]—Archimago's initial pose of severe monastic detachment would invite hostility from an audience conditioned to the newly revised self-depiction of an active clergy, living in the world and attending to the practical needs of the flock for assurance and comfort.[42]

Archimago presently discards his reclusiveness and, when it is in his interests to do so, joins Una in giving advice to Redcrosse by seconding her recommendation to rest at Archimago's dwelling: "Right well Sir knight ye haue aduised bin" for "the way to win / Is wisely to aduise" (1.33). Earlier Redcrosse has rashly ignored Una's counsel (about "stay[ing] the steppe" [1.13] at Errour's cave); here he accepts it, to their detriment. Redcrosse is unable, here and elsewhere, to discriminate between good and bad advice; he has not, in Perkins's trope, developed a "saving hearing" (3:280). Hence he is not suspicious to find they have "all things at their will" (1.35) in Archimago's environment. Nor can he discern the diabolical in Archi-

mago's speech, even when the old man flaunts it so no Protestant audience could mishear—or would have heard from its godly divines:

> With faire discourse the euening so they pas:
> For that old man of pleasing words had store,
> And well could file his tongue as smooth as glas;
> He told of Saintes and Popes, and euermore
> He strowd an *Aue-Mary* after and before.
>
> (1.35)

His words may please, but they neither instruct nor comfort. And
if these hints are not enough, Archimago soon "choos[es] out few
wordes most horrible," the satanic negation of the preacher's Word:

> He bad awake blacke *Plutoes* griesly Dame,
> And cursed heauen, and spake reprochfull shame
> Of highest God, the Lord of life and light.
>
> (1.37)

The scene parodies the relation between preacher and hearer. Archimago's hearer is an infernal deity, whom he commands to do his bid-
ding. And presto, "the God obeyed" (1.44). In fact, the parody works
in two directions: on one hand, Archimago mimes the Roman Catholic priest, often accused of superstitiously trying to propitiate or
manipulate heaven with sacraments;[43] on the other, he parodies the
Protestant preacher, whose goal is to induce "obedience" in the faithful hearer, certainly not in the deity. Like Redcrosse, the infernal
hearer of Archimago's words obeys. The subsequent campaign to se-
duce Redcrosse during the night continues the parody of preacherly
motifs. The knight's encounter with the infernally summoned spright
anticipates the one already examined between Arthur and Una at the
end of canto 7, exactly half a book later. Like Una, the spright begins
tearfully and then pauses:

> Her swollen hart her speach seemd to bereaue,
> And then againe begun, My weaker yeares
> Captiu'd to fortune and frayle worldly feares,
> Fly to your faith for succour and sure ayde.
>
> (1.52)

Key words such as "speach," "faith," "sure ayde," and "succour"
signal the correspondences between the two scenes. In a parodic
foreshadowing of Arthur's later pastoral office, Redcrosse assumes
the role here of comforter. "Assure your selfe," he tells the imposter,
"I deeme your love, and hold me to you bound" (1.54). He thus pro-

leptically mimes Arthur's later words to Una: "Assure your self, I will you not foresake" (7.52). Redcrosse also tries to verify what he hears "and gan himself aduise / To proue his sense" (1.50). He does not seem to be able to rely on his own advice, and he has taken the wrong advice from others. Although the spright's "doubtfull words made that redoubted knight / Suspect her truth" (1.53), he nonetheless misreads, "fed with words, that could not chuse but please" (1.54), becomes a redoubter, misplaces his faith, and abandons Una. The spright's words "could not chuse but please" because Redcrosse himself has so few choices, if he has any at all. Having failed to curb his will to the only words demonstrated to please (i.e., genuine homiletic words, reflecting the Word), he diminishes his power of choice.

A selection from a Reformed catechism, Perkins's "The Foundation of Christian Religion," might serve to gloss this scene and others: "Q. How must we heare Gods word, that it may be effectuall to our saluation? A. We must come vnto it with hunger-bitten hearts, hauing an appetite to the word; we must marke it with attention, receiue it by faith, submit ourselues vnto it with feare and trembling, euen then when our faults are reproued. Lastly, we must hide it in the corners of our hearts, that we may frame our liues and conuersations by it" (1:7). The demanding auxiliary verb "must" suggests the hearers' duty: we must *mark, receive, submit, frame*. Hearing becomes a moral and spiritual obligation that will result in submission to yet more duties: framing lives and conversations. Redcrosse errs because he will or cannot hear anything but "doubtfull words."

In the following episodes, as Redcrosse's errors and mishaps deepen, the moral ambiguities of the first canto are not simplified. The text continually draws attention to the power of words, in Perkins's phrase, to "pearce the heart"—or, in Redcrosse's declining state, to fail to do so. The narrator remarks that the knight "wandred" and that "Will was his guide" (2.12), but the extent that this is a theological judgment, expressing a corrupt will, saturated with sin, is not certain. On the other hand, his wandering is certainly a feature of his epistemological biography. In the second canto, for example, Redcrosse succumbs to Duessa disguised as Fidessa. As she recounts her story, riddled with inconsistencies, Redcrosse responds in this fashion:

> He in great passion all this while did dwell,
> More busying his quicke eyes, her face to view,

Then his dull eares, to heare what she did tell.
(2.26)

His ears have been "dull" from the beginning. He listens only with
what Perkins calls the "bodily eare," neglecting the "sauing hearing
which bringeth eternal life: all other hearing doth increase our sins to
our further condemnation" (3:280). Relying on the "other hearing,"
he offers Duessa rash assurance, heard now in two other contexts:
"Henceforth," he tells her, "in safe assuraunce may ye rest" (2.27).
His later paralysis may be a result of his presumption of this preacherly task, of offering assurance. Duessa has just asked Redcrosse for
"mercy" because she is "subiect to hard mischaunce, / And to [his]
mighty will" (2.21). So she is, and so perhaps is he. Subject to his own
misguided will, he cannot yield to others' counsel, except when it
misleads. Duessa then heightens the wordplay on free will. She is, she
says, "made thrall to your commandement" and one whom "false
fortune betraide . . . to your powre" (2.22), just as Sansfoy had "per-
force me led / With him away" (2.25). Redcrosse, of course, is far
more thrall to her than she to him. Furthermore, her phrasing apes
the putative obligations of Redcrosse, wearer of Christian insignia:
made thrall to commandment(s).

Oddly enough, however, although he is spiritually hard of hearing, Redcrosse recognizes that some words can deceive. No sooner
has he given assurance to Duessa than Fradubio's "piteous yelling
voyce was heard" (2.31). The knight at this point is still sufficiently
aware of his own frailty to ask

What voyce of damned Ghost from *Limbo* lake,
Or guilefull spright wandring in empty aire,
Both which fraile men do oftentimes mistake,
Sends to my doubtfull eares these speaches rare[?]
(2.32)

Despite his claims to alertness, his ears are not "doubtfull" in any
morally useful sense (although perhaps they are full of doubt, in a
theologically harmful sense). He fails to recognize that he has already
been victimized by his dull ears and that Fradubio's words apply to
his own situation—nor does he heed Fradubio's plea to "fly, fly"
(2.31).

Whatever other literary precedents lie behind the Fradubio episode, it also derives from the medieval homiletic exemplum, perhaps
one drawn from "natural phenomena, especially the life of plants,"

still current in the sixteenth century, despite changes in the Reformation sermon.[44] The auditor, in this case, conspicuously fails to make the desired personal application. This Fradubio shortly makes plain in his tale of woe, when he tells how a "cruell witch her cursed will to wreake, /Hath thus transformd" (2.33) him so that *his* will is utterly impaired, "enclosd in wooden wals full faste" (2.42): "We may not chaunge (quoth he) this euil plight" (2.43), a summation of his immobility and perhaps of his auditor's as well.[45] In refusing to apply Fradubio's exemplum to himself, or to heed Fradubio's advice to "fly," Redcrosse insures that his own story becomes in turn an exemplum, as the narrator makes explicit when he later resumes the knight's tale and exhorts us to "Beware of fraud, beware of ficklenesse": "That doth this *Redcrosse* knights ensample plainly proue" (4.1).

That proof is perhaps most effective in the house of Pride, where the narrative technique underscores Redcrosse's widening separation from the saving power of words (and the Word). The episode up until the joust has relatively little dialogue. We hear nothing directly, for example, of what Lucifera says. And the procession of the Seven Deadly Sins is depicted as an exclusively visual event.[46] Nobody speaks until Sansjoy's rude entrance. Redcrosse's ominous response to the Saracen's challenge confirms his deepening insensitivity to the power of language: "He neuer meant with words, but swords to plead his right" (4.42). Swords have replaced words in his armory of defenses against the world's perils. No wonder, then, that Redcrosse so easily misinterprets Duessa's famous words in the ensuing joust. When she cries out from the stand to Sansjoy on what appears to be the verge of his triumph, "Thine the shield, and I, and all" (5.11), Redcrosse mishears, mistakenly applies her words to himself, and ironically rises to the danger. His interpretive powers have been crippled. In these cantos it is Duessa and Sansjoy who communicate accurately and profoundly. In their secret parley she approaches him "with speaches seeming fit" (4.45), and he in turn "With gentle wordes . . . can her fairely greet / And bad say on the secret of her hart" (4.46). They have access to a language able to communicate feeling and reveal secrets (however debased)—this is yet another parody of the colloquy between Arthur and Una. In his own way, meanwhile, Redcrosse himself has coarsened language. By wishing to respond with swords, not words, to an infidel's reproaches, he literalizes and so distorts the Pauline metaphor of the sword of the spirit (Heb. 4:12). As Bullinger notes,

> Neither do we euer reade it any were sent of the Lorde as souldiers, which with armed force shuld bring the world in subiection. But rather the Scripture witnesseth the great enemie of God, Antichrist, shalbe destroied with the breth of Gods mouth. Where fore there is no doubt, that all those thinges which are reade in diuers places of the prophets . . . concerning wars to be made against all nations, and by the apostles and apostolical men, ought to be figuratively expounded. For the Apostles according to their manner, fight as apostles: not with speare, sword, and bowe of carnal warfare, but of spiritual. The apostolical sword is the word of God.[47]

Lacking the readerly skills to interpret the world figuratively, Redcrosse is a crude and naive literalist who prefers swords to words. Any English Reformer (before 1588) could tell him that the Word and its attendant words have far more powerful claims to defeat Antichrist or his infidel minions. For example, Richard Taverner points out that the original disciples "preached [the gospel], according to theyr commission, and lefte it in mens free lybertie to come to it or not. They said not, eyther beleue it or I wyl kyll the. So ye se that infidels, as Turkes, Sarasens and Jues, ought not violently to be drawn to our faith, but louingly rather prouoked and allured."[48] Whether Redcrosse has "faith" is an open question, but he has certainly shown a greater aptness for swords than words.

The profundity of Redcrosse's spiritual illiteracy and deafness deepens by the interlacing of his trials with Una's wandering in separate cantos. Already vulnerable without Redcrosse's protection, she is reduced to helplessness by the incomprehension of the characters she encounters. Corceca can neither "heare, nor speake, nor vnderstand" (3.11) and is hardly bettered by her mother, whose speech is limited to "nine hundred *Pater nosters* euery day / And thrise nine hundred *Aues* she was wont to say" (3.13). They swing to the opposite extreme, equally ineffective, after the death of Kirkrapine. They "loudly bray" at Una "with hollow howling, and lamenting cry / Shamefuly at her rayling all the way" (3.23). Una's plight in the midst of this inarticulateness reinforces the text's insistence on the salvific power of language as a way out of the wilderness. Furthermore Una's adventures in the savage nation also reflect upon Redcrosse's simultaneous exploits in the house of Pride. In the forest Una herself now becomes miserably speechless—"Such fearefull fit assaid her trembling hart / Ne word to speake, ne ioynt to moue she had." And yet she is understood more clearly, one suspects, by others than by Redcrosse: "The saluage nation feele her secret smarte, / And read her sorrow in her count'nance sad" and "comfort her" (6.11)—still more therapeutic counseling. Despite their superior powers as readers of secret feeling, the satyrs are nonetheless incapable (though perhaps no more so than Redcrosse at this point) of comprehending the Word:

> During which time her gentle wit she plyes,
> To teach them truth, which worshipt her in vaine,
> And made her th'Image of Idolatryes.
>
> (6.19)

Like a preacher—she is, of course, one of Book I's chief sources of uncorrupted homiletic discourse—Una instructs them in "Trew sacred lore" (6.30). She also teaches Satyrane "wisedome heauenly rare" so effectively that he "learn[s] her discipline of faith and veritie" (6.31).[49] This is the discipline marking the successful transaction between preacher and hearer. Una has taken on for them the role of the preacher: "Teaching the Satyres" (6.30). The irony is obvious: the lower creatures hear Una's advice and "learn . . . her discipline," again implying the obedience advocated in sermon theory, a yielding that leads the satyrs to "faith and veritie" (6.31). The wandering in this book of the poem centers precisely in this issue, in the relation of the Word/word to moral and spiritual errancy. On the question of how are we saved, Taverner offers the answer that the "worde, which beyng preached vnto vs reproueth vs of our wanderyng and strayeng abroade."[50] Becon describes the hearer who does not hear: "For as shepe, whan that they be without a shepeharde, wander they cannot tell whither, hang on euery bush, are rent wyth euery brier, and in daunger to be deuoured of the rauening wolfe at all tymes, euen so lykewise, those people that are wythout a Preacher and techer of gods word, run astray without order, heare the voice of euery straunger, fal into all kynde of vicious abhominacion, are rent and torne with wycked spirites, and ready at euery houre to be swalowed up of Satan our olde aduersary."[51] Hence the throng surrounding Satan in the procession of the Seven Deadly Sins stands atop the "bones of men, whose life had gone astray" (4.36), while the satyrs respond as obedient hearers to Una's teaching.

Canto 7, meanwhile, cuts to Redcrosse, stretched out with Duessa and "pourd out in loosnesse on the grassy grownd" (7.7). This looseness leads only to captivity, to his enthrallment, as the "eternall bondslaue" (7.14) of Orgoglio. Having failed to read or hear, the knight is paralysed, even as he appears to be loose. After their victory, the giant and the sorceress now play out a teasing minuet of the will: "So willingly she came into his armes / Who her as willingly to grace did take" (7.15) and for whom "He chose" (7.16) a monstrous beast. They seem to have choices, while Redcrosse, having disregarded advice that might have freed him, finds himself a "caytiue thrall" (7.19) who can neither "see, nor heare at will" (7.13).

Because preaching weds rhetoric and theology, the Reformation finds it the ideal medium for the Word to save and regenerate. Two episodes pertaining to Redcrosse's salvation in the second half of Book I need to be situated in the Reformation *ars praedicandi*: the one in Despaire's cave, where Redcrosse is exhorted to suicide, and the other in the house of Holinesse, where Redcrosse learns about mercy and salvation. Both episodes have been the focus of considerable attention, from both theological and rhetorical perspectives. The advice Redcrosse receives from Despaire constitutes what Perkins calls "unprofitable hearing" (a danger Perkins associates with despair in his scheme of "tentations to the godly"), and what the knight finds in the house of Holinesse comprises "effectual preaching and hearing" (an advantage Perkins lists among the "causes of salvation").[52] Or to state the matter in the terms of another contemporary sermon theorist, in the last part of this book Redcrosse hears two major categories of homily: from Despaire he hears a "chidinge" sermon; from Contemplation he hears a sermon both doctrinal and "perswasible."[53] The two forms of preaching are closely linked, not least in how they help transform Redcrosse from private individual to national protagonist in the combat against Antichrist.

Critics have skillfully traced the origins of Despaire's speech in a number of religious discourses.[54] Two treatments are especially pertinent. Patrick Cullen extends earlier perceptions that Despaire's forensic strategy is to segregate the Covenants of Justice and Mercy by pointing out that Despaire delivers an "infernal sermon" based on a distortion of Scripture, particularly of Pauline texts. By "parodying New Testament doctrine" Despaire's speech becomes a "profanation

of divine [i.e., Pauline] metaphor."[55] Ann E. Imbrie demonstrates
that Despaire's rhetoric is based on a parody of biblical interpretation and that his method relies on the "fault of quoting out of context," condemned in Reformation hermeneutics.[56] Both examinations show how Despaire distorts Scripture. He also maims the
contemporary art of preaching.

Redcrosse gets ample warning of Despaire's methods. Trevisan,
who directs him to Despaire's cave, cautions against the "wounding
words and termes of foule repriefe" by which Despaire plucks "from
vs all hope of due reliefe" (9.29). When Redcrosse naively asks how
"idle speach" could harm, Trevisan tells him that "His subtill tongue,
like dropping honny, mealt'th / Into the hart" (9.31). Despaire's rhetorical ploys (conveyed in now familiar terms of *words-heart-hope*)
are the diabolical counterpart of those Arthur has employed to con-
sole Una. Redcrosse, however, has become so deafened to whole-
some advice that he ignores this warning and quickly proves vulnerable to Despaire's cunning.

Despaire's deforming of the Reformation sermon parallels his
warping of Scripture: he suppresses half the text. According to some
Reformation theorists, the sermon has two equally important functions: on the one hand, to preach repentance; on the other, to teach
forgiveness of sins. One sermon manual stresses the parity of the two
functions by noting that the congregation must be convinced not
only that they are wicked but also that "God will pardon and forgive
their sins and that he will withdraw his anger and punishment."[57]
The culmination of Despaire's speech, with its universalizing and
sweeping questions, skillfully mimics the preacher's bid for repentance:

> Is not he iust, that all this doth behold
>> From highest heauen, and beares an equall eye?
>> Shall he thy sins vp in his knowledge fold,
>> And guiltie be of thine impietie?
>> Is not his law, Let euery sinner die:
>> Die shall all flesh?
>>> (9.47)

By ending here, Despaire truncates the preacher's obligation to bal-
ance the warning about penitence with the good news about forgiveness.[58] Niels Hemmingsen warns in his manual, *The Preacher*, that
the "chidinge sermon," used to correct "the loytring or offendinge,

or the stubburne and disobediente hearer," has an inherent danger, strictly to be avoided. "Condition of repentance," he says, ought to "be mingled, lest any being discouraged, with somewhat more rougher chidinges, should fall into desparation or wilfullye kill him-selfe."[59]

Despaire also parodies sermons based on popular Reformed understandings of the depravity of human nature. One need only compare Despaire's final words with those of the celebrated Elizabethan preacher, Henry Smith. In a characteristic sermon Smith dwells vividly on the consequences of sin: "An Arrow is swift, the Sun is swifter, but Sin is swiftest of all: For in a moment it is committed on earth, it comes before God in heaven, and is condemned to hell . . . For the wrath of God taketh us up on high, and throweth us down low upon the rocks of shame and contempt, and terrour of conscience: and so having crushed us with double death, the grave devouring us, hell swallowing us."[60] Smith's words have their visual counterpart in the tableau Despaire shows Redcrosse near the end of the temptation:

> He shew'd him painted in a table plaine,
> The damned ghosts, that doe in torments waile,
> And thousand feends that doe them endlesse paine
> With fire and brimstone, which for euer shall remaine.
>
> (9.49)

Despaire's performance, then, parodies sermons of the age not so much by distorting them (he actually mirrors them—or elements of them—quite accurately) as by simply omitting what normally follows fulminations against sin, namely assurance of salvation for the righteous. He parodies, then, the Reformation preacher's obligation to bring assurance that salvation is the hearer's; instead he brings assurance of damnation. His is the diabolic counterpart to the assurance Arthur has brought to Una.

Critics have noted that Despaire's counsel contains fundamental rhetorical contradictions; his speech also embodies theological contradictions focusing on questions of voluntarism. On the one hand, like a good determinist (both pagan and Christian), he asks,

> Who then can striue with strong necessitie,
> That holds the world in his still chaunging state,
> Or shun the death ordaynd by destinie?
>
> (9.42)

On the other, he seems to present Redcrosse with choices, namely suicide. When he brings Redcrosse the implements of self-destruction, he bids "him choose, what death he would desire: / For death was due to him, that had prouokt Gods ire" (9.50). Having foolishly ignored good advice from Una (or, quite recently, Trevisan) and now faced with these false choices, Redcrosse faithfully attends to Despaire's decidedly bad advice. When she intervenes to subvert Redcrosse's willful course, Una places Despaire's advice in the homiletic context of hearing with the heart's ear: "Ne let vaine words bewitch thy manly hart," she reproaches the knight. Her words ("ne let") presume Redcrosse's freedom in this matter and put the emphasis on choice: "Why shouldst thou then despeire, that chosen art?" (9.53). The interchange poses—although it does not answer—a fundamental question of sixteenth-century religious thought: has Redcrosse here revealed his will to be free, even if it sometimes makes the wrong choice, or has he evidenced a will so blighted as to be forced to choose evil?

Despaire employs other sermon parodies as well. His speech is larded with homiletic idiom, for example. A number of his sentences would be quite at home in *The Book of Homilies*: his corrective parlance ("is then vniust to each his due to giue?") or his admonitory tone ("Is not great grace to helpe him ouer past, /Or free his feet, that in the myre sticke fast?" [9.38–39]). Like all great parodists, Despaire succeeds by imitating the original quite closely: no, it is not unjust to give each his due; yes, it is good to free someone stuck in the mire. Stanza 39, for example, could easily be inserted into commonplace sermon remarks against excessive grief. It mimes, with only the slightest off-coloring, an unexceptionable funeral homily. In this sense, Despaire is the book's consummate advice-giver. That his counsel is infernal underscores Redcrosse's gravel-deafness.

Hence the effect of Despaire's speech on Redcrosse is supremely parodic—of the hearer's response, summed up in Perkins's Pauline phrase that the "word preached must pearce into the heart" (cf. Heb. 4:12: "the worde of God is liuelie, & mightie in operation, and sharper than anie two edged sworde"):

> The knight was much enmoued with his speach,
>> That as a swords point through his hart did perse,
>> And in his conscience made a secret breach.
>
> (9.48)

Although Redcrosse appears to respond with his heart (the choice of a distancing simile is telling), he hears this homily with only a "bodily ear." Despaire's sermon may heighten his listener's awareness of sin, but it discourages another kind of hearing that brings with it "faith, conversion, and obedience. . . . This is that saving hearing which bringeth eternal life: all other hearing doth increase our sins to our further condemnation" (Perkins, 3:280).

Finally Despaire should be seen *sub specie et temporalis et aeternitatis*—for he is a major antagonist in the book's project of vanquishing Rome, perceived as the chief threat, both spiritual and temporal, to sixteenth-century English Protestants. As a distorted version of the Reformation preacher, Despaire incarnates Antichrist, at loose abroad in Roman Catholic forces threatening to undo the godly work of the English church. In the arena of international religious conflict enacted in this book, Despaire plays the historical role of what in sermon theory is called (after the figure from Revelation) a False Prophet, a particularly sinister counterfeit who seems to have held special terror for English Protestantism: "There are three kinds of false prophets. The first teacheth false doctrine. The second teacheth true doctrine but applieth it falsely. The third teacheth and applieth it well, but liue ill."[61] Despaire embodies in varying degrees all three aberrations. In this book he divides with Archimago the work of the False Prophet. As the narrator points out, Redcrosse has been "charmed with [Despaire's] inchaunted rimes" (9.48), different only in degree from the "mighty charmes" and curses of Archimago (1.36–37), to whom Despaire is akin. Despaire, then, takes his place in the book's infernal triumvirate, who populate the allegory in a variety of shifting characterological manifestations: Whore, False Prophet, Beast. All three taken together incarnate Antichrist, who can be crushed only with the power of the Word.[62]

That Word is uttered, quickly and powerfully, by Una. In one stanza (9.53) she delivers all five major types of homily, as classified by the sermon manuals.[63] Una now plays the role of the doctrinal homilist ("In heauenly mercies hast thou not a part?"); redargutive homilist ("Why shouldst thou then despeire, that chosen art?"); admonitory homilist ("Arise . . . and leaue this cursed place"); corrective homilist ("Ne let vain words bewitch thy manly heart"); as well as consolatory homilist ("greater grace / . . . doth quench the brond of hellish smart"). Una plays her homiletic part as savior from despair quite differently from

Arthur in his earlier rescue of her. Arthur functions solely as a consolatory homilist, giving assurance and comfort of "faith" (7.42). Una embraces a wider sweep of homily. She rehearses all the subgenres of homily, including the consolatory: she brings the hearer assurance that the
good news of the gospel applies to him.[64]

Her succinct speech—with its mordant question, "in heauenly
mercies hast thou not a part?" indebted to the Protestant commonplace of "greater grace"—needs to be juxtaposed to two other relevant homiletic passages. The first is the narrator's exordium before
the house of Holinesse, with its fervent Reformation generalizations
and its exalted exhortations:

> Ne let the man ascribe it to his skill,
> That thorough grace hath gained victory.
> If any strength we haue, it is to ill,
> But all the good is Gods, both power and eke will.
>
> (10.1)

These lines have been the subject of intensive commentary in Spenser
criticism.[65] They have usually been taken as articulating Spenser's
theology, which seems here uncomplicatedly antivoluntarist. If all
the good is God's, including whatever good is done by human will,
then human autonomy to do good is profoundly diminished. The
stanza seems to insist upon God's absolute power to do good and
upon the absolute inability of the human will to do good in the absence of God's grace ("good"). From the perspective of the sermon
discourses implanted in this book of the poem, the stanza would appear to verify the claim that only by submission to the Word can the
will be free. For this passage cannot be isolated from its two fellow
homiletic passages nearby. The centrifugal force of the narrator's
homily expands the earlier lines of Una to Redcrosse to encompass
the human condition. Both passages prepare for yet another homily,
Caelia's in the house of Holinesse:

> So few there bee,
> That chose the narrow path, or seeke the right:
> All keepe the broad high way, and take delight
> With many rather for to go astray,
> And be partakers of their euill plight,
> Then with a few to walke the rightest way;
> O foolish men, why haste ye to your owne decay?
>
> (10.10)

All three sermons center on the will. Yet taken as a homiletic trio, they fail to map out a unified theological position. Each passage, segregated from the others and from surrounding circumstances in the text, has been—often with considerable persuasiveness—offered as evidence of one or other position on the will available in the disputes of the Reformation. Does God by grace bend the depraved will to do good (10.1); or, alternatively, can the creature cooperate with grace and choose the narrow path to heaven (10.10)? What exactly is the "part" in "heauenly mercies" of the fallen creature; if he can "choose" despair, can he also help choose a more hopeful course (9.53)? On the extent of Redcrosse's will, its iniquity or its nascent ability to choose and cooperate with the good, the text is far from clear, as the very existence of the multitudinous glosses on these passages verify.

It is tempting to bracket the scholarly quest to situate Spenser's theology and concentrate instead on Redcrosse's drama. All three homilies occur only when Redcrosse's heart has been sufficiently bruised, softened, and humbled to be pierced readily by their (s)wordplay. As Una recognizes, he is ready to enroll in Fidelia's "schoolehouse" so "That of her heauenly learning he might taste, / And heare the wisedome of her words diuine" (10.18). At last Redcrosse will learn how to hear obediently, and so learn how to develop what Perkins calls that "sauing hearing which bringeth eternal life." Perkins warns that the hard of heart "must know that Gods judgement is on them; and if they would be saued, they must labour to come out of this estate, and endeauor to hear with their hearts, that they may be turned vnto God both in minde, heart, and life . . . We must use all good meanes to become good hearers of Gods word, bringing not only the bodily eares which wee have by creation, but the spiritual eares of the heart, which we have by regeneration" (3:280). *Labor, endeavor, bring, use*: Perkins's verbs imply choice, available after regeneration: to yield and bend, to eschew what is heard by the bodily ear and attend instead to the heart's ear.

This is exactly Redcrosse's condition; hence he responds to the Word offered in Fidelia's preaching, described in a stanza replete with the language of Reformation sermon theory:

And that her *sacred Booke*, with bloud ywrit,
 That none could *read*, except she did them *teach*,
 She vnto him disclosed euery whit,

And *heauenly documents thereout did preach,*
That weaker wit of man could neuer reach,
Of God, of grace, of justice, *of free will,*
That wonder was *to hear her goodly speach*:
For she was able, *with her words* to kill,
And raise againe to life *the hart,* that she did thrill.
(10.19; emphasis added)

At last Redcrosse learns to "read," a skill he has lacked since the cave of Errour. And he learns at last how to "hear her goodly speach," a hearing different in kind from that of his "bodily eares." "So it is," says Greenham, "that preaching brings hearing, hearing breeds beleeving, and by beleeving we are saved."

Redcrosse has now become what Perkins calls a "hearing hearer," one of those who have "eares pierced in their hearts by the spirit of grace, whereby they do not only heare the word outwardly, but their hearts are also affected with it, and made pliable unto it" (3:280). He listens to Fidelia's preaching—figured as disclosure of heavenly documents—and is given access to what his "weaker wit" had been denied. "None could read, except": a formulation that privileges the preacher (Sandys, "To stand before the preacher is to stand before God") with disclosures concealed from others, with truths that "thrill" (pierce?) the heart. Hence "the faithfull knight now grew in litle space, / By hearing her" (10.21). Hearing her preach, chief among the comforts and ministrations of the house of Holinesse, makes the knight's heart pliable, or pierceable.[66]

Revived by this new hearing, Redcrosse can profit from further instruction. "If we do heare the Lord," says Greenham, "he will heare us and communicate unto us the graces of his holy spirit and whatsoever is needful for our salvation."[67] Rogers suggests that preaching helps those "who have had weake beginnings in the Church of God . . . cast off that which would hinder them, their inward corruptions especially; they prepare themselves to follow the rules which lead and guide them to their duty: by this they espy their weaknesses, and how they are hidden backe when they have fallen, and which is the right way of proceeding."[68] *Lead-follow-guide-right way*: the prescriptive language of the divines is mirrored in the narrative of Redcrosse's recovery. The various therapies and counselings Redcrosse receives have exactly this purpose, to "communicate . . . whatsoever is needful for our salvation." The surgeon Patience, for instance, applies not only "salues and med'cines" to "that soule-diseased knight" but also "words of wondrous might" (10.24). When the knight is in danger of being overwhelmed by recognition of his "sins," Speranza gives "him comfort sweet . . . to take assured hold" (10.22). Caelia, too, enacts the role of comforting preacher—as Una and Arthur have at earlier stages—and so ministers to Una's "perplexitie" on the knight's behalf: "Her [i.e., Una] wisely comforted all that [Caelia] might / With goodly counsell and aduisement right" (10.23). Caelia becomes yet another comforter/advisor/preacher. And Redcrosse, in turn, remains the protocomforted/assured/preached-to hearer of "words of wondrous might."

While all these figures "instruct . . . with great industree" (10.45), none does so more effectually than Contemplation, who reveals to Redcrosse the vision of the New Jerusalem as well as the knight's saintly destiny. Contemplation conforms to the various homiletic postures struck by earlier characters. Moreover, his roles as private advice-giver to Redcrosse and as public spokesman of a national vision signal the book's widening scope. "*Instruction,*" says Perkins, "is that whereby doctrine is applied to frame a man to liue well in the family, commonwealth and Church" (2:668). Something of the complexity of Contemplation's function is suggested by the structure of the episode: after an introduction by Mercie, he presents the vision of the New Jerusalem (10.55–56); he then interprets the vision (57); he next debates with Redcrosse the pragmatic and ethical import of the vision (58–63); and finally he reveals Redcrosse's identity and role as national saint (64–68).

Contemplation assumes his responsibility as spiritual counselor from Mercie. When she escorts Redcrosse to him, Contemplation intuits that she "doth lead, /And shewes the way, his sinfull soule to saue" and that (in the trope tirelessly reiterated since the first episode) she "can the way to heauen aread" (10.51). Contemplation's duties as Redcrosse's spiritual advisor take two forms. First, like any good doctrinal preacher, he explicitly points the way to salvation:

> Then seeke this path, that I do thee presage,
> Which after all to heauen shall thee send
> . . . .
> Where is for thee ordaind a blessed end.
>   (10.61)

Second, he acts as a specifically ethical guide, as an admonitory preacher. He enjoins Redcrosse to complete his worldly chores, temporarily to "forgo" a desire to renounce his calling as a knight. In this hortatory capacity Contemplation's advice comprises a "perswasible" sermon, intended to "perswade the hearers, either to due, to suffer, or to forsake some thinge."[69] His guidance conforms, then, to the exhortations directed toward Redcrosse from the beginning of the book. The difference here, of course, is that Redcrosse follows the advice.

In addition to his role as a private counselor, Contemplation functions as a public homilist, as the canto distills apocalyptic elements featured from the start of the book. The mountain to which Contemplation leads Redcrosse closely resembles the "great and hie mountaine" (Rev. 21:10) from which John of Patmos sees the New Jerusalem. Contemplation's vision and his pronouncements on the value of "*Cleopolis* for earthly frame" (10.59) expand the boundaries of both the episode and the poem as a whole from the individual to the nation and usher the book into the sphere of contemporary apocalyptic exegesis. Recent investigation of Tudor apocalypticism has brought vividly to light the prominent role of this kind of preaching—particularly, as we shall see below, in the chapter titled "Post-Armada Apocalyptic Discourse"—by those exegetes contributing to, and capitalizing on, post-Armada fervor.[70] Contemplation's vision has close affinities with apocalyptic discourse proclaiming international triumphs for Protestant England, presided over by its monarch.[71] Hence Contemplation's praise of both Cleopolis "the fairest peece, that eye beholden can" and of its "soueraigne Dame" (10.59).

We have long recognized that Book I is modeled on apocalypse.[72] What has not been noticed is how apocalyptic *preaching*, so fundamental to Tudor apocalypticism, plays a part in this book. Following Luther's lead, most English commentators before 1588 agreed that Antichrist would be overthrown by preaching.[73] In defining the role of the preached Word in this combat, apocalyptic divines repeatedly cite two prooftexts: "And then shal the wicked man be reueiled, whom the Lorde shal consume with the Spirit of his mouth, and shal abolish with the brightnes of his comming" (2 Thess. 2:8)—the spirit of his mouth is glossed in the Geneva version as "his worde," a reading followed by apocalyptic commentary between 1540 and 1590; and "And this Gospel of the kingdome shal be preached through the whole worlde for a witnes vnto all nacions, and then shal the end come" (Matt. 24:14). However violent their diction, the apocalyptic exegetes insist upon the pacific nature of the means: the Word preached will defeat Antichrist. Hence, for example, Sandys declares:

> We haue left that man of sinne, that rosecoloured harlot with whom the kings of the earth haue committed fornication, that triple crowned beast, that double-sworded Tyrant. . . . This wicked man of sinne is at length reuealed by the sincere preaching of the Gospell. . . . This wicked man the Lord shall destroy with the breath of his mouth, and then shall be the ende. The blaste of Gods trumpe hath made him already stagger: he hath caught such a crampe, that he beginneth now to halt . . . the Gospell shall be preached in the whole world, and then an end . . . Gods word neuer sounded more shrill, neuer was preached more sincerely then at this day.[74]

The notion of preaching advanced in the propagandist apocalyptic literature conforms, then, to the role Contemplation plays, for his preaching, so effectual in motivating his now alert hearer, is one means to rout Antichrist. Tudor apocalypticism had a huge political task before it, to renounce centuries of tradition and institute a new religion. In Contemplation's apocalyptic preaching, this book has become part of that historical project. It demonizes Rome and offers instead a politically acceptable and culturally stable state religion. Preaching will effectuate this historical overturning.

A final dimension of Contemplation's homiletic vocation is to bring assurance and comfort. Indeed his chief narrative function is to assure Redcrosse of this future victory, both temporal and spiritual. In this respect Contemplation bears strong affinities to Arthur. They share responsibility for promulgating many of the book's "spiritual" values, which now apply to both the national, political realm and Redcrosse's individual biography. The stichomythy in which Arthur rescues Una from despair (7.41) has its counterpart in that between Redcrosse and Contemplation (10.62–63). The hermit predicts Redcrosse's destiny as a saint:

> Vnworthy wretch (quoth [Redcrosse]) of so great grace,
>   How dare I thinke such glory to attaine?
>   These that haue it attaind, were in like cace
>   (Quoth he) as wretched, and liu'd in like paine.
>   But deeds of armes must I at last be faine,
>   And Ladies loues to leaue so dearely bought?
>   What need of armes, where peace doth ay remaine,

(Said he) and battailes none are to be fought?
As for loose loues are vaine, and vanish into nought.
(10.62)

The terms of the debate here, however, differ significantly from those in the dialogue between Arthur and Una. The focus of the earlier conversation is "faith": it corresponds to justification, an early stage of the Protestant *ordo salutis* in which the individual first believes he has been saved by faith given him by grace. The exchange between Redcrosse and Contemplation corresponds to a later stage of the *ordo* (Redcrosse having already understood justification from his experiences in the house of Holinesse). Here attention centers on the later prospect of how Redcrosse will "suche glory to attaine." Contemplation's insistence on the inevitability of Redcrosse's later good works, imaged as "deeds of armes" and "ladies loues," corresponds to sanctification. Moreover he directs Redcrosse to glorification, the final stage of the *ordo,* the life eternal:

Where is for thee ordaind a blessed end:
For thou emongst those Saints, whom thou doest see,
Shalt be a Saint.
(10.61)

The assurance Contemplation offers Redcrosse of his ultimate triumph fulfills the preacher's goal of kindling fervent hearts to yearn for salvation. Comforted by Contemplation's counsel of assurance, Redcrosse can now sally forth to slay the dragon.

Contemplation's assurance has public dimensions, characteristic of his (and Redcrosse's) apocalyptic roles. He assures both Redcrosse and a larger (reading) public that the victory will be both private and national and that public and personal domains will overlap and intermingle. Hence the ecclesiological movement of the final cantos. Redcrosse's victory is the nation's and the national church's. To slay the dragon is to slay the Beast threatening from abroad. Both victories, private and public, will be accomplished by preaching. The poem itself has become part of that historical venture, for it has assumed its place among the homiletic and apocalyptic discourses of the era. As we shall see in examining Book V, this apocalyptic ambition will take on dimensions not envisioned (or at least not intimated) in the 1590 version of *The Faerie Queene.* But for now, the victory over the Beast, the False Prophet, and the Whore will be executed by a special form of language, by the figurative sword of the spirit. And so it is no coincidence that in the general rejoicing at the conquest of the Dragon, Book I ends, as it began, with advice: papers and words are read, revealed, mastered. The papers of Duessa, like Errour's wordy spew, are exposed and demystified. Una's faithful word undoes Duessa as simply—and as impermanently—as it vanquishes Errour.

Sermon Parody and Discourses
of the Flesh in Book II

Book II's first glimpse of the hero suggests his confined estate: "in harnesse meete, /That from his head no place appeared to his feete" (1.5). The simultaneous harnessing and concealing of Guyon's body suggests how this book of the poem approaches the site of its own subject. Temperance, that body-centered virtue, is strangely exercised by covering its locus and constricting its medium, by hiding the body or harnessing it. Despite such protection, as well as custody by his sober Palmer, Guyon makes an easy target. At moments of crisis, if we may call his adventures that, he is often the object of others' will. Hoping "to win occasion to his will" (1.5), Archimago weaves a "web of wicked guile" (1.8) to trap his victim with images of erotic violence. He entices Guyon with a tale of a maid raped by a

> lewd ribauld [who] with vile lust aduaunst
> Layd his filthie hands on virgin cleene,
> To spoile her dainty corse so faire and sheene.[1]
>
> (1.10)

The focus on the body (or "corse"), here and throughout, is worth investigating, for in its vexed anatomy is found the essence of Spenser's peculiar virtue of temperance.

In this episode, the body is either concealed, as in Guyon's case, or violated, as in the false tale of Duessa's rape. In fact, the body is lexically dismembered, often vehemently. Having found Duessa "naked" (1.22) after her humiliation in Book I, Archimago now concocts an account of her assault by cannily cataloging body parts and strewing them through his yarn:

> Her looser golden *locks* he [her assailant] rudely rent,
> And drew her on the ground, and his sharpe sword
> Against her snowy *brest* he fiercely bent,
> And threatened death with many a bloudy word;

Toung hates to tell the rest, that *eye* to see abhord.

(1.11; emphasis added)

The anatomical dispersal typifies Book II, curious in a narrative dedicated to containing the body's unruliness. Even more surprising is the violence by which the text disjoints the body while urging restraint of fleshly errancy. This is a legend of the flesh, the primary locale of the hero's challenges, and it will carefully inspect and dissect bodily disobedience and corruption. Book II does not, then, celebrate the body. It instead inscribes Becon's orthodox view that "the lyfe of man upon earth is nothyng els then a warrefare . . . also that the flesh wythout ceasing throughe the subtile suggestion of sathan lusteth contrary to the spirite."[2] One of the text's primary projects, as the first stanza of the proem quietly puts it, is to achieve "no body," to construct the allegory so as to erase the body. For, as the narrator says of the reader in the fourth stanza of the proem, "let him . . . / . . . yield his sence to be too blunt and bace."

Certainly Archimago's images of lustful violence have their desired effect. Guyon is "amoued from his sober mood" (1.12) to "fierce ire / And zealous haste" (1.12). His unharnessing is easily accomplished, however worthily he fulfills the chivalric ideal of rescuing a lady in distress. We see more here than the simple lesson readers have drawn from the episode, that Guyon must grow in temperance. The episode highlights the human body as a problem in itself. Archimago's lies not only (textually) dismember the alleged victim but also (figuratively) discompose Guyon's body: he is unharnessed and inflamed to action by Archimago's narrative dismemberment and catalog of Duessa's bodily harm. Upon meeting her, Guyon sympathizes with Duessa for being "thus dismaid" (1.14)—a pun that works in several directions: she has been emotionally dismayed, sexually dismaid, physically dis-made. All three significations apply, too, to Guyon, who has been chivalrously dismayed on a wronged lady's behalf, unharnessed and so dis-made, and, in being righteously aroused by erotic violence, himself dis-maid.

Book II, then, immediately attends to the flesh. Coming from the first book, we may ponder the second book's connection with Redcrosse's quest, for surely he too had his own struggles with carnality.[3] Redcrosse's trials with the flesh seem to be at an end, for as he tells Guyon, God has "made my hand the organ of his might" (1.33). His flesh finally tamed to the spirit, he has accomplished one of his chief tasks and can now pledge his "good will" (1.34) to Guyon. Will Guyon's hand—and his will, too—become the organ of God's might? Or will this book of the poem remain fixed on taming the body, leaving the spirit to another realm? Since A. S. P. Woodhouse's reductive division of Book I and Book II into the realms of nature and grace, critics have sought some such connection between the two books.[4] Their links are various and intricate, broadly centering on the relation of matter and spirit: both books could be glossed by the Petrine homiletic admonition, "Derely beloued, I beseche you, as strangers and pilgrims, absteine from fleshie lustes, which fight against the soule" (1 Pet. 2:11). Book II, though, has been subjected to more diverse interpretation than its predecessor. A perusal of the *Variorum* and relevant entries in *The Spenser Encyclopedia*, for example, yields a trove of sources, analogues, and homologies rivaled by few works in English. During the middle decades of this century, scholarship firmly rooted the second book of *The Faerie Queene* in Christian soil, but we have not yet determined how this book weights classical and Christian discourses.[5] Recent scholarship has sidestepped these issues (perhaps they are unresolvable) in favor of other forms of social, political, and psychological interrogation. This chapter, too, offers indirect responses to the questions of several decades ago, for I do not believe we may definitively locate Spenser's "position," either theologically or philosophically, on many of Book II's chief issues. The wide critical diversity indicates the book's discursive opacity, and so this chapter does not offer yet another reading of Book II. Instead it shows that, by situating the book in Protestant discourses hitherto overlooked or insufficiently appreciated in scholarly discussion, we may better understand how the book configures the life of the body.[6]

One of the chief links between the first two books of *The Faerie Queene* is parody, particularly of the sermon discourses that are traced in the previous chapter of this study.[7] For example, in his interview with Duessa, the feigned rape victim, Guyon finds himself in the role Arthur plays to Una in Book I. The lexical echoes are plain. As Arthur bids Una, Guyon asks Duessa to "tell the cause of your conceiued paine" (1.14; cf. I.7.40) and twice offers her "comfort" (1.15,18). When he hears Duessa's bogus tale, Guyon says to her, "faire Lady, comfort to you make" (1.18; cf. I.7.52). In playing Arthur to Duessa's Una, Guyon also parodies the comforting role of the

Protestant preacher, a role Arthur homologously fulfills in Book I. In this way Spenser represents his characters echoing both his own text (Book I, canto 7) as well as other texts (homiletic discourse). As Arthur "saves" Una from despair, so Guyon "saves" Duessa: "Now therefore Ladie, rise out of your paine, /And see the saluing of your blotted name" (1.20; cf. I.7.42). Of course, he cannot really save her but instead is dominated by Archimago, who "*Guyon* guides an vncouth way" (1.24). At the start, Guyon's freedom seems severely restricted by his own gullibility, perhaps also by his subordination to the Palmer. The Palmer guides Guyon and "with words his will, / From foule intemperance he oft did stay" (1.34). Will words, even homiletic words, be sufficient to stay the will from intemperance? Because the advice-giving that is crucial to Redcrosse's decline and eventual resuscitation takes on new dimensions here, it is worth examining how Book II represents homiletic discourse.

The pattern of advice-giving that we trace in the previous chapter is reversed in Book II by Guyon's being the source of advice at least as often as its beneficiary. In nearly every episode his character is constructed in the lineaments of a Reformed homilist. The Palmer, too, participates in this counseling, sometimes by providing Guyon with advice, often by joining Guyon to dispense it; sometimes they sermonize in tandem. Simply to list the instances of their moralizing is to recognize that homiletic discourse forms a rich intellectual cache in this book of the poem, largely unexplored by Spenser scholarship.[8] Guyon counsels Duessa, Amavia, Phedon, Pyrochles, Mammon, and Verdant, and in turn is repeatedly admonished by the Palmer and several other characters, including Arthur. Other characters disseminate counsel generously, including Medina, Occasion, Phedon, Atin, Phaedria, and Mammon. Much of this counsel replicates, transforms, and parodies Reformation sermons, as this popular genre is formulated in the Protestant *artes praedicandi*. The advice-giving is of several varieties, and a brief taxonomy will help make clearer in later discussion how the text deploys homiletic discourse.

Following the precepts of classical rhetoric, as developed and adapted by both Augustine and Erasmus, Reformation sermon theory identifies five basic homiletic genres.[9] Two address matters of faith: doctrinal sermons seek to confirm doctrine, and redargutive sermons seek to refute doctrinal error. Three other genres are identified as pertinent to matters of behavior or attitude: admonitory ser-

mons seek to persuade the hearer to observe ethical obligations toward others, corrective sermons seek to reprove corrupt manners
and behavior, and consolatory sermons seek to comfort the afflicted
and instill hope. The five sermon genres, then, are divided roughly
into two categories: the first two genres address issues of faith; the
second three address works. Book II abounds with reworkings of all
five genres. The various pieces of counsel offered throughout the
book may be readily identified according to the generic categories set
forth in Reformation sermon theory. Parody is the chief rhetorical
mechanism by which Book II represents sermons. The various sermon parodies enacted over the course of the book comprise a species
of creative imitation that Thomas M. Greene has identified in humanist discourse: "superior parody always engages its subtext in a
dialectic of affectionate malice."[10] In Book II of *The Faerie Queene*,
the malice is usually reserved for the character doing the parodying,
but, as we shall see, it applies often to the hero and his quest as well.
We may locate an abundance of characters engaged in moralizing or
advice-giving, their discourses forming a weblike series of parodies
of the codified sermon genres in the Reformation.

For example, Guyon's conversation with Amavia, like that with
Duessa, again finds him playing Arthur's unwitting avatar by assuming the posture of the consolatory homilist. He provides her with
"goodly counsel": "help neuer comes too late" (1.44), he says, asking
her to "tell the secret of your mortall smart; / He oft finds present
helpe, who does his griefe impart" (1.46; cf. I.7.41,42). He delivers
what is known in the Reformation art of preaching as a consolatory
sermon. As his ministrations continue, however, his counseling frays
out to parody. He will, he tells Amavia, "die with you in sorrow, and
partake your griefe" (1.48). The Reformed preacher is enjoined to
comfort his listener, not to "die with" her. Guyon's role as counselor
has become that of would-be redeemer.

It is challenging to untangle Guyon's various roles in this scene.
First he pledges himself to Amavia as avenger of her wrongs.[11] Then
after her death, he sermonizes—indeed, he moralizes—the spectacle
before him: "Behold the image of mortalitie," he proclaims to the
Palmer. His homiletic style would make it a straightforward corrective sermon (reproving intemperate behavior) but for its verging on
the hackneyed, if not the self-satisfied. "The strong through pleasure
soonest falles," he observes, "the weake through smart" (1.57), as

though these conditions were detached from his own. The Palmer immediately matches his moralizing with an equally platitudinous stanza, a version of an admonitory homily on temperately measuring a golden mean (1.58). Surely one may doubt the propriety of these commonplaces at such a moment. The Palmer's pronouncements next inspire Guyon to more homily, this time the doctrinal kind— "after death the tryall is to come /When best shall be to them, that liued best" (1.59). Together they intone a homiletic counterpoint. They next conduct a funeral service—the dead couple's "utmost obloquy" (1.60) and "due rites and dolorous lament" (2.1)—indeed a pagan funeral service, complete with strewing locks of hair on the grave, that plausibly parodies the Christian rite of burial.[12] Then, continuing in his self-appointed clerical duties, Guyon conducts the rite of baptism—or so his washing of Ruddymane's bloody hands has been taken to signify—a service accompanied by yet more bromides ("Such is the state of men," and so on [2.2]).[13] Guyon has carried clerical role-playing as far as it can go—in fact, a good deal further than it conventionally should. Not only has he provided counsel, delivered himself of universal truths on the human condition, and conducted two liturgical-like rites, but he also vows to fulfill the incompatible role of revenger of the dead couple's wrongs. Guyon's moralizing makes him appear more sanctimonious than sanctified. He broadcasts temperance to the point of caricature.

Let us closely inspect the tortured flesh of Amavia and Mortdant, on display throughout the episode.[14] The human body is here represented in its widest and most disarrayed aspect, from the babe's "little hands embrewed in the bleeding brest" (1.37) of the mother to Mortdant's "ruddie lips" and "chearefull cheekes" (1.41). The episode itemizes more than forty references to an individual's body parts, unparalleled elsewhere in *The Faerie Queene*, strewn across the text as though dismembered—the hands, breast, heart, head, lap, joints, eyes, hair, cheeks, veins, eyelids, sides, chest, tongue, womb, even blood and tears, a jumbled inventory of *membra disjecta* testifying to Amavia's famous description of her husband: "For he was flesh: (all flesh doth frailtie breed)" (1.52). Carol Kaske has suggested Romans 7 as the primary subtext of this episode, where Paul ascribes his moral progress to a knowledge that "in me, that is, in my flesh, dwelleth no good thing" (7:18). "I see," says Paul, "another law in my membres, rebelling against the law of my minde, and leading me captiue vnto the law of sinne, which is in my membres" (7:23).[15] The one member prominently absent in this episode's tally has led the family to this impasse, the *membrum virile* that draws Mortdant to the "pleasure and delight" (1.52) of the witch Acrasia. That frailest of flesh plays its part in every episode, however inconspicuously, and is the absent signifier of the book's "image of mortalitie." From Duessa's (a)rousing tale of rape to the final tableau of Grill "delight[ing] in filth and foule incontinence" (12.87), the book represents the flesh as enthralled to eros and gravely needing regulation—or erasure.

In fact, the flesh of Amavia and Mortdant is portrayed as both dead and alive, a grim spectacle of the body in pain. This sad couple emblematizes the Pauline combat between flesh and spirit. When Guyon first sees Amavia, she is depicted as a "sad portrait . . . halfe dead, halfe quicke" (1.39). Mortdant is both an image of life (ruddy lips and cheerful cheek) and a "dead corse" (1.41). Together the couple betoken the fleshly condition, poised between life and death, and form an icon of the combat between flesh and spirit. The Geneva gloss of Romans 6 admonishes that "no man shulde glorie in the flesh, but rather seke to subdue it to the Spirit," exemplified in Paul's injunctions: "Let not sinne reign reigne therefore in your mortal bodie, that ye shulde obey it in the lustes thereof. Neither giue your members as weapons of vnrighteousnesse vnto sinne" (Rom. 6:12–13). Amavia and Mortdant incarnate, as Guyon sermonizes the instant after Amavia expires, "feeble nature cloth'd with fleshly tyre" (1.57). Just seeing their misery on death's brink has a similar effect on Guyon. His "fresh bloud did frieze with fearfull cold" (1.42), a kind of transference from them to him—verging, as is all flesh, between life and death. The Palmer later hypostatizes Amavia as "a sacred Symbole . . . dwell[ing] / In her sonnes flesh" (2.10).

As the Geneva glosses suggest, contextualizing this book of *The Faerie Queene* in Reformation discourses of the flesh makes plainer how Guyon functions as Redcrosse's successor. Reformation writers are preoccupied with the combat of the flesh and the spirit. Taking Galatians 5, Romans 6, 7, and 8, and other salient passages primarily from Paul as their prooftexts, the Reformers consistently sustain a view of the flesh that helps both to define their characteristic understanding of the human condition and to distinguish them from their Roman Catholic adversaries. By "the flesh," Reformation commentators mean not simply the body but also everything unregenerate in humanity, including reason and the will. The term becomes short-hand for all "relics of corruption, which after regeneration, doe still remaine in us."[16] Becon frames the issue neatly: "What is the flesh? Euerye affection, the hearte, the minde, and the thought of man, and what soeuer elles man doth or can do by al the powers of his reason, destitute of the worde of God."[17] Tyndale defines flesh as "the whole man, with lyfe, soule, body, wit, will, reason."[18] Calvin repines that the flesh is heir to every ill in the human condition: "There remaineth in man regenerate a feeling of euill, from whence continually spring desires that allure and stir him to sin." Even the elect, "vntill they be vnclothed of the mortall bodie," suffer "in their flesh the peruerse-nesse of lusting that fighteth against vprightnes" (4.3.10; fol. 195ʳ–96ᵛ); "all the lusts of the flesh are sinnes," he continues, "and that the same disease of lusting, which they [who would disagree] call a feed-ing, is the wellspring of sinne"; "all desires of men are euill" because they are "inordinate" and "appeareth a continuall disorder and in-temperance" (3.3.12; fol. 196ʳ). Like his English followers, Calvin in-dicts the lusts of the flesh as the inevitable effect of original sin: "whatsoeuer is in man, euen from the vnderstanding to the will, from the soule to the flesh, is corrupted and stuffed full with this concupis-cence: or, to end it shortlier, that whole man is of himselfe nothing else but concupiscence" (2.1.8; fol. 74ʳ–75ᵛ). Elizabethan Protestan-tism codified this view in article 9, "On Original Sin," of the Thirty-nine Articles: "the fleshe lusteth alwayes contrary to the spirite, and therefore in euery person borne into this worlde, it deserueth Gods wrath and damnation. And this infection of nature doth remayne, yea in them that are regenerated, whereby the luste of the fleshe . . . is not subiect to the lawe of God."[19]

Against the threat of our own omnipresent fleshly depravity, Ref-ormation commentators counsel—often within the same text—two distinct measures for us to take: one is an extreme asceticism that calls for the expulsion of fleshly longing, the other a more moderate response that seeks to contain the wanton flesh. The austere position, which has direct ties to the discourse of *de contemptu mundi* and other medieval discourses, is limned with considerable vehemence.[20] Taking their lead from Paul's martial tropes, the Reformers depict the struggle as a to-the-finish combat, waged with no little violence on both sides. Edwin Sandys avers that "our flesh . . . rebelleth, *and lusteth contrary to the spirit.* Fleshly lustes *fight against the soule.*"[21] Even after justification, says Tyndale, "there remaine in us yet euill lustes and synne, which fight agaynst the spirite." Or more vividly: "the flesh driueth, compelleth, craueth and rageth, agaynst the spirite, and wil haue her lustes satisfied. On the other side driueth the spirite, crieth and fighteth against the flesh, and will haue his lust satisfied. And this strife dureth in us, as long as we liue, in some more and in some lesse, as the spirite or the flesh is stronger, and the very man his owne selfe is both spirite and the fleshe, which fighteth with his owne self untill sinne be utterly slayne, and he all together spirituall." The spirit, on the contrary, "laboureth and enforceth to kyll the remnaunt of sinne and lust: which remaine in the fleshe after our iustifying."[22] This mortal combat is inherently divisive of the human being, for "euery man is two men, flesh and spirite, which so fight perpetually one agaynst an other, that a man must go either backe or forward, and cannot stand long in one state."[23] Life is a "continuall matter of strife," says Calvin. Becon points out that our intimacy with our flesh makes its conquest difficult, for it is "an householde enemye euer at home and neuer without, euen wyth in our own brest caryed about with us whersoeuer we goo, and accompanynge us what so euer we do, and continually prouokyng us unto those wicked actes."[24] Becon reviles "synne, which boyleth in the fleshe," and so he would "knocke down, quench, oppresse, crucifie and kil the workes of the flesh." Here we see the violent asceticism for which followers of Calvin are almost stereotypically famous, a severe denial of the value of the body and a wish to eradicate its compulsions. It is a thinly veiled longing to erase the body altogether, as Becon evidences when he says in the same essay in response to Paul's dictum "he that is dead is freed from sinne" (Rom. 6:7), "I desyre nothyng more than to be cleane and utterly deliuered from sin."[25]

Yet the Reformers also voice a more moderate view of the flesh, one that seeks not to annihilate it but to contain its disorderliness. Commenting on Rom. 6:12, Calvin claims that Paul "saieth not, let [sin] not be, but let it not reigne. So long as thou liuest, sinne must needes be in thy members at least, let reigne be taken from it. Let not that be done which it commandeth" (3.13.3; fol. 196^r–97^v). Calvin's words highlight a tendency in Reformation commentary toward the hope that the flesh can be regulated by an effort of will. Both positions are present in Paul, who first insists that the "bodie of sinne be destroyed" (Rom. 6:6) and then, some verses later, warns that we must "let not sinne reigne . . . in your mortall bodie" (Rom. 6:12). Reformation commentators, too, champion such oppositions: on the one hand, the sinful body is hopelessly corrupt and is vanquished only at death; on the other, the will can subdue the unruly body and exert limited authority over its corruptions. Hence Tyndale claims on one page that "Sinners we are, because the fleshe is not full killed, and mortified" and, on another, that "we haue inough to doe all our lyves long, to tame our bodies, and to compell the members to obey the spirite, and not the appetites."[26] One position is a radical Calvinist mortification of the flesh that sees corruption in all human action. The second is a more moderate one, a stance closer to the humanist and classical concept that puts temperance within the grasp of individual agency.

Book II responds to the threat of fleshly rebellion by simultaneously representing both the extreme Calvinist asceticism and the less radical, classical view of continence familiar in scholarly glosses on this book of the poem. The text foregrounds classical temperance by persistently reiterating a host of words that suggest binding, constriction, containment, and the like. This regulation is imaged frequently by equestrianship—mildly witty, given Guyon's horselessness, but appropriate to the Platonic trope of taming the horses of passion or the hope that the flesh can be contained. Temperance is a willed act or series of acts, a discipline that responds to bodily disintegration by tying the body together. This emphasis on the willed dominion over the flesh is similar to Aristotelian continence and other classical views, codified for the Renaissance most notably in the *Nicomachean Ethics* as well as the *Tusculan Disputations*.[27] In this respect Book II of *The Faerie Queene* seems to allegorize classical views that put temperance under the surveillance of the will. Hence, for example, in the instructive opening stanzas of canto 11, the poet commends "a body, which doth freely yeeld / His parts to reasons rule obedient" (11.2). The tropes and actions of this "rule" are figured elsewhere in Guyon's harnessed body, Medina's and Alma's self-control, the lock on Occasion's tongue, the netting of Acrasia, and so forth. In its reiteration of temperance as a containing of the flesh, the text answers the classical-humanist hope—echoed in strains of moderate Reformation discourses of the flesh—that fleshly waywardness be dominated by the will, that temperance stop Acrasia from dividing body from spirit. Acrasia herself enacts the combat between the flesh and the spirit—she "the feeble sprightes / Can call out of the bodies of fraile wightes" (5.27)—and the text shows she can be controlled with effort and force.

Book II concurrently develops another view of temperance, based on a different conception of the body. Far from seeking to contain the flesh, the text dismembers and obliterates the body. Often torturing it in the process, the text disassembles and erases the body, thus fulfilling the proem's forecast of "no body." To do so answers the Reformation asceticism that impugns fleshly life. The text combats the body, fights successfully to the finish, and so conquers its waywardness by annihilation. Hence, some stanzas after commending "reasons rule obedient" (11.1) over the body, the poet laments, in Pauline fashion, "mans state," which remains "vnsound . . . / Till it dissolued be from earthly band" (11.30).[28] This dissolution is waged variously: literally, for example, in the scenes of fighting that exult in dismemberment or in the narrator's warning that Guyon will be rent to pieces if he succumbs in Mammon's house; or figuratively, in the multiple anatomizing descriptions throughout the book. The afflicted bodies of Amavia and Mortdant are merely the first in a series of dismembered bodies that figure forth its combat of flesh and spirit, and their dismemberment suggests how this book of the poem will portray that combat.

The book's dual attitude toward the body takes its most curious form in the portrait of Belphoebe, the longest in the poem as a whole. As a blazon, the portrait has its very purpose in a cataloging of her body parts, by devoting often an entire stanza to a single corporeal feature. Her face, eyes, forehead, eyelids, legs (both knees and hams), her "snowie brest, and . . . daintie paps" (3.29), her hair, her shoulders—each is carefully parceled and inventoried. This description is meant to celebrate her beauty and preserve it in the artifice of the blazon.[29] But as that blazon emphasizes the individual aspects of her person, Belphoebe simultaneously and paradoxically exemplifies the mutability of the flesh. Her members are as *disjecta* as those of Amavia, at least in the way the text represents the two bodies, each of which is anatomically disjointed. Amavia incarnates the body's frailty and mortality, Belphoebe its chaste strength and impermeability—instances respectively of the Bakhtinian grotesque and classical bodies.[30] In both figures, though, the flesh is hedged by concupiscent forces that threaten to harm, overpower, and deteriorate it, whether those forces be Amavia's intemperate reaction to her husband's death, or Mortdant's wandering eye, or Braggadocchio's lust. Belphoebe's weaponry preserves her intact, but the text dismembers her more effectively than Braggadocchio would have.

In a well-known essay, Nancy Vickers has demonstrated how the *Rime sparse* presents Laura (Belphoebe's emblazoned original) as a "part or parts of a woman" and how Laura's fragmentation is determined by the subtext of the Diana-Actaeon myth. "Woman's body, albeit divine, is displayed to Actaeon," Vickers writes, "and his body, as a consequence, is literally taken apart. Petrarch's Actaeon, having read his Ovid, realizes what will ensue: his response to the threat of imminent dismemberment is the neutralization, through descriptive dismemberment, of the threat. He transforms the visible totality into scattered words, the body into signs."[31] Something similar can be said of Book II's presentation of Belphoebe, explicitly modeled on the Diana-Actaeon myth. Compared to "*Diana* by the sandie shore" (3.31), Belphoebe mistakes Trompart spying her for a "bleeding Hind" (3.32). Braggadocchio, too, "gan burne in filthie lust" and tries to embrace her in his "bastard armes" (3.42). The poet, yet another onlooker, is reduced to "fear" by the threat of Belphoebe's beauty. But none of these male gazers is harmed by Belphoebe, who is, instead, herself dismembered and "scattered" (3.30) over nine stanzas of portrait. "How shall fraile pen descriue her heauenly face," asks the poet, "For feare through want of skill her beauty to disgrace?" (3.25). His response to his own fear is to inventory and scatter her body throughout subsequent stanzas.

One of Belphoebe's primary achievements is to subdue lust, an agenda the portrait accomplishes by emblazoning the body and by transforming Belphoebe into something other than human. The portrait tends toward stasis by preserving Belphoebe's beauty in the artifice of Petrarchan conceits. Her flesh becomes a "soueraine moniment" before which even the poet is fearful. She has a "heauenly face," a "glorious mirrhour of celestiall grace" and is "borne of heauenly birth" (3.25).[32] In this sense, her body is not merely neutralized but obliterated. Although her face mirrors celestial grace, it is significantly a "mirrhour"—the very spelling suggests Belphoebe's attachment to time and decay. Her "face so faire as flesh it seemed not" (3.22), but flesh she certainly is—and finally as frail as Amavia and

Mortdant, however guarded she is by her virginity, her celestial beauty, her Diana-like aggression, her status as avatar of the queen, or the encasing artifice of the blazon. Despite its avowed purpose of celebrating Belphoebe's virginal power, the text insists, by its very taxonomy of her flesh, on her bodily frailty and its similarity to that of Mortdant and Amavia. These multiple protections cannot altogether rend an "iuorie forhead" (3.24) out of a mortal skull. Trompart speculates that Belphoebe is "some powre celestiall" (3.44), but the textual insistence on the human dimensions of her fleshliness belies, or at least works to counter, his hypothesis.

Reformation strictures against the flesh, which form a subtext to Book II throughout, mediate between Petrarchan discourse and Belphoebe's portrait. The text envisions the flesh, sees its imminent decay and dismemberment, and responds by descriptively amputating the human corpus—at the same time, paradoxically, that it calls for moderate, classical constrictions of temperance to contain the flesh and prevent its disjointing. Belphoebe's flesh represents that dismemberment most poignantly, all the more because the text strains to deny her mortality by glorifying it as quasi-divine. The portrait of Belphoebe inscribes the combat of the flesh and the spirit. In her very beauty that battle is waged. As the antithesis of Acrasia, Belphoebe demonstrates the *discordia concors* of the combat itself. But she is hardly typical. Indeed the poet asserts her uniqueness variously, not least by her figuration of the queen—herself an all-too-fleshly being in whom her courtiers attempt to deny fleshly imperatives, including eros, and to preserve from mortal ravages.

Guyon, meanwhile, proceeds through his own adventures as notoriously unvarying in his temperance as Belphoebe. As to whether he actively restrains himself or is impervious to temptation—the distinction between Aristotle's continent and temperate men that once exercised Spenser scholars—critics are now rightly uncertain. In either case, Guyon rarely demonstrates chivalric success. His adventure at the castle of Medina lands Guyon in the squabble between Huddibras (his name suggests his anatomical disarray; the center of his being is located in his arms) and Sansloy. This is an altercation Guyon is powerless to quell or ameliorate. However much he aspires to the role of homilist in the episode with Mortdant and Amavia, Guyon is impotent to propitiate these dyspeptic knights in the first combat he finds himself in, despite the narrator's praise of his "great prowesse and heroick worth" (2.25). That task falls to Medina, whose "gracious wordes their rancour did appall" (2.32)—words with a decidedly homiletic cast, with their Christian truisms of peace and brotherly love (2.29–31). Delivering "with pitthy words and counsel sad" what sermon theory calls a corrective homily, she demonstrates herself an able preacher: the squabbling knights "hearken to the sober speaches, which she spoke" (2.28). She proves far more efficacious than Guyon in correcting destructive behavior. He can do nothing, even by dint of arms, to stop the violence. What has become of his earlier high-minded platitudes—uttered, it may now be noted, before the *dead* Amavia and Mortdant? His intervention in the present argument fails altogether, whereas Medina's homily brings "grace to reconcile" (2.32–33). She fulfills, therefore, two of the primary roles of the Reformation preacher, to correct vice and then to bring comfort and reconciliation. In this episode Guyon has neither effectively borne arms nor proved himself a productive counselor. In fact the only valuable homily he delivers has been at the funeral of Amavia and Mortdant, when his audience consisted of Ruddymane and the Palmer, who vied with Guyon for confecting the more hackneyed funeral sermon.

The episode with Furor, Occasion, and Phedon is exceptionally rich in homiletic rhetoric. The narrator begins by praising Guyon as an exemplar of temperance, as one who through sheer willpower "well could manage and subdew his pride." Rehearsing both admonitory and corrective homiletic genres, the Palmer "Teach[es] him the weake to strengthen, and the strong suppresse." Control of "strong passion, or weake fleshlinesse" (4.2) lies within the compass of volition; sin is not inevitable. If Guyon succeeds at subduing the flesh, Phedon is surely his opposite. Guyon and the Palmer deliver an extended homily in counterpoint to Phedon on the need to eschew wrath and embrace temperance (4.33–36), a skillful intermingling of admonitory and corrective genres. In doing so, they condescend to poor Phedon, who, by his own admission (4.31), needs no proof of his trespasses or moralizing reminders to "guide [his] wayes with warie gouernaunce" (4.36). If Guyon proves adept (albeit redundant) at reproof, what comfort (that other preacherly obligation) does he offer? Before he preaches to him, Guyon "gan to comfort [Phedon], and his wounds to dresse" (4.16). Guyon reverses, in other words, the order prescribed in sermon theory: first he comforts; then he reproves.[33] The parodic inversion of the prescribed sequence may suggest only Guyon's maladroitness, rather than any serious failing. But it indicates his limitations. His reaction to Phedon's tale, for example, built on apothegms about the monstrosities of jealousy, is neither sympathetic nor especially constructive. Although he clamps down on Occasion's tongue, Guyon exercises little control over his own.

The power of rhetoric informs the episode. The most obvious example occurs when Occasion "with many a bitter threat" (4.9) goads Furor against his victim:

> And euer as she went, her tongue did walke
>> In foule reproch, and termes of vile depight,
>> Prouoking him by her outrageous talke,
>> To heape more vengeance on that wretched wight [Phedon].
>
> (4.5)

Occasion's ambulatory tongue emblematizes the dissociation of the body's members from the will, which, from one perspective, is designated to keep the flesh well-managed. Her autonomous tongue provokes not merely Furor but also Spenser's critics, who have unearthed a wealth of iconographic signification. To this richness belongs a pertinent commentary from the Epistle of James, whose third chapter in the Geneva version is glossed "Of the tongue." The tongue, says James, "set among our members . . . defileth the whole bodie, and setteth on fyre the course of nature, and it is set on fyre of hel" (James 3:6). The Geneva gloss advises that "the intemperancie of the tongue is as a flame of hel fyre," a point corresponding to the Palmer's advice to Guyon: restrain Occasion, for she "kindles" (4.11) Furor.[34] Her speech is the infernal opposite of the homiletic speech exercised by Guyon and the Palmer, but it is vastly more effectual. Occasion's tongue kindles her listener to action, however reprehensible. So her speech parodies an admonitory homily, intended to improve manners. Guyon's admonitory homilies, on the contrary, fail to alter the behavior of these unhappy characters.

James's words about the tongue "set among our members" also indicates how the episode dismembers the body—most visibly, of course, in the amputation of Occasion's tongue: "her tongue did walke" (4.5). But bodily disarray is evident throughout, particularly in the episode's rich iconography. Drawn by his hair, for example, Phedon has "cheekes with teares, and sides with bloud" (4.3). Both

Furor and Occasion, too, are enumerated by jumbled body parts: legs, hair, face, tongue, hands, teeth, beard, eyes, skull. This anatomical anarchy shows the explosive effects of intemperance upon those who fail to govern themselves. It also conveys the impact of intemperance on those proximate to the ungoverned. Occasion and Furor are not merely allegorical projections of Phedon: they are allegorized examples of a well-known passage in Galatians, glossed in the Geneva version as antitypes of desired "temperancie": "use not *your* libertie as an occasion vnto the flesh, but by love to serve one another. For all the Law is fulfilled in one worde, which is this, Thou shalt loue thy neighbor as thy self. If ye bite and deuoure one another, take heed lest ye be consumed of one another. Then I say, walke in the Spirit, and ye shal not fulfill the lustes of the flesh" (Gal. 5:13–16). In Occasion's goading and Furor's biting, the text allegorizes an occasion unto the flesh. Hence the flesh is literally distributed across the narrative. Guyon's homiletic counsel reproduces Paul's injunction to walk in the spirit, but because his counsel is closer to sermon parody than to actual sermon, the results are unsatisfactory. Phedon's disappearance from the text after his counseling contributes to the inconclusiveness of his tale and to the sense that the episode does not enhance Guyon's prestige as an exemplar of temperance. He preaches more than he practices.

Phedon's story provides the chance to consider the role of the Palmer in Book II. In this episode he advises Phedon, as Harold Weatherby points out, not merely to control the passions but to "expell" them (4.35), for the passions inevitably overpower the "fort of Reason" (4.34).[35] Elsewhere, however, the Palmer has called for a less extreme asceticism, advising instead that the passions be tempered and controlled. In the Palmer, then, the text dramatizes both extreme and moderate attitudes toward the flesh. At one time the Palmer urges moderation, at another mortification of the flesh. In his utterances we see the book's dual responses to the life of the flesh—the one suggesting that reason can control the anarchic flesh, the other that the flesh must be subordinated to the spirit.

The encounter with Pyrochles grows directly out of Phedon's tale before that tale is satisfyingly concluded. Guyon first proleptically beheads Pyrochles' horse and then disarms Pyrochles himself by literally dismembering him: he strikes so "Deepe in his flesh" that "it did quite disarme" (5.7). Having "dismayd" his adversary, Guyon then provides Pyrochles with the now-expected sermon, this one a parody of the corrective kind that warns of damnation and then offers hope of salvation. Anger, he reproves Pyrochles, will "thee to endlesse bale captiued lead" unless "thou didst my mercy proue" (5.16). Styling himself as dispenser of mercy, Guyon evaluates Pyrochles' plight as an analogue of the human condition. His salvific posture proves almost comic when he deludes himself into thinking his improvident agreement to Pyrochles' request to free Occasion as "great mercy sure, for to enlarge a thrall." "I yield them free" (5.17), says Guyon, with no little sense of his own magnanimity. In this encounter, then, parody works quite against Guyon's sense of his own importance. He first functions as a knight of temperance not by managing Pyrochles' unruly flesh but instead by dismembering it. Again the text pushes toward violent elimination of the body rather than merely managing its unruliness. Guyon then counsels Pyrochles on the infernal consequences of intemperance by fashioning himself as the source of the "mercy" that will save him. This gesture, of course, proves futile, for Guyon's mercy only renews the anger of Furor, who "his redeemer chalengd for his foe" (5.20).

Even more than in the episode with Furor and Phedon, discourses of the flesh and sermon parody are inextricably joined in Phaedria. Her person and her actions embody the life of the flesh—or "loose desire," as argument of canto 6 puts it. And her every utterance—her "stile" (6.22)—parodies sermon rhetoric, "For all her words . . . wanted grace" (6.6). Since Upton we have recognized in her song to Cymochles a parody of Matt. 6:25–34, the Sermon on the Mount, a primary example in Reformation hermeneutics of an effective sermon.[36] Ann Imbrie has demonstrated that Phaedria's is also a parody of Reformation sermons that "offer a concentrated exposition of a particular biblical text."[37] In this fashion Phaedria's seduction impersonates texts (sermons) that themselves represent texts (in this case, Matthew 6). Her parody, then, apes two generations of discourse, Reformation sermons as well as the protosermon on the Mount. In the first instance, Phaedria "his eyes and senses fed / With false delights" (6.14), thereby distorting the mission of the preacher to speak to the heart. Cymochles' reaction is equally parodic: lulled fast asleep—"That of no worldly thing he care did take" (6.18)—he is the somnolent icon of the converted sinner, a burlesque of the hearer who is moved by preaching to abandon worldly vanities for love of

God. In the second instance, Phaedria parodies Jesus' sermon by mis-representing its essence. In advising Cymochles to abandon the "fruitlesse toile" of chivalric endeavor for "present pleasures" (6.17), she exhorts her listener not to the Kingdom of God urged in the Sermon on the Mount but rather to the kingdom of the flesh. Sermon parody, then, is here used to promote the works of the flesh, for Phaedria employs the devices of both Reformation and Gospel sermons to beckon Cymochles, not to the love of God but to the love of "pleasures vaine" (6.14).

The result is anatomically to disjoint Cymochles. The tableau of the young knight recumbent in Phaedria's arms wittily recalls a pietà and anticipates Acrasia's separation of flesh and spirit. The icon of Cymochles' "laying his head disarm'd / In her loose lap" (6.14) graphically shows how both bodies are dismembered. The text continually strives to demonstrate how intemperance not only disarms in the chivalric sense but also disarms literally—and beheads and un-laps.

Guyon, on the other hand, holds the body together when confronted by Phaedria's blandishments and "euer held his hand vpon his hart," a bodily discipline demanding he "subdew" his "fond desire" (6.26). But to maintain his mastery, he has to fight Cymochles, who threatens to reduce Guyon's flesh to a "carcasse for [the birds'] pray" (6.28). The ensuing battle literally exposes the flesh: they "naked made each others manly spalles" by planting their swords "Deepe in their flesh" (6.29). Their flesh has now been exposed, invaded, and made as vulnerable as possible—Cymochles has "bared all his head vnto the bone" (6.31). The discourses of the flesh are here made completely literal. In a witty pun suggesting how Phaedria will erotically apply her arts, the knights are said to be "dismayld" (6.29). Engaged in the most male of activities—combat—the males lose the protection of their mail just as they are about to become the (decidedly male) objects of Phaedria's seductions. She bodily inserts herself between them and then delivers yet another sermon parody. She now exhorts them to what seems like brotherly love ("louely peace, and gentle amitie"), but is actually another love of the flesh in the form of sensual "Amours" (6.35). Her counsel in this case parodies not the doctrinal sermon that advocates love of God (or faith) but instead the genre urging love of fellow human (or good works). Rather than delivering an admonitory sermon exhorting charity, she recommends erotic self-indulgence. And indeed she effectively quells their animosity, for "Suche powre haue pleasing words" (6.36).

The very sequence of Phaedria's sermon parodies, then, mimes the Reformed relation between faith and works, the latter a necessary consequence of the former. In her first sermon parody (6.15–17) Phaedria substitutes love of flesh for love of God, eros for faith. In her second sermon parody (6.33–35) she substitutes love of flesh for love of neighbor, eros for charity or *agape*. The Reformation conflict between the flesh and the spirit is consummately reconfigured in her seemingly high-minded apothegm:

> wo worth the man
> That first did teach the cursed steel to bight
> In his own flesh, and make way to the liuing spright.
>
> (6.32)

The antinomy she sketches is between life and death, but the opposition summons up that combat in its more inclusive sense in contemporary religious discourse. Both of Phaedria's sermon parodies can be ironically illustrated by Calvin's salty words on the opposition between flesh and spirit: "But in the whole law there is not read one sillable that appointeth to man any rule of suche thinges as hee shall doe or leaue vndone to the commoditie of his owne fleshe. And surely . . . men are so borne of such disposition naturally that they bee too much caried all headlong to loue of them selues, and . . . still they keep that selfe loue. . . . not loue of selues, but the loue of God and neighbor is the keeping of the commaundements" (2.8.54; fol. 131ʳ). Phaedria's sermon parodies urge a love of self in its most nakedly erotic form. Both parodies have called attention to the conflict between flesh and spirit. She offers a resolution to the combat that the Reformers would find not only offensive but self-defeating. Rather than vanquish the power of the flesh by means of the spirit, Phaedria offers only to substitute concupiscible works of the flesh for irascible works. To repair the dismembered flesh of the wounded combatants, she offers not the spirit but more flesh.

Guyon's response to Phaedria is odd. Having demonstrated his fondness for sermonizing, he would seem to have met his homiletic match. But for once he does not moralize. He does not counter blasphemous versions of the Word with authentic sermons, or even parodies of it. Instead he keeps his counsel, in a way atypical of earlier episodes, where he has shown himself (all-too) eager to offer advice and pseudosermons. By "turning taile" (6.40), he leaves Phaedria's island with no debate. Are we to understand by Guyon's unprecedented silence that "strong reason maistred passion fraile" (6.40) and thus that speech is made unnecessary? Or does his silence indicate his impotence before challenges both homiletic and fleshly? These questions will be central to his encounter with Mammon. For now, we may hypothesize that the office of sermon parody has passed from Guyon to Phaedria, from whose mouth it proves blasphemous and destructive. In retrospect, Guyon's earlier sermonizing seems relatively harmless.

On the other hand, the remainder of this canto—when Pyrochles reappears in flames—casts doubt on Guyon's capabilities. Archimago's entrance prompts Atin to cry out, "Helpe with thy hand, or with thy counsell sage: / Weake hands, but counsell is most strong in age" (6.48). These alternatives have been Guyon's throughout: counsel and hands—and he has been readier with counsel. In fact, though, neither his counsel nor his hands have much helped the troubled characters he has encountered. What, then, are we to make of Archimago's apparent success in rescuing Pyrochles? After searching Pyrochles' wounds, Archimago

> balmes and herbes thereto applyde,
> And euermore with mighty spels them charmd,
> That in short space he has them qualifyde,
> And him restor'd to health, that would haue algates dyde.
>
> (6.51)

Archimago substitutes mighty spells for Guyon's platitudes. Whereas Guyon has been helpless to save those in distress, Archimago pragmatically heals wounds. At the halfway point in Book II, Archimago in one stanza accomplishes more than Guyon's many stanzas of moral instruction have done. In fact Archimago performs a signal work of charity in this episode, more effectual than anything Guyon has accomplished. As the narrator says two stanzas into the next canto, Guyon "euermore himselfe with comfort feedes, / Of his own vertues, and prayse-worthy deedes" (7.2). Anne Prescott calls this famous couplet a description of a spiritually risky state, expressing Guyon's confidence in human merit or works.[38] Previous events provide ample reason to expand this insight to characterize his performance throughout the first half of Book II.

Readers have long puzzled over these well-known two lines. Given Guyon's lackluster achievement hitherto, they seem negative, or at least highly suspect. Having failed to minister to anyone else, Guyon provides himself with comfort, that keynote of Reformation homiletics describing the preacher's duty to his wounded charges. The word "feedes" gives pause, too, for the flesh must be fed, but not at the expense of the spirit. Feeding is rarely a positive word in the poem, particularly in this book, where it has recently described how Phaedria "fed" (6.14) the senses of Cymochles and anticipates how Mammon "feede[s] his eye / With couetous desire" (7.4, cf. 7.24) or how Acrasia "depastur[es]" (12.73) Verdant. And so the famous couplet resonates to both sermon parody and discourses of the flesh, and it appropriately introduces a pivotal episode where both motifs will profoundly change. Guyon will shift from homilist to hearer, and he will, for the first time, subjectively experience the combat between flesh and spirit.

Mammon is a supreme parodic homilist. The temptations he offers are not so much fleshly as more generally worldly. Prescott points out that as god of the world, Mammon encourages, by "parodic usurpation," the illusion that the world is sufficient, that the world can be understood without reference to its Creator. Like God he offers bliss and grace; like Christ he says, "Come and see," and an iron door opens for him as for Peter. The episode has, of course, been the subject of massive scholarly investigation, much of it focusing on the precise nature of Guyon's temptations and the rich allusiveness of the environmental details. We have long recognized that Mammon tempts Guyon as Satan tests Jesus in Matthew 4. Missing from earlier analysis is that Mammon, in addition to figuring Satan the tempter, also functions as a parodic preacher.[39] In earlier episodes this has been Guyon's role; Mammon inherits the mantle from Guyon and proves himself not merely an adept parodist but an infernal parodist, a false preacher. When he announces to Guyon that "of my plenty [I] poure out vnto all, / And vnto none my graces do enuye" (7.8), he substitutes himself for God. In this way Mammon's words parody two discourses: he imitates Satan in Matthew 4, a primary example in Reformation hermeneutics of a false preacher;[40] and he parodies Reformation sermons, specifically the doctrinal subgenre, intended to enforce the truths of Scripture. Mammon's offer of grace burlesques the preacher performing the ultimate act of pride, extending his own form of salvation rather than preaching God's gift of salvation. He can, says Mammon in that biblical commonplace, provide all Guyon wants "in twinckling of an eye" (7.11). At various stages of the temptation, Mammon further parodies doctrinal and redargutive sermons (e.g., 7.32,38), with their characteristic universalizing solemnity and exclamations—"Loe here the worldes blis, loe here the end" (7.32); "Behold . . . the fountaine of the worldes good" (7.38). This homiletic idiom has earlier been Guyon's (e.g., "Behold the image of mortalitie" [1.57]) and has made it easy for critics to accuse Guyon of smugness.[41] Mammon's usurpation of God's offices, delivered in the inflections of homiletic discourse, displaces censure from Guyon to Mammon. Mammon's blasphemy thereby helps enhance our estimate of Guyon. When their sermon parodies are compared, Guyon rises in rhetorical and perhaps even in moral stature.

It is curious that Guyon says so little after he agrees to be led by Mammon. He is as silent as he is in the Phaedria episode—and perhaps this is one reason why the two episodes have been seen as mirrors of temptation.[42] Once he has followed Mammon, Guyon ceases sermonizing. He does not counter Mammon's infernal homilies with his own. Nor, on the other hand, does he maintain the strict silence he has observed as a hearer of Phaedria's false sermons. His responses to Mammon are unprecedentedly straightforward and unmarked by the platitudes of his earlier dicta. "Suffice it then," says Guyon, "all thine idle offers I refuse" (7.39). He comes closest to his accustomed preaching when tersely (and perhaps self-righteously) answering Tantalus's request for food and drink with the suggestion he become an exemplum: "Ensample be of mind intemperate" (7.60). Prescott points out that the next step would be for Guyon to examine himself, but this he does not do. Nor indeed would it be consistent for him to do so. In the temptation offered by Phaedria, Guyon has not refuted her sermon parodies with authentic examples of the kind. In the house of Richesse, too, Guyon does not contradict Mammon's parody of the Word (7.38) with a legitimate counterexample.

Nor is Guyon tempted in the episode. Instead, as in the Phaedria episode, Guyon's response to temptation is taciturnity. Perhaps Guyon's terseness, so unusual for him, signals his change as an exemplar of temperance. Confronting others' weaknesses, Guyon has been prolix. But faced by Phaedria and Mammon with temptations of his own, he maintains a dignified reticence betokening moral strength. This may be part of the point of providing him with sermon *parody* earlier. Now the parodists are his tempters, ones to whom he responds brusquely, if at all. He becomes a hearer as opposed to a (parodic) preacher of the (parodic) Word. This role-reversal seems healthy, particularly since the hearer proves immune to blasphemous sermon parody. If Mammon is an avatar of the devil, and the mediating discourse in the temptation is Reformation homily, then Guyon's shift from homilist to hearer surely enhances his rhetorical posture.

Guyon's behavior is not explicitly judged in the episode. We are not told his motivation for following Mammon, an act that is neither condemned nor commended by the poet. We may be asked to infer a judgment, or perhaps we are asked *not* to judge Guyon. We are, however, told of the consequences to Guyon if he were to accept Mammon's offers: "If euer couetous hand, or lustfull eye, / Or lips [Guyon] layd on thing"—a formulation that textually dismembers Guyon before the fact—a watchful fiend would "rend [him] in peeces" (7.27). Indeed, we are told twice: his succumbing, it is later stressed to the reader, "Would him haue rent [him] in thousand peeces strayt" (7.64). Although the temptations here do not specifically appeal to the flesh (the focus of every previous episode), in Mammon's house the human body remains vulnerable—or at least Guyon's flesh is made to seem so to the reader, if not to Guyon himself. The opportunities in this environment to display the dismembered persons of the inhabitants would seem rife. Dante stands as a precedent. But the long description of life in the house virtually ignores the bodies of the inhabitants. Even Philotime is not physically described. The closest depiction of the flesh comes when Guyon archly responds to Mammon's offer of his daughter: "I, that am fraile flesh and earthly wight, / Vnworthy match for such immortal mate" (7.50). Guyon's adroit response is meant to ward off temptation, but he has not before said anything so savvy. He has not acknowledged the frailty of his own flesh (indeed, he has never acknowledged he has flesh), although he and the Palmer have repeatedly indicted the frailty of others' flesh.

This change may help explain Guyon's faint, perplexing to several generations of scholarship.[43] The temptations are manifestations of the life of the flesh, broadly understood in the Pauline-Reformation sense, and Guyon's refusal of their power leads to the faint. Guyon's longstanding denial of the flesh, so basically formulated, is surely significant, particularly at the end of his sojourn through the house of Richesse. His own fleshly needs overtake him: "For want of food, and sleepe, which two vpbeare, / Like mighty pillars, this fraile life of man" (7.64). A. C. Hamilton avers that explaining Guyon's faint as merely the result of his lacking food and sleep, as the text plainly states (7.65), is to explain it away. And of course that is true if we mean by food and drink mere physical sustenance. But these items have taken on much greater significance than the merely physical.[44] They stand for "vitall powres [that] waxe both weake and wan" (7.65), signatures of the life of the flesh and human frailty—what the Reformers mean when they speak of the unregenerate flesh that remains even in the regenerate. This is one function of the apples and the stool: emblems of Guyon's fleshly frailty, icons of food and rest. Guyon has ignored these requirements throughout, most notably in his indifference to Phaedria's enticements. Unlike Redcrosse, Guyon has seemed impervious to fleshly compulsions. He preaches the containment of the flesh, and indeed he himself, unlike Redcrosse, has remained outwardly untouched by its imperatives, even when, as in his heated response to the news of Duessa's rape, he has shown himself covertly vulnerable to carnal excitements. Now, though, when subjected to extended reminders of his fleshliness, he faints. As Calvin observes when explaining that works of the flesh will continue until we are "by death deliuered out of the body of death": "they should not faint and be discouraged, which are tickled and pricked of their flesh. Let them rather thinke that they are yet in the way, and let them beleeue that they haue much profited, when they feele that there is dayly somewhat minished of their lust, till they haue attained thither whither they trauaile, namely to the last death of their flesh, which shall be ended in the dying of this mortall life" (4.15.11; fol. 438^r–439^v). Guyon certainly now shows himself to be a fleshly creature, whether threatened by dismemberment or prone to faint from hunger and thirst. So there are two major shifts in the presentation of Guyon in this pivotal episode: first, he becomes a hearer, rather than the source, of sermon parodies; second, he clearly demonstrates his fleshliness.

Several readers have noted that the fainted Guyon is described not merely as unconscious but as dead, that the faint is depicted as fatal:[45]

> But all so soon as his enfeebled spright
> Gan sucke this vitall aire into his brest,
> As ouercome with too exceeding might,
> The life did flit away out of her nest,
> And all his senses were with deadly fit opprest.
>
> (7.66)

The opposition between flesh and spirit is teasing. Guyon's "spright" is revitalized upon escape from the infernal regions of Mammon's house. His "brest" is overcome, and his senses die. Has the flesh been defeated and the spirit made "vitall"? These details could indicate he has undergone a spiritual regeneration. Alternatively, the flesh has been merely contained, thereby enhancing the spirit. The text is not explicit. In either case, throughout the next scene he is portrayed as a carcass.

But not before the narrator has his say. Although Guyon has ceased preaching, the narrator has not. The next canto begins with two memorable stanzas of homiletic:

> And is there care in heauen? and is there loue
> In heauenly spirits to these creatures bace,
> That may compassion of their euils moue?
> There is: else much more wretched were the cace
> Of men, then beasts. But O th'exceeding grace
> Of highest God, that loues his creatures so,
> And all his workes with mercy doth embrace,
> That blessed Angels, he sends to and fro,
> To serue to wicked man, to serue his wicked foe.
>
> How oft do they, their siluer bowers leaue,
> To come to succour vs, that succour want?
> How oft do they with golden pineons, cleaue
> The flitting skyes, like flying Pursuiuant,
> Against foule feends to aide vs millitant?
> They for vs fight, they watch and dewly ward,
> And their bright Squadrons round about vs plant,
> And all for loue, and nothing for reward:
> O why should heauenly God to man haue such regard?
>
> (8.1–2)

These stanzas, which are *The Faerie Queene*'s purest form of Reformation doctrinal homily, implicitly rebut Mammon's parodic examples of the kind. The lines would grace the most unexceptionable sermon on divine love, for they praise heavenly spirits, the grace of highest God, the perfect love of God for humanity.[46] No trace of parody is here. Furthermore, they introduce to Book II the theme of "succour" and mark a shift from homiletic speech to action—signaled, of course, with the angel's and Arthur's "succour" (8.8) of Guyon. Indeed, Arthur himself delivers the only other homily in this canto, and like the poet's, it is not parody. Arthur's is straightforward exposition on Scripture, what sermon theory calls "corrective," intended to refute erroneous manners. The error in this case is Cymochles' intention that Guyon's "dead carrion" (8.28) be mutilated to atone for his guilt. Taking as his text Exod. 20:5, Arthur points out that though iniquity be passed from generation to generation, it is shameful to desecrate the dead. Arthur, then, appropriates the role of homilist from the incapacitated Guyon. The two knights play this role, however, quite differently. Unlike Guyon, Arthur combines effective action with homiletic word. He both preaches and practices. He defends the helpless, playing a salvific role explicitly aligned with care in heaven. The word *grace* attaches to him repeatedly. His antagonists are God's antagonists, who, even when offered it, "wilfully refused grace" (8.52). Arthur acts as interpreter of Scripture (7.29), guardian of the defenseless (7.27), agent of heaven's care (7.25,40), judge and punisher of the wicked (7.51–52), and grace-giver (7.52,55). Homiletic has vastly expanded its scope in this canto, not only to encompass the poet's and Arthur's utterances but also to include heroic and salvific action.

This canto also fully dramatizes the combat of the flesh and the spirit. Pyrochles and Cymochles have earlier established themselves as knights of irascibility and concupiscence, those dual afflictions of the flesh. Arthur triumphs by repeatedly mutilating their flesh, making this the most violent and fleshly episode in Book II (e.g., 8.32,45,52). Arthur's sword

> did deep inuade
> [Cymochles'] head, and cruell passage made
> Quite through his braine.
> (8.45)

As for Pyrochles, Arthur "left his headlesse body bleeding all the place" (8.52). The corrupt body is forcefully subdued, indeed dismembered. Arthur here literalizes what the text has figuratively accomplished in earlier episodes by its fragmenting descriptions of the body. Acting as divine protector, judge, and redeemer, he leaves behind "carcases on ground" (8.54) and reduces these bodies to oblivion. This condition replicates Guyon's throughout the scene. His senses are "with deadly fit oppresst" (7.66), and Cymochles refers to him as a "carkasse" and "dead carrion" (7.28). After their defeat, though, his assailants become the carcasses, Guyon's slain surrogates. In both cases, the flesh is vanquished to the point of extinction, a bodily condition the text has aimed at from the start.

Something of a psychomachia takes place in this episode.[47] In ritual combat, Arthur dispatches Pyrochles and Cymochles, those representatives of the irascible and the concupiscent flesh. Does this mean that these fleshly parts of Guyon himself have now been slain? If so, may we then say, following Reformation discourses of the flesh, that he will now live solely in spirit?[48] The scene can be read as enacting a ritual of redemption. Reduced to spiritless flesh, Guyon is then redeemed by his "dayes man" (8.28). The struggle to resurrect Guyon is dramatized as a combat of flesh and spirit. Guyon is literally resurrected, saved in the spirit and released from the flesh. This is a question criticism has been unable to resolve: does Arthur redeem Guyon? Again the text will not readily yield definitive answers. On one hand, the scene is rich in the language of redemption; parody has dispelled. And after the episode Guyon moves purposefully to Alma's house and completes his quest. It is therefore tempting to conclude that Guyon, saved by the "Patrone of his life" (8.55), has achieved a sanctified status and may proceed purposefully through the world's trials to a glorified reward. On the other hand, the text has not abandoned its focus on carnal corruption and hence on discourses of the flesh. Although Guyon is revived, he is far from bodiless spirit. Sermon parody, too, prevails in later episodes. Both types of discourse—sermon parody and discourses of the flesh—continue to play problematic parts.

It is no wonder, then, that the narrative turns to the poem's most carefully wrought description of the body, in Alma's house of Temperance. The narrator introduces the episode with a stanza of homily that spotlights the human anatomy:

Of all Gods workes, which do this world adorne,
    There is no one more faire and excellent,

> Then is mans body both for powre and forme,
> Whiles it is kept in sober gouernment;
> But none then it, more fowle and indecent,
> Distempred through misrule and passions bace:
> It growes a Monster, and incontinent
> Doth loose his dignitie and natiue grace.
> Behold, who list, both one and other in this place.
>
> (9.1)

Adopting the preacherly tones of Guyon as he contemplates the corpses of Mortdant and Amavia ("Behold the image of mortalitie," [1.57]), the narrator's homily ("Behold, who list") replicates two prescribed genres of sermon: the admonitory, which enjoins the hearer to exercise ethical duty (hence he urges that the body be "kept in sober gouernment") and the corrective, which cautions against corruption in manners (hence he proscribes "misrule and passions bace"). The next cantos grow directly out of these homiletic objectives. These cantos allegorize "both one and other" bodies, the one kept in sober government and the other monstrous and incontinent. So the two cantos describing Alma's house and Maleger function as extended exempla of the narrator's opening homily.

It is therefore puzzling that the description of Alma's house seems so remote from the human body.[49] Until now the text has most often depicted the body as disarrayed, unstable, vulnerable. Although Alma's house is besieged from without, canto 9 allegorizes the body as an integral and integrated structure. The canto reverses the repeated portrayal of the human anatomy as frail, dismembered, exposed. To the contrary, the house itself is ably protected from the assaulting rabble outside. Although the house is composed of "earth" and "slime" (9.21), which suggest its mortality—indeed, it is partly "imperfect, mortall" (9.22)—it is constructed of stone and framed of "more worthy substance" (9.23) than even brass (and flesh?). Order, management, and invulnerability have informed the blueprint. The house, then, illustrates the moderate ideal that seeks to contain the unruly flesh. But its "sober gouernment" is achieved contradistinctively from the extreme asceticism the text has earlier used to represent (and obliterate) bodily reality. It is more "worke diuine" (9.22) than human. For example, although the tour of the house bravely descends through the body's lower regions, it notably avoids the sexual organs—the body parts most consistently implicated in

the book's various earlier travails and the source of so much anatomical disjointing.[50] The pointed sidestepping of genital carnality and
the highlighting of the hardness, durability, and immunity of the
body suggest several issues about how this canto represents its ideals.

First, if this house allegorizes the flesh, it does so without fleshliness. Not only are the various components of the house strong, integral, impermeable. They are only remotely, abstractly, and deco-
ratively related to the flesh as the text has represented it previously.
What now substitutes for earlier (troubling) representations of the
body is an allegory rightly called quaint, for this episode is but feebly
related to the discourses of the flesh as the text has represented them.
The management of the body here suggests the flesh be transformed
into something unfleshly. Before they enter the house, Arthur and
Guyon are urged to "saue your selues from neare decay" (9.12), embodied in the rout outside. If the environment within counters the
threat of fleshly decay, it does so by expelling or forbidding fleshly
mandates. The allegory of Alma's house suggests the futility of such a
wish. To annihilate desire is to elide not just the genitals but all flesh,
exactly what has happened in this canto. Hence Shamefastnesse, for
example, is figured as "polisht yuory" (9.41) rather than as a bodily
woman. In Alma's house the body, having been managed, disappears. No wonder, then, that critics have condescended to this canto.
The episode does not correspond to the discourses of the flesh as they
have been represented earlier. To pretend the genitals do not exist is
to ignore their imperatives, and yet earlier episodes have demanded
their recognition. Alma herself "had not yet felt *Cupides* wanton
rage" (9.18). What, we may ask, will happen to her well-managed
household when she has? The canto's idealizing simplistically ignores what has troubled (and enriched) this book of the poem: the
body's tendency to disintegrate, and the text's tendency to fragment
the body.

Furthermore, the canto does not offer the orthodox answer to the
unruliness of the flesh—namely, the life of the spirit. That spiritual
alternative would seem to be advanced, though, at the canto's outset.
Guyon tells Arthur about his devotion to the Faerie Queene, whose
"beautie of . . . minde" vastly surpasses her "mortall hew" and directs "desire" into "spirite" (9.3). But the opposition between flesh
and spirit is dropped as they enter the walls of Alma's house. It is a
place without either flesh or spirit. Nothing like the rich spiritual ex-

periences in the house of Holinesse is here. Guyon and Arthur do not find in Eumenestes' chamber traditional spiritual iconography. This canto is sundered from *all* the book's earlier representations of the flesh. The tour of the house causes the knights to reflect that "neuer had they seene so straunge a sight" (9.33), and indeed nothing has prepared us to accept this environment as an ideal alternative to the conflicts of the flesh repeatedly presented. If this is the ideal of "sober gouernment" (9.1), as the narrator had promised, it idealizes by truncating the real, by simply ignoring what has proved uncomfortable in the text's previous illustrations of the body.

In the narrator's two stanzas of instruction after the interlude of "*Briton moniments*" (9.59) he resumes the opposition between the "fraile flesh" and the "soule" (11.1). This canto will now concentrate on the unruly body, the tyranny brought "Upon the parts" of the body when the soul is captive to the passions. The canto reverts, then, to the book's earlier preoccupation with the frail flesh. In a repetition of Guyon's initial encounter with the dismayed/made/maid Duessa, Arthur "recomfort[s]" the "dismayed" Alma, the assaulted "noble virgin" (11.16). The correspondence is ironic, of course, for unlike Duessa, Alma is both maid and dismayed, and, unlike Guyon, Arthur is the poem's genuine protocomforter. Uncharacteristic of Guyon, too, is the skill by which Arthur joins comfort to deeds: the remainder of the canto concerns how he is able to overcome the infirmities of the body. The initial attack by the twelve troops resumes the text's preoccupation with disjointing the body. Indeed, the senses are now allegorically disjoined and classified. Each is assaulted for one integral stanza, each textually segregated from its fellows as it is rent, decayed, de-formed, and dis-made (11.9,10,11,12,14), all in "ransack of that peece" (11.14). Here the text accomplishes literally the dismemberment it has attempted lexically in earlier episodes.

The battle between Arthur and Maleger is the book's locus classicus of the combat between the flesh and the spirit. Maleger embodies pure misruled carnality, appropriate to his association with Antaeus, whom Renaissance mythographers claim to embody lusts of the flesh.[51] Maleger and his hags are as textually fragmented as many earlier characters. Skin, head, locks, visage, feet, legs: all disassembled and itemized as models of fleshly instability (11.22–23). Indeed Maleger is pure carnality, "Flesh without bloud, a person without spright" (11.40), a "carkasse" (11.38,42) and a "dead corse"

(11.37,42,46), that Arthur cannot easily kill. This "dead-liuing swaine" (11.44) is Book II's most palpable icon of the threatened triumph of flesh over soul.[52] The violence necessary to subjugate him highlights the conflict between flesh and spirit—and quite differs from the idea that reason's rule will control and govern the flesh. Only a violent suppression will release the spirit, "now loosd from sinfull bands" (11.46). This episode dramatizes the struggle animating Reformation discourses of the flesh; Arthur's crushing of Maleger fulfills the proem's forecast of "no body."

The final canto variously fuses sermon parody and discourses of the flesh. First, Guyon's voyage and the Bowre of Blisse depict the flesh in two distinct aspects. The voyage represents the body primarily as threatening, the Bowre as seductive. Both environments continue the text's project of dismembering the body. To take the voyage first: the Gulfe of Greedinesse "engorgeth," "swallow[s]," "vomit[s]," and "belcheth" (12.3). The locales of the sea voyage are figured as a corrupt body, with "griesly mouth . . . / Sucking the seas into his entralles deepe" (12.6). The Rocke of Reproach is stuck with "carkasses inanimate" (12.7). Both hazards symbolically portray the body as vile, violent, and perilous. Guyon's voyage traverses a landscape-as-body that threatens him, in the fashion of the irascible characters or Maleger. The flesh here repels, for it is a place of "Most vgly shapes, and horrible aspects" and "All dreadfull pourtraicts of deformitee" (12.23). Even the sirens, who attempt the only seduction en route, are half "Transform'd to fish" (12.31), denatured flesh.

The Palmer exercises a corrective function throughout the voyage. He continually warns against the corruption embodied in the *paysage moralisé*. Moreover, his homiletic duties expand beyond overseeing Guyon; he exercises a curiously public homiletic role. "Let all that liue," says the Palmer, "hereby be counselled, / To shunne *Rocke of Reproch*, and it as death to dred" (12.9). Even to Phaedria, over whom he has no charge and to whom he can feel no obligation, he acts as corrective homilist: "the Palmer gan full bitterly / Her to rebuke" (12.16). We need hardly wonder about the content of his rebuking, since Spenser's original readership heard it repeatedly in corrective sermons and repeatedly in Book II's representations of sermon discourse. Toward Guyon, too, the Palmer's role continues to be both admonitory and corrective, as when he "With temperate aduice discounselled" (12.34) Guyon and steers him away from danger.

The Palmer also reprises his earlier harsh counsel against "foolish pitty" (12.29). Guyon resists none of this advice; indeed he becomes the ideal hearer of Reformed sermon theory. "He hearkned" unvaryingly to "his sage Palmer that him gouerned" (12.38). Guyon sustains and enhances the role of hearer he has assumed in the book's second half. He is "ruled" (12.29) consistently by the Palmer's edifying counsel and so is "firmly armd"—in flesh and spirit?—"for euery hard assay" (12.38).

If the landscape of the voyage illustrates the flesh as menacing and violent, the Bowre and its environs represent the flesh as deceptively alluring, in the long tradition of the *hortus conclusus*.[53] Once the voyagers arrive at the island, the representation of the body becomes as weirdly enticing as it has been in the concupiscent experiences allegorized earlier. The fence enclosing the Bowre, for example, is "weake and thin," the gate "of substance light, / Rather for pleasure, then for battery or fight" (12.43). And yet its ivory frame encloses a prototypical tale of erotic violence, the "mighty charmes" (12.44) of Jason and Medea. The porch with its "embracing vine" (12.54) beckoning passersby, the fountain with its ivy and its "lascivious armes" (12.61), the bathing women in the fountain with their "snowy limbes" (12.64) and "lilly paps" (12.66): the environment does not merely beguile. It also itemizes and fragments the body and so continues to impugn the life of the flesh.

But it does so slightly differently from earlier. Here the body as alluring object is represented in its didactic fullness for the first time in Book II. The dismemberment of the body is now projected onto the environment, so that the discrete features of the landscape are represented as body parts. The effect is both seductive and repellent, not unlike the book's tales of erotic violence—a fact that may account for some of the ambivalent responses to the Bowre critics have registered. The body is as literally and repugnantly dismembered as it has been throughout. But it is also bewitching in its individuation. In that sense the text emblazons the Bowre. Belphoebe's discretely represented body parts have been reformulated as perilously seductive in the emblazoned landscape. Its independent features, like hers, are both scattered and alluring. But enticing as it is, it continues the combat between flesh and spirit, figured by Acrasia's predatory dominance over Verdant: "And through his humid eyes did sucke his spright" (12.73). Acrasia's goal is to complete the separation of flesh and spirit allegorized throughout—to fulfill, that is, the goal of "no body" heralded from the outset. Her lexical beheading of Verdant—his "sleepie head she in her lap did soft dispose" (12.76)—accomplishes what the text has performed repeatedly in its anatomical disposing. Acrasia fulfills a process the text itself has been performing: the dismemberment of the body. The effect on Verdant is telling—"his bodie he did spend" (12.80)—but is this expense deplorable or desirable?

Only by tying up Acrasia can Guyon halt Verdant's beheading. Throwing a net over Acrasia to prevent the unhinging of Verdant has little logical meaning. But it is a paradox the text has consistently allegorized, with its pervasive images of tying and constriction. This is the ostensible lesson of temperance, a controlling and binding of otherwise unruly bodily impulses. Stephen Greenblatt has written persuasively of the dual response inspired by Acrasia and her Bowre: they offer sexual gratification as well as "self-abandonment, the melting of the will, the end of all quests; and Spenser understands . . . the appeal of such an end." Repression of longing for such intensity is necessary, says Greenblatt, lest Guyon be "absorbed" into the sensual.[54] The book's ongoing drama of the flesh and its discontents has insisted on the repression, indeed the obliteration, of the flesh. Less extremely, temperance answers the dismembering impulses of the uncooperative flesh: it literally holds the body together. This is what the Palmer has done for Guyon all along. His homiletic advice keeps the body from dismemberment. When Guyon gazes longingly at the women in the fountain, the Palmer "much rebukt those wandring eyes of his / And conseld well" (12.69). The Palmer keeps the body's discrete parts from "wandring" and so unhinging the corpus. He does so by counsel, by means of his timely, homely homilies to correct—or repress—vice. In the Palmer's function in the final canto, then, homily and the discourses of the flesh dovetail. His homilies prevent wandering flesh. They now more closely replicate rather than parody sermons.

Sermon parody and discourses of the flesh again converge in the final stanzas. As Acrasia sucks Verdant's spirit from his flesh, a song is chanted (12.74–75). This consummate example of the *carpe florem* lyric celebrates the life of the flesh even as it fearfully acknowledges its frailty. Ann Imbrie has demonstrated that it is also a parody of Isa. 40:6–7: "all flesh is grass"—a scriptural *topos* to illustrate the brevity of life and the need to trust in God.[55] The song also needs to be embedded more fully in Reformation discourses of the flesh, where it is seen to be a parody of sermons exhorting the hearer to live not by the flesh but by the spirit. The second selection in *The Book of Homilies*, "Of the Miserie of Al Mankynd," urges, by way of Isaiah's prooftext, remembrance of "our mortall and earthly generacion" and our "manifold miseries" (71). The final lines of the song bear this out: "Gather the Rose of loue, whilest yet is time, / Whilest louing thou mayst loued be with equall crime" (12.75). The final words suggest the universality of the fleshly condition: it is a "crime" shared by all flesh equally. Guyon escapes this equal crime through an effort of the will, abetted by the Palmer's advice. Temperance is an option available to human volition. It hedges the body.

Hence the final stanzas about Verdant and Grill. Verdant is paradoxically untied, only to be preached to about temperance. At the end Guyon resumes the role of preacher. "But *Verdant* (so he hight) he soone vntyde, / And counsell sage in steed therof to him applyde" (12.82). Having bound Acrasia in "chaines of adament" (12.82) and untied Verdant, Guyon reties him by applying to him the constraining "counsel sage" of the life temperate. To win the combat between flesh and spirit, the body must be tied with temperance and so prevented from being (prematurely) dismembered. But the scene implies that few want temperance. The book concludes with one last homiletic counterpoint. Using the spectacle of Grill to generalize, Guyon and the Palmer draw an appropriately homiletic lesson: Guyon's injunction "See the mind of beastly man" is matched by the Palmer's "The donghill kind / Delights in filth and foule incontinence." Temperance and its opposite are matters of volition: "he chooseth . . . / To be a beast" (12.87). Having totalized the exemplum of Grill to pronounce, in unexceptionable homiletic fashion, on the human condition, they turn and depart.

Reformation Continence and
Spenserian Chastity in Book III

As Guyon and his Palmer contemplate the destruction of Acrasia's bower in the final stanza of Book II, they moralize the spectacle of Grill—who has elected to remain in hoglike degradation—as an example of "the mind of beastly man." Guyon rues the sight as a matter of corrupt volition: "he chooseth, with vile difference [i.e., preference], / To be a beast," willfully disregarding the "excellence / Of his creation" in favor of a "hoggish mind." Generalizing from the perverseness of such a decision, the Palmer opines that the "donghill kind / Delights in filth and foule incontinence" (II.12.87). While perhaps a disconcerting note on which to end the Legend of Temperance, this is a fitting transition to the Legend of Chastity, which presents a broader array of self-degraded and hoggish sort than any other in the poem. Book III widens the Palmer's focus on incontinence—and, even more, on continence, its desirable opposite—key terms uniting the second and third books of the poem and resonating throughout contemporary Protestant discourses on marriage and sexuality. When John Calvin recommends marriage on the grounds that "the most part of men are subject to the vice of incontinence" (2.8.44; fol. 128ᵛ), like Guyon and his Palmer he attributes sexuality to the inherent sinfulness of human nature. A major subtext of the Legend of Chastity is the considerable corpus of English Reformation erotic discourse, strongly Calvinist in disposition. To inlay Book III within contemporary Reformation texts on sexuality and marriage is to accent how the poem interrogates that discourse. This book dramatizes the power of eros and inspects contemporary Reformation prescriptions for taming that power. But the book is vastly more skeptical about the human ability to contain erotic forces than are the contemporary divines, with their proffered remedies for "incontinence."

A memorable maxim in Book II pronounces it a "Harder lesson to learne Continence / In ioyous pleasure, then in grieuous paine" (II.6.1). Like its predecessor, Book III allegorizes this aphorism; the overlaps between the two books show how hard a lesson continence can be. Britomart learns a lot about its vexations in the first canto, her adventure in Castle Joyous. The "harder lesson" of continence is generally ignored in that sexually uncontrolled environment, and by none more than Malecasta, Grill's immediate heiress, in whom "incontinence," "lust," and "sensuall delight" (III.1.48) signal a conspicuous failure to bridle eros. Malecasta's incontinence underscores how effectively Britomart has controlled her own longings by converting them to martial energy. But she is not free from turmoil. Although reassured of Artegall's worthiness by her conversation with the Redcrosse Knight and armed with a keen knowledge of her wondrous destiny, she is gravely wounded by erotic fantasies and a thousand thoughts of her future husband's image. At the seacoast in canto 4, held miserably in Cupid's thrall, she cries out for succor in a well-known Petrarchan complaint in which she beseeches Aeolus for continence: "Thou God of winds, that raignest in the seas, / That raignest also in the Continent" (4.10). Britomart's wordplay signals Book III's complex representation of Reformation discourses on love, sex, and marriage.[1] These discourses consistently center on continence, the ability to restrain and channel sexual power. Amid the collection of erotic discourses informing Book III—Ovidian, Neoplatonic, Petrarchan, Chaucerian, Ariostan, a wealth of erotic discourses with classical and Christian antecedents—Reformation attitudes toward sexuality may be clearly discerned.[2] Moreover, as illustrated in Britomart's complaint and its pun on *continent*, this book recasts cognate issues about temperance from the previous book, where "continence" and "temperance" play an elegant discursive counterpoint. These two bodies of thought—Reformation discourse about sexuality and the Spenserian allegory of temperance from Book II—intermingle in Book III and help configure Spenser's inclusive anatomy of love.

The purpose of this chapter, then, is twofold: to inspect the representation in Book III of Reformation discourses on sex and to examine Book II and Book III as a diptych of continence. These purposes are closely joined. Reformation erotic discourse, largely ignored by Spenser's critics, is reproduced and severely tested in the third book of *The Faerie Queene*.[3] Recent scholarship about gender and the family has developed tools for investigating this discourse more amply and has given Renaissance studies the impetus and vocabulary to explore literary representations of sexuality from fresh perspectives. This chapter and the next employ methodology developed by recent feminist scholarship to track the peculiarly Reformation character of marriage and sexuality in the central books of Spenser's poem. To isolate the role of Reformation constructions of desire—that ideology of marriage and sex codified in an outpouring of treatises and manuals in the period—is to show at the least how those constructions inform Spenserian chastity. More important, Book III only qualifiedly reproduces the Reformation ideals of married chastity found in the manuals and elsewhere, or reproduces them only to resist them. The book is deeply ambivalent about this discourse and does not fully endorse its idealizing of married chastity. The book instead dramatizes how desire is too mighty to be accommodated by the normative prescriptions of Reformation pronouncements on marriage. Despite its projection of one of the poem's major marriages in the union of Britomart and Artegall, Book III is not "about" marriage but rather "about" desire and its discontents. Especially as it progresses, the book allegorizes how Reformation idealizings about marriage cannot satisfy the dark imperatives of sexual desire.

The second purpose of this chapter, to illustrate the intimacy between Book II and Book III, responds to Spenser's fondness for synchronicity and to the multitudinous connections among the various episodes and books of the poem. Despite the work done on revealing such links, little attention has been paid to those uniting these two books of the poem.[4] When they are examined as companion allegories of continence, fundamental structural features emerge. Spenser transmutes an assortment of episodes from the Legend of Temperance in the following book, under the auspices of chastity. Book III extends and comments on Book II and so explores chastity by way of temperance and continence. Hence the wordplay on *continent* at several key junctures, puns that serve as radiating sources of signification. Spenserian chastity is a form of continence—it contains, reins, bridles, and controls desire (or tries to)—and so it augments and reflects upon cognate issues about continence and temperance from the earlier book. Moreover, Book III refashions the earlier material by way of the mediating discourse of Reformation marriage and sexuality. In notable instances this discourse bridges the two books and helps transform the allegory from the earlier to the following one.

The profusion of Reformation treatises, manuals, sermons, conduct books, and other practical and devotional texts marks a heightened cultural interest in redefining marriage and its attendant sexuality. The Roman Catholic privileging of virginity and lifelong celibacy—extending back at least to Paul's Epistles and evident throughout the strains of Christian discourse that impugn the life of the body as sinful—yields generally and officially to a new celebration of marriage as the preferable and godlier condition.[5] Conjugal affection is praised as the basis of sound Christian living; holy matrimony is promulgated as the source of both individual and social happiness. Celibacy, long hallowed as the holier state, is dethroned, and marriage is acclaimed as the divinely commanded condition for most of humankind. Now marriage, not celibacy, more effectively banishes lust, relegating it to its rightful place, as the marriage service in *The Book of Common Prayer* formulates it, among "brute beasts" (290). William Perkins states the matter concisely in Pauline echoes: "for those who have not the power to abstaine, [marriage] is expressly enioyned by God as necessarie" (cf. 1 Cor. 7:9).[6]

That Perkins limits the recommendation of marriage to "those who have not the power to abstaine" suggests the ambivalence about sex that makes this discourse so elusive. Despite the chorus of praise for the married state, deep qualms about its attendant sexuality may be discovered not far beneath the surface. Such reservations are not surprising, of course, given the tensions sexuality seems to induce in most of humanity. Among Reformation commentators these uncertainties are expressed variously: for example, those who *do* have the "power to abstaine" are generally commended. Abstinence, or continence (the commentators use the terms interchangeably), is a gift of God, as *The Book of Common Prayer* pronounces: marriage is the alternative for "such persons as have not the gift of continency" (290). I Corinthians 7, a prooftext for all contemporary opinions on the relative virtues of marriage and celibacy, avers that "every man hath his proper gift of God," whether marriage or abstinence. Employing a commonplace figure from the cultural lexicon that treats sexuality as illness, the gloss in the Geneva Bible adds: "[Paul] commandeth not precisely all men to marie, but that God hath granted this remedie vnto them who can not liue chaste." Hence even a Pro-

testant exalting marriage, such as Thomas Pritchard, tempers his en-
thusiasm with a conceding acknowledgment of the merits of celibacy: "Let others prayse Chastitie much as they list, which (they say)
filleth Heauen: (I pray God it do so) yet will I commende Matrimonie."[7] His outlook, like that of other Reformation commentators, is
not hostile toward celibacy per se: even clerical celibacy, when freely
chosen, is frequently praised as a godly state. Instead, the hostility is
directed toward "fornication" and "whoredom," habitual words to
describe sex outside marriage. Reformation commentators extol
marriage, rather than celibacy, as the most efficacious means of com-
batting the dictates of desire that too often result in illicit sex, which
is depicted as a defilement and uncleanness. *The Book of Common
Prayer* proclaims that matrimony, in addition to its procreative and
companionate purposes, is "ordained for a remedy against sin, and
to avoid fornication, that such persons as have not the gift of continency might marry, and keep themselves undefiled members of
Christ's body" (290). The Reformation exaltation of marriage, then,
is not specifically an attack on virginity, which is often praised as a
good for some and as an imperative, before marriage, for all. The residual reverence for virginity in Reformation culture is felt powerfully in Book III, not only in its tribute to Belphoebe's virginity but
also in the description of Chrysogonee's parthenogenesis, an act described as "Pure and vnspotted from all loathly crime, / That is ingenerate in fleshly slime" (6.3). In such highly charged imagery, Book
III, like other Reformation erotic discourses, preserves traditional
distaste about sexuality. Reformation praise of marriage does not exclude praise of virginity, for both combat the "crime" of fornication.[8]

Recent scholarly investigations of English Reformation views of
marriage have not agreed about the sexual ideology of these discourses. A longstanding position holds that Reformation writers idealize married companionship and so sanctify relations between husband and wife, including sexual pleasure. According to this account,
married sexuality is respected, even consecrated, as the "Puritan art
of love."[9] Another scholarly explanation of Reformation attitudes
toward marriage posits that patriarchy and male dominance continue to prevail and that women, still regarded as the source of sin
and sexual debility, are thus felt to need their husbands' control.[10]
This patriarchal model stresses the continuity of attitudes about gender relations by pointing to the prevalence of a conservative social

consensus in the conduct books and other discourses about the family. Other commentators are currently making a compelling case for the heterogeneity of Reformation thinking about marriage and sexuality. Heather Dubrow, for example, has argued persuasively that we need to talk about "Protestant discourses of marriage, not the Protestant discourse, of Puritan arts of love rather than a unified and monolithic art."[11] Stephen Greenblatt, on the other hand, has pointed out that Augustinian and early Christian hostility to sexual desire "remain[s] essentially unchallenged" by Reformation marriage discourse.[12]

Leaving aside for the moment how the discourses portray *married* sexuality, we can certainly claim that Reformation commentators agree about sex outside marriage: they do not approve. These writers tirelessly reiterate that the threefold purpose of marriage is to encourage procreation, to provide companionship, and to prevent fornication. The third of these purposes inspires not only unanimity but also special zeal. The intensity of the attack on unmarried sexuality indicates the anxiety unregulated sex seems always to engender, whether in Reformation culture or elsewhere. Most Reformation unease centers in how the sexual drive is to be controlled. Fear and distrust of sex, even when eros is bridled and firmly controlled by the reins of matrimony, permeate Reformation discourse on marriage.

Commentators consistently focus on continence, the ability to restrain and channel the sexual drive, and endlessly repeat that marriage is the key to such mastery. John Dod and Robert Cleaver state the issue forthrightly: marriage "serveth as a strong bridle to pull backe the force and headines of carnall, naturall, and brutish lust" lest "any person, man or woman, should abuse their bodies . . . vpon euery instigation & lust, like brute beasts."[13] "Let them that are troubled with incontinence, and striuing with it, can not get the vpper hand," echoes Calvin, "resorte to the helpe of marriage, so that they may keepe chastitie" (2.8.42; fol. 127ʳ). Marriage is the way to get the upper hand on incontinence, not only the last resort but also the sole legitimate recourse for the creature not endowed with self-control. It is the "onely remedie," asserts Calvin, "wherewith vnchastitie is resisted" (2.8.44; fol. 128ʳ). Even within the antimonastic context that gives Calvin's endorsement of marriage a polemical edge, marriage—more pragmatically than monastic celibacy—eases the threat of sexual incontinence. Says Calvin: "Continence I call, not whereby the body is onely kept cleane from whoredome, but whereby the minde keepeth chastity vndefiled" (2.8.41; fol. 125ʳ). Within marriage lies the means to "remedie the intemperance of the flesh": those who "woulde dedicate themselues wholy to the Lorde, shoulde binde themselues to the vow of [marital] continence" (2.13.17; fol. 425ʳ). Matrimony, says William Gouge, is a "meanes of preuenting whoredome."[14] *The Book of Homilies* pronounces wedlock a means by which "a good conscience might be preserued on both perties, in brideling the corrupt inclinations of the flesh, within the limits of honestie."[15] As Gouge puts it, "they that keepe the lawes of wedlocke are as chaste as they that containe."[16] William Perkins employs the same figure, with a reminder of what "continence" suggests etymologically: "God hath ordained [marriage] to bee a remedy of incontinence to al such persons as cannot contain."[17]

The figuring of marriage as a "container" and a "remedy" suggests other tropes the conduct books find to describe the married state. The very term "wedlock" implies a similar control, a suppression of the unregulated in humanity. All societies, of course, construct sexual regulations. What is intriguing about Reformation ideology is the anxiety located, quite physically as it were, in the formulations. Hence the concept of matrimony as a yoke: the commentators habitually refer to married couples as "yoke-partners." Hence, too, the popular figure of the marriage knot: "Wedlocke or Matrimonie, is a lawfull knot, and vnto God an acceptable yoking and ioyning together of one man, and one woman."[18] Married love "knitteth louing heartes, in an insoluble knot of amitie."[19] Marriage, then, subjugates the unruly tendencies flesh is heir to. It masters this anarchy by locking eros in an indissoluble knot. It places the couple under a yoke and bridles the inclination toward untamed sexual expression. As Calvin puts it, "the fellowship of mariage it selfe, was ordaind for the remedie of necessitie, that we should not runne out into vnbridled lust" (2.8.42; fol. 127ᵛ). Thomas Gataker warns the married man from "giuing way now to any raunging affections."[20] The word *continence* itself carries just such a richness of meaning: its etymological connections are with *contain* and *container*; both *continent* and *contain* derive from *continere*, the Latin verb meaning "to hold together"; its present participle, *continens*, is the etymological source of *continent*, land mass.[21] Hence Book III's recurring pun on "continent" at critical junctures of erotic distress, its use of "remedy" at others. When the characters face or fall on the continent, they are in need of continence, an available remedy for dangerous sexual passion. They need to be contained, held together. They need to be *reigned* and *bridled*, other tropes from both Book III and the marriage discourses to express the best means of taming otherwise anarchic human impulses. They need a remedy.

The widespread iteration of marriage as a "remedy" suggests that marriage is a medicine and that sexuality is an illness, or, as Calvin says, an "infirmitie," needing a cure. In his popular tract on the subject Henry Bullinger states that "God hath given [humanity] the medicine of marriage, and wyl not esteeme the worke thereof as synne, whoredome, or vncleanes."[22] Pritchard is emphatic: "God ordained mariage for a remedy or medecine to asswage the heat of the burning flesh."[23] The unmarried state is ever perilous, likely for most to entail sin, filth, degradation. Calvin avers that "the honestie of mariage do[es] couer the filthines of incontinence" (2.8.44; fol. 128ʳ); Bullinger claims that marriage is given by God to "auoyde whoredom, and al maner of unclennesse."[24] Even those already married must be ever on the alert. Above all, adultery would cast them into a state of incontinent degradation, and only "for the attainment of a short, momentary, impure, brutish, and sensual pleasure, or for the satisfying of a foolish, sinfull, shamefull, vnreasonable, and vnbridled passion, which will neuer be so satisfied."[25] Those couples who do not defile their marriages with adultery must nonetheless be ever on the ready to bridle their passion even toward one another: "So that marriage is not a mad or dissolute estate, neither are husbandes to turne their wiues into whores, or wiues their husbands into whoremasters, by immoderate, intemperate, or excessiue lust."[26] The commentators are often keen to curb passion within the confines of married intimacy and hence repeatedly urge sexual moderation, usually on the grounds that "excessive" passion between married partners provokes rather than slakes "lust." Calvin warns "married folkes" not "to defile [marriage] with intemperate and dissolute lust . . . commit nothing vnseeming the honestie and temperance of marriage" (2.8.43; fol. 128ᵛ).[27] *The Book of Common Prayer* warns that marriage is not "to be taken in hand unadvisedly, lightly, or wantonly, to satisfy men's carnal lusts and appetites" (290).

Such suspicion is longstanding, of course, and fully consonant with the Pauline revulsion against sexuality that found ample confirmation not only in late classical Gnosticism but also in wider Christian ideology that impugns the flesh. Early Christian culture codifies this unease, most influentially in the writings of Augustine. His essay "The Good of Marriage," for example, is riddled with restrictions and qualifying provisions that tend to undermine the very "good" he putatively supports: "Marriage has also this good, that carnal or youthful incontinence, even if it is bad, is turned to the honorable task of begetting children, so that marital intercourse makes something good out of the evil of lust. Finally, the concupiscence of the flesh . . . is repressed and becomes inflamed more modestly."[28] One of the more conspicuous features of later attitudes toward sex is the ease with which Reformers adapt to their celebration of matrimony the Pauline-Augustine aversion to the flesh.

These sentiments, though hardly unique to Reformation Protestants, distinguish their views from what we may identify as a humanist position on marriage, one notable for its tolerance and its downplaying of the Pauline-Augustinian distaste for carnality.[29] It is instructive to measure the distance between the humanist and Reformation views on sexuality. If one takes Erasmus as the standard-bearer in this field, one does not observe a comparable aversion. Erasmus's colloquies on marriage and his widely read *Encomium Matrimonii* (popularized by its inclusion in Thomas Wilson's *The Arte of Rhetorique*) betray little of the characteristic misgiving observed in much Reformation writing on the subject. Indeed, Erasmus displays an unashamed admiration of the joys of sexuality: "And yet what is he that is so sower of witte, and so drouping of braine (I will not say) blockheaded, or insensate, that is not mooued with such pleasure?"[30]

English Reformation commentators, almost without exception, prove themselves sour and unmoved by the pleasure Erasmus takes to be the human norm. One may search—if not in vain, then certainly with some labor—for comparable praise of sexual pleasure in Reformation marriage discourse or indeed for extended recognition that marriage involves much sexual enjoyment at all.[31] Dod and Cleaver, in a popular manual, phrase it this way: "Honestie of marriage grounded upon Gods ordinance, doth couer the shame of incontinencie."[32]

This cover is available to human volition. Reformation marriage commentators consistently recommend marriage as readily securable to remedy sexual drives. The relief from sin, in this case, is fully within humanity's grasp—unlike, for example, grace itself, which is subject to the inscrutable will of God and not deserved by sinful humanity in any event. Calvin states the matter directly: "For they cannot conceiue this word [chastity], if they do not succour their owne intemperance with the remedie that is offered and graunted them" (2.8.42; fol. 127ʳ). This remedy requires a willed discipline, a reining in of the anarchic in humanity. Britomart's complaint at the seacoast to the god who would help her "raign . . . in the Continent" (4.10) craves precisely such a discipline. Two puns are at work here, both congenial to Reformation sexual ethos, signifying her wish to rein in her perilously incontinent fantasizing.[33]

Britomart's characterization draws on Reformation erotic discourses. The flashback in canto 2 to her initial vision of Artegall illustrates how she fulfills the roles of both yearning Petrarchan lover and prospective Protestant wife. The androgyny implicit in this dual role comprises a signal feature of her characterization, this female warrior who figures both Mars and Venus. Britomart assumes the role not of the Petrarchan *woman*, distant and sought-after; instead she plays the part of the conventionally *male* lover, desiring from afar a beloved unaware of either her passion or even her existence.[34] She is also a chaste woman, of course, but not a Petrarchan lady. As a woman, she unknowingly fulfills the ideal of the prospective Protestant wife and mother. Gazing into the mirror, she is depicted as tyrannized by "imperious Love," a commonplace Petrarchan conceit usually applied to a man. The convention is abruptly altered at the end of the stanza:

> Not that she lusted after any one;
> For she was pure from blame of sinfull blot,
> Yet wist her life at last must lincke in that same knot.
>
> (2.23)

Here the depiction has taken a decidedly Protestant turn. Her passion must be distinguished from the "filthie lust" inflaming "brutish minds" (3.1) on the one hand, and on the other, the Neoplatonic love whose goal is the contemplation of heaven.[35] Britomart's destiny is the marriage "knot"—that popular figure to express the control of passion. Such a knot will bring forth "Most famous fruits of matrimoniall bowre" (3.3). Britomart's nascent affection mirrors, then, conceptions of married love in Reformation commentary. The pointed disavowal of lust and sin echoes Reformation erotic discourse, which determinedly domesticates eros, never denying its power but always leashing it until it can be released (paradoxically) in the knot, the "lincke" of marriage. Britomart is caught in a struggle best resolved by matrimony, the most effective means of channeling disruptive passion.

Until she is married, the "sighs and anguish" (2.32) of her Petrarchan longing threaten to remain unalleviated: as she tells Glauce, "no reason can find remedy" for her "wound" (2.36). The bringing together of "reason," one of cardinal words of signification from the previous book, and "remedy," one of the chief sources of signification in Reformation erotic discourse, suggests how Reformation marriage ideology has bridged Book II and Book III. Neither note, reason or remedy, is sounded in the story that Spenser closely imitates from the pseudo-Virgilian *Ciris*.[36] Glauce responds that

> though no reason may apply
> Salue to your sore, yet loue can higher stye
> Than reasons reach.
>   (2.36)

Reason is often proposed as a remedy for the problems manifest in Book II, but for Britomart's wound another cure is needed: "Ne can my running sore find remedie," she again complains (2.39), a yoking of Petrarchan illness to its Reformation cure. Glauce proposes an equally Reformation solution:

> But if thou may with reason yet represse
>   The growing euill, ere it strength haue got,
>   And thee abandond wholly doe possesse,
>   Against it strongly striue, and yield thee not,
> . . . .
> . . . compasse thy desire, and find that loued knight.
>   (2.46)

Here we see the prescription of Reformation erotic discourse linked to the economy of Spenserian temperance. Glauce urges repression, a compassing of "euill" sexual desire and joins it to exhort a temperate "reason." But unlike erotic discourses (such as those in Petrarch) that offer reason as a remedy for passion, Glauce here draws upon a Pauline-Protestant remedy: marriage. Such a healing will lead Britomart toward the altar, where her repressed passion will find its appropriate release in matrimony. This scene inscribes the dynamics of temperance in a new key, facilitated by the mediating Reformation marriage discourse.[37]

Glauce's advice, however, goes unheeded, for Britomart is not yet able to exert such self-control. It is not at all coincidental that Glauce next leads Britomart "vnto the Church" (the first location to be so named in the poem and the only one in the 1590 version), there to apply a variety of folk medicines. These nostrums, too, prove ineffectual, for Britomart's malady is of a different order:

> Returned home, the royall Infant fell
> > Into her former fit; for why, no powre
> > Nor guidance of her selfe in her did dwell.
>
> (2.49)

Her struggle to achieve continence ("guidance of her selfe") will be resolved gradually. Her final remedy will only come in another church at the appointed time of her wedding, a scene proleptically figured in the dream vision of Isis Church in Book V, though the actual wedding is deferred beyond the limits of the poem.[38]

Meanwhile in the early cantos of Book III, Britomart strives to become a model of two kinds of continence: Reformation chastity, which most often finds its fulfillment in matrimony, and Spenserian temperance. She looks forward to marriage, but in the meantime she channels her erotic energy into knightly wrath, a familiar process from Guyon's quest.[39] Hence the scene at the seacoast, where she pleads for continence from Aeolus, the god who according to Natalis Comes "contains" the winds.[40] Immediately after her plea, Glauce again intervenes and offers the Reformation remedy for lovesickness. Glauce "restraine[s]" her and grants her "reliefe, / Through hope of those" who will "fetch their being from the sacred mould / Of her immortall wombe" (4.11). Moreover, as a result of her struggle against incontinence, Britomart is able to resist other temptations. Having pleaded for continence, she can turn away from the wealth on Marinell's shore as easily as Guyon turns away from the wealth in Mammon's house, an episode we are surely meant to recall: "But them despised al; for all was in her powre" (4.18; cf. II.7.9,19,64).

Britomart's struggle with desire, depicted at length in the first four cantos and by implication throughout Book III, differs markedly from that of other (male) characters similarly afflicted. The comparison is plain in the case of Arthur, whose complaint to Night in canto

4 compares closely to Britomart's complaint earlier in the same canto. Neither here nor, for that matter, in his vision of the Faerie Queene in Book I is marriage promised as the fulfillment of Arthur's yearning. His complaint trails off inconclusively with the ending of the canto. Unlike Britomart, he is provided with no comfort. Her characterization is constructed on a different understanding of sexuality, for her longing will find its satisfaction in marriage. Arthur's lovesickness—and, as we shall see, that of the other male characters—finds no remedy in this book. The contrast is between two conceptions of eros, Petrarchan and Reformation.

The intimacy between Book II and Book III is dramatized at the outset of the third book by Arthur's tying of Guyon and Britomart with a "golden chaine of concord" so that "reconcilement was betweene them knit, / Through goodly temperance, and affection chaste" (1.12). Actions of binding and constricting, already familiar from the previous book, mark Book III as pervasively as contemporary Reformation prescriptions concerning sex. Not an episode in the book passes without mention of controlling, tying, containing—continence, in short—and so allegorizing chastity and linking it to the previous book.[41] As Arthur's golden chain suggests, the titular heroes are also strongly allied. Britomart is portrayed as Guyon transfigured. Like him she has a "constant mind" that does not "lightly follow beauties chace" (1.19; cf. II.6.21,26). She is praised as "stedfast"—Guyon's characteristic epithet, which is also applied to the chaste female figures of this book.[42] Britomart and Guyon are the only two figures in the poem entitled to the term "magnanimity" (II.8.23; III.11.19). Unlike other protagonists of *The Faerie Queene*, neither succumbs to sexual or other worldly blandishments. Each moves steadfastly through peril, armed in innocence against various temptations.

The superiority of chastity, that "fairest vertue, farre aboue the rest" (III, proem 1), is evident from the start: Britomart's "secret powre vnseene" (1.7) enables her to overcome Guyon in their initial clash. Some readers have puzzled over Britomart's defeat of Guyon in this episode: why should these virtues be in conflict?[43] What exactly constitutes the superiority of chastity? Arthur provides a clue when he says that Guyon has been bested by losing control over his horse (conventionally associated with the passions): the harness was "not firmly tyde" (1.11). This will be exactly Britomart's advantage, as the next cantos will illustrate: she is learning to tie her passions, and she can thereby channel her energies, sublimate them perhaps, into purposeful martial derring-do. Even the knight of temperance may have lapses of self-command, at least when confronted by Britomart. At any rate, her "secret powre" depends upon self-control, which gives her the advantage even over Guyon, who could hardly be considered deficient in this property. Such self-restraint comprises the defense of her chastity. To guard herself she must learn how to rein the horses of passion.

Differences between the two titular heroes help reveal their virtues. Spenserian temperance is a notoriously colorless virtue, whose challenges produce in Guyon little of the turmoil stirring Britomart.[44] For the most part horseless, Guyon habitually stands prosaically with his feet firmly on the ground, looking neither above nor within. While the Palmer must direct Guyon away from "vanity" (II.12.34) or from gazing on the bathing nymphs en route to Acrasia's Bower (12.69), the task is relatively effortless, for Guyon is compliant. His virtue does not require activity but a calm shunning of temptation: he struggles little because he usually feels little. Britomart is the more sympathetic of the two figures, at least to modern readers, both because her inner life is more fully realized and because she is given a compelling past and future. Her associations with Elizabeth I have always exerted a powerful claim on readers, not least because in this respect, too, she incarnates and enfolds both male and female, Mars and Venus.[45] Britomart engages our attention because she is active, martial, and embattled both within and without.[46] Whereas Guyon ties up an adversary in Acrasia, hardly a fierce one at that, Britomart binds both Busirane, a violent adversary, as well as her own threatening incontinence. Her control over her inner life, especially in the early cantos, taxes her. In this sense Britomart is not merely the more complete and interesting character; she also defends a virtue more challenging and complex, and more at the heart of human existence, than that defended by Guyon.

Britomart's career, more than Guyon's, embodies continence as Aristotle defines it in the *Nicomachean Ethics*, where he distinguishes between the temperate man and the continent man, noting that the continent man feels strong emotion but restrains himself from acting upon his passions.[47] Britomart exemplifies Aristotelian continence in this sense, the more strikingly so since, from Aristotle on, the assumption is that such a virtue can be figured only in a man. Spenser's adaptation of Aristotelian continence is syncretized, in this book, with Reformation notions of sexuality, which emphasize the power of desire and the need to harness it. In this way the virtue Britomart defends is close to continence as defined by Philipp Melanchthon, who in the *Enarrationes* yokes Aristotle's continence to Protestant doctrine.[48] Critics early in the twentieth century, notably H. S. V. Jones and F. M. Padelford, aver that Spenser knew Melanchthon's text and used it as a "source" in shaping Chastity. But they fail to verify the claim and make little of it interpretively, and so later Spenser criticism drops it.[49] It is nonetheless worth speculating that Melanchthon's synthesis of Aristotelian continence and Reformation continence advocates a containment of desire sympathetic to the construction of Britomart's character.

Reformation sexual ideology is also inscribed in Malecasta. She is an icon of Reformation incontinence, not to mention the culturally expected womanly unruliness that serves to highlight Britomart's difference. Upon glimpsing Britomart decked out in man's attire, she is overcome by a fire that "brent into extreme desire, / And ransackt all her veines with passion entire" (1.47). Her uncontrollable "fleshly lust" soon "into termes of open outrage brust, / That plaine discouered her incontinence" (1.48). She suffers from a longing as insistent as that of Britomart, who, however, does not "discouer her incontinence" but instead bridles it. Malecasta, on the contrary, looses the "bridle to her wanton will" (1.50). Furthermore her sighs and sobs and plaints are those of the Petrarchan (male) lover as well as a throwback to the intemperate characters of the previous book of the poem: she exemplifies "strong extremitie" (1.53).

The atmosphere surrounding Malecasta is mephitic with intemperance: "The image of superfluous riotize / Exceeding much the state of meane degree" (1.33). The tapestry depicting Venus and Adonis suggests how Acrasia's spirit has invaded this midst, for it elaborately recreates the terminal episodes of the previous book, an Acrasia figure overwhelming both Mortdant and Verdant.[50] Britomart cannot decipher this tapestry, for, as the flashbacks will dramatize, she is in process of acquiring continence. Nor can she foresee the assault by Malecasta and the subsequent wound from Gardante. Along with all the other richness of its signification, this wound suggests her need to guard her own erotic vulnerability.[51] Castle Joyous, then, incorporates the menaces Britomart must grapple with, especially in the early cantos. In its confines she is beset allegorically from within. Its residents try to harm her intimately.

Such vulnerability would not fit Guyon's character. When he faints, he is providentially aided. Guyon's biography calls upon him to prove himself, but not on his own, for he is supported all along in concealed or indirect ways—by the angel who comes at his faint, by Arthur, by the Palmer.[52] After the intervention of the angel, Guyon moves purposefully to the conclusion of his quest. Britomart is never the beneficiary of a ministering angel. Nor is she favored at times of crisis or attack in the way Florimell is, by the intercession of "heauens . . . voluntary grace" (8.29). On the other hand, Merlin tells her that "heauenly destiny, / Led with eternall prouidence" has guided her to the vision of Artegall in the mirror so as "to bring [its] will to pas" (3.24). From the start, heavenly powers support her, but unlike Guyon (or Redcrosse) she is never rescued by providential mediation. Merlin's information does not, for that matter, diminish her emotional distress, for despite the mage's comforting prophecy she continues to pine for Artegall. After leaving Redcrosse in canto 4, for example, she is not said to be guided by destiny, as Merlin had avouched, but "Following the guidaunce of her blinded guest" (4.6). However guaranteed of the purposes of heaven, she is emotionally unsupported (e.g., "With such selfe-pleasing thoughts her wound she fed" [4.6]) and must rely on her own resources to combat her enemies.

Chief among those resources is her virginity, which is temporary, since her eventual estate is marriage. Despite their praise of "continency" as a legitimate alternative to marriage, virginity and celibacy may have caused Reformation commentators more uncertainty than they acknowledge. Calvin's hedged endorsement is not anomalous: "Virginitie, I graunt, is a vertue not to be despised" (2.8.42; fol. 127ʳ). Though committed to a new erotic ideology that glorifies marriage, many commentators, as we have seen, are loathe to devalue virginity—particularly, of course, for women but also for men. Frequently prooftexts from Paul are adduced in its support, always with the proviso that it not be automatically privileged as the superior state, as was the case for so long.[53] Richard Hooker is the great exemplar of this position among the English Reformers ("the single life," he says in the *Laws*, is "a thing more angelicall and divine" than the married).[54] He has ample confirmation from Luther, Calvin, and others.[55] As Calvin says: "If virgins haue of faith dedicate themselues to God, let them continn[u]e shamefastely, and chastly without any faining. So being strong and stedfast, let them looke for the reward of virginitie" (4.13.17; fol. 425ʳ). Like Calvin, other commentators emphasize that celibacy must be a conscious choice and not the result of an arbitrary or institutional compulsion such as clerical requirements.

In thinking about the part played by virginity in Book III, one turns to the central cantos, beginning with the mysterious figure of Marinell. His arrival at the seacoast complicates the allegory surrounding Britomart's character. No sooner has she beseeched that containing god Aeolus for continence and listened yet again to Glauce's advice "to restraine" her passion and to hope for "reliefe" (4.12) than Marinell charges into the narrative in a familiar pattern of Spenserian cause-and-effect. Marinell's intrusion bears strenuously on the poem's pageant of Reformation continence. His is an ironic continence, unnaturally and unhealthily inflicted from without, that is, by his mother and in a pagan-sounding prophecy. His future, made barren by maternal imposition of celibacy, contrasts with that of Britomart, who anticipates fruitful marriage. Britomart confronts in Marinell her opposite, a denatured exemplar of continence. Marinell serves, then, as a reminder that Britomart's is a temporary and hale continence, leading toward marriage.

Marinell functions more than to highlight Britomart's good fortune and health. He also serves an ideological purpose in this episode. He embodies a residual form of Roman Catholic continence, usually associated by Protestants with the clergy. His continence is involuntary. Marinell's is emphatically unlike the "gift of continence" Reformation commentators never weary of praising. Marinell has obtained his continence as unwholesomely as the monkish celibate scorned by Reformation polemicists—Calvin, for example, urges monks not to "despise the remedy that is offered to them" by marriage (4.13.17; fol. 425ʳ). Marinell's aberrant celibacy provides a "lesson too hard for liuing clay." Hence the narrator's flat assertion: "he was loues enimy" (4.26). Marinell is a male version of Britomart whose characterization and destiny are constructed from Roman

Catholic rather than Protestant notions of chastity. His monkish celibacy signifies a residual (the divines would say *retrograde*) ideology of Roman Catholic sexuality.

When Cymoent hears of her son's defeat at Britomart's hands, she throws "her selfe downe on the Continent" (4.30). The wordplay and her histrionic gesture emblematize the destructive imposition of virginity upon her son.[56] The continence she has sought on his behalf would result not in marriage or even a chosen celibacy but rather in the condition suggested by his name, "marry-nil."[57] Alternatively, the play on "Continent" could suggest her jealousy: she herself would then be a sinister example of incontinence, a mother lusting after her son. Her lament (4.36–39), by this account, would then take its place among the other lovelorn complaints of this canto and would serve, by contrast, to underscore the robust hope of Britomart's prospects.

The episode recalls Book II. Upon Marinell's appearance, Britomart "Conuert[s]" her passion into "suddein wrath" (4.12) and "vengeance" (4.13), an action characteristic of Guyon, especially in the first half of his book as he confronts examples of anger. Similarly, after pleading for continence, Britomart converts sexual energy into wrath. Other details of Marinell's story align it with the previous book. He is an avatar of Mammon: the younger figure, too, commands and protects a cache of wealth in his "perilous glade" (4.21; cf. II.7.3), riches and treasures that comprise the "spoyle of the world" (4.23; cf. II.7.8) and suggest his estrangement from human companionship.[58] Furthermore, the episode is fraught with the intemperate behavior that is routine in the world of Book II. Cymoent, for example, reacts to her son's overthrow with a zeal worthy of Occasion. Her handmaids likewise respond "with yelling outcries, and with shrieking sowne" (4.30). These extreme responses voice the frustration of Marinell's concocted continence, which is so artificial that it appears divorced even from him. He cannot rage, and so his mother's handmaidens do. These and other resonances from the previous book are mediated by a specifically Reformation erotic ideology that here shapes an episode germane to Britomart's allegory. The incontinence of Cymoent and her handmaidens, which would have illustrated the excesses of intemperance in the earlier book, in Book III express the indignity of abnormal continence—or, again alternatively, of Cymoent's abnormal lust, which leads her to try to enforce her son's continence out of jealousy. And so the Marinell episode resurrects two different but connected forms of incontinence: one, Marinell's culturally residual parody of monklike continence; the other, the regressive intemperance of Cymoent and her attendants.

Continence continues to play its pageants diversely in the next canto when Timias is wounded while slaying the three lustful fosters. Unlike Marinell's, his is an overt and conscious struggle with continence. His story in Book III suggests that the defense against incontinence cannot always match its power. He decapitates the third foster, whose head falls "backewarde on the Continent" (5.25). Here the wordplay and the action of separating head from body may at first seem to mark the beginning of Timias's deliverance into continence from the forces of lust. But the dismemberment of the foster allegorizes Timias's own sexual dilemma. The head has fallen on the continent, but it has been sundered from the body, which, one may presume, continues to lust. However earnestly Timias wills continence, his body pines with desire. He lives, the narrator says, but joylessly.

Stronger remedy is needed, hence the intervention of "Providence heauenly." He is now comforted by "grace or fortune" (5.27) in the person of Belphoebe. She offers him nothing less than redemption—though a highly ambiguous one demanding from him superhuman self-sacrifice. Belphoebe's intercession is depicted in terms explicitly biblical: an "Angel" of God, "full of diuinities," brings "heavenly grace" to a "sinfull wight" (5.34,35). She offers him herbs as a "remedy" (5.32). Indeed she brings him back to life. But the remedy she proffers is not the Reformation remedy for incontinence tendered to Britomart in the form of a prospective companionate marriage. Belphoebe offers no cure for lust. Against that, Timias must struggle differently from Britomart. And so he implores heaven "From whence descend all hopelesse remedies" (5.34).

Timias's story in this book suggests that no remedy exists for the incontinence threatening him, or at any rate that such a restorative is not the hope of union with Belphoebe. Although this "gracious Lady, yet no paines did spare, / To do him ease, or do him remedy," she offers only "sweet Cordiall" (5.50), merely a physical cure, like those of Glauce for Britomart's earlier lovesickness. Like Britomart's, Timias's sickness can be remedied only by sexual congress. Of course, Belphoebe cannot provide that help: "A loue-sick hart, she did to him enuy [i.e., deny]" (5.50). And so he struggles to squelch incontinence: "Long while he stroue in his courageous brest / With reason dew the passion to subdew" (5.44). But in Timias's case, the bridling of passion will issue not in Britomart's "hope" (4.11) of marriage and children but in desperation only: "To be captiued in endlesse duraunce /Of sorrow and despaire without aleggeaunce" (5.42).

This important strand of the allegory initiates the undermining of Reformation certainties about marriage as the remedy to the pervasive distresses of sexuality, of which Timias's futile desire comprises one of the most plangent reminders in the Spenserian canon. The very exaltedness of Belphoebe, as well as the abyss her inviolable chastity puts between her and Timias, subverts facile assurances that the book replicates Reformation "solutions" to the enigmas of sexuality. Her remoteness can be only partly explained by Belphoebe's status as a figure for Elizabeth I, for the text at this point stresses Timias's desire more than the historical referent of Belphoebe's virginity.[59] If we interpret the episode, as some have, as figuring the relationship of Raleigh and the queen, we must downplay the obvious accent on Timias's erotic suffering, which is simply too sharp and indelicate to be read merely as an extended figure for courtly disappointment. Timias is trapped, at least in this episode, in an insoluble quandary—one to which the Reformation answer is of little value. He may restrain his incontinence, but he cannot rid himself of desire. Marriage is not a possibility, and so he is cornered in hopelessness. For the Reformation commentators, continence is a chosen skill, at the disposal of the will. For Timias the answer is not so handy: "Thus warreid he long time against his will" (5.48), a disagreeable conflict that Belphoebe, despite her attempt to "do him remedy" (5.50), is unequipped to assuage.

The episode also suggests how the Legend of Chastity reinscribes the concerns of Book II, where Belphoebe has made a memorable appearance and rebuffed a suitor far less noble and sympathetic than Timias. In Book III she recreates the role of the angel sent to succor Guyon and bring him "grace" (II.8.1, III.5.35).[60] The verbal echoes are too strong to be insignificant. She is an agent of "grace" sent by providence to "comfort" (5.27) him, and as she herself says, her mission is to "succour wretched wights" (5.36). Timias feels that she has brought him "from deathes dore" (5.46).

Belphoebe also transfigures Acrasia. Timias sees her as God's "Angell from her bowre of blis" (5.35). When she first chances upon him, she recreates the tableau of Acrasia standing dominatingly over Verdant: "His mayled haberieon she did vndight" (5.31)—with wordplay on "mayled," for Belphoebe has un-maled him, however unwittingly. In retrospect Acrasia is now revealed, in Spenserian fashion, to be a demonic parody of Belphoebe. Acrasia has been refashioned and spiritually retamed. In this episode Belphoebe functions, in addition to the many roles commentators have noted her playing, as recreating both the role of Guyon's protecting angel as well as a transmuted Acrasia. Hence the purposeful echoes of earlier scenes: for Timias, struggling with desire, Belphoebe is both protector and seducer—the former willingly, the latter unknowingly and inevitably. The result is his simultaneous rescue and incapacitation.

His conflict is perplexing. His is another futile Petrarchan agon: the unrequited anguish of the love-smitten male for the chaste and unapproachable beloved.[61] His complaint (5.45–47) echoes those of Britomart and Arthur. But his yearning will never be satisfied, and the text does not imply it should be. The poem instead endorses Belphoebe's chastity, for she is "Pure and vnspotted from all loathly crime, / That is ingenerate in fleshly slime" (6.3). No irony clouds this presentation of Belphoebe's virtue and chastity, which, as we saw, is sanctioned in Reformation erotic discourse.[62] But the pain of unrequited male desire is a reality, as Petrarchan discourse amply testifies, and its weight falls heavily on this portion of the narrative. The Reformation remedy for the demands of desire has no potency to cure Timias's illness.

This episode challenges that remedy as the best response to the predicament of human sexuality. Timias must struggle—and the struggle is redolent of the temperance of Book II. He exerts reason to conquer his erotic impulses: "Long while he stroue in his couragous brest, / With reason dew the passion to subdew" (5.44). He is said to be "restraind" and "constraind" (5.44) by the circumstances of his convalescence. His conflict is depicted as a matter of volition: "Thus warreid he long time against his will" (5.48). Continence is something that can be chosen. Or can it? How much choice does the desirous lover have, at least about his feelings? Timias's conflict reproduces that of Britomart at the seacoast. But willpower fails him, and, unlike Britomart, he cannot channel his incontinence into knightly wrath, at least not as long as he remains in proximity to Belphoebe. He can do little but feel anguish. His desire will never be recipro- cated, and there are no textual indications that it ought to be.

To contextualize this episode in Reformation erotic discourse is to recognize it as a test of the values regarding sexuality advanced there so univocally and certainly. This episode endorses Belphoebe's chas- tity, in a way consonant with contemporary views of virginity, at the same time that it equally sympathizes with Timias's heartache. In this episode Petrarchan and Reformation erotic discourses intersect—or, more accurately, clash irreconcilably. Timias cannot be gratified, whether he acts as a celibate, as a prospective marriage partner, or as a desire-driven young male. It may well be that Timias is portrayed, at least in this book, as both a model of continence, laboring to main- tain integrity in the face of passion, and a victim of hopeless desire. These roles cannot be readily squared. The gap between them high- lights the ambivalence of the text toward the marriage discourse it represents, a resistance that in later episodes becomes a challenge.

In comparison to the witch's son, however, Timias seems a model of continence. The allegory goes to considerable lengths to incarnate in this churl the forces of incontinence, and we are asked to measure other young male characters against him. Moreover, he seems plucked directly out of Book II, especially in the initial descriptions where he seems (as Hamilton says) one of Acrasia's knights. He also recalls Cymochles, for he is "stretched forth in idlenesse alwayes," and "vs'd to slug, or sleepe in slothfull shade" (7.12; cf. II.6.14). Fur- thermore, in the witch and her son we are surely meant to recall an- other mother-son duo, Occasion and Furor. Both hags provoke and enflame their sons, one to anger, the other to lust (II.4.7; cf. III.7.16,20,21). The witch's son, like Furor, "scratcht his face, and with his teeth did teare / His rugged flesh, and rent his ragged heare" (7.20; cf. II.4.3). But at this point the episode changes from seeming to belong in the world of Book II and emerges as an episode fitting to Book III. Eros now becomes sinister, brutal, and violent. The witch both eggs him on and responds to his intemperate reactions to Flo- rimell's escape by calling the hideous Monster to pursue her—a crea- ture that will be subdued only by its being tied with the girdle of chas- tity. The Monster itself, as Hamilton points out, "is strengthened by being wounded, and may be compared to Maleger."[63] Here again a situation from Book II has been transformed to suit the allegory of chastity. Maleger, the embodiment of misruled flesh generally, is reincarnated in the Monster as unbridled sexuality in particular: it "feeds on womens flesh, as others feede on gras" (7.22). The witch's son is a close kinsman of Grill: as he looks on Florimell, he "cast to loue her in his brutish mind; / No loue, but brutish lust, that was so beastly tind" (7.15). In this respect he typifies several characters in the second half of the book—Argante and Ollyphant, the fisherman, Proteus, Malbecco and Hellenore—who are associated with the forces of degraded lust. These forces will rage unless taken in hand, exactly what Satyrane does when he binds the beast with Florimell's ribbon. The Monster, like the forces of tamed lust itself, then trembles like a lamb that has "long bene learned to obay" (7.36).[64]

While the Monster looks back to a variety of texts and more primordial discourses, it may also be recognized as the embodiment of the unbridled flesh, a monstrous version of the fallen condition of ungoverned sexuality continuously feared in Reformation marriage discourses. The witch's son exemplifies a similar anxiety, for he degenerates over the course of the episode from a lazy lout to a rapacious sexual predator. Occasion and Furor, allegorical illustrations in Book II of intemperate anger, have in the witch and her son been eroticized into representations of unregulated sexual appetite. Reformation marriage manuals abound in animal imagery to describe lust, but the use of such imagery is also commonplace throughout the culture. When we contextualize that imagery in the Reformation fear of ungoverned eros, we must hypothesize that the lustful characters in Book III allegorize profound reserves of suspicion and anxiety found in Reformation discourse on marriage and sexuality.

The most notable lustful figures are Hellenore and Paridell, who embody the antithesis of the chaste and temperate union endorsed by the commentators. Their adultery, however, cannot be said to violate an idealized marriage. The alliance of Malbecco and Hellenore is mocked by its very presentation as a fabliau.[65] The best that can be said of their affiliation is that it provides an admonitory antitype of a marriage. The narrator labels Hellenore an "ensample of the bad" (9.2), and the term applies to both as a couple, for they compose a model of an unhappy marriage. "Vnfitly yokt together in one teeme" (9.6), these yoke-fellows "finde no remedie" (10.3) in wedlock. Theirs reads like a textbook case (not to mention the standard fabliau pretext) of what the marriage manuals claim will prevent marital contentment: separated from her husband by "far vnequall yeares" (9.4), Hellenore is "mewe[d] from all mens sight / Depriu'd of kindly ioy and naturall delight" (9.5).[66] Paridell shrewdly notes that in constricting his wife's freedom Malbecco has in fact enslaved himself "In dolefull thraldome" and golden "fetters" (9.8). The bridling and restriction recommended as Reformation remedies to incontinence are here turned to different purpose. The miser containing his gold becomes a parody of continence.[67] Malbecco's imprisonment is the psychic enslavement of an ill-advised marital yoke, a prospect continually cautioned against in the marriage texts.

The tale challenges the ideal of marriage as a certain means of achieving continence. The narrator pronounces this the story of a "wanton Lady" guilty of "loose incontinence" (9.1), but the episode blames all parties. The threats to their union are both internal and external, the latter embodied in Paridell's "fierce youngmans vnruly maistery" (10.2). Certainly the bad marriage Malbecco and Hellenore endure makes them prey to adultery, although Hellenore is condemned for having chosen to betray her husband. Satyrane comments disapprovingly on the futility of "yron bandes" and other artificial constrictions to achieve a happy marriage. These constraints will not "containe" (9.7) her and, in fact, result instead in Malbecco's own imprisonment.

Certain aspects of this tale would be comfortable in the world of Book II, for it tells of "loues extremitie, / That is the father of foule gealosy" (10.22).[68] Malbecco's is a refashioning of Phedon's story. Both are accounts of married love, betrayal, and jealousy. (Phedon is said to be an almost-married man: the nuptials have been celebrated [II.4.21]). Both tales record how a deceived lover's anguish is deepened by his becoming "the sad spectatour of [his] Tragedy" (II.4.27), watching (or seeming to watch) his beloved in the act of betraying him. Both tales suggest that, though each lover is traduced, his misery is primarily the result of self-betrayal, for both are injured by their own failures at self-control. Like Phedon, Malbecco is seized by "extreme fury" (10.54) when faced with what he takes to be treachery in love. For the older character, though, the loss of money rather than his wife instigates intemperance. He attempts to win Hellenore back to "bandes of fresh accord" (10.51), but by coupling with satyrs she has already degenerated to the level of Grill.[69]

Malbecco's story amplifies that of Phedon, for it is a richer version of the effects of extreme passion on nuptial alliance. The endings of

the stories are tailored to the needs of each book. In a fit of intemperate wrath Phedon slays his betrothed as well as his betrayer, putting
him readily in the clutches of Occasion. Malbecco instead turns his
"Griefe, and despight, and gealosie, and scorne" (10.55) inward
against himself. His jealousy makes him victim of a perverse chastity.
He elects a sterile celibacy, freezes in suspended animation, fragmented and utterly isolated. He has chosen his misery, a willful and
destructive continence motivated by the agony of jealous despair.
Trapped by his own misguided celibacy, Malbecco fashions himself
into a sad, hermitlike figure, similar to the kind whom the Reformers
deride as the celibate living a life of punishment for exile from nor-
mal social life.[70] He exemplifies what endangers Timias and Marinell, trapped in their own forms of injurious celibacy. Both Phedon's and Malbecco's responses to their unhappiness in love are
forms of incontinence, each appropriately allegorized. The different
denouements reveal how Reformation marriage discourse bridges
these two books of Spenser's poem, for Malbecco, unlike Phedon, is
reduced not to a furious intemperance but to a perverse lovelessness
condemned by Reformation manuals. At the end, Malbecco becomes a parody of continence.

It is significant and perplexing that this tale is the primary example of married love in Book III and one of the most memorable marriages depicted (as opposed to projected) in *The Faerie Queene*. Because it stands in such solitude as a marriage tale, the episode of
Malbecco and Hellenore challenges the Reformation ideal of companionate wedlock. The deeply ambivalent views about sex in Reformation marriage discourse are matched by the less than affirmative
attitude toward marriage seen throughout *The Faerie Queene* and
especially in Book III. Indeed, the distrust of eros not far beneath the
surface of Reformation discourse on marriage is much in evidence in
this book's treatment of marriage and sexuality. Unlike its Reformation contemporaries, however, Book III does not glorify marriage except in prophesied or anticipated or deferred unions. By drawing on
the lexicon of Reformation discourse, the text reproduces the exaltation of marriage as remedy for the insidious effects of fallen sexuality.
The early cantos of this book depicting Britomart's erotic career
seem to privilege the redemptive powers of married love. But the text
does not continue to idealize companionate marriage in the fashion
of contemporary Reformation discourse as a remedy for fallen sexu-

ality. As the book progresses, even Britomart's (or is it, in retrospect, Glauce's?) trust in marriage begins to seem naive. In its cumulative impact, Book III questions the marriage discourse it foregrounds, but it also displays anxiety about marriage and sex.

That uncertainty is not assuaged by the final episode, Britomart's rescue of Amoret from Busirane. If Spenser had wished to offer a alternative to the grim "ensample" of the marriage of Malbecco and Hellenore, one presumes he would not have presented a union so interpretively taxing as that of Scudamour and Amoret. For example, Britomart's meeting with Scudamour results directly and enigmatically from her chasing of Ollyphant, an episodic ordering of Spenserian cause-and-effect not designed to inspire confidence in Scudamour's emotional integrity. None of the initial details of this encounter leads us to expect a chivalric tale of a lover's devotion to his betrothed. Britomart finds Scudamour by a fountain wallowing on the ground stripped of his armor, groaning and sobbing, almost a parody (as critics have noted) of a Petrarchan lover.[71] His tale takes a more sinister turn as he cries out to God for vengeance against his enemy, who has pierced Amoret's chaste breast. Assuming him to be at life's end, Britomart counsels him to submit to "high prouidence" (11.14). But she then offers herself as the agent of vengeance: "Perhaps this hand may helpe to . . . wreake your sorrow on your cruel foe" (11.15), who, Scudamour claims, has "pen[ned]" Amoret with "enchauntments and blacke Magicke" (11.16).[72]

This episode recreates Guyon's encounter with Amavia at the beginning of Book II. The parallels are too strong to be insignificant. Guyon hears the piercing shrieks of Amavia questioning why the "carelesse heauens" refuse the "doome of iust reuenge" (1.36). Guyon finds *her* alabaster breast pierced by a knife as she lies beside a bubbling fountain. He offers counsel as well as vengeance. Amavia then describes how *her* mate was "beguiled" by a "false enchaunteresse" (1.51) and was "In chaines of lust and lewd desires ybound" (1.54).

Neither of these spectacles of extravagant emotion will be alleviated until the protagonist completes an act of just revenge against the enchanter. Guyon ties Acrasia in a net and releases Verdant. Britomart defeats Busirane, having "vnbound" and "restor'd" (12.38) Amoret by binding him up. What are we to make of these parallels?

When the two episodes are juxtaposed, as their similarities ask us to do, salient differences emerge. Amavia's tale and Guyon's deferred

avenging of it comprise a relatively straightforward story of justice
done and order restored. It is not primarily a tale about Guyon. Acrasia, Amavia, Mortdant, Verdant: none directly reflects his struggle to
achieve temperance or figures his emotional life. But when this tale is
transmuted at the end of Book III, a multitude of changes take place,
many as a result of the book's intertextual formation, notably in Ital-
ian romance. If we posit that one discourse mediating the two books
is Reformation erotic discourse, we can draw important conclusions
about the differences between the two tales. Britomart completes her
assistance of Scudamour, whereas Guyon fails to help Amavia. That
cause is lost before Guyon begins, and he is left only to seek revenge
and (almost incidentally, certainly without prior intention) to prevent Verdant's undoing. Britomart, on the other hand, heroically rescues Amoret, Scudamour, and—most readers feel—herself. Britomart's penetration of Busirane's house allegorizes her own struggle
with the challenges of desire at least as much as it does Amoret's, and
arguably more. Britomart must brave Busirane on his terms, in his
house, with fearless skill. To regulate erotic turmoil Britomart must
act aggressively. She must, as Judith Anderson points out, defeat
Busirane where he resides: hence the penetration within, the determined movement to the interior with sword drawn.[73]

Britomart must outperform Scudamour, to whom we are surely
meant to compare her. Scudamour's self-absorbed, unattractive Petrarchan mannerisms are put to shame by Britomart's bravery. In
Scudamour she is presented with another male version of herself, as
she is with Marinell at the seacoast. In the earlier encounter, she converts her incontinence into wrath and exits the narrative with martial
purposefulness. Scudamour offers a more complex challenge. In him
she faces a male version of the Petrarchan lover she is in danger of becoming in the early cantos. Now, however, through the mysterious
process of *entrelacement*, she is changed into a figure of more directed energies, and she can shoulder Scudamour's burden.[74]

Britomart also fights for her own erotic integrity. Her temperate
persistence (Be Bold/Be Not Too Bold) defeats Busirane's malice and
the sexual disruption incarnated in his environment. She ties, regu-
lates, controls Busirane, who embodies a sinister mutation of Scudamour's rantings and of the human propensity for unregulated erotic
desire, including her own. In so doing she exercises continence.[75]
When entreating Britomart not to kill Busirane, Amoret says that

otherwise "her paine / Should be remedilesse" (12.34). Unlike Guyon, Britomart does not wreck the enchanter's environment. Passion cannot be eliminated if the lovers are to be joined, but it must be tightly contained. The tying of Busirane expresses the ideology of healthy continence ("Restore vnto her health" [12.35], says Britomart to the enchanter) of erotic longing, to be released in the knot of marriage.

In the 1590 version, the remedy Amoret calls for is emblematized in the famous hermaphroditic image of the couple joined as one being. Amoret and Scudamour, united in a "long embracement" (12.45) and "growne together quite" (12.46), embody the phrase from the marriage service (and Genesis 2) that proclaim married man and woman as one flesh. Britomart is moved by the spectacle, for "to her selfe oft wisht like happinesse" (12.46), seeing in their union what she has from the start craved for herself. Many readers have admired the image as an ideal of Book III's allegorized virtue—a "creative revision," as Lauren Silberman puts it, "of constricting attitudes towards love" that "accounts for sexual difference and sexual desire."[76]

It is also, as others point out, an uncharacteristically simplified ending. It suggests that obstacles to chaste love disappear when separation becomes reunion.[77] The whole force of the book, however, has militated against such an easy and uncomplicated solution to the challenge of incontinent sexuality as suggested by the tightly contained, marble image of "two senceles stocks in long embracement" (12.45). The previous "ensample" of Malbecco and Hellenore—not to mention the many other characters burdened with the inherent weight of sexual desire—expressly subverts such a monolithic ending. The continuation of the lovers' tale in later episodes also undermines any certainties that the 1590 ending might encourage. The dynamics of continence, especially in the second half of the book, are exacting at best. A union of the lovers, however sexually idealized, does not leap the hazards of desire that the text has been at pains to allegorize.

As Reformation commentators admit, the illness of sexuality is not easily amenable even to the remedies they themselves propose. Nor have the ambivalences about eros inherent in other episodes been dispelled. By granting to sexuality greater power than its predecessor, Book III reinscribes concupiscence in a darker key. In the canto depicting the Garden of Adonis, sexual power finds elaborate cosmological celebration. But that canto is counterbalanced and arguably offset by the cumulative weight of individual episodes depicting erotic distress. Those episodes project darkly against the visionary canto depicting the mysteries of generativity. Elsewhere— perhaps, in effect, throughout—Book III is preoccupied with the negative power of eros, especially in the second half with its array of lustful characters charging in and out of the narrative. Even the worthier characters (except Belphoebe) are troubled by sexuality, the turmoil of which is not calmed by the solutions offered in Reformation marriage discourses. The text taps those resources only to find, as the allegory proceeds, that they are shallower than they appear. The deferred union of Scudamour and Amoret in the 1596 version testifies to the degree this discourse has disquieted the text and to the dissatisfactions Spenser evidently felt as he contemplated Book IV.

Revenge and Companionate
Marriage in Book IV

The attention to marriage we may have expected in Book III finds its place in Book IV in the Legend of Friendship, which records more betrothals and marriages than elsewhere in *The Faerie Queene*. We may well ask why the poet deferred representing matrimony until the later book, when Book III, with its celebration of chaste love, would, on the face of it, have been the more likely forum. Simply to list the marriages contracted or projected in Book IV is to register the scarcity of nuptial unions in other books. Britomart and Artegall, Amoret and Scudamour, Florimell and Marinell, Æmylia and Amyas, Poeana and Placidas, Cambina and Cambell, Canacee and Triamond—each couple is said in this book either to wed or to engage to marry, and indeed Amoret and Scudamour do both (though in reverse chronological order). Moreover, the great set piece of the book, the marriage of the Thames and the Medway—however abstractly related to flesh-and-blood concerns of matrimony—can certainly be said to honor that institution. The union of so many couples, then, would seem to indicate a profound shift in the presentation of marriage from the 1590 version, where it is rarely depicted, or, as in Book III, where it is presented with considerable reservation, if not outright skepticism. The hesitancy about marriage that I argue in the previous chapter would seem to have dissipated, or at least diminished, as the second half of the 1596 version begins. But, in fact, that hesitancy is deepened. Book III investigates marriage as one expression of sexual desire. Book IV explores marriage, or at least courtship, under a different auspices, as an expression of companionship. Yet the violence of this book—surely one of its notable hallmarks, even in a poem noted for its violence throughout—seriously compromises the idealizing of marriage it struggles to present.

The decision to interrogate matrimony more fully in the book "Of Friendship" is supported by a considerable body of contemporary Reformation writing on marriage. Having little to say directly on the subject of friendship, Reformation writers more often confine their remarks on the issue to the lauding of companionate marriage. Perhaps this is why so many projected marriages are stockpiled in Book IV. As scholarship has fully documented over the past fifteen years, writers during the Reformation, whether Protestant or humanist, consistently privilege marriage over virginity on the grounds that it fosters "true and perfit loue, that maketh the Flower of Friendship betweene man and wife freshle to spring."[1] Marriage manuals of the period unfailingly commend friendship between husband and wife as one of the chief benefits of the institution. As Henry Bullinger's popular manual *The Golden Boke of Christen Matrimonye* puts it, wedlock is established so that man and woman "may dwel together in frendship."[2] It is surprising, then, that Spenser's book "Of Friendship" has not before been situated among Reformation discourses of marriage, where it would seem to find a hospitable environment.[3] *The Book of Homilies*, to take a notable example, begins the sermon on the state of matrimony by claiming that it "is instituted of God, to the intent that man and woman should liue lawfully in a perpetuall frendly felowship." The sermon represents marriage as grounded in the same standards as Book IV: "married persons must apply their mindes in most earnest wise to concorde, and must craue continually of God the helpe of his holy spirite, so to rule their hartes and to knit their mindes together, that they be disseuered not by any deuition of discorde."[4]

Although concord and discord also structure Book IV, God and his holy spirit do not. The book taps Reformation discourses of marriage, but it remains distant from the theological underpinnings of that discourse. Indeed, this is the least theological book in the poem. It reveals less evidence of God, providence, the afterlife, and the supernatural—or of the theology buttressing these religious concepts—than any other in *The Faerie Queene*.[5] Reformation discourses, then, are thoroughly absorbed into other domains, some of which seem remote from religion. Book IV portrays, for example, the greatest number of chivalric contests, the most frequent ritualized combat, the most brutal knightly standoffs. As tedious as most readers probably find those scenes, with their lavish bloodletting, their duration (some extending over two cantos or several days), their repetitions and substitutions, their doublings, triplings, and quadruplings—for all their multiplicity, the tournaments repeat one chivalric formula: male warriors fight for and before female beauties. As the poet says in an introductory stanza:

> It hath bene through all ages euer seene,
>> That with the praise of armes and cheualrie,
>> The prize of beautie still hath ioyned beene;
>> And that for reasons speciall priuitie:
>> For either doth on other much relie.
>
> (5.1)

This chapter investigates how Book IV tries to consolidate arms and beauty, violence and love, those ancient and incompatible adversary-allies. The hermaphroditic Venus, on the altar of her temple in a climactic moment of the book, mysteriously joins "Both male and female, both vnder one name" (10.41), a cryptic emblem of the often pained engagements between the sexes. While these encounters frequently lead to betrothal, certainly here more than elsewhere, it is only after bitter strife and misunderstanding. Those conflicts often erupt between the prospective marriage partners, of course, but more often the contests pit male antagonists squaring off for a woman.[6] Under the guidance of gender theory, recent scholarship has begun to recognize the implications of these homosocial relations. This chapter may be seen as a part of the scholarly investigation of the poem's endlessly fascinating representations of gender and sexuality.[7] More specifically, recent scholarship can help in recognizing how the book's homosocial conflicts are constructed in the language of Reformation discourse, most notably in the emphasis on revenge. Here is a subject that attracted Reformation writers keenly, as students of English Renaissance drama have long known.[8] Just as marriage is Book IV's chief figure of concord, so revenge is its chief emblem of discord. The exploitation of the Reformation discourses addressing these issues, already bedfellows in the drama of the period, permits the text a complex construction of gender relations. The first half of the book dramatizes male violence waged for the sexual conquest of women. Women are repeatedly treated as objects, reduced to prizes to be won or lost by dint of arms. In this respect the poem is prolonging a chivalric discourse that seems even by 1596 not to have altogether staled.[9] The poem revitalizes this rapidly disappearing discourse by echoing contemporary Reformation concerns, notably those pertaining to revenge and companionate marriage. How the allegory foregrounds these distinctively Reformation preoccupations is the concern of this chapter. A chief problem the allegory confronts is how to reconcile two conflicting structures of desire: homosocial rivalry and heterosexual companionate marriage. Book IV idealizes marriage but undermines the ideal by presenting it simultaneously with an equally idealizing discourse of male violence and homosocial revenge.

Having alerted us in the proem that his subject will be the time-tested one of "braue exploits which great Heroes wonne, / In loue" (proem 3), the poet immediately returns us to the story of Scudamour and Amoret, left so tantalizingly incomplete with the 1596 revised ending of the previous book, and flashes back to their wedding and the disruption that led to Amoret's imprisonment. Sketching narrative background to be later elaborated at the Temple of Venus, the poet reveals that "Scudamour her bought / In perilous fight" and that "he with force her brought /From twentie knights" (1.2). We are instantly introduced to the connection between chivalric prowess and its effect upon women: "both the shield of loue, / And eke the Ladie selfe he brought away" (1.2), a formulation suggesting that shield and lady, both plundered from the temple, are related in Scudamour's chivalric agenda. But which has the greater value in that agenda? His is a conquest that results in marriage, and indeed marriage is much on the poet's mind at the outset of this book. It begins with Scudamour and Amoret's wedding, an event frustrated by not leading to the bedchamber (the bride is "conueyed quite away" by Busirane before she is "bedded" [1.3]). The impediments to marriage—the "vnknowen mischiefe" (1.2) that breaks the union of the newlyweds—link this book to the preceding one, particularly since that mischief is the "sinfull lust" (1.4) of Busirane. A comic situation arises in the aftermath of Amoret's rescue. Thinking her deliverer from Busirane's house is a man, she feels herself torn between two dominant male figures, her husband and her disguised defender. In a provocative echo of the marriage service, Amoret ponders her obligations to her second champion, who she thinks is her "liues Lord" and so "deserue[s] as his duefull meed, / Her loue, her seruice, and her vtmost wealth" (1.6). She sees herself as many female figures in this book do: a passive third party between competing male rivals.

This short episode functions as a prolegomenon to Book IV, for it touches upon the complex of bonds joining the sexes and forces separating them. Having won a woman in chivalric conquest, a man is prevented from asserting his sexual claim to her by the disruption of a lustful competitor; a woman finds her allegiances torn between knights she thinks compete to dominate her sexually.

The unnamed knight whom Britomart and Amoret encounter in the book's first full episode regards her with similar proprietorship, claiming that "fairest *Amoret* was his by right" (1.10). The very environment of this episode fosters ownership of women.[10] Any knight wishing entrance to the castle must "winne him one, or lye without the dore" (1.9). Britomart's martial prowess undoes the challenger, who is "made [to] repent that he had rashly lusted / For thing vnlawfull, that was not his owne" (1.11), a formulation not geared to refute the custom of regarding women as chivalric trophies. One may well speculate about the poem's attitude toward this convention, here and throughout the book. Because the motif is so relentlessly, indeed often brutally asserted, especially by unattractive characters, it is tempting to conclude simply that the poem disapproves of esteeming women as spoil. And of course it does, if the issue is formulated as such. But in fact, as Amoret's dilemma suggests, women in this book are positioned between men and competed for, and the poem does not necessarily reject the premise of this dynamic and may in fact idealize it. As the book's reliance on Reformation marriage values makes clear, Amoret, like the other female figures, is held thrall to discourses that result in her inevitable subordination—a position that the poem gives no indication of disavowing, even if the result is degrading.

Britomart's role in this initial episode is worth examining. She wields the might of arms, fights for justice, and defends an endangered female charge. She acts, that is, in the role of the idealized chivalric (male) hero protecting a threatened woman. But her motives do not seem compromised by the standard male desire to possess the woman he fights for. Furthermore she differs from many of the male characters in this book and in much other chivalric literature: when she triumphs, she does not hold grudges or seek revenge against her adversary. After her victory she asks that her antagonist be admitted to the chivalric company. She then creatively finds a solution to the demands of the local custom, by revealing her sex and offering herself as the knight's female companion, a switch of genders that makes for reconciliation and harmony.

Britomart's gender is complexly constructed in this scene, more so than at other points in the poem. By acting out the male role of battling another man over a woman, she forms an almost stereotypical homosocial bond with her male adversary. Furthermore, when she triumphs, she enacts a male fantasy of ownership by literally sleeping with the embattled woman. The homoerotic ambience of the stanzas following Britomart's victory is conspicuous.[11] Now "freed from feare," Amoret extends "franke affection" to Britomart and "to her bed . . . / Now freely drew." Once the two women are bedded, "all that night they of their loues did treat" in accounts "That each the other gan with passion great" (1.15–16). Dorothy Stephens has recently analyzed the erotic subtext of these stanzas and notes that "it is wonderfully puzzling that the one happy bed scene in the whole poem appears here."[12] Surely that happiness is attached as much to Britomart's chivalric success in defeating the males who would lay claim to Amoret as it does to the private realm the two women remove themselves to. After Britomart's martial achievement, the homosocial bond between the warring knights is refocused toward the homoerotic bonds between the two women.[13] Having triumphed over contenders, Britomart sleeps with the woman, enacting a male desire to share the bed of the woman he defends. Yet this is not a claim she implements as a man might assert a sexual claim over a woman, for Amoret is released the next day at will. Their intimacy is enhanced by their private joking:

> Long wandred they, yet neuer met with none,
> That to their willes could them direct aright,
> Or to them tydings tell, that mote their harts delight.
> (1.16)

Presumably "none" includes men, for the women have fashioned a privacy for their "willes" to wander freely without male direction. When Amoret thought Britomart a man, "His will she feard" (1.8); now they provide one another "harts delight." In this episode, then, because Amoret is bedded by a knight, Scudamour's later jealousy of Britomart is ironically fitting: this rival knight *has* slept with Amoret, perhaps (though perhaps not) in the sense Scudamour presumes. In either event, placed as it is in the first canto, this scene of love/friendship seems an especially apt instance of the book's titular virtue, all the more compelling because its private dimensions are subject to multiple (mis)interpretation both by readers and by other characters.

In the next episode Blandamour tries to goad Paridell into fighting Britomart by portraying her as a knight who has usurped Amoret, "his [Britomart's] conquests part" (1.33). The male characters again automatically project proprietorship onto Britomart, with no conclusive evidence. When Paridell resists the goad ("ne list I for reuenge prouoke new fight"), Blandamour steps in to claim Amoret and so challenges Britomart "for my fee [i.e., possession]" (1.35)—with no success. Scudamour duplicates the motif, for when he abruptly arrives, he claims that Amoret "he wonne by right" (1.39). Ate slanders Amoret and Britomart (1.49)—or does she? "I saw him sleepe," says Ate, "with her all night his fill"—enraging Scudamour to seek "reuenge" (1.52) against Britomart ("What vengeance due can equal thy desart," he asks [1.53]). His anger, in turn, gives Blandamour great pleasure—another homosocial coup: he "gan thereat to triumph without victorie" (1.49). Here the homosocial bonds are strong, ironic, and various: Blandamour's unprovoked assault on Britomart; Paridell's attempt to unhorse Scudamour; Scudamour's jealousy of Britomart (disguised as a male rival); Blandamour's emotional triumph over the inflamed Scudamour. The emotional focus is exclusively homosocial, at least for the male characters, who think Britomart is a man. For example, Scudamour rages (unjustifiably, shamefully) at Glauce:

> Why doth mine hand from thine auenge abstaine,
> Whose Lord hath done my loue this foule despight?
> Why do I not it wreake, on thee now in my might?
>
> (1.52)

Clearly, however, Scudamour perceives the offense as more to himself than to his "loue." Revenge yokes him to Britomart, and it seems to supercede even the matrimonial bond in his emotional calculus. As the canto ends with an infuriated Scudamour's clamoring for revenge and threatening Glauce, Amoret has faded from the forefront of his emotions. The bonds of matrimony have been displaced by the homosocial ties of vengeance. Revenge—the passion guiding most of the male characters in this book—more deeply engages Scudamour's desires than marriage does.[14]

As the chief homosocial bond in Book IV, revenge needs investigating in the context of Spenserian friendship. From the perspective of the book's virtue, the discordant vengeance most of the male characters heatedly seek hinders concord. Vengeance is portrayed as a male activity—the sole female character to seek revenge is Britomart, and then only when armored as a man in the excitement of combat. It is the primary signification of male violence in the book and the leading indicator of male gender assumptions. Because vengeance constitutes the chief mode for the male characters to win mates, it is also fully implicated in assumptions about female gender. For the sake of peace and social harmony, the male propensity for violent vengeance must be quelled by female armistice and tamed by the civilizing institution of matrimony. For one to make a marital match, ties of revenge must be broken. But those ties comprise a form of desire, a compelling bond between males that exercises powerful claims upon their allegiances. These polarities structure the action: homosocial revenge and heterosexual marriage. Revenge obstructs friendship, but it yokes men to one another. Marriage suggests the ultimate form of friendship, but it breaks the bonds of homosocial desire. These tensions need to be understood in the discourses of an age that generally idealizes marriage and consistently condemns revenge.

The subject of vengeance excited Reformation moralists to uncommon agreement. Their views are uniform and predictable: all condemn personal revenge for the same reasons, based on the same precepts and scriptural passages, as have centuries of Christian discourse. The prooftext cited repeatedly is Rom. 12:19: "Dearly beloued, auenge not your selues, but giue place vnto wrath: for it is written, Vengeance is mine; I will repaye, saith the Lord."[15] Echoes of this Pauline ordinance reverberate throughout sixteenth-century English culture. William Tyndale echoes its truisms with this pronouncement: "If thou aduenge thy selfe, or desyrest more then that such wrong be forboden, thou synnest agaynst God in takynge the auctorety of God upon the, without his commaundment, God is Father ouer al, and is of ryghte, Judge ouer all his chyldren, and to hym onlye parteyneth all aduenging. Who therfore without his commaundement aduengeth, ether with hert or hand, the same doth cast him selfe into the handes of the swerde, and loseth the right of his cause."[16] As Tyndale's diction suggests, revenge is clearly a masculine sin, at times almost inseparable from male violence. "Agaynst Contencion and Braulinge" in *The Book of Homilies* cautions against revenge by claiming that "he that cannot temper ne rule hys awn yre is but weake and feble, and rather more lyke a woman or a childe, then a stronge man. For the true strength and manlines is to overcome wrath, and to despice injury and other mennes folishnes" (195).Although revenge is unanimously denounced in all Christian discourse, Protestants adapt the proscription against private vengeance to their own theology and their special views of salvation. The desire for revenge illustrates the distinctive Reformed relation of works to grace. Works, whether good or bad, do not determine salvation but follow from a status divinely predetermined. Those who are saved will inevitably perform good works and so manifest the grace that has redeemed them; the damned will inevitably deepen with further evil the destruction they, and all fallen humanity, abundantly deserve. *The Book of Homilies* fits revenge exactly into this paradigm: "And in so goynge about to revenge evil, we shew our selves to be evil, and while we punysh and revenge another mannes foly, we double and augment our awnc foly" (195). The homily captures the peculiarly Reformed tenor of the ban on revenge. Vengeance is censured not merely because it is unethical, or violates scriptural dictates, or constitutes an act that will result in punishment after death. Revenge follows from, rather than simply leads to, reprobation. Thomas Becon states the matter clearly: "if we are vengeaunce-thirsty against our neighbour . . . it is a sure sign our sins are not forgeuen, that the hot wrath and fierce vengeaunce of God abideth still upon us and we remayne in a most damnable state."[17] Conversely, to be free of the desire to avenge is to be assured that one has been elected to be saved. Forgiveness of our enemies signifies assurance, that paramount and comfortable Reformed condition. Thus is the general Christian interdiction against revenge incorporated into the specific Protestant drama of salvation.

On the other hand, Reformation commentators' almost automatic response to the subject suggests that the situation is not quite as simple as it may seem on the surface or as convincing as the divines would have it. Censure of revenge, as well as converse pronouncements on the requirement of universal brotherhood, is generally characterized by abstractness of diction and barrenness of tone. More than most ethical discourse, Reformation prohibitions against revenge lack conviction and fail to account for the subtle complexities of human passion. This is an aspect of a problem that has long vexed scholars of drama of the period. Given the widespread con-

demnation of vengeance in moral and theological writing, how do
we account for the undeniable popularity of revenge on the stage?
This quandary has given rise to an assortment of hypotheses on the
place of revenge in Elizabethan and Jacobean culture. Some critics
have simply (and accurately) pointed out the ubiquitous denuncia-
tion of private revenge and have deduced (less convincingly) a similar
condemnation by playwrights.[18] Others have found "counter-codes"
justifying or exonerating revenge.[19] Still others have sensed a gap between orthodox piety and popular sentiment on the suitability of revenge.[20] Little consensus has been achieved on the role of revenge in
drama and, by extension, in the wider culture of the period. Another
approach to the problem is needed, one that bears on the underinvestigated preoccupation with revenge in *The Faerie Queene*, specifically in Book IV.

    Reformation moral discourse gravely undermines its disapproval
of revenge by the qualifications and exceptions it quietly finds to its
prohibitions. These are of three varieties of such extenuation. First,
Reformation writers distinguish between public and private revenge.
They condemn revenge, counsel patience, and advise forgiveness as a
response to injury. They then offer recourse to the law, a form of justice they call public revenge. Hugh Latimer addresses the issue: "But
ye must know that there be two manner of vengeance. There is a priuat vengeance, and there is a publique vengeance: the publique vengeance is alawed of God: the priuat is forbidden."[21] Public vengeance, administered by the state acting with the authority of God,
has the legitimacy of quasi-divine sanction. So Tyndale, for example,
can say, "If the wrong that is done, be greater then thou art able to
beare, trust in God, and complayne with all meeknesse unto the officer, that is set of God to forbid such violence"—to which the gloss
adds "Referre the reuenge of thy cause to the Magistrate whom God
appointeth to forbid such violence."[22] Second, vengeance is in fact
permitted, as long as it is accomplished under the auspices of the
ruler and so can be labeled public vengeance, having thereby quasi-
divine authority. Indeed, it is fully sanctioned by Rom. 13:4, which
avers that the prince "is the minister of God to take vengeance on him
that doeth euil." The ruler, says Tyndale, may "send the[e] to use violence uppon thy neyghbour to take him, to prison him and happlye to
kyll him to. And thou must euer loue thy neybour on thyne herte by
the reason that he is thy brother in the fyrste state, and yet obaye the

ruler and goo wyth the constable or like officer and break open thy neiboures door, if he wyll not open it in the kynges name: yea, and if he wyl not yeld in the kinges name thou must lay on, and smite hym to the ground tyll he be subdued."[23] A marginal gloss adds the comforting words: "Thou mayest fight with or slay thine enemie, and yet love them." Third, one may even take pleasure in vengeance—so long as the vengeance can be justified as God's. Bullinger states the matter straightforwardly: "And although the saincts do not rejoyce at the destruction of their persecuting enimies, whom they could wish rather to be conuerted, and so saued, than in this present world to be punished, and in the world to come to be damned for ever: yet they are gladd, when they see the Lord punish their afflicters, because therby they perceiue that God hath a care over those that be his servants."[24] In this fashion is revenge conflated with justice. All three qualifications suggest how vengeance as a cultural and human fact is accommodated in Reformation to religious and moral strictures against it and is normalized by religious discourse.

So, too, in *The Faerie Queene*. In the first two books in particular we find evidence of the era's standard censure of revenge. For example, as Hugh MacLachlan has demonstrated, personal revenge preoccupies Guyon throughout his early, unsuccessful adventures, as he struggles on his own to avenge injustice and defeat the wrongs of a world ruled by force and human failure.[25] Guyon surrenders his desire for private revenge upon his rescue by Arthur, who acts in the role of divine vengeance and so manifests "care in heauen" (II.8.1). By this reckoning, Guyon's allegory would satisfy Bullinger's view that God will sometimes punish the wicked and so show care for his servants. But when Book IV resumes the issue of revenge, it is with considerably more complexity than in earlier books. For one thing, this book shows no "care in heauen" attached to the issue of vengeance. What revenge the characters undertake and what care is offered are without heavenly intrusion. Although the text avails itself of contemporary discourse about revenge, it dramatizes the subject without a theological substructure. In this sense, this book reconstitutes contemporary animadversions about revenge. Its reformulations highlight the qualifications and exceptions within Reformation discourse. Finally the poem vastly widens the dimensions of that discourse by employing it to interrogate gender assumptions and relations.

The cantos following the initial clash between Britomart and Scudamour amplify the issues raised there about revenge, male rivalry, and relations between the sexes. Each of the next encounters repeats with variations the initial formula: males clash violently for sexual monopoly over a woman. It is worth looking rapidly at each episode in the sequence, for it becomes a challenge to unravel the poem's endorsements. Does the poem simply condemn the incessant quarreling? Why are these squabbling characters and turbulent episodes so closely duplicative to the point that one cannot easily distinguish some segments of the action or even the characters, both good and bad, from one another? What interpretive sense do we make of the poem's repeated display of women as objects of male rivalry? How is marriage, toward which several of these episodes lead, intended to resolve the conflicts they describe in such lavish and gruesome detail? Contextualizing these episodes in Reformation discourse can at least sketch preliminary answers to these questions.

The initial competition between Scudamour and Britomart over Amoret is parodied in the next canto, where the false Florimell, focus of lustful attention from Blandamour and Paridell, is described as a "glorious theft" (2.4), "so fayre a spoyle" (2.5), one "ygot" (2.8) from a rival and put on display. Ate takes advantage of their rivalry by "stirr[ing] vp strife, twixt loue and spight" (2.11), an apt formula to describe the homosocial confrontations in this book. Occasionally these standoffs are played for comic effect, as when Blandamour and Paridell skirmish over the false Florimell and Paridell protests that "euery spoyle or pray / Should equally be shard betwixt vs tway" (2.13). His words parody not only Spenserian friendship but also the equality of married partners in the Reformation marriage service. "Like two mad mastiffes" (2.17), these erstwhile friends rapidly degenerate to "fell auenges end" and "pitilesse remorse" (2.14). The knights temporarily abate their animosity by agreeing to a tournament in which Florimell will be the prize. Although their competition seems intended to contrast the earlier conflict of Scudamour and Britomart for Amoret, the homosocial triangle is less a parody than a duplication. In both cases the woman in question is reduced to helplessness. Although Britomart is not motivated by lust or possessiveness, she nonetheless forms a triangulated bond with a male over a female. Her motives may be different, but the effect upon the women is the same. The male characters in these early scenes do not regard Amoret differently from the false Florimell.

This incident is linked to the following story about Cambell and Triamond, who, like Blandamour and Paridell, are "foes the fellonest on ground" (2.32).[26] The enmity between these first two will be resolved by each of them marrying: a signal instance in which the homosocial bond of revenge is replaced and tamed by the bond of marriage. The text clearly juxtaposes these consecutive episodes as opposites: the false friendship of Blandamour-Paridell is contrasted with the true friendship of Cambell-Triamond. But how are these two stories different in their gender assumptions? Cambell is the brother of the woman in question, not her prospective sexual partner. Still, he plays the role of the rival by challenging her suitors "That with himselfe should combat for her sake" (2.38). In both episodes the woman links the men in violence, and in both she is regarded by the combatants as a reward for besting a rival. The connection between male violence and the role of women comes together explicitly in the following description of Canacee. Because she refuses to love,

> So much the more she loued was and sought,
>> That oftentimes vnquiet strife did moue
>> Amongst her louers, and great quarrels wrought,
>> That oft for her in bloody armes they fought.
>>> (2.37)

Her unwillingness to marry, then, incites and heightens male violence. Cambell institutionalizes this savagery by devising a public tournament "to weet whose she should bee" (2.38), an overt auctioning off, through feats of arms, of his sister. This event does not dissipate but rather rechannels male violence over a woman. The chief difference in the two episodes seems to be that in the second, both brutality and lust are institutionalized (the tournament and the betrothal) and thereby normalized. The effect upon the women in question is virtually identical. Both Florimell and Canacee are passive objects of male fury, sexual prizes to be awarded to the victor. One will be a concubine, the other a wife: in neither case are the woman's wishes in the matter an issue. In both cases vengeful ferocity is glorified and rewarded sexually.

The text gives no hint of disapproval. On the contrary, Cambell is said to be "wise" (2.38) for devising the tournament as a means of determining Canacee's husband. It appears to be simply a fact of culture/nature that males will strive in brutal competition for a mate. To socialize that natural violence by means of a public tournament earns the poem's approbation as much as "public" vengeance wins the approval of the Reformation divine. That Cambell himself serves as the combatant against his sister's suitors positions him as one of those suitors. His is a barely sublimated incestuous role, and one for which he wins praise.[27] In the following canto this reifying of Canacee continues. Winning her becomes the objective of the tournament between Cambell and the three brothers ("For Canacee with Cambell for to fight" [3.3]). Indeed she is placed like a prize on a dais "to be seene" by those who "could her purchase with his liue's aduentur'd gage" (3.4). Here as elsewhere the woman's views in the matter remain unvoiced, indeed unconsidered by either the male combatants or by the poet. The text takes it as a matter of course that Canacee, like the other women who form the pretext for the male clashes, have no opinions—or, at any rate, cannot publicly express any—on the disposition of her matrimonial future. The males who wage battle before her eyes decide who her mate will be.

In the ensuing tournament, described with considerable elaboration and obvious relish as an orderly and stately ritual, Diamond is "stird to vengeance and despite" (3.14) by Priamond's death. Diamond then makes "chaleng[e of] the Virgin as his dew" (3.14). The description of the tournament is long, bloody, and engaged with no little aesthetic self-indulgence for forty-six stanzas. It seems clear that the narrator enjoys describing how "cruelly these Knights stroue for Ladies sake" (3.16). The resolution is achieved not by any action of the contestants, whether by force or negotiation, but by the intrusion of Cambina's pacific wand and cup of nepenthe. First, though, she tries a familiar female tactic, conventional in epic and chivalric literature: "downe on the bloudy plaine / Her selfe she threw, and tears gan shed amaine" (3.47). When these ploys prove ineffective, she resorts to magic to negate or at least defuse the violence. Only by this agency of magic can the conflict be solved and a double affiliation formed, the marriages of Cambell and Cambina, and Triamond and Canacee. Both couples are now "Allide with bands of mutuall couplement" (3.52). Again, marriage is the means by which vengeance and male violence are overcome, in this case abetted by magical agents.[28] In this episode the homosocial bond of vengeance is supplanted by the link of kinship as well as marriage (the men become brothers-in-law). But the unions do not arise naturally, as it were; they must be imposed upon the combatants from an outside magical source. The bonds of vengeance seem more instinctive than those of peace and marriage. In fact the narrator's summarizing comment on this action suggests that the institutional attachment of matrimony can supercede more primordial bonds of both enmity and friendship:

> For enmitie, that of no ill proceeds,
> But of occasion, with th'occasion ends;
> And friendship, which a faint affection breeds
> Withouten regard of good, dyes like ill grounded seeds.
>
> (4.1)

Is marriage (here the "regard of good") therefore useful to cement bonds that (male) humanity, left to its own violent devices, would not otherwise form? Or are revenge and male rivalry interrupted by marriage? The text is deeply ambivalent.

The links between revenge and eros are represented in canto 4 quite starkly. The canto reinforces the nexus between physical might and beauty, even at the expense of considerable digression, stop-and-start action, and uncertain narrative ends. Two quarrels spring up and are quickly deferred, once the opportunity of solving the disputes in a tournament for Florimell's girdle presents itself: that "prize of her, which did in beauty most excell" (4.5). Braggadocchio reenters the narrative, laying claim to the false Florimell "as his owne prize, / Whom formerly he had in battell wonne" (4.8). All parties, sympathetic and unappealing characters alike, regard turning the woman into a prize in a contest as the ideal means of resolving the dispute. Violent male competition is thereby directed along socially approved routes. Blandamour's response to the coward's claim likewise brings the two motifs together: Braggadocchio will have to "winne" her; like a trophy, she will be "placed here in sight" before the combatants. The loser will get the Hag and, in a parody of marriage, "with her alwaies ride, till he another get" (4.9). Cambell further institutionalizes the practice by urging the contestants to defer their animosity until the tournament, "And then it shall be tried, if ye will, /Whether shall haue the Hag, or hold the Lady still" (4.12). During the meet Satyrane appears holding the girdle, "that precious relicke in an arke" (4.15):

That same aloft he hong in open vew,
    To be the prize of beautie and of might;
   . . . .
    . . . all men threw out vowes and wishes vaine.[29]
                   (4.16)

Men take vows for this prize, as opposed to wedding vows, another socialized method for men to win women. But in fact this tournament will also lead to projected wedding vows, those of Britomart and Artegall. Meanwhile the tournament itself, extending over three days and dozens of stanzas, is marked by a variety of vengeances. Cambell "cast t'auenge his friends indignitee" (4.28). Wearing Cambell's arms in the Achillean manner, Triamond fights with

                  dreadfull might,
Both in remembrance of his friends late harm
And in reuengement of his owne despight.
           (4.35)

So, too, when Britomart enters and defeats Artegall and Cambell, Triamond "cast t'auenge the shame doen to his freend" (4.45). Britomart "restore[s] / That prize" (4.48), and although she appears to be the only combatant with no vengeful motives, she is motivated, like the males, by violence.

The emphasis on revenge seems at first to be in keeping with the condemning values we find both elsewhere in the poem and in the moral literature of the day. And indeed, like contemporary pronouncements on revenge, these episodes demonstrate considerable moral ambivalence. Reformation moralists find grounds enough to vindicate various kinds of violent revenge, even as they invariably advance a rather knee-jerk condemnation of it. Likewise the poem seems to savor its descriptions of the bloody revenge throughout these cantos. The role of women is yoked to this pervasive revenge, at least in the early cantos. Men fight vengefully over women as booty. As Scudamour has exhibited at his first jealous challenge of Britomart, the claims of love can be secondary to the homosocial bond, even if (especially if) the bond is violent. Yet in other episodes, marriage dissolves the homosocial bond. Which of these alternatives does the text encourage? With vengeance as its leitmotif, the poem can have it both ways: it can condemn and justify simultaneously. So, too, with the object of that vengeful violence: women are demeaned by being reified and are glorified by being fought over. In both cases, the text seems to disparage values that extol the merely physical, arms and beauty. In doing so, it exhibits an unexceptionable, orthodox piety. But the text also explicitly glamorizes both arms and beauty. Hence the narrator's approving generalization:

> For he me seems most fit the faire to serue,
> That can her best defend from villenie;
> And she most fit her seruice doth deserue,
> That fairest is and from her faith will neuer swerue. (5.1)

In Book IV, male defense from villainy is figured by violent vengeance, and never swerving from faith leads to marriage. So the poet can portray relations between the sexes as valid and noble when they result in conjugal union, even if the route to the altar is bloody. Hence the married tetrad of an earlier episode, which ends by romanticizing a union of family and friends:

> For *Triamond* had *Canacee* to wife,
> With whom he ledd a long and happie life;
> And *Cambel* tooke *Cambina* to his fere,
> The which as life were to each other liefe.
>
> (3.52)

Here we have a lionizing of values endorsed throughout the Reformation. The bloody tournament becomes a means of achieving an incipient sacralized household, a companionate marriage—two marriages, in fact. The text projects for this group of characters a socialized network of friendship and marriage. Far from being impediments to that concord, revenge and the treatment of women as objects help to achieve marriage. The poem ritualizes and glamorizes both of these seemingly disparaged evils.

Let us take Britomart as a case in point, for she is fully implicated in this book's moral ambiguities, particularly in her gender performances. In the aftermath to the tournament over Florimell's girdle, Britomart displays a remarkable multivalence. The participating knights bring "vnto . . . view" their ladies as trophies, unveil and "vnheale" them (5.10). This competitive "display" (5.13) Britomart participates in fully: "At the last the most redoubted *Britonesse,* / Her louely *Amoret* did open shew" (5.13). In the ensuing farce over the girdle, it is judged that Britomart is to be given the false Florimell "as wonne in fight" (5.20). Britomart refuses, not on the grounds that it is shameful to traffic in women but because Amoret's "vertuous gouernment" (5.20) is preferable to Florimell's looseness. Britomart rejects only the specific criterion on which these women are to be negotiated as prizes, not the negotiation itself. She departs triumphant, "taking with her louely *Amoret*" (5.29) and having fully joined in the commerce of women and their degradation into chattel.[30] In playing the role of the male warrior, Britomart here engages in what the text constructs as a male practice. Is she thereby paradoxically preparing herself for marriage, which, when she has exchanged her armor for the wedding veil, will demand that she subordinate herself to her husband?

The previous chapter of this study considers the third of the agreed-upon purposes of marriage: procreation, companionship, and relief of concupiscence. The concerns of Book IV demand that we now examine the role of marital companionship or friendship. On this subject scholarship has been deeply divided for some years. One theory has it that because Protestant "arts of love" privilege marriage over celibacy and specify one of the chief purposes of that union to be companionship, marriage during the Reformation greatly enhanced the status of women by exalting the wife to the equal or near equal of her husband.[31] Mutuality is the keynote of this theory. A chorus of Reformation marriage tracts has been adduced to demonstrate that the Protestant emphasis on companionship of husband and wife marks the emergence of a new ideal based on mutual love and respect. Another scholarly position, led by Lawrence Stone and others, challenges whether the status of women is in fact enhanced by the wife's being proclaimed the partner and companion of her husband.[32] Indeed, despite rhetorical assertions of companionship, male dominance and female subordination do seem to continue unabated throughout the sixteenth and seventeenth centuries. The Reformation emphasis upon male superiority militates against polemical claims of equality or even mutuality within marriage, a situation Stone has termed "paradoxical."[33] More recently commentators dispute the novelty of this Reformation paradox, pointing out that companionship and hierarchy comprise dual ideological tenets about marriage from Augustine through Milton. They argue that Stone and his followers have exaggerated the degree to which Reformation writing about marriage, with its constant focus on the dominance of husband and the subordination of wife, represents change. They stress instead the continuity among Reformation and earlier discourses of marriage, extending back at least to Augustine and probably to Aristotle.[34]

Salutary as these recent correctives are, they have not fully dislodged the innovative character of Reformation views of matrimony. Reformation writers highlight and bring to the forefront of cultural consciousness this paradoxical ideology: each marriage partner is recognized as equal to the other, and they share in all things, yet one rules and the other obeys. Reformation writers *do* celebrate the companionate virtues of matrimony, they elaborate the benefits therein, they insist upon male dominance, and they shape all these opinions into an orthodoxy more systematically and broadcast them more widely than their predecessors. Hence William Perkins on one page pronounces that the husband's duty to his wife is "in making account of her as his companion, or yoke-fellow" and on the next page admonishes the wife to "submit herselfe to her husband, and to acknowledge and reuerence him in all things."[35]

However much companionship is privileged, the woman remains subordinate. The dissonance of the formulation is worth briefly investigating. Companionship is extolled and then almost instantly revoked. Marriage makes a man and a woman yoke-fellows and partners, a condition that implies equality. But one commands and rules the other, though she is a partner.[36] As Bullinger states it in his influential *Golden Boke of Christen Matrimonye*: in Paradise woman was made for man as a "companion lyke unto himselfe and mete for him," and "yet she was not made of the head. For the husband is the head and master of the wife."[37] No Reformation writer about marriage seems to recognize the contradiction in this position: although each is the equal in the marriage partnership, one is naturally superior and therefore is fit to rule the other. William Whately maintains that the "husband must be as carefull to please his wife as she him." But he then says that the "wiues speciall duty may fitly be referred to two heads: first, she must acknowledge her inferiouritie: secondly, she must carry her selfe as an inferiour."[38] William Gouge's hedging comes closest among the English commentators to recognizing the difficulty of maintaining both hierarchy and companionship. The wife's place "is indeed a place of inferiourity, and subiection, yet the neerest to equalitie that may be: a place of common equitie in many respects, wherein man and wife are after a sort euen fellowes, and partners: Hence it followeth that the husband must account his wife a yoke-fellow and companion."[39]

Book IV engages and foregrounds the contradictions within the Reformation ideology of marriage. These contradictions help illuminate the recognition scene between Artegall and Britomart, which takes place in a tournament whose main sightline is initially staked out as revenge. Artegall has "greatly grudged" Britomart her unhorsing of him in the previous tournament and "Fit time t'awaite auenged for to be" (5.9). Because he reckons her as a male adversary, he longs (naturally?) for revenge. Artegall's ignorance of Britomart's sex serves comic purposes and also highlights the gender issues surrounding his thirst for vengeance. Why will his passion change once he finds out Britomart is a woman? Why should his revenge be transformed by her gender into desire? In canto 6, while Artegall is once again tracking Britomart, "On whom I waite to wreake that foule despight" (6.5), he allies himself with Scudamour as a companion-in-vengeance: "If to that auenge by you decreed," says Scudamour, pledging Artegall his troth, "This hand may helpe, or succour ought supplie / It shall not fayle, when so ye shall it need" (6.8). They form one of the book's more amusing homosocial ties. These men are now impassionedly bonded by revenge, directed not, as in previous encounters, toward one another but instead toward Britomart: "so both to wreake their wrathes on *Britomart* agreed" (6.8). One of the several twists to this association is that Artegall will soon replace this shared longing for revenge with another form of longing, erotic desire for the object of that revenge. As long as he thinks Britomart a man, Artegall will be satisfied with nothing less than "spoyle and vengeance" (6.11). But when he sees that his adversary is a woman, he "From his reuengefull purpose shronke abacke" (6.21) and falls down on his knees in a religious posture of erotic worship. Britomart, though, continues to crave revenge, to "bene ywroke" on her assailant (6.23). This is the only time she is described as vengeful, otherwise in this book exclusively a male trait.

Artegall continues begging her for pardon, even while she covets vengeance. Here is the book's first yoking of revenge and forgiveness. These actions will recur in the second half of the book and will be intimately joined to its construction of gender and its exploitation of Reformation resources. When Britomart doffs her helmet and reveals her sex, he "At last fell humbly downe vpon his knee, / And of his wonder made religion" (6.22). The revelation of her sex impels him to seek forgiveness: "But her of pardon prayd more earnestlie, /

Or wreake on him her will for so great iniurie" (6.23). When Britomart, in turn, recognizes him to be the Artegall of her vision in the glass, she, too, cools her ardor for revenge and "therewith her wrathfull courage gan appall" (6.26). It is Glauce, acting as conciliator, who introduces the idea of forgiveness most explicitly by aligning it figuratively with a sacrament: "Graunt him your grace," she says to Britomart, "but so that he fulfill / The penance, which ye shall to him empart" (6.32). Here we have the first of several incidents in the second half of Book IV in which mortals forgive and thereby lead one another to a form of salvation, but one drained of theological reserves.[40]

At this juncture Reformation writers can be of considerable help. Forgiveness is their universally prescribed (and utterly predictable) antidote to the poisonous urge for revenge. Spenser configures forgiveness with betrothal, an association familiar from Shakespearean comedy and romance.[41] Perhaps the key here is salvation. Like the divines, Spenser associates forgiveness with salvation. But in Book IV that salvation is unattached to theology and yoked to prospective marriage. Revenge forgiven leads to the altar. The grace that Britomart grants to Artegall's repentance leads them to a kind of temporal redemption. The result is a betrothal: "till they with marriage meet might finish that accord" (6.41). So the homosocial alliance Artegall formed with Scudamour is supplanted by the betrothal bond with Britomart—as the homoerotic bond between the two women is supplanted by the heterosexual bond. Scudamour, too, loses all his jealousy, of course, upon learning that Amoret's protector is a woman and replaces his vengeful wishes with gratitude for her protection of Amoret (however uninformed he may be about their friendship). His homosocial bond, however, is not altogether broken but is deflected, rather, into male joking about gender dominance and submission:

> Certes sir *Artegall*,
> I ioy to see you lout so low on ground,
> And now become to liue a Ladies thrall.
> (6.28)

In fact, though, it is Britomart who exchanges chivalric parity for submission, who exchanges a (male) yearning for vengeance with a (female) consent to subordinate herself. The canto ends with their betrothal, when she

> yeeld[s] her consent
> To be his loue, and take him for her Lord,
> Till they with mariage meet might finish that accord.
>
> (6.41)

Artegall has now succeeded Amoret in Britomart's affections. The halfway point in the book focuses on the changes in Britomart: she has become betrothed, she accepts her wifely inferiority, she ceases to participate in male violence, and she replaces Amoret with Artegall in her emotional hierarchy. Amoret is now "her second care, though in another kind" (6.46), subsidiary to the new allegiance to her future husband—and yet, as the final line of this stanza says in its claim for the ties between the women, "True loue and faithfull friendship, she by her did set" (6.46). Equal to Artegall in arms, Britomart becomes his subordinate in betrothal. Her submission to her future husband fulfills the ideal of Reformation marriage—as summarized, say, by Perkins: "A couple, is that whereby two persons standing in mutuall relation to each other, are combined together as it were in one. And of these two the one is alwaies higher, and beareth rule, the other is lower, and yeeldeth subiection."[42]

The alliance between Britomart and Artegall that emerges from their animosity carefully balances that of Belphoebe and Timias. The later episode provides significant contrasts, if not outright contradictions, to the view of marriage implied in the first match. When she takes offense at the squire's attentions to Amoret and accuses him of a breach of "faith," Belphoebe, like Britomart in the previous episode and like so many of this book's male cast, is enraged—"yet held her wrathfull hand from vengeaunce sore" (7.36). Not even Arthur can help him "restore to former grace againe" (7.47). The scene of their reconciliation is carefully imbued with the language of forgiveness. First, Timias has to undergo the process of "penaunce sad" (8.2). Then, the Dove that brings the two together "seeing his sad plight, her tender heart / With deare compassion deeply did emmoue" (8.3). When Belphoebe witnesses the squire's misery, she is "mou'd with ruth" and asks what "wrath of cruell wight on thee ywrake?" (8.14). Timias claims that Belphoebe has "wreake[d] on worthlesse wight / Your high displesure" (8.17). His begging for restoration has its desired mollifying effect: "her inburning wrath she gan abate" (8.17). Human forgiveness, not divine absolution, leads to a "happie life with grace" (8.18).

The parallel with the reconciliation of Britomart and Artegall is not exact, of course, for the later one does not lead to matrimony. In preserving her virginity, Belphoebe preserves her independence, indeed her dominance. Unlike Britomart, she does not exchange her autonomy for a recognition of a husband as her lord. The episode between Belphoebe and Timias ends with "grace and good accord" (8.18) on both sides. Belphoebe has made her last exit from *The Faerie Queene* without being betrothed. Timias departs this book in much the same way that the married and betrothed couples of this book do: "he long time afterwards did lead / A happie life" (8.18). The implication is that both have preserved independence and happiness simultaneously and that reconciliation between a man and a woman is possible without marriage.

Is this what is meant by friendship between the sexes, that it need not be subsumed by marriage? If so, Belphoebe and Timias have an unusual friendship, for after their reconciliation they are not again depicted as having any contact whatever.[43] This episode has the effect of undermining or at least resisting the certainties about marriage advanced elsewhere in the book, particularly those attached to the betrothal of Britomart and Artegall. Belphoebe serves the function in this book, as she does in the previous one, of exposing contradictions implicit in episodes about the principal figures. Her independence and power, like those of the monarch she represents, call into question the suppositions about gender and the inequalities of married partners here. It may be that Spenser was compelled by the queen's singular relation to marriage and gender assumptions to create a character who defies the dominant view of matrimony upheld elsewhere in the book (and the culture). The effect, however, is to expose contradictions and anxieties about that view, anxieties that later episodes reinforce and develop.

The two stanzas of instruction initial to canto 9 are important in this respect. Following classical and Renaissance commonplaces, the poet claims that companionship is superior to passion: "Cupids greater flame" is an ardor that "faithfull friendship doth . . . suppresse" (9.2).[44] This assertion is then abundantly and paradoxically illustrated by the story of Placidas and Amyas. This episode depicts a strong homoerotic friendship, all the more pronounced because the story is largely narrated by Placidas, the friend with the greater degree of affection. Placidas initiates the ruse that puts him in the prison

with his friend because of "the feruent zeale / Which I to him as to my
soule did beare" (8.55). When the two are thrown into the same dungeon, Placidas claims wishfully (or defensively) that "Æmylia well he
lou'd, as I mote ghesse; / Yet greater loue to me then her he did pro-
fesse" (8.57). In a phrase that recalls the bonds between Britomart
and Amoret, Placidas says that "There did I finde mine onely faithfull
frend" (8.57; cf. 6.46). This devotion leads to the stratagem against
Poeana. Again the woman is secondary to the bond between the men,
but here that bond is no longer revenge. That homosocial tie has been
supplanted by one with a more patently homoerotic nuance. Placidas
speaks the language of romantic love when he claims that he has acted for the sake of Amyas, "For whose sole libertie I loue and life did
stake" (8.60). He also claims he is able to accept the amorous advances of Poeana, who mistakes him for his look-alike, Amyas, because "I . . . was not bent to . . . loue, / As was my friend" (8.60). By
this means he justifies wooing Poeana with feigned affection. Here is
an obvious case of homoerotic fondness transferred to a heterosexual alliance—formed, says Placidas, "for my friends good, more then
for my own sake" (8.60). Upon Amyas's release from prison,
Placidas and Æmylia "both vnto him ran" (9.9). The three form an
odd parody of the homosocial triangles the poem repeatedly constructs. The two rivals are now a man and a woman, and the object of
their (unstated) competition is a young man:

> And him embracing fast betwixt them held,
> Striuing to comfort him all that they can,
> And kissing oft his visage pale and wan.
>   (9.9)

The solution to this nexus of crossed affections will be the second
marriage tetrad in the book, one that mirrors the double union of
Cambell-Triamond and their wives. The barely disguised incestuous
attachment of Cambell to Canacee, which was dissolved (or at least
suppressed) in the double marriage of canto 3, has its counterpart in
the overt homoerotic attachment of Placidas to Amyas. This passion,
too, is dissolved (or suppressed) by a double marriage.[45] Placidas resolves not to "despise that dame, which lou'd him liefe," and instead
"to accept her to his wedded wife"—an acceptance that sounds like
little more than a marriage of convenience. Certainly Placidas benefits materially from the match, for he acquires from Poeana "all her
land and lordship during life" (9.15). Placidas also retains continuing

contact with Amyas: Arthur leaves the four of them as "paires of friends in peace and setled rest" (9.17).[46] As Cambell's chivalric exploits gain him the companionship of both wife and sister, so Placidas's adroit maneuvers obtain him the companionship of both wife and friend.

On the other hand, Placidas and Poeana are said to have "liu'd together long without debate / Ne priuate iarre" (9.16). They form, from this perspective, an acceptable companionate marriage, entailing as it does simultaneous companionship and wifely submission. Poeana "reform[s] her waies" (9.16): she is brought to an ethical renewal from her "too loose . . . life" (8.49). (The text does not say whether Placidas renounces his kissing of Amyas.) Again penance and forgiveness lead to a marriage, indeed two of them. Æmylia-Amyas and Poeana-Placidas are "shut vp all in friendly loue" (9.15), and nothing can "shake the safe assuraunce of their state" (9.16)—language that figuratively summons up the Reformed Protestant hope that one find assurance of the saved state of one's soul. But this double marriage has been achieved at some cost. Not only has the dangerous passion of Placidas for Amyas been quelled (or at least masked), but also Poeana has been used. Her respectability has been achieved by her "reformation" and by Placidas's elevating her social status to that of a married woman. In this episode, too, forgiveness leads to marriage, but a marriage with a dubious foundation. Poeana is "enlarged free" (9.13) from her father's tyranny and from the sins of her past, but Placidas manipulates her as much as any of the men in Book IV do the women. Although she is not the focus of male violence as women in earlier cantos are, she is as lavishly exploited. The episode has further exposed insecurities about companionate marriage as exemplified in several of the book's dominant characters. The homoerotic features of the courtships would alone be enough to undermine the governing model of marriage elsewhere in the book. Because that homoeroticism lies at the heart of one of these matches, the episode is subversive. The union of Poeana and Placidas, emotionally hollow at its core, is presented in the same idealizing terms as the other companionate marriages of the book and so serves to deconstruct the ideology that celebrates every marriage *qua* marriage. The difficulty the text dramatizes (and indeed has) here—also evident in the association of Britomart and Amoret—is how to claim that friendship flourishes best in marriage, when plainly it seems to work best in homoerotic unions.

The final three cantos detail two major unions of the poem, Scudamour's abduction of Amoret and the betrothal of Florimell and Marinell. These episodes, linked by the marriage of the Thames and the Medway, form a marital double. All three cantos sustain the book's focus on matrimony and on the forces inhibiting concord between men and women. The framing episodes, of course, postpone matrimony. For Scudamour and Amoret, sexual fulfillment is deferred beyond the limits of the (1596) poem, while Florimell and Marinell are wed in the next book.

As he begins his narrative, Scudamour is the same self-pitying fellow we saw at the end of Book III (e.g., "I wast my life, and doe my daies deuowre / In wretched anguish and incessant woe" [9.39]). His hackneyed Petrarchan complaints undermine his credibility as hero of his own adventure to win a wife.[47] When he says that he "purchased this peerlesse beauties spoile" (10.3) by sojourning to the Temple of Venus, he echoes the now familiar note about women as plunder.[48] At the porch of the temple, he encounters Dame Concord, flanked by her twins, two young men, Love and Hate, whom she holds in uneasy equipoise. These figures embody the tension between marriage and revenge that reigns throughout Book IV. Their *discordia concors* emblematizes the book's repeated conflicts. The youths also aptly mirror Scudamour himself, the young man who more than any other in this book embodies love and hate and who has been one of its primary revengers and its primary married partners. One need only recall the episode in canto 5 where he is "Bent to reuenge on blamelesse *Britomart* / The crime, which . . . like thornes did pricke his gealous hart" (5.31) for being the "companion" (5.30) of Amoret. These stanzas repeatedly stress his hunger for revenge, explicitly a function of his characteristic jealousy. In typical Spenserian fashion, jealousy leads him directly to the house of Care, where he seeks vengeance even while being tormented (5.44).

As a would-be bridegroom in the temple, Scudamour is faced with symbols of the married state he aspires to. The statue of Venus exhibits an iconography said to represent fidelity, adopted in the Renaissance as an emblem of marital concord.[49] The serpent that binds Venus depicts conjugal loyalty and the joining of man and woman in the one flesh of matrimony. Hence this statue is superior to "All other Idoles, which the heathen adore" (10.40). When he finds Amoret in the lap of "an amiable Dame" who "in her semblant shewed great womanhood" (10.31), she is surrounded by a "beuie of fayre damzels" (10.48) who configure traditional female virtues, including the Obedience of marital subordination.[50] As her lover and prospective husband, Scudamour regards Amoret, seated in the lap of womanhood, as a "glorious spoyle" (10.55). His seizure of her is accomplished against both her will and that of her protectors in the temple. As he says, he is not there to free her,

> but yet for nought
> That euer she to me could say or doe,
> Could she her wished freedome fro me wooe.
>
> (10.57)

Her imprisonment as Scudamour's booty forecasts her incarceration in both Busirane's house and in Lust's cave. Their union, founded as it is on force and fear, is depicted as an imprisonment, especially for Amoret. But in retrospect, Scudamour, too, has remained a prisoner to his own jealousy and vengeful anger. He has been consistently portrayed as an inadequate lover, from his initial meeting with Britomart in Book III through to this end of Book IV, a being consumed by these passions—feelings which are repeatedly shown to degrade Amoret as well as himself.[51] Her passivity and helplessness over the course of these two books are allegorized as a response to his selfishness and violence. The result has been to debase and transform her into an object. Even though the couple is joined in matrimony—a state forecast by her place in the lap of Womanhood—they never achieve, within the (1596) poem, the satisfactions, erotic or friendly, promised by contemporary marriage polemic.

Nor are they shown as reunited (in the 1596 version) after Amoret's release from the house of Busirane. This seeming oversight—the poet has the opportunity to rejoin them in canto 9—may suggest the poem's reservations about marriage in general.[52] The oversight is more plausibly consonant with the largely negative presentation of *this* married couple and their attachment, based as it seems to be on fear and jealousy. Amoret and Scudamour are consistently depicted as thralls of various kinds, both extrinsic and intrinsic. Scudamour has been imprisoned in the house of Care, an environment that suggests his enslavement to jealousy. In addition to her several physical imprisonments, fear and submissiveness hold Amoret captive at every stage of the narrative. She never achieves the freedom of any of the other major female figures of these two books. A series of male figures subjugate her—or so she thinks, even when, as in the case of Arthur and Britomart (in male disguise), they protect or liberate her. Of the married or betrothed figures in Book IV, Scudamour and Amoret are the only couple who do not forgive one another—do not, that is, partake of the salvation the book makes available to other couples.

The marriage of the Thames and the Medway intervenes between the two major human unions of the final cantos. It is the primordial wedding of the whole poem, a "bridale feast" (11.9) solemnized by the sea gods "In honour of the spousalls" (11.8)—spousals that are decidedly nonhuman.[53] Perhaps this is why the canto has never won many readers' hearts. But this union serves a useful function in the book's disposition of matrimony. It expands the allegory beyond the peculiar private concerns of individual couples. The marriage is both a public occasion involving "some most famous founders . . . / Of puissant Nations" (11.15)[54] and a celebration of nature. Unlike its counterparts in other books, this canto does not expand beyond nature to encompass heaven, the soul, or the supernatural. It maintains the book's nontheological focus by acclaiming a union that in its coloration lies somewhere between the georgic and the chthonic. It reaches into the earth rather than upward to the heavens. It sanctions the book's unions with a celebration of mysteries deep in the landscape, tied to natural rhythms. Its function is to link the two halves of the marital double episodes in the book's last quarter. As such, the episode exalts the natural, as opposed to the supernatural, and suggests how the characters may find redemption. And yet this is not a union of *characters*. For all its concern with courtship and projected marital unions, the text chooses this peculiar ceremony most fully to represent a marriage. Most of the other would-be unions remain just that, or less: frustrated weddings, planned weddings, broken nuptials, projected or hoped-for marriages, marriages of convenience. The text repeatedly shows that marriage cannot be idealized or even dramatized in its own terms. Book IV undercuts every union but that between the rivers and leaves those between the flesh-and-blood characters deeply ambiguous.

But the text tries to celebrate one, the final match presented in the book: the union of Florimell and Marinell. Florimell's incarceration in Proteus's cave is the counterpart to Amoret's imprisonment in the

Temple of Venus or the cave of Lust. Marinell hears her in prison: "So feelingly her case she did complaine / That ruth it moued in the rocky stone" (12.5).[55] "I suffer prisonment" (12.7) is Florimell's lament, and she speaks for other of the book's women who are freed by men. Book IV seems to relish this role for its female characters. Florimell's is yet another love lament, like Arthur's, Britomart's, and others in Book III and Book IV. "Know Marinell that all this is for thee" (12.11), cries Florimell. Unlike earlier laments, however, hers finds a response. Indeed, its effect on Marinell is instant: "His stubborne heart, that neuer felt misfare / Was toucht with soft remorse and pitty rare" (12.12). He sees his own culpability for Florimell's suffering: "Backe to him selfe he gan returne the blame, / That was the author of her punishment" (12.16). His recognition of his own responsibility is something Scudamour, by contrast, has never achieved. It marks the almost official end to the recriminations and vengeance of earlier episodes in Book IV. Marinell recognizes his guilt and responds accordingly, action that takes the form of mercy and compassion: "He could no more but her great misery bemone" (12.12). None of the salvific language of these stanzas marks the earlier union of Amoret and Scudamour, which is achieved through force and typified by fear and jealousy. That couple has remained imprisoned, whether by self or other or by the confining discourses of a bygone eroticism. Florimell and Marinell, by contrast, seem to conquer separation and mistrust through sympathy and compassion.

Florimell and Marinell are not freed by Reformation conceptions of salvation.[56] Whatever freedom is theirs they find on their own. When Florimell cries out for care in heaven and hears but silence (12.6,9), the book indicates that redemption is the responsibility of the human heart: Marinell's "stony heart with tender ruth was toucht" (12.13). The allusion to Ezekiel is fitting: "And I wil giue them one heart, and I wil put a newe spirit within their bowels: and I wil take the stonie heart out of their bodies, and wil giue them an heart of flesh" (Ezek. 11:19). The allusion is also mildly ironic, for this change of heart is not divinely accomplished but rather attained by the lovers themselves. Similarly, in an echo of Redcrosse's despair after his imprisonment in Orgoglio's dungeon, Marinell is said to die (12.20; cf. I.8.41). The remedy for Marinell's despair, however, is not heavenly grace. He performs instead an act of decidedly secular penance:

> Backe to him selfe he gan returne the blame,
> That was the author of her punishment;
> And with vile curses, and reprochfull shame
> To damne himselfe by euery euill name.
>
> (12.16)

After the fashion of a Shakespearean romance, then, the text at the last moment inscribes traditional patterns of forgiveness. When this couple pardon one another, they project a marriage. The text does not appeal to the supernatural at this point any more than earlier in the book. Guyon's and Redcrosse's failures find supernatural remedies, but this book tenders no heavenly intercession. Human agency alone restores wounded characters to health. When the narrator first resumes Florimell's plight in canto 11, he laments that she must remain "In bands of loue and in sad thraldoms chayne" unless "some heauenly powre her free / By miracle, not yet appearing playne" (11.1). But in marked distinction from the first two books of the poem, no heavenly power appears. The miracle that frees her has a (quasi-)human form. When Proteus "enlarge[s]" (12.32) and "deliuer[s]" (12.33) Florimell to Marinell, he merely completes a deliverance the characters have already achieved on their own, for salvation now has no ostensible supernatural attachment. Book IV incorporates into its allegory the topics of revenge and marriage, preoccupations Spenser's contemporary moralists treat from a religious perspective. The book draws upon those discourses but remains silent about their specifically religious sanctions. Instead, the book subverts the very ideals it seems to endorse. By pitting the discourse of revenge against that of companionate marriage, and then idealizing the former but leaving the latter equivocal, the book dramatizes an unresolved struggle about one of the era's most celebrated institutions. In the next book, a different solution is sought to the conflict between violence and virtue. In tapping apocalyptic discourse, Book V aims at a religious sanction of a more radical kind than elsewhere in the poem. Here the Legend of Justice turns to a form of religious expression—apocalypse—that greatly expands the poem's realms of discourse and so attempts authorization and resolution from well beyond the characters' ken.

Post-Armada Apocalyptic
Discourse in Book V

In his treatise of 1587, "A Fruitfull Dialogue concerning the End of the World," William Perkins fabricates an eschatological exchange between Worldling and Christian. Naturally they consider the arrival of the Final Day. Worldling offers the popular opinion of the moment: "They say euery where, that next yeare eighty eight, Doomes day will be."[1] Although Christian prudently denies the feasibility of exact calculation, he agrees that the Day of Judgment is inevitable and possibly at hand. Their debate typifies late Elizabethan preoccupations. In the 1580s, as the great struggle with Spain reaches a crisis and war seems certain, voices both religious and political become increasingly apocalyptic. After England's defeat of the Spanish Armada in 1588, eschatological zeal continues to grow and remains unabated for over a decade, often nationalistic and always anti-Catholic in emphasis. With the triumph of international Protestantism now so clearly visible in England's victory over the Armada, belief grows certain that the apocalypse is near and that the Reformation will be at last complete. Among those joyous voices is Book V of *The Faerie Queene*, whose final episodes not only partake of but contribute to the religious and political fervor following that great confrontation between European powers. The second half of Book V is constructed as an apocalyptic exegesis of contemporary history and is inseparable from a variety of post-Armada apocalyptic texts. The Protestant historiography of which these texts comprise a chapter has recently been the subject of extensive scholarly investigation—research that documents the degree to which the self-determination of Tudor England is shaped by apocalyptic discourse.[2] Spenser's Legend of Justice needs to be located squarely among these apocalyptic texts, for the final "international" episodes of Book V are a product of this peculiar historical moment. They also reformulate the issues of late Elizabethan apocalyptic discourse and thereby contribute to a striking confluence of religious polemic, the formulation of foreign policy, and prophetic historiography.

Book V has frequently alienated readers who object to its political views and particularly its presumptive support of the Elizabethan imperium. The book is often pronounced a literary failure, even by critics who have taken pains to interpret the topical allegory.[3] Attention over the last decade and a half to the book's negotiation of distinct and often contradictory voices about power and its justification has not fully dislodged these negative estimates.[4] While this historicist criticism has revitalized our understanding of the poem's political assumptions, it has not centered Book V within the contemporary religious upheavals inseparable from England's political life and hence has missed how the book is embedded in the crucial public questions of the period. But with the efflorescence of Protestant studies, Book V has now begun to attract scholars who see how it incorporates biblical apocalypse.[5] The most richly detailed of these studies is by Kenneth Borris, who supplies irrefutable evidence that the final three cantos employ Revelation as their main textual source.[6] This chapter draws on Borris's work and that of recent historians of Tudor religion and politics to document how Book V not only is shaped by biblical apocalypse but also, just as pervasively, confronts and so becomes a part of apocalyptic commentary of the post-Armada period. Accomplishing this task requires an examination of exegetical texts that are insufficiently appreciated in previous criticism but are central to a comprehensive reckoning of Reformation England's national self-description.

The earlier generation of apocalyptic commentators, represented notably by John Bale and John Foxe, center their concerns in the remote future or the remote past and the history of the church and its martyrs.[7] Those of the late 1580s and the 1590s, in contrast, focus upon the political affairs of the present and the recent past and largely exclude the wider frame of historical reference evident in their predecessors. More specifically, their commentary is distinguished by its view of the English Reformation as a national struggle whose concerns are manifested in current political events, including foreign relations. And while they are pointedly aware of many immediate political events that can be interpreted in the light of apocalypse, it is the Armada—as the most pressing example of the perils facing England from Antichrist and his adherents, embodied most alarmingly in Spain and its Roman Catholic allies—that looms largest among the contemporary occasions occupying these exegetes' attention. This post-Armada commentary mediates between biblical apocalypse and Spenser's poem. To sort out the complex hermeneutical status of Book V, this chapter determines how the Legend of Justice partakes of biblical apocalypse throughout the final six cantos, how it forms part of late Elizabethan apocalyptic commentary, and how that commentary bridges biblical texts and the allegory that comments on current events. Finally, the chapter suggests that in the last canto Book V of *The Faerie Queene* transcends some of the more nakedly polemical features of post-Armada hermeneutics.

Spenser's fascination with apocalypse was lifelong. Indeed, for Jan van der Noot's *A Theatre for Worldlings* the young poet translated *Visions from Revelation*, a series of four verse commonplaces capitalizing on the ecclesiological meaning that the Reformation saw in the last book of the Christian Bible.[8] As apocalypse continues to play greater and lesser parts throughout the Spenserian canon, it figures most weightily, as we have seen, in Book I of *The Faerie Queene* in the Legend of Holinesse.[9] Almost from its inception, readers have recognized that the first book of the poem is modeled on Revelation and draws its primary images from that enigmatic testament.[10] The book exploits the rich visions of apocalypse not only to allegorize the Redcrosse Knight's individual struggle for redemptive faith but also to comment congruently on the fortunes of the English Reformation church in a titanic struggle against its sinister and mighty opposite.

Book I's employment of biblical apocalypse to allegorize ecclesiastical history accords with how most English commentators between 1540 and 1590 generally understand the genre. Luther identifies Antichrist with the papacy and then in 1530 initiates a historicist exegesis of Revelation, interpreting it as a prophecy of church history.[11] His goal is to "take from history the events and disasters" of Christianity and to find in them exegetical lessons about the monumental tasks he and his followers are caught up in.[12] For early Reformation England these lessons require reading apocalypse primarily as a history of persecution and a theology of history. The chief subjects of such writing are three: the doctrine of the two churches—one true and oppressed, the other false, idolatrous, and powerful; the identification of the papacy as Antichrist; and the imminence of the

Last Judgment.[13] These themes remain fairly consistent throughout the century, as apocalyptic commentary comes to provide both the primary means of unfolding church history and the chief instrument for Protestants to proclaim their historic destiny and justify their rebellion from Rome.

Developing an idea first propounded in England by William Tyndale, Bale's *Ymage of Both Churches* (1540–47) sets out in vivid detail the doctrine of the two churches. Bale claims that historical research should be guided by apocalyptic exegesis; therefore, he says, in an apothegm that will direct exegetes for several generations, "the texte [is] a lyght to the cronycles, and not the cronycles to the texte."[14] Apocalypse becomes a light by which history may be made fully visible. It reveals the wickedness of Rome and the truth of Protestantism. By closely correlating apocalypse and history, Foxe's *Actes and Monuments* and other works amplify Bale's dichotomies and historiographic outlines into a fully articulated church history. Particularly in his late unfinished work, *Eicasmi*, Foxe represents a signal historiographic advance on Bale.[15] In Foxe's hands Bale's doctrine of the two churches becomes a guide to history and a means of judging truth and falsehood in the consuming crises of the Reformation. By establishing the historiographic principles of apocalyptic exegesis Bale, Foxe, and their followers make possible many of the great commonplaces of Reformation discourse, such as the universal belief that the papacy is Antichrist—or as when William Fulke pronounces in his popular and quite unoriginal *Sermon Preached at Hampton Court* (1570), "I shal plainly shew and proue that Babilon is Rome."[16]

Apocalypse, especially Revelation, is an attractive subject to early Reformation commentators because it offers readers burdened with a strong sense of persecution a theodicy and a hope for future redress. Its clashing dichotomies foster this hope: Christ and Antichrist, Mother and Whore, right and wrong, true and false. Daniel and Revelation, written in times of crisis, have as their purpose to rouse suffering readers to a faith in the ultimate justice of history and God's vindication of the faithful. Their goal is to give a higher meaning to history by correlating the particularities of fallen experience to transcendent patterns accessible to the prophetic vision. Reformation apocalypticists see themselves in this line of vision, as latter-day prophets as well as exegetes. Finding multiple links between history and apocalypse, they not only justify their own theological convictions but also find ample evidence of a teleology in the historical and political maelstroms swirling about them.

It comes as no surprise, then, to find apocalyptic exegesis and political polemic so closely intertwined in the period. As Bernard Capp has pointed out, this is a natural link, for princes were instrumental, indeed essential, to the success of the Reformation.[17] Throughout the century, as apocalypse is scrutinized for evidence of papal corruption, the monarch is increasingly hailed as the hope of Antichrist's destruction and the instrument of the elect. Foxe dedicates *Actes and Monuments* to Elizabeth I. The frontispiece to the 1563 edition depicts the queen enthroned in triumph over a defeated papal Antichrist, declaring her the apocalyptic hope of the nation.[18] Just after her accession John Aylmer (later Bishop of London) writes that the queen wields the "sworde of our defence" to "cutt the head of that Hidra, the Antichrist of Rome, in suche sorte, as it neuer growe againe in this realme of England."[19] Both Bale and Foxe are partly responsible for the nationalistic strain that runs through later apocalyptic commentary. Foxe, for example, claims apostolic roots for the English church and promotes the crown as the source of God-given government.[20] But these voices are sporadic; the nationalism that becomes a chorus in apocalyptic commentary late in the century is, on the whole, relatively muted between 1540 and 1590.

Instead most English commentators follow Luther's lead and stress the "preaching of God's word in history" as the key to squelching the dark forces of Antichrist.[21] Although no commentator appears to have doubted the ultimate overthrow of Antichrist any more than his identification with Rome, many worried about his interim perfidies. Hence the chief question centered on how he was to be overpowered. Given the Protestant supremacy of the preached Word, it is natural that commentators promote this activity as the instrument of victory. The great apologist of the English church, Archbishop Jewel, may be the most representative spokesman for this position. His sermon on 2 Thessalonians typifies Reformation apocalyptic exegesis before the Armada. He rejects the notion that Antichrist will be routed literally "by Michael." Instead, he says, "The preaching of the Gospel . . . shal consume the kingdome of Antichrist. . . . Princes make their conquests by power and strength, by fyre and sworde, and engines of warre, but God shal beate downe his aduersarie with the rod of his mouthe. By true preaching of his worde. His worde is mighty, it is his sworde, it is his mace: it is the rod of his mouth."[22] The opposition Jewel draws between preachers and princes (and his implicit admission that the power of the ruler is available as an option) underscores that Reformation polemicists are often unsure about where to look for leadership in resisting Antichrist. Aylmer has endorsed the queen's sword as the preferred weapon. The fact remains, though, that early in the reign of Elizabeth I, preaching was endorsed as the most suitable means of subduing Antichrist.

A quite different approach to the issue comes from Arthur Dent, writing *The Ruine of Rome* at the end of Elizabeth's reign (and published thereafter). He considers the question explicitly: is preaching the most effectual means of conquering Antichrist? "Of all other meanes, the Gospell is strongest, but the thing is this. First, the Gospell being set abroach, shal detect and discouer the Whoore of Rome, and all her abhominable doctrine and filthinesse, which the Christian Princes espying, shal renounce her, make warre vpon her, and slay in the field thousande thousandes of her soldiers."[23] The gospel alone is insufficient; to complete the great task the arms of a godly leader are needed. In his *Sermons Vpon the Whole Booke of Revelation* (1596) George Gifford makes a similar point. After acknowledging the role that preaching might play, he turns to the power of statecraft: "we . . . stand in neede of noble warriors and mighty men, who in so great and waighty causes are to be guided by the most high God, euen by the light of his sacred worde. . . . Among other bookes of the holy Scripture, this Reuelation doth giue both special instruction and direction, and also incouragement vnto these warres."[24]

The Protestant princes, says Gifford, "are the ministers of the true Gospell upon earth, and all the right valiant men of warre which fight with the material sworde against Antichrist."[25] Jewel's spiritual reading has been literalized and materialized. The physical sword of the righteous leader has replaced the spiritual armor of Ephesians donned by the Redcrosse Knight. Laurence Deios, in *That the Pope is That Antichrist*, observes that while faith and prayer are appropriate as "spiritual armour, . . . as men, we must arme our selues if neede require otherwise."[26] Anthony Marten asks: "When had euer England so iust a cause to fight as now? . . . When had we euer a more louing Prince to her subiects then now?"[27]

As the nation edges toward war with Spain and a general mood of crisis deepens—particularly after the execution of Mary, Queen of Scots, making armed conflict virtually inevitable—apocalyptic commentary, increasingly politicized, intensifies the already vital role demanded of the monarch by the events of the Reformation. In 1593 John Napier writes to James VI of Scotland in *A plaine discouery of the whole Reuelation of Saint Iohn* that "it is the dutie of Gods seruants in this age, interpreters of Prophecies, as well as (according to examples of Prophets) to incourage and inanimate Princes, to be ready against that greate day of the Lords reuenge."[28] James himself has already virtually invited such a call-to-arms. His own apocalyptic pronouncement of 1588 warns that Antichrist has "sent out the Iesuites, his last and most pernicious vermin, to stirre vp the Princes of the earth his slaues. . . . And are not the armies presently assembled, yea vpon the very point of their execution in France against the saints there? In Flanders for the like?"[29]

James's urgency characterizes the moment. The Armada and its attendant national furor heightens the expectation, already prevalent from Luther and Bale on, that the Reformation signaled the end of the world.[30] After the Armada, exegetes assume a combative posture far different from Jewel's pacific confidence that preaching will bring victory. English Protestants see themselves not as preachers but as warriors, determined to trounce Antichrist with the force of dire arms.[31] Their exegesis takes on a bellicose tone commensurate with the current mood of political crisis. Napier claims that Revelation entreats "most speciallie of the destruction of the Antichristian seat, citie, and kingdome, doth directe the execution of that great work of Gods Iustice and iust iudgement to the kings of the earth."[32] Deios asserts that "popish legions . . . make warre vpon vs only for religion, & in those wars in *France* and *Germanie* & the low countries, & in all places where by inuasion or rebellion they can preuaile, haue made infinit slaughters."[33] Marten exhorts his countrymen to take up arms against "this very Antichrist" even as he asks God to "stretch out the Arme of Moses, that thy Christian Souldiers may valiantly fight for their Prince, their Countrey, and thy true Religion." He entreats God to "destroy their Armies, confound their forces, terrifie their Captaines. Scatter, breake, and sinke into the Sea, their huge and strong vessels."[34]

This militancy corresponds closely with shifts in foreign affairs and policy. From 1558 until the 1580s Elizabethan policy was on the defensive, and relations with Philip II relatively amicable. But by the late 1580s foreign relations had deteriorated markedly. The Netherlands, France, and Ireland were all areas of danger, and increasingly the English saw themselves sequestered by Roman Catholic adversaries, led of course by Spain. In the Netherlands the situation was especially perilous (especially after the fall of Antwerp in 1585), for the inviolability of England was, in the view of Elizabeth and her advisors, dependent upon the defense of the Low Countries. The danger from Spanish troops in those nearby lands was reinforced by hazards on other fronts: at home, fears persisted of papal plots against the queen's life, carried out by the Jesuits, often in collaboration with the Spanish and (before 1586) Mary, Queen of Scots; Irish resistance to English rule continued to prompt worries about European Roman Catholic intervention; the Roman Catholic Guise party in France was now subsidized by Philip II, a fact leading to renewed anxieties about a Guise invasion of England led by Spanish troops.[35] The Armada invasion has brought these mounting apprehensions to a climax, and in the years following that heady event, there is little diminution of the alarm over Roman Catholic encroachments. As Gifford puts it: "The enemies prepare themselues with mighty forces, threatening great terror vnto this land, euen as the waues of the sea, ready to ouerwhelme vs."[36] The passion of the apocalyptic commentators is that of the nation at large; the nationalistic zeal so marked in the commentary after 1588 is proportionate to unease about national self-preservation in the discourses of the moment.

Book V responds to this historical urgency when in its second half it becomes both fully topical and apocalyptic. The national and historical drama now unfolds, and so the allegory shifts to the spacious arena sanctioned by the late Elizabethan apocalyptic habit of viewing political events of the present and recent past hermeneutically. It is appropriate, then, that the figures of the conflict assume the contrasting proportions of good and evil typical of apocalypse. Mercilla, figuring Elizabeth, a maiden queen of "soueraine grace" (8.17), is oppressed by that "mighty man" (8.18), the Souldan, figuring Philip II, who would slay her "sacred selfe" (8.19).[37] Upton in 1758 was the first to note the Souldan's associations with the Roman Catholic enemies of England, associations evident in the apocalyptic battle between Arthur and the Souldan.[38] The "pagan" is "Swearing, and banning most blasphemously" (8.28); he "bannes, and sweares, and rayles" (8.39). In view of the maritime threat the Armada epitomizes, it is hermeneutically appropriate that the Souldan figure the beast from the sea that has upon its heads "the names of blasphemy" (Rev. 13:1, 5–7; cf. Dan. 7:3, 11:36). The Souldan's activities illustrate how this book of *The Faerie Queene* employs simultaneously both apocalypse and its mediating post-Armada exegesis. Revelation and Daniel are the source of the Souldan's blaspheming; the commentary is the source of his "banning," one of the papacy's more notorious ecclesiastical practices, tirelessly denounced by the Reformers.

It is challenging to untangle the scriptural from the exegetical sources of the episode. The Roman Catholic Mass is condemned in article 31 of the Thirty-nine Articles as "blasphemous," an epithet the exegetes persistently malign the papacy with.[39] In the same fashion, the Souldan, who "neither religion hath nor fay," is said to serve "Idols" (8.19), a term attached to Antichrist in apocalyptic writings (e.g., Rev. 17:3 and gloss; 21:8; cf. Dan. 11:31) as well as a common charge from the 1540s on in other anti-Catholic writings.[40] The Souldan is guilty of "cruell tyranny" (8.20) and is vilified as a "tyrant" (8.45), one of the favorite terms of execration heaped on the papacy throughout the period, especially by the apocalyptic commentators, and an objurgation transferred to Philip as he became increasingly fearsome.[41] The battle between Arthur and the Souldan is based on both the triumphant accounts of England's Armada victory as well as the victories in Revelation and Daniel. Acting the apocalyptic role of the conquering Christ, Arthur's arms "glister" and shine "as bright, as doth the heauen sheene" (8.29), terrifying his enemy with a vision of Judgment Day (cf. Rev. 1:16, 19:11–12, 22:16; cf. Dan. 10:6). The aftermath is portrayed with eschatological joy: Arthur is declared "victour of that day" (8.51); Artegall's "warlike rout" is accomplished with "finall force" (8.50), when, Michael-like, he dispatches the pagan's followers "lyke wyld Goates" (8.50; cf. Rev. 12:7; Matt. 25:32–33). As Dent comments on the victory in Revelation 19: "Now all this is to be vnderstood of the battels betwixt the Papists and the Protestants in these last dayes."[42] The triumph over the Souldan, then, is modeled on a variety of apocalyptic battles as mediated by the commentary that saw Philip as the tyrant representative of Antichrist.

In this respect Book V is part of a wider cultural self-understanding, what we might label the discourse of foreign policy and also a newly developing discourse of nationalism. Post-Armada commentary contributes to this discourse by encouraging England to think of itself as oppressed, righteous, and engaged in a struggle under providential auspices. Critics earlier in this century make this point: Edwin A. Greenlaw maintains that the "whole Book treats of the danger to England from Spanish aggression"; H. S. V. Jones that "its main themes present different aspects of the Catholic danger in England, France, the Low Countries, and Ireland."[43] Recently Richard Helgerson has amplified our understanding of how the language of a developing nationalism shapes a variety of discourses in the period.[44] The rapid political shifts in the sixteenth century that lead English people by the 1590s to write about themselves as a "state," when they have not done so before, has startling manifestations; such changes can lead Aylmer (a post-Armada apocalypticist *avant la lettre*) to the conclusion that "God is English."[45]

Like other apocalyptic and patriotic polemic, the Souldan episode has little moral nuance, for the struggle is simply between right and wrong. Hence the poet claims that the Souldan "breakes all bonds of law and rules of right"; Adicia is "mortall foe to Iustice." The dichotomy is pellucid: the Souldan "Sought onely slaughter and auengement / But the braue Prince for honour and for right" (8.30). The apocalyptic outcome is suitably public and providential: "How worthily, by heauens high decree / Iustice that day of wrong herself had wroken" (8.44). As part of post-Armada apocalyptic commentary, the episode elicits a patriotic frisson, not to mention a quelling of fears about national self-preservation. It surely provided Spenser's original audience the same hopeful satisfaction that Dent does: "let us obserue for our comfort, that whensoeuer we shall see Kings and Captains, Nobles, and Potentates of the earth, being solicited by the Iesuites, priests, and False Prophet, to leuy great armies . . . they shal not preuaile, but bee vtterly ouerthrowne and destroyed. As in part we see fulfilled in the yeare our Lorde 1588 when the great and inuincible Armado of the Spaniards . . . came to Armegeddon."[46]

The long, vexed history of apocalyptic exegesis reflects the dichotomy of right and wrong it finds in its biblical originals. These dualities are also those of political polemic, to which the genre has been tied throughout its history. Here, too, we see what has alienated so many readers of the Legend of Justice. The nation is at war, hemmed in by the enemies of truth, justice, and international Protestantism.

Alfred B. Gough speaks for many later critics of Book V when he observes that "very recent history is seldom a fit matter for poetry, especially when the poet's country is engaged in a fierce national and religious struggle."[47] Doubtless, though, this is exactly why apocalypse attracts Spenser in this book. Drawing upon the intense interest of apocalypse in justice, and with the example of both Bale's and Foxe's identifying the papacy as the source of injustice in church history, post-Armada exegetes repeatedly appeal to supreme standards of justice, usually in political and military terms.[48] Addressing James VI, Napier calls for "iustice to be done" against the "enemies of Gods Church, and . . . most cruell oppressors." If James will "ministrate Iustice to them, God the supreme Iudge shal ministrate Iustice to you against your enemies."[49] Marten claims that the Spanish have "neither Iustice nor religion, nor charity, nor conscience, nor yet good cause on their side. If they had been iust, they would not have pretended peace, and yet swear our destruction . . . neither have they God on their side."[50] Justice derives from God in all apocalyptic commentary, most emphatically in post-Armada commentary, as it does in the Legend of Justice. The power of the prince needs to uphold and defend that originating source of Justice's authority.[51] She engages her statecraft on behalf of both God and justice: "Power is the right hand of iustice truely dight" (4.1). The proem explicitly links this God-given virtue to the monarch:

> That powre [God] also doth to Princes lend,
> And makes them like himselfe in glorious sight,
> To sit in his owne seate, his cause to end,
> And rule his people right, as he doth recommend.

(proem 10)

Book V cannot be comprehended as apocalyptic commentary without appreciating, then, the role of Elizabeth in this text. Readers have always seen the queen in both Britomart and Mercilla, as warrior and ruler. The imagery of apocalypse contributes significantly to Britomart's vision in Isis Church; the New Jerusalem surely figures in the extended description of Mercilla's throne and person. The two loci comprise the iconographic centers of Book V, where the queen's presence is felt keenly. In Isis Church, Britomart's vision before an "Idoll" (7.6,8) proleptically summons up and transfigures apocalyptic imagery of later cantos. Her "Moon-like Mitre" becomes a "Crowne of gold"; her "linnen stole" a "robe of scarlet red"; she is "adorn'd with gems and iewels manifold" (7.13). Imagery later associated with figures modeled on the Whore and the Antichrist (e.g., the scarlet robe and the mitre) in the environment of Isis Church instead summons up the New Jerusalem and also makes Britomart the "woman clothed with the sunne" (Rev. 12:1). In her subsequent dream vision she fights a flaming battle with a beast (a crocodile) that she overcomes with her rod (7.15).

With similar iconographic fluidity the description of Mercilla follows another great contest, the defeat of the Souldan. Her depiction, too, taps a variety of scriptural and iconographic sources; unnoticed perhaps are the echoes of the New Jerusalem (which itself follows a great victory in Rev. 21:9–27):

> Vpon a throne of gold full bright and sheene,
> Adorned all with gemmes of endlesse price,
> . . . .
>
> All ouer her a cloth of state was spred,
> . . . .
>
> . . . sunny beams,
> Glistring like gold . . .
> . . . .
>
> Seemed those litle Angels did vphold
> The cloth of state, and on their purpled wings
> . . . .
>
> Besides a thousand more of such, as sings
> Hymnes to high God, and carols heauenly things,
> . . . .
>
> Whilest kings and kesars at her feet did them prostrate.
>
> (9.27–30)

Both scenes have a nationalistic dimension. Britomart, the "Magnificke Virgin" (7.21), is promised union with Artegall, ultimate deliverance from the "raging flames, that many foes shall reare," and inheritance of her "countrey deare" (7.23). Mercilla's court recalls both Parliament and the grandeur of the Elizabethan court.[52]

But Elizabeth I in her own person, as it were, plays the leading apocalyptic role, right from the start in the proem. Artegall is named as an "instrument" (proem 11) of her justice, the only time any knight is joined so clearly to Elizabethan policy. The depiction of the queen, one of the most fervent in Spenser's canon, is explicitly apocalyptic (cf. Dan. 7:13):

Dread Souerayne Goddesse, that doest highest sit
    In seate of iudgement, in th'Almighties stead,
    And with magnificke might and wondrous wit
    Doest to thy people righteous doome aread
    That furthest Nations filles with awfull dread.

(proem 11)

The "doome" (a word that has an apocalyptic career of its own in this book: it is employed variously over twenty times) delivered to the queen's subjects is a version of the divine doom, the ultimate justice of the last day when God shall sit in the "seate of iudgement" now occupied by the queen. These lines reverberate throughout the final cantos, where, as the proem has forecast, the "furthest Nations" are filled with "awfull dread" (cf. Rev. 15.4). In the proem the queen exercises the authority attributed to her by some post-Armada exegetes, who praise her as the hope of Protestantism, the agent of divine retribution, and the instrument of justice.[53] They say, with Leonard Wright in his perfervid tract *The Hunting of Antichrist* (1589), the queen has "so hunted, tossed, and chased that Romish Antichrist, with all his superstitious trash and traditions, out of the forests of England: as (except by stealth in priuie corners) he dare not shew his head."[54] Gifford asserts that the queen has "made the whore desolate and naked"; although "Antichrist and his adherents" will attempt the "subuersion of our religion, Queene, and countrie," the "wars and enterprises" of the "Romish beast" are "to smal purpose, vnlesse they could first supplant and destroy her Maiestie."[55]

Many critics have observed close affinities between the first and fifth books of *The Faerie Queene*. Like the Legend of Holinesse, Book V turns to apocalypse as a generic model.[56] It is worth sketching the relation of the two books to apocalypse, for the differences between each book's handling of the genre suggest some of the distinctive features of the Legend of Justice. Florence Sandler has suggested that Book I be understood as apocalyptic insofar as Spenser reads Revelation primarily as a moral and spiritual allegory where "historical" elements are subordinate.[57] Redcrosse's individual struggle to add "faith vnto [his] force" (I.1.19) compels the reader's attention at least as powerfully as the national saga that his story allegorizes. In Book V this situation is somewhat reversed, or at least considerably altered. The Legend of Justice, far from subordinating "historical elements," draws upon contemporary apocalyptic commentary that eagerly seeks historical and immediately topical application in Revelation. The struggles of the final cantos are comprised not merely of spiritual warfare but of literal, physical warfare, grounded in the material of history and politics. The difference partly resides in the general movement of the poem from the "private" virtues of the first half to the "public" virtues of the second half. In apocalyptic terms, Book I dramatizes the individual's thwarting of Antichrist by faith and the Word at least as much as (and arguably more than) it allegorizes the fortunes of the national church. Book V, however, stresses the aspect of Elizabethan apocalyptic commentary that is preoccupied with the nation's overthrow of Antichrist. Its contests have historical, national referents—situations impinging daily on the lives of the original readership. Furthermore, in the earlier book contact with Scripture is more direct and immediate than in the later one, where apocalypse is mediated more thoroughly by contemporary commentary.

A consequence of these differences, then, is that Book V uses apocalypse more obliquely than Book I. In the earlier book, Redcrosse journeys toward the New Jerusalem encountering en route figures modeled on those from Revelation. The False Prophet and the Whore of Babylon, to take two outstanding examples, are incarnated in Archimago (and Despaire) and Duessa. In Book V the relationship to apocalypse is less systematic and direct. The characters are not modeled as closely and uniformly on figures from Revelation. Instead we find in them refractions of apocalyptic figures. The chief villains of the book—Radigund, Duessa, the Souldan, Geryoneo, Grantorto—form a composite portrait of Antichrist.[58] Furthermore, these characters are heavily bridged by contemporary exegesis, which itself refracts Antichrist. Some commentators locate Spain in the Beast, others in the Whore, still others in Antichrist.

Let us take Duessa as a case in point. Her manifestation in Book I is anything but simple; but there is no doubt, from her first appearance on, that we are encouraged to recall the Whore of Babylon. Those powerful affiliations remain through her exposure and defeat. In Book V, Duessa has a rather more limited role, of course, as an avatar of Mary, Queen of Scots, and as such, she is indebted to the Elizabethan conception of Mary as the representative of a pernicious "papism." Among Protestants Mary was commonly regarded as one of the current embodiments of the Whore or, as she was called in the English Parliament, a "professed member of Antichrist."[59] Duessa is a political threat, and the allegory treats her accordingly. With typical Spenserian flexibility, the episode of her trial pays almost no attention to what is a principal focus in Book I, her danger as a seductive woman.[60] The Geneva gloss of Rev. 17:2–3 concurs: "Antichrist compared to a Harlot because he seduceth the worlde with vaine wordes." Nor does the post-Armada commentary treat the Whore as an erotically alluring woman but rather as a political and even a military peril. Her role in Book V is almost exclusively public; she has virtually nothing of the personal menace she had in Book I. The judgment delivered on Duessa in Book V is political, mediated by the apocalyptic commentary—hence the eschatological diction: she is "brought to her sad doome" (9.42); her "doome" is heard "a-right"; and she is "damned" (10.4). Furthermore this judgment is rendered in the international context favored by the late Elizabethan exegetes (cf. Dan. 7:26):

> And then the law of *Nations* gainst her rose
>
> . . . .
>
> Next gan *Religion* gainst her to impute
> High Gods beheast, . . .
>
> . . . .
>
> And lastly *Iustice*.[61]
>
> (9.44)

The judgment against Duessa—political and transparently figuring the trial of Mary, Queen of Scots—is the second defeat in the poem of the Scottish monarch, for she is recognizable in Radigund. Mary, then, is twice demonized in this book (or three times: since her mother was a Guise, she is also implicated in the Burbon episode). Radigund is labeled a "harlot" and a "Tyrannesse" (6.11), terms from both apocalypse (*Whore*) and its exegesis (*tyrant*). The combat between Britomart and Radigund signifies not merely the triumph of Elizabeth over Mary but also a version of an apocalyptic battle urged on the Protestant prince against England's Roman Catholic adversaries. Indeed, after the contest Britomart "there as Princess rained / . . . changing all that forme of common weale" (7.42). She rules as the idealized mighty sovereign, who, through power of arms, institutes a just peace: "There she continu'd for a certaine space" (7.45). Britomart brings about what in the proem is attributed to the queen: a political peace issuing from her might.

It is significant that intervening between the Souldan episode and the Duessa episode is the incident with Malengin. This protean figure, with his numerous literary forebears, has been persuasively identified as an allegorical representation of the Jesuits.[62] Known for their treasonous guile and their efforts to assassinate the queen, the Jesuits are the targets of ceaseless excoriation in apocalyptic commentary and elsewhere. The Geneva gloss of the "croking frogs" of Rev. 16:3 singles out the Jesuits, "who speak nothing but lies all manner of craftie deceite." Dent glosses the same verse similarly and adds that the Jesuits show forth the Harlot and the Antichrist, "liuing dayly in whoredom, Sodomitrie, and al kind of outragious beastlinesse."[63] Malengin epitomizes "forged guile" (7.7), one of the obstacles to justice. His deviousness also aligns him with Despaire, on whom he appears modeled in part. Both live in hollow caves (I.9.33,35; V.9.10) and have wild hair and hollow eyes. Malengin's "crafty" practices and "forged guyle" (9.25), his "guilefull words" that his "false intent to shade" (9.12), his "slights and iugling feates . . . of legierdemayne" (9.13)—all recall Despaire's subtly deceptive rhetoric. As we saw in the first chapter of this study, Despaire himself is certainly modeled in part on the biblical False Prophet (e.g., Rev. 19:20), an especially pernicious example of religious abuse. In "quoting" himself, a typically Spenserian as well as an apocalyptic trait, the poet draws attention to the uses he makes of scriptural narrative technique. By recalling both Despaire and the biblical False Prophet (among others), Malengin fits the bill as a cunning enemy of justice. As the representative of the Jesuits, he is vilified as a religious and political enemy of the nation, one of the exegetes' chief straw men.

These three consecutive episodes—the Souldan, Malengin, Duessa—incorporate the apocalyptic triumvirate of Beast, False Prophet, and Whore. Together they sum up this book's emphasis on "forged guile, /And open force" (7.7) as the principal antagonists of justice.[64] All three stand in for Antichrist, acknowledged throughout the Reformation for his ghastly strength as well as his deceit (Jewel: "He is suttle and cunning, hee that shal deceiue the learned and the wise").[65] In post-Armada commentary, too, Antichrist is condemned for both his duplicity and his might.[66] But as England's Roman Catholic enemies figure more ominously in the national life, force becomes the dominant theme. Especially in the wake of the invasion, commentators concentrate on the military power of "the Romish beast and his company," who "prepare themselues with mighty forces, threatening great terrour vnto this land, euen as the waues of the sea, ready to ouerwhelme vs."[67] Geryoneo and Grantorto impress their brutality on the final cantos of Book V, where the allegory downplays the earlier emphasis on guile. Given the contemporary dread of invasion and other military depredations, it is not surprising that in the international episodes of Book V the preponderance of indictment falls on force.

The locus of these fears in Book V, as in other political discourse of the period, is Spain. Anticipation of Spanish hostility, not to mention actual examples of it, is of the greatest urgency in the last two decades of the Elizabethan reign. Hence Spain is repeatedly detracted in apocalyptic exegesis, which finds considerable evidence in Scripture of Spanish perfidy as well as its ultimate vanquishing.[68] It bears examining how Philip II is depicted in the Legend of Justice. Besides his most obvious manifestation as the Souldan, he is reproduced in Geryoneo and Grantorto, perhaps even in Dolon and in the Samient episode.[69] His role in Book V reflects his multiple international crimes in late Elizabethan discourse. He is held responsible for plots to assassinate the queen (Dolon) and to monopolize the seas (Samient), for the oppression of the Low Countries (Geryoneo), the troubles in France (Burbon), and the subversion of Ireland (Grantorto). Philip is demonized repeatedly in this book of the poem, even more strenuously than Mary is. He is also crushed repeatedly. That he is variously condemned speaks to his minatory role, one commensurate with the historical facts of Philip's seemingly ubiquitous presence in western Europe. The multiplicity of Spenser's portrayal of Philip is unmatched in *The Faerie Queene* by that of any historic personage, with the exception of Elizabeth I. Philip's daunting presence in Book V bears witness to his military, political, and religious importance and to the magnitude of the anxieties he instilled in his Protestant English contemporaries.

His continuous reappearance also reflects his apocalyptic function. The narrative principles of incremental repetition and overlapping operate powerfully throughout apocalypse, not only from Daniel to Revelation and other Christian loci but also within the confines of a single text. Antichrist enjoys numerous modes and faces in Scripture; Philip and Spain have multiple modes and faces in post-Armada commentary. Sometimes Philip is identified as the Beast, at other times Antichrist—even, in the "maiden face" of Geryoneo's monster, as the Whore.[70] The fluidity of Philip's representation in this book exemplifies the apocalyptic view of the world, where a multiplicity of figures represent either good or evil. Throughout Reformation commentary apocalyptic figures are interchangeable. The numerous trouncings of Philip express the longing of apocalypse for the undoing of the wicked and the triumph of divine justice.

In the Belge episode Philip appears most complexly as a politico-religious malefactor. We need not examine these episodes in detail because Kenneth Borris has recorded conclusively the multiple correspondences between the episode and Revelation, particularly the ways its monsters are modeled on apocalyptic beasts. Borris clarifies how Geryoneo refers to both the papacy and Spain, "the monstrosities of tyrannical government and religion," and he has pointed out how Spanish rule in the Low Countries had become a byword for tyranny.[71] Hence Geryoneo is "tyrannizing, and oppressing all" (10.14), forcing the people of Belge's land to "beare the yoke of inquisition" (10.27). His parent Geryone, "that whylome in Spaine so sore was dred / For his huge powre and great oppression" (10.9), expresses English fear of the Spanish menace. "Are not all places full of forraine powres?" (10.23), asks Belge. She herself, a "woman fled into the wildernes" (Rev. 12:6) who has been banished "mongst the croking frogs" (10.23; cf. Rev. 16:13), is a Mercilla *manquée*, a monarch shorn of her rightful sovereignty by a predatory invader. She embodies the most sinister peril the English fear for their own monarch and nation. England's distress over the impingement of those "forraine powres" on the nation's autonomy, as well as panic over the loss of Antwerp, formed the basis of Elizabethan intervention in the Low Countries. This worry is reflected in the commentary as outrage against the Spanish Antichrist. One may then modify Borris's remark that "it would be wrong to identify the abuses of Gerioneo and his Beast with Roman Catholicism exclusively. The episode allegorically attacks political as well as religious tyranny."[72] For the post-Armada apocalypticists these tyrannies are inseparable, and so it is in this book of Spenser's poem.

The description of Geryoneo's Chapel is worth looking at from this perspective. It is described fully twice (10.28–29; 11.19–20), with detailed horror rare even in Spenser's most vivid depictions of idolatry. Geryoneo has erected a "cursed Idole," proclaims it God, and offers it in "sinfull sacrifice / The flesh of men" (10.28; cf. Dan.7:19). A "hideous monster" accepts these sacrifices, one whose "dreadful shape was neuer seene of none / That liues on earth" (10.29). In the next canto Belge repeats the description, adding that before being fed to the monster on the altar, the victims are tortured and "burnt in flame" (11.19–20). A "huge great Beast it was" (11.23) and one that has been recognized since Gough's edition of *The Faerie Queene* as an allegory of the Spanish inquisition and its idolatrous papism.[73] As conflated allusions to the Mass and the Spanish Inquisition, these reiterated depictions comprise a ferocious attack on Roman Catholic religion.

They are surpassed in their zeal, however, by the narratives of Arthur's battles, first against Geryoneo and even more in the subsequent combat against the monster beneath Geryone's altar. Critics often remark that the defeat of Geryoneo recalls Arthur's defeat of Orgoglio. But the two contests differ in this major detail: Orgoglio is a mythical giant; Geryoneo refers quite specifically to a historic personage (or nation, led by Philip). This battle is in turn outstripped in its violence by Arthur's encounter with the Beast in Geryoneo's Chapel. The event is portrayed as an apocalyptic battle, which we may legitimately see as the English wish fulfillment in the conflict with Spain. Belge hopes Arthur's

> victorious arme will not yet cease
Till ye haue rooted all the *relickes* out
Of that vilde race.
> (11.18; emphasis added)

Arthur does just this. As Geryoneo goes down to defeat, he "curst and band, and blasphemies forth threw" and "gnasht his teeth" (11.12; cf. Matt. 25:30; Rev. 16:10, 11; Dan. 7:11, 12, 26)—a conflation of terms exemplary of how the commentary bridges apocalypse and the poem. Having begun to rid Belge of that "yoke of inquisition" (10.27), Arthur then fells the beast, a creature of "fowle blasphemous speaches . . . / And bitter curses" (11.28).

As religious invective, the episode is matchless. The narrator fiercely attacks Spain; the hatred of Roman Catholicism (the "hideous monster" [11.20] in its defeat becomes, as Borris points out, a "deformed Masse" [11.32]) is the equal of any contemporary anti-Catholic diatribe.[74] Philip is demonized here even more bitterly than in the Souldan episode. The allegory is becoming more belligerent with each incarnation of the Spanish monarch. The intensity of the episode must lead one to conclude that if it does not actually celebrate violence in the name of religion, it surely relishes the violence deemed necessary to defend religion and punish the sacrilegious. After the slaying—a public gesture, as it were, that is this book's eschatological counterpart to Redcrosse's slaying of the dragon as well as a repetition of the vanquishing of the Souldan—the public reaction echoes those found in Rev. 19:1: "Then all the people, which beheld that day, / Gan shout aloud, that vnto heauen it rong" (11.34; see also Dan. 7:9–10).

In the Burbon episode Philip is attacked yet again, albeit indirectly, for it was generally reported, quite accurately, that the rebellious subjects of Henry IV were supported by Spain. The two episodes—Belge and Burbon—need to be understood as apocalyptic counterparts. They represent the two approaches we have seen taken by the exegetes to the question of how Antichrist is to be defeated, by preaching the Word or by wielding the Sword. Arthur's success against Geryoneo and his Beast answers the call of the post-Armada exegetes that the prince's arms smite Antichrist. On the other hand, Artegall's encounter with Burbon is presented as an example of what may be expected if Antichrist is confronted mainly by the more pacific, traditional Reformist strategy of preaching the Word to enhance faith.

The poet takes considerable trouble to link the episode expressly with Book I and its concern with faith as the agency of redemption. Burbon announces that he has been "dubbed knight / By a good knight, the knight of the *Redcrosse*," from whom he received his shield with his "deare Redeemers badge vpon the bosse" (11.53)—a shield he has forsaken. He presents his problem as one of faith: he has been "forelore" (11.49) by Flourdelis, who has withdrawn "her faith" (11.50) from Burbon. Artegall upbraids Flourdelis, who is figured as a harlot ("richly clad / In roiall robes, and many Iewels dight" [11.60]) and impervious to "prayer [and] meed" ([11.61]). Furthermore, Burbon thanks Artegall for "sauing him from daungerous despaire" (11.48). But the episode is, as one commentator puts it, "remarkably unheroic."[75] Artegall barely rescues anybody; indeed he must deploy Talus to effectuate what limited heroic success the episode has. In apocalyptic terms the questions are clear: can Artegall "save" Burbon by means of the Word? Is preaching the Word of faith enough to defeat Antichrist, as earlier Elizabethan apocalypticists had averred? Can France be rescued from the forces of the Beast by nonviolent measures?

Here, I believe, we may detect a reason why Spenser chose to place this episode in the same canto as the defeat of Geryoneo. The argument to the final canto indicates that the Burbon episode may have originally been included in canto 12, along with the Grantorto episode. Josephine Waters Bennett's conjecture that a last-minute change took place as the poem went to press is supported by other bibliographic evidence.[76] But the final disposition of the episodes is just: Arthur's conquest of Geryoneo and Artegall's meeting with Burbon belong together in the same canto as twin examples of how the faithful may confront Antichrist. Arthur's purely military exploit is unequivocally triumphant: the power of his arms gets the better of the Beast. Artegall's rescue of Burbon is patently less heroic, for he employs almost no physical might of his own but rather relies on almost exclusively verbal resources to end the episode. His homily about a "breach of faith" (12.62) seems feeble when compared to Arthur's victorious purging of Belge's lands.

The episode asks us to compare Burbon's situation with that of Redcrosse for this very purpose. For Redcrosse, too, the issue is one of faith. Una's salvific words about "heauenly mercies" and "grace" (I.9.53) snatch him from the brink of suicide in the cave of Despaire and direct him to the house of Holinesse, where he learns to deepen his faith so as to destroy the dragon. The Burbon episode, with its explicit links to Redcrosse's situation, calls into question the reliance placed in the earlier book on the Word of faith as the most efficacious means of foiling Antichrist. Arthur's sword rids Belge's land of bestial "forraine powres"; Artegall's nonbelligerent homily fails to rid Burbon's land of its molesters. Burbon, of course, is freed from his assailants, at least temporarily, but the episode lacks the aura of a final victory or the conclusive emergence of the good. Flourdelis has been held "by force" (11.54), and the two episodes taken as companions suggest that force may be needed to free her for the long term. As the poet says, "No faith so firme . . . / . . . that may enduren long" (12.1), a truth to which "Witnesse may *Burbon* be" (12.2). Certainly the historical events motivating the allegory would bear out such a disheartened conclusion. Elizabeth has bowed to the dictates of realpolitik in not opposing the right of Henry IV, a newly converted Catholic, to sit on the French throne in 1595, a practical political compromise that could not but offend those who advocated an aggressive opposition to the advances in Europe of Antichrist. In the international political arena, where he rages, the Word alone is insufficient: "loue of Lordship and lands /Made [Burbon] become most faithlesse and vnsound" (12.2). Although Henry IV enjoys English support, his recent apostasy can hardly be seen as affirming the value of nonaggressive tactics against Rome. The post-Armada apocalypticists assert instead that the Book of Revelation encourages war and, in the words of Gifford, "setteth forth how the Lord himselfe doth as it were sound the trumpet vnto this battaile against *Babel*, saying Reward her euen as she hath rewarded you, and giue her double according to her works, and in the cup that she hath filled vnto you fil her the double."[77]

In canto 12 this is exactly what happens. The previous paired episodes of Geryoneo and Burbon dramatize the superiority of Arthur's weaponry in overpowering the Beast. Why, then, is the Belge episode not placed at the conclusion of Book V? If that episode were the book's ultimate one, we could say confidently that the Legend of Justice replicates the recommendations of other post-Armada apocalyptic exegesis: use the sword to subdue Antichrist. Instead, this book concludes with not only the most vexing and ambiguous test case in English foreign policy but also the unleashing of yet one more Beast, the Blattant Beast. Why is the Irena episode last, where it is certain to generate doubt and protest and controversy? Why does this book move from the chivalric rescue of the beleaguered Belge to the ironies and perplexities of the contest on Irena's behalf?

Book V has always been faulted for its presentation of violence. Critics have noted that its presiding genius appears to be Talus, his merciless iron flail mowing down all resistance. If we examine the second half of the book under its apocalyptic aegis, we find that violence is legitimated in biblical terms. When Gifford cries out for vengeance against the foreign Antichrist, when Dent forecasts the beneficent slaughter of thousands of the enemy, when exegetes call out for the shedding of blood as demanded by prophecy, the violence of Book V seems less extreme—more the pronouncement of a nation at war, hedged in by bloodthirsty enemies. Post-Armada commentaries are often calls-to-arms based on fears of persecution, responses to the crises of the moment. Richard McCabe has noted that Book V's villains are more easily defeated once transformed into monsters.[78] However that may be, this book of the poem is but one of a number of texts of the day to treat the enemies of England like beasts from Daniel and Revelation. Biblical apocalypse dehumanizes God's enemies, and much of its exegesis treats the enemies of the faithful similarly. (Dent: "The popish armies [will] go downe by heapes in all countries and kingdomes, and be made meate for the foules of the aire.")[79] Hermeneutics is used to validate bloodshed, particularly when the exegete advocates the "material sword" as the divinely sanctioned weapon to destroy Antichrist.

Little sanction is needed in the case of the Souldan, who is, after all, an invader—and a universally loathed one. There can be no question why Spenser violates chronology and places this first among the international episodes. From a contemporary English perspective the moral issue is plain and needs little justifying. But as the righteous triumphs of self-defense give way to the quandaries of foreign intervention and colonialism, the allegory becomes more ambiguous. Grantorto is both man and monster, "Tyrant" (12.25) and "Giant," less monstrous than Geryoneo's Beast but more so than the Souldan: "whether man or monster one could scarse discerne" (12.15).

The episode is presented in apocalyptic terms similar to its predecessors. The battle is heralded by trumpets to take place on a "dismall [i.e., *dies mali*] day" (12.11)—an Eschaton of sorts but also morally overcast. As she awaits the "doome of her decaye," Irena "no redemption nigh . . . did nor heare nor see" (12.11). The Burbon episode has demonstrated the insufficiency of defeating Antichrist by peaceful, homiletic means. Artegall now follows the example set by Arthur in performing apocalyptic violence so prosperously in the Belge episode. And indeed at first Artegall proves the equal of Arthur and fully overcomes Grantorto. He acts out the Arthurian role of both Michael and Christ, who are themselves interchangeable in apocalyptic commentary. Having quashed this "tyrant" (12.3) in the fashion advocated by the exegetes, Artegall faces a problem that has plagued English rulers in Ireland since: "How to reforme that ragged common-weale" (12.26). Here is an issue not addressed by the exegetes, who confidently champion Arthur's policy and who (to my knowledge) make no mention of Ireland.

But, better informed by bitter experience, Spenser does, both in Book V and in *A View of the Present State of Ireland*. Considerable notice has been taken of this document in recent years, particularly its links to the Irena episode.[80] We may best approach the *View* from its estimates of the religion of Ireland. When the interlocutors turn specifically to the issue, Irenius laments that the Irish are "all Papistes by theire profession but in the same so blindelye and brutishly." His phrase implies a kind of patronizing exoneration, for indeed "what other Could they learne then suche trashe as was taughte them[?]" The Irish have been instructed with all other Christians ("Corrupted with . . . Popishe trumperie") to "drinke that Cupp of fornicacion with which the purple Harlott had then made all nacions drunken." Therefore "purgacions" are needed to remove these pernicious practices, but they will have to await quieter times: "it is ill time to preache amongest swordes." Instead of endorsing the violent coercion he sees as imperative to reform most other aspects of Irish society, Irenius implies that nonviolent preaching will best serve the purpose of bringing religious truth to Ireland. He sets up an opposition between preaching and violence that we have seen elsewhere and develops it in this section of the *View* as he segues from matters of religion to matters of civil order. He does not, in fact, keep the terms in opposition but rather as complements. Reformation must come first in matters of government: religious reform will be the effect of political reform. When Eudoxus asks how such "reformacion" is to be achieved, Irenius responds that "the sworde"—the "Royall power of the Prince"—must help bring into effect "Lawes and ordinaunces." Although he disavows widespread slaughter and endorses only limited bloodshed as a short-term policy, Irenius's proposed solution to Irish disorder is that championed by the exegetes and Book V: "must needs this violente meanes be used."[81]

The proximities, associations, and connections among colonial policy, religion, and violence in the *View* are distanced in Book V by its multivalent and syncretic allegorical methods. The sharp pragmatism of the *View* is blunted in the allegory—although perhaps not thoroughly enough, for realpolitik emerges despite the amelioration and alienates modern readers. As an apocalypse the book makes no attempt in the final victories to downplay the bloodshed or its celebration. To impose on the allegory a distaste for violence is both sentimental and anachronistic—especially against a foreign enemy, especially in a religious war—as any cursory reading of the chronicles demonstrates. Throughout *The Faerie Queene* we find ample evidence of violence; it appears to embarrass and outrage twentieth century (idealist) critics, however, chiefly when the allegory becomes "historical" or "topical." Religious discourse has always been deployed to justify war ("neither is God on their side"), and this book of the poem is no exception. Scripture and its commentary serve the purpose, as they have in countless cultures and crises, of legitimating aggression.

Book V is distinctive not in advocating warfare to enhance the aims of foreign policy nor in its harnessing of Scripture and hermeneutics to justify the goals and methods of the prince. What finally makes Book V unusual as a commentary on contemporary history is its conclusion. One presumes Spenser could have chosen to place the Belge episode last or to give the Irena episode a Belge-like triumph and end the book at that. Had Spenser elected some such course, he would have been following one set down by his exegetical contemporaries in locating the ideal patterns of apocalypse behind the chaotic particulars of history. In fact the Belge episode reflects just such a plan of action, for its unqualified triumphs do not conform closely to the often ignoble events of Elizabethan intervention in the Low Countries. Instead the book ends on the distressing notes of the inconclusive Irena episode, followed by the unleashing of the Blattant Beast.

It seems certain that the final stanzas are intended to provide an unsettling conclusion—or inconclusiveness—to the issues raised in the international episodes. The hags Envy and Detraction represent two more harlot figures, more deformed than any others in the book, and the Blattant Beast is obviously designed in part on the beasts of apocalypse. These "griesly creatures" (12.28) resurrect the book's emphasis on deceit (the hags "weaue false tales" [12.36], which they "make much worse by telling /And take great ioy to publish . . . to many" [12.35]) rather more than force, although they are nothing if not aggressive. They reflect the emphasis throughout the book (indeed throughout the Spenserian canon) on fraudulent speech. Like blasphemy, with which it is consonant, this speech cannot easily be contained.[82] (Bonfont's tongue is nailed to a post for his "blaspheme" of Mercilla "for forged guyle" [9.25].) On the other hand, the coloration of the final vignette is decidedly domestic. The malice of these creatures seems contained at least by the borders of England: gone is the interest in foreign affairs that has been motivating the allegory for several cantos. Nonetheless when the final stanzas are examined from the apocalyptic perspective encouraged by the second half of Book V, we may discern how hesitant the book has been to advance a complete eschatology. The widespread Reformation belief in the imminent end of the world is not part of this book's apocalypticism. Its refusal to advance a more certain eschatology is certainly consonant with the tendency of *The Faerie Queene* to defer, dilate, and put off all absolute gestures of ending, a structural feature documented by much recent Spenser scholarship.[83] The final dour notes also suggest that evil will continue to rule the world indefinitely. Most readers have felt that the ending suggests a deep skepticism about the operations of justice. In fact, such a doubtful vision accords with the apocalyptic view of temporal justice. History cries out for a providential judge to dispel its corruptions and impose a higher form of justice. But as Merlin says to Britomart in his prophecy in Book III: "yet the end is not" (III.3.50). Book V is an Apocalypse Postponed.[84]

The ending of the book conforms closely with the image of the present advanced in the proem: the world "growes daily wourse and wourse" (proem 1), as it moves "toward . . . dissolution" (proem 4) and its "last ruinous decay" (proem 6). However fervently the monarch may be looked to for relief from injustice, her might is limited and evil is widespread. The apocalyptic view of the world comprehends human failure as deeply as tragedy does. The Eschaton may be imminent, but it is also delayed. Artegall is no exception to the rule that Spenser's heroes, like the policy of the queen whom Artegall represents, are radically limited. No more than Redcrosse does he establish a New Jerusalem. He is not even vouchsafed a vision of it. Nor, for that matter, can he so much as "reforme that ragged commonweale" (12.26). Apocalypse and its exegesis dwell on the degradations of the present. Few see much hope of human redress of that deterioration. What future the world has will be marked by chaos and suffering.

Providence, Fortune, and
Free Will in Book VI

In the final canto of Book VI, Pastorella is reunited with her parents, a scene sonorous in the language of salvation. Melissa, the servant who had abandoned the infant Pastorella "to fortunes spoile," runs to Claribell with the news that "the heauens had her graste" (12.16), for the "same is yonder Lady, whom high God did saue" (12.17). I want to listen carefully to the phrase "whom high God did saue," for it would reverberate in a soteriological age. Heaven, Melissa decides, has elected "To saue her chylde, which in misfortunes mouth was plaste" (12.16). Several stanzas later, however, the narrator rather confusingly reports that "chance . . . presents" (12.20) Pastorella to her mother. At the scene's end, the auspices of Pastorella's rescue remain tantalizingly and emblematically unspecified. Has she been the child of fortune or the beneficiary of heaven? Has she been saved by God, or is she a fortuitous target of chance? Claribell herself takes no stand on the issue but simply rejoices that her lost daughter, whom she has "thought long dead, she fyndes aliue" (12.21): "And liuest now my daughter now againe? / And art thou yet aliue, whom dead I long did faine?" (12.19). The romance convention of the lost child restored ought not to muffle the echoes of redemption here and throughout Book VI. More than any book since the first, this one is pervaded with the discourses of salvation, and, like the first book, it inscribes contemporary concerns about freedom of the will and its relation to both providence and fortune.

Critics have often noted that fortune appears to dominate Book VI more powerfully than others, to determine the lives and actions of the characters.[1] What, then, is the role of God? Does he "saue" any characters in this book? Is providence at work in this narrative?[2] If so, what is its relation to fortune, and how does each of these forces play its part? Although criticism has often noted the prominence of both fortune and providence in this book, it has yet to formulate the relation of the will to these determining powers. This chapter, then, focuses on how Book VI interrogates the nexus of individual will, providence, and fortune—not, I hasten to add, with the intention of securing Spenser's "position" but rather with the aim of clarifying some of the poem's difficult questions about conduct and its external limitations. The ontology of human behavior, both virtuous and evil, is the subject of speculation right from the start, when the poet seeks the origins of courtesy. Imploring the muses to reveal the "sacred noursery / Of vertue," he says that it "deriu'd at furst / From heauenly seedes of bounty soueraine" (proem 3). To this unexceptionable proposition, one supposes, any orthodoxy would assent, implying as it does that virtue originates with God. What, then, to make of the statement two stanzas later that "vertues seat is deepe within the mynd" (proem 5), strongly intimating that the wellsprings of good lie in the will? Is virtue innate, or is virtue infused by grace? Is the will (wholly) infected, or is it capable of cooperating in redemption? The proem merely hints at relations among a constellation of forces bearing on courtesy: to vary Sidney's famous apothegm, our erected wit maketh us to know what courtesy is, but our infected will keepeth us from reaching unto it.

Several critics of Book VI have argued that grace is central to its concerns—a fact evidenced, for example, in the vision of the Graces on Mount Acidale or in the reiteration of the word itself in nearly every episode.[3] Having to overcome a tradition that long condescended to this book as the least intellectually serious in *The Faerie Queene*, scholarship has for some time recognized the book's religious affiliations, although that recognition has often reflected an essentialism that perhaps overcompensates for earlier trivializing criticism.[4] Defenses of Book VI, essentialist or otherwise, no longer need to be made, though in recent years its religious dimensions have been downplayed. When Melissa cries out that Pastorella has been saved by God, her words might be understood allegorically, namely that Pastorella's rescue figures her spiritual salvation. But this reading would raise more problems than it would solve, for it would fail to account for the textual insistence on the place of fortune in human affairs. How does the human will overcome the promiscuous and too often baleful effects of fortune? Hamilton's edition observes that "events seem to be governed by chance or fortune rather than by individual will or divine providence" (626). This is exactly right: fortune seems to rule. Events in the book often seem random, such as the intrusions of the Blattant Beast, the depredations of the Brigants, the various interruptions that characterize so much of the plot.[5] The characters seem to be subject to indiscriminate disturbances, frequently harmful, sometimes benevolent.

More problematic is Hamilton's yoking of the phrases "individual will or divine providence," for they are neither antinomies nor self-evident allies. When the Hermit advises Serena and Timias how to cure the wounds inflicted by the Blattant Beast, wounds specifically associated with original sin, his counsel plays on these fundamental issues:

> For in your selfe your onely helpe doth lie,
>> To heale your selues, and must proceed alone
>> From your owne will, to cure your maladie.
>
> (6.7)

These words, too, resound in the soteriological zeitgeist and seem to contradict, or severely qualify, Melissa's claim that God sometimes saves the unfortunate. It sounds pious to suggest providence helps the luckless. It is within the bounds of (at least one) orthodoxy to imply that the wound of sin may be healed by cooperating with grace, but it is downright Pelagian and heterodox to aver that the cure "must proceed alone / From your owne will," especially if we emphasize his word "alone." The Hermit limns a self-sufficiency much at odds with contemporary religious pronouncements on the nature of fallen humanity and its relation to God and grace. His advice, which demands lengthier analysis in due course, is part of a network of concerns prominent in Reformation discourses. Embedding this book in contemporary religious polemic puts this issue in high relief.[6] No problem strikes more piercingly at sixteenth-century religious culture than the relation of the will to the purposes of God, for the will, as we have seen, is the fulcrum of Reformation understandings of humanity.

From Paul's Epistles and the writings of Augustine, Reformation writers fashion a view of sinful human nature against which the drama of salvation is enacted. The fallen creature suffers from an inherent and inherited depravity that leaves salvation altogether out of the reach of natural ability. As Martin Luther states the matter in an early translation, Adam's fall means that humanity is "borne in sinne, liue and dye, and must be condemned to euerlasting death" if not for Christian redemption.[7] On this point Protestant writers across the spectrum agree. But the dominant position of Reformed commentators gives their views special interest. John Calvin's position is particularly noteworthy for its emphasis and enhancement of the Lutheran conception of human insufficiency: "Yet of such perverseness of nature [man] is that he cannot but be moved or driven to evill" (2.3.5; fol. 89ᵛ). Both Calvin and his followers find venerable precedent for this view: "Man . . . is subject to the necessitie of sinning . . . Augustine ech where speaketh of it" (2.3.5; fol. 89ᵛ).[8] This theological determinism is intended to point to the utter uselessness of good works in achieving salvation, a futility pertaining closely to the role of the will. Edwin Sandys can therefore maintain that free will is not "sufficient to enable man to do good workes," for "our will is in such thraldome and slaverie unto sinne that it cannot like of any thing spirituall and heauenely."[9] The tenth of the Thirty-nine Articles echoes the point that human nature, unaided by grace, is incapable of redemption: "The condition of man, after the Fall of Adam, is such that he cannot turne, and prepare himself by his owne naturall strength, and good workes, to Faith, and calling upon God, wherefore we have no power to doe good workes pleasant and acceptable to God, without grace of God preventing us, that we may have a good will, and working with us when we have that good will."[10] Salvation, in short, is attributable solely to God, for we cannot earn it.

But Calvin and his followers go further than this statement would indicate. Not only is salvation unavailable to good works, to human effort; sinful human beings can do no good at all. Calvin's belief in the "unvarying corruption of our nature" extends to all unregenerate human action: "the soul, being drowned in this gulfe of destruction [i.e., the body] is not only troubled with vices, but also altogether voide of all goodnesse" (2.3.2; fol. 87ʳ). In shaping this assessment of human nature, Calvin focuses on the will: "the bondage of sin" constricting the will prohibits it from moving "itselfe toward goodnesse . . . libertie is by necessitie drawen or led into evill" (2.3.5; fol. 88ʳ). Calvin's deterministic view of the infected will is echoed by his many followers among the English Reformers. John Jewel's remarks are typical: "But as touching the freedome of the will, and power of ourselves, wee say with St. Augustine [that] man mis-using his free will, spilt both himselfe and his will," with the result that human nature is "wounded, it is mangled, it is troubled, it is lost."[11] "Man hath free-will," says Thomas Rogers, "to performe the workes of Satan, both in thinking, willing, and doing that which euill is."[12] The followers of Calvin, then, impeach all unregenerate human activity. As Reformed theology's chief English spokesman, William Perkins, puts it: "originall sinne is nothing els but a disorder or evill disposition in all the faculties and inclinations of man."[13]

Against the intransigence and determinism of the Reformed construction of human nature, there remains also in Reformation England a more moderate view of the unaided human capability to do good. Certainly all Protestants, across the spectrum, agree that salvation comes only through God's grace. But following the lead of Erasmus in his debate with Luther in the 1520s over the nature of the will, some English Protestants later in the century stop short of the Reformed position that impugns all human agency.[14] A number of these moderate English Protestants (as I shall refer to them) find some value, and therefore less than complete corruption, in the natural human faculties, including the will. Richard Hooker, who develops and makes better known Erasmus's view by privileging reason, is the preeminent exponent of this position, though it is present, at least potentially, in many otherwise Reformed writings. Thomas Becon, for example, asks, "What is free-will? It is the libertie that man hath in doyng outwarde thinges, and the naturall worke of man in suche thynges as be not spirituall: as in ordering hym selfe after a ciuill and political fashion, and outwarde fulfilling of moral virtues."[15] The exalted role Hooker assigns to reason leads him to attribute also to the will the capability of right action: "the object of wil is that good which reason doth leade us to seeke."[16]

Hooker sets forth this view with considerable clarity. "Freedom is a part of man's nature," he says, and, though original perfection is lost, "Man hath still a reasonable understanding, and a will thereby framable to good things." In countering the Reformed view of absolute depravity, Hooker claims that "experience teacheth us, that wee never doe any thing well, but with deliberate advice and choice." In his desire to refute the Reformed and predominant position, he is unequivocal in granting to the will freedom to choose the good: "I conclude therefore, the naturall aptnes of mans will to take or refuse things presented before it; and the evidence which good things have for themselves, if reason were diligent to search it out, may be sound-lie and safely taught without contradiction to any syllable in that confession of the Church, or in those sentences of holy Scripture."[17] Indeed "the Church," in its Roman Catholic—and, as Harold L. Weatherby has recently demonstrated for Spenser studies, in its Eastern communions—has long averred the ability of the will to do good.[18] Moderate Protestant defenses of the will, such as Hooker's, reaffirm Roman Catholic and pre-Augustinian belief in the will's ability to cooperate in salvation.[19] Recent scholarship has demonstrated that this moderate position, granting to the will an autonomy and a capacity to choose the good, runs as an undercurrent in sixteenth-century English Reformation thought and continues to swell throughout the next century.[20]

These issues are dramatized shrewdly in the Legend of Courtesy.[21] The first episode, as readers often observe, is intricately linked with the business of the previous book, which closes on a bleak note, suggesting (as its proem has forecast) that the world "growes daily wourse and wourse" (proem 1). Artegall and Calidore meet at the outset of Book VI, and their journeys intersect: "where ye ended haue," says Calidore, "now I begin" (1.6). His quest—the pursuit of the Blattant Beast left at large by Artegall at the end of the previous book—is repeatedly described as a combat against the forces of evil, for the Beast is "bred of hellishe race" (1.7) and has been sent into the "wicked world" to be the "plague and scourge of wretched men" (1.8). Although the world Calidore enters is palpably fallen, the first episode demonstrates its susceptibility to amelioration. This amenability helps to make it, as critics have consistently noted, different from the landscape of Book V.[22] The story of Briana and Crudor fashions not simply a fall but also a redemption. It is a tale couched in the language of deliverance.

　　Calidore comes upon a "comely Squire" (1.11) tied to a tree and inquires what has occasioned his "disgrace," a "shame" the squire blames on "misfortune" rather than "misdesert" (1.12). The victimized squire, however, is not the center of the episode. He serves merely to call attention to often confusing discriminations between culpability and misfortune. Defying our expectations in a way characteristic of how this book slyly evaluates moral accountability, the focus quickly shifts to Briana and Crudor, who are responsible for this "shamefull vse" (1.14). The words "shame" and "shameful" designate their fallen state. Deployed throughout the book, these terms suggest how, in Maurice Evans's phrase, "its evils are most commonly stigmatised . . . and the most pervasive symptoms of Original Sin."[23] If "shame" signifies their fallen status, so do other keynotes from the fund of Western moral mythography: Briana is said to be "proud" (1.40) and to have a "wicked will"; Crudor is "proud" (1.17) and "vnblest" (1.17); their seneschal is a "lumpe of sin" (1.23). Calidore's role, like that of Artegall before him, is to mete out punishment, for as he says, "it is no blame / To punish those that doe deserue the same" (1.26). Until Calidore slays Briana's seneschal—whose very name, Maleffort, designates his volitional function, the one who "executes her wicked will" (1.15)—the episode could easily have been plucked from the first half of the previous book. Two reprehensible characters will be justly punished for their "inhumanitie" (1.26) and "pryde" (1.30,40).[24] Theirs is a case of simple injustice and castigation, and their tale a rather obvious allegory of sin and damnation.

Two elements transform the episode into something quite different and embed it firmly in Reformation controversy over the will. First, after Crudor has stumbled to the ground in combat with Calidore (a mishap that is called a "fall"), he is spared certain death by virtue of his own efforts: "Nathlesse at length him selfe he did vpreare / . . . as if against his will" (1.35). Briana, too, seems "ready . . . to fall" when she sees Crudor "dead on ground" (1.34). Theirs is not so much a *felix culpa* as a moral faux pas. They fall only to rise and cooperate fully in their own rehabilitation. Crudor uprears himself and, in a posture of "meeke humilitie" (1.38), cries to Calidore, "Ah mercie Sir, doe me not slay / But saue my life" (1.39). His will is fully engaged in his recovery. The incident depicts no death, no permanent fall. The pride-driven sinner helps to save himself by participating in the process of his regeneration.[25] Though sin and fortune have brought him low—"lot [i.e., fortune] before your foot doth lay [me]" (1.39), says Crudor while he begs for mercy—his own will searches out and asserts the humility he needs to surmount pride and ask for mercy.

Second, Calidore dispenses mercy. Playing a part that is unfamiliar in the poem, particularly after the bloodbaths of the previous two books, he spares his enemy's life. Instead of an execution, Calidore delivers a sermon—the first of several in Book VI. He exhorts Crudor to eschew "pride and cruelnesse" and "him selfe . . . to subdew" because "all flesh is frayle" and "Subiect to fortunes chance" (1.41). Platitudinizing like a preacher, Calidore urges a series of Christian virtues that culminate in his gesture of forgiveness:

> Who will not mercie vnto others shew,
>> How can he mercy euer hope to haue?
>> To pay each with his owne is right and dew.
>> Yet since ye mercie now doe need to craue,
>> I will it graunt, your hopelesse life to saue.
>
> (1.42)

Calidore's triumph allows him to enjoy two roles, that of homilist and that of deliverer. He preaches mercy as a desirable ethical norm and then practices what he preaches.[26] Salvation is literally his to bestow: "I will it graunt, your hopelesse life to saue." Furthermore, Crudor collaborates in his own redemption in two respects: after mustering sufficient humility to beg for mercy, he "promis[es] to performe [Calidore's] precept well." Both of these actions result in Crudor's release from "dread of death" (1.43). Briana, too, has her "life and loue restord" (1.45) and is "wondrously now chaung'd, from that she was afore" (1.46). The agent, then, cooperates in his or her own salvation and is thereby "release[d] from his former foule condition" (1.43).

The episode suggests that the "fall" (1.35) is not everlasting and that human failure is not permanently impairing. The tale would hearten a moderate Protestant examining this book for its stand on human volition. The will is injured, but it is not altogether incapable of effecting good, even in order to abet its own salvation. Human beings can reverse the effects of willful malice. Indeed this is exactly the point of Spenser's conception of courtesy and the reason this virtue proves so effective a means to contemplate the nature of the will. Courtesy is a product of human intelligence, compassion, and effort. It is an act of volition. Although Calidore's manners "were planted naturall," his own deliberate "adding comely guize withall / And gracious speech" (1.2) help make him this book's titular hero. The courteous being extends charity and helps others restore themselves.[27] Calidore enjoins Crudor to show others mercy in order to receive it himself (1.42). Just as Calidore is said, in the book's opening description of his social skills, to have "purchast greatest grace; / Which he could wisely vse and well apply" (1.3), so, too, Crudor is bid apply to others the grace his liberator has bestowed on him.

But what kind of mercy is Calidore speaking of? The characters here help to effect their own salvation, to mend themselves and one another so that they may "hopelesse life . . . saue" (1.42). Hence this "wretched man that all this while did dwell / In dread of death" is suffered to "rise" and is "release[d from] his former foule condition" (1.43). This episode, serving as a prologue to the book (Calidore afterwards proceeds to his "first quest" [1.47]), suggests that the will is capable of at least partial regeneration, that human effort can reverse the effects of the "fall," and that the world is not doomed (as it is indeed said to be in Book V) to grow daily worse and worse. Yet the episode resists easy theologizing. The problem of the will is dramatized nontheologically and is not overtly attached to the inventory of factional contention over good works and their relation to redemption. Although the episode's language draws on the storehouse of theological discourse, it is surely not engrossed centrally with spiritual salvation, as Spenser's theological contemporaries delimit the terms of that issue. The episode inscribes the language of redemption and so heightens issues of moral responsibility. The afterlife—which is, after all, the fundamental crux of Reformation theology—is not at issue in this episode or anywhere else in Book VI. Unlike, for example, the first two books of the poem, this one does not "decide" the status of any character's afterlife. Book VI inscribes contemporary understandings of the will in order to allegorize the virtue of courtesy. Its use of Reformation discourses about the will, as later episodes show, makes Spenser's partisanship all but impossible to ascertain—a slipperiness that, far from debilitating, in fact enriches the allegory.

Canto 2, for example, challenges the points made in the first episode about the nature of the will. It draws a sharper distinction between good and bad characters. The good are constructed as immutably virtuous; the wicked do not rehabilitate themselves and are damned and discarded. The canto begins with the narrator's instructive taxonomy of how courtesy is arrayed among humankind. On the one hand, it is a "skill" (2.1) and, on the other, an inherent trait— "by kind":

> Thereto great helpe dame Nature selfe doth lend:
> > For some so goodly gratious are by kind,

> That euery action doth them much commend,
> And in the eyes of men great liking find;
> Which others, that haue greater skill in mind,
> Though they enforce themselues, cannot attaine.
> For euerie thing, to which one is inclin'd,
> Doth best become, and greatest grace doth gaine:
> Yet praise likewise deserue good thewes, enforst with paine.
>
>   (2.2)

The narrator sharply distinguishes those capable of attaining courtesy by dint of willpower ("enforst with paine") from those whose courtesy "dame Nature" has predetermined. In this second category, he further distinguishes between the naturally courteous (the "goodly gratious . . . by kind") and those who "cannot attaine" courtesy, whatever their efforts. Neither nature nor skill, "though they enforce themselues," is sufficient for these beings to gain "greatest grace" on their own. A Reformed Protestant reading this stanza allegorically would readily concur: the will is inherently incapable of participating in its salvation. Humanity is divided between those who have been saved and those whose wills remain depraved.

But how are we supposed to read these lines (and many others) that attach *courtesy* to "grace"? That depends, of course, on how we understand "grace" here and elsewhere in this book of the poem.[28] The text does not seem to mean it solely in its theological sense, but neither can that sense be dissociated from the way the text employs the term. For example, we are immediately told that Tristram is a "goodly youth of amiable grace" (2.5). Is this a social or theological state? The text is surely tapping the discourse of redemption to enrich a social signification. If the term were understood only theologically, Tristram would be either an unfallen being, something traditional Christianity would not assent to, or a regenerate one, something the text takes no stand on. Yet the text insists on his goodness. Tristram's heavily stressed youth reinforces the moral innocence that is his chief hallmark. Upon interrogation, the lady who accompanies Tristram's defeated opponent "cleard that stripling of th'imputed blame" (2.14), a theologically pregnant phrase. Calidore, acting once again as judge, finds that he, too, cannot "Him charge with guilt," for "what he did, he did him selfe to saue" (2.14). If Tristram is not only morally guiltless but also capable of saving himself, the text quietly challenges Reformed theology. If we put this stanza among Reformed discourses of salvation, it argues a strong counter-statement on the possibility of human freedom and self-sufficiency. It implies that the will is free to execute good and effect its own salvation. As Calidore goes on to aver, "For knights and all men this by nature haue, / Towards all womenkind them kindly to behaue" (2.14). The pun on "kindly" underlines the connection between natural behavior and goodness.[29] Calidore's dictum that "all men" are obliged to ("haue . . . to") do good presupposes the freedom to do so. By this reckoning, as the first episode has in fact dramatized, free will is the natural human condition, and "grace" is obtainable through human effort. Just as Crudor and Briana can be restored to a state of virtue, so Tristram is naturally good ("cleard . . . of th'imputed blame"). Virtue's seat is deep within the mind and with some civilized effort can be cultivated.

On the other hand, such a reading ignores Tristram's slain opponent, repeatedly charged with "pride" (2.8,11,23,40). His wronged lady's account, buttressed by that of Tristram, is enough to convince Calidore, again acting as adjudicator—this time of the dead—of the knight's guilt. The offending knight, like the Souldan of the previous book, does "curse and ban" (sure signs of reprobation) and so manifests his "guilt" (2.21; cf. V.8.39). Having pronounced the dead knight to be "proud" and one who "falles in his owne assault" (2.23), Calidore casts him into outer narrative darkness and turns back to Tristram, on whom he again confers the titles "grace" and "gratious" (2.23,24). By this reading, then, the text posits a principle at odds with the previous episode. Indeed the first two cantos can be viewed from this perspective as theological opponents. The first presents the possibility of limited human self-sufficiency, with the characters cooperating with the forces of salvation. Restoration is possible by means of human agency, cooperating with the forces of good, in this case Calidore. In contrast, though, the second, when read as an instance of the inherence of moral traits, presents a quite different picture. Here the characters are either innately and irresistibly good, as in the case of Tristram ("surely," says Calidore to Tristram, you are "borne of some Heroicke sead / That in thy face appears and gratious goodlyhead" [2.25]), or innately and hopelessly wicked, as in the case of his opponent, the "cause of all this euill" (3.17), whose very name has been expunged from the narrative. Calidore's function in the first episode is to further the restoration of Briana and

Crudor to moral health. In the second episode, he merely judges what is self-evident, namely, that some are innately good (saved?) and others are innately fallen and damned. Which of these two views of humanity does the text encourage? Book VI comprises a kind of psychomachia on the nature of the will, some episodes illustrating the Reformed position, others the moderate, and some, such as Tristram's, illustrating multiple and shifting perspectives.

The following episodes comprise variations on the theme of redemption and rescue. On the one hand, the text presents a series of malign figures: the unnamed knight who has wounded Aladine; the Blattant Beast that wounds Serena; Turpine; the Bear. All are allegorically aligned with sin and the forces of destruction. The severed head of the unnamed knight, "the cause of all this euill," is "the signe of shame" (3.17). The bite of the Beast, which gives a "rankling wound" (4.9) described as "mortall" (5.28), is implicitly associated with original sin (its effect on Serena is to make her feel despair: "being of all hope forelore" [4.10]).[30] Turpine, the knight of "pryde" (3.36,47) and "malice" (3.47), refuses aid to the wounded Serena and, with "the fury of his bloudy will" (3.49), wounds Calepine. The Bear embodies naked destructiveness: a "cruell Beare, the which an infant bore / Betwixt his bloodie iawes, besprinckled all with gore" (4.17). On the other hand, struggling against these pernicious figures are virtuous characters: Calidore, in his "deliueraunce" (3.19) of Priscilla to her father; Priscilla, in her ministration to wounded Aladine; the "saluage man," in his rescue of Serena and Calepine from Turpine and his stanching of their wounds; Calepine and Mathilde, in the "rescue" (4.18) of the bloody babe. Each episode is carefully linked to the next by the dramatizing of how each of these benevolent figures delivers those in distress. More important is the motivation and the means by which aid is offered in these crises. What is said of Priscilla and Aladine applies to all: "His care more than her own compassionate, / Forgetful of her owne, to minde his feares" (3.12). She saves Aladine by washing his wounds with her tears so thoroughly

> That of the deadly swound . . .
> . . . she at the length dispacht him
> And droue away the stound, which mortally attacht him.
>   (3.10)

Calidore, in turn, "restore[s]" (3.19) Priscilla to her father and presents her "guiltlesse innocent / Of blame" (3.18). The salvage man is moved by Turpine's assault to "feele compassion" (4.3) for Calepine's and Serena's plight. Having been "Recured well" (4.16) from Turpine's wound, Calepine in turn rescues the infant from the Bear. His "pitying" (4.23) of the infant's plight and his "tender ruth for [Mathilde's] unworthy griefe" (4.34) lead him to the "remedie" (4.28) of uniting stepmother and child. Each of the benevolent figures, then, surmounts evil by an act of good will, by responding compassionately and acting charitably to relieve another's adversity.

These rescues are notably secular. The means of "succour" (3.29,49) is not the intrusion of the supernatural but human pity. Help comes from within, not from above. Rescue has its wellsprings in human compassion—though it is abetted by a mysterious fortune ("so fortune him did ayde" [4.21]; "Such chaunces oft exceed all humaine thought" [3.51]). When the salvage man first bursts into the narrative, Serena is terrified and seeks "Gods sole grace, whom she did oft implore, / To send her succour, being of all hope forelore" (4.10). The text does not suggest that God ignores her. But neither does it suggest that God aids her. Although the salvage man may act as the agent of God (his name suggests his salvific function, and salvaging others is his raison d'être), the text gives no indication that he acts as anything but a natural man, whose motivation is "deepe compassion . . . which nature did him teach" (4.11). Moved to charity by the sheerest good will, the "wyld man did apply / His best endeuour, and his daily paine" (4.16) to cure the wounds of Calepine and Serena. After their rescue, though, Calepine and Serena

> thanked God for all,
Which had them freed from that deadly feare,
And sau'd from being to that caytiue thrall [i.e., Turpine].

(4.15)

This piety rings oddly. God is nowhere demonstrated as responsible for their rescue. An act of human will, emerging from the salvage man's solicitude, saves them—"The gentle minde by gentle deeds is knowne" (3.1). No intercession of heavenly powers brings about the characters' rehabilitation. They are "sau'd" not by grace but by human volition, in this case by the salvage man, who employs natural herbs to help cure their wounds—injuries which the text carefully associates with sin and human failure.[31] The chief antagonists of these episodes, Turpine and the Blattant Beast, are repeatedly constructed with traditional lexical indications (*pride, malice, wound*) of sin, even original sin. The assaulted characters are delivered by human resources from the inflictions of malevolence.

The chief rescuer of *The Faerie Queene* reenters the narrative during these episodes, only to play a role significantly different from one anywhere earlier. Although Arthur appears in this more frequently than in previous books, his magnitude is paradoxically diminished, particularly from Book V, where, as we have seen, he assumes the part of an apocalyptic agent. Here his motivation for rescuing Timias, for example, is decidedly less impersonal than his most recent intrusions to crush the Souldan or Geryoneo. In the flashback to their reuniting, Arthur finds Timias in mortal danger, surrounded by predators, and is moved by "pitty" to "reskue him and his weake part abet" (5.22). His embrace of Timias and his tender greeting— "My liefe, my lifes desire / Why haue ye me alone thus long yleft?" (5.23)—are more emotional and personal than any of his earlier, rather detached encounters with the poem's characters. His personal engagement with Timias upon his entrance to this book signifies, too, that Arthur is not aligned with the supernatural, as he has been elsewhere in the poem. Nor is he responsible, as we learn when the narrative flashes forward to Arthur's entrance into this book, for the rescue of Serena. At first he mistakes the salvage man for a harmful predator. Serena must prevent Arthur from dispatching the salvage man, who, she says, exemplifies "milde humanity, and perfect gentle mynd." She elaborates:

> I had surely long ere this bene dead,
> Or else remained in most wretched state,
> Had not this wylde man in that wofull stead
> Kept, and deliuered me from deadly dread.
>   (5.29)

Surely these lines could apply to the role Arthur has played in previous books. His part has now been assumed by an ostensibly lower being, and the reversal suggests his shrunken authority in this book. Far from serving as a moral and spiritual beacon to this episode's embattled characters, Arthur now follows the salvage man's lead, by acquiring his characteristic emotion of "pitty" (5.30), and then joins him in escorting Serena and Timias to the Hermit, at whose hermitage they will find deliverance. Arthur's salvific capacity is severely provisional and circumscribed, a diminution that suggests how obliquely this book works out its concerns. The term *grace*, which has been his in the early books, lights nowhere near Arthur in this book.[32]

Neither Arthur nor the salvage man can cure the Beast's wounds, which will respond only to a spiritual cure. If, as I have been arguing, this book does not look to supernatural remedy, the religious language deployed to identify the Beast's wound is problematic. The wound is inflicted by a "poysonous sting," recalling that of the Dragon of Book I (see I.11.11), and "by no art . . . / It euer can recured be againe." No skill "Can remedy such hurts; such hurts are hellish paine" (6.1). The "ranckling wounds" (6.3) are clearly associated with original sin—"The seede of all this euill first doth spring," and "It neuer rests, till it haue wrought this finall bane" (6.8). And the Beast is said to have diabolic origins—"bred of hellish strene," it is "Begot of foule Echidna," who is "a Monster direfull dred, / Whom Gods doe hate, and heauens abhor to see" (6.9,10). Over this malignity the Hermit appears to triumph. The events of the early episodes are propelled toward his Hermitage, which, along with Mount Acidale, forms the spiritual core of the book—the only time the term *hermitage* is used in the poem outside of Book I, where it designates the dwellings of Archimago and Contemplation. Indeed, these three are the only hermits per se in the poem, and each of them embodies a distinct form of the spiritual life. If Archimago "cursed heauen, and spake reprochfull shame / Of highest God" (I.1.37), and if Contemplation "God . . . often saw from heauens hight" (I.10.47), where, we may ask, does the Hermit of this book locate himself spiritually? Clearly we are meant to align him more closely with Contemplation, if only because both come to the rescue of the spiritually distressed. The Hermit, like Contemplation, has removed himself from the world, but only after a life of heroic action, which he continues to practice in the form of good works—he "could his good to all" (5.36). In the Hermit, we appear to be faced with a specifically religious figure, presented with no irony as a spiritual savior. At first glance it would seem that his job is to provide the expected wisdom of Christian orthodoxy, not unlike the truths Redcrosse was nursed by in the house of Holinesse. As Contemplation leads Redcrosse to a vision of the New Jerusalem and "shewes the way, his sinfull soule to saue" (I.10.51), so we expect this Hermit to seek divine assistance in the recovery of Timias and Serena.

The Hermit quickly disavows himself as the source of their rescue: "in vaine of me ye hope for remedie / And I likewise in vaine doe salues to you applie" (6.6). Nor does he proffer the customary spiritual remedy, faith. Finding that they need "counsell to the minde" (6.5), the Hermit administers a salve that is not salvation:

> For in your selfe your onely helpe doth lie,
>> To heale your selues, and must proceed alone
>> From your owne will, to cure your maladie.
>>> (6.7)

Their wills, then, are not infected but capable of originating a cure. Though the Hermit has denied his healing power, he does serve as a conduit for them to realize their own powers of self-rehabilitation. He exhorts them with a secular homily, as did Calidore to Crudor and Briana—the "holesome reed of sad sobriety" that gives "salues to euery sore, but counsell to the minde" (6.5). The Hermit thus plays the secular counterpart of the Reformation preacher, whose primary function, as we saw in the chapter on Book I, is to provide advice and comfort. The salves he dispenses, like those of his Reformation counterparts, assist in salvation, "As he the art of words knew wondrous well" (6.6). In a stanza abundant in the lexicon of redemption, the Hermit stresses his limited efficacy as a physician and highlights his function as a counselor:

> In vaine therefore it were, with medicine
>> To go about to salue such kynd of sore,
>> That rather needes wise read and discipline,
>> Then outward salues, that may augment it more.
>> Aye me (sayd then *Serena* sighing sore)
>> What hope of helpe doth then for vs remaine,
>> If that no salues may vs to health restore?
>> But sith we need good counsel (sayd the swaine)
> Aread good sire, some counsell, that may vs sustaine.
>>> (6.13)

In a pun calling attention to his affiliations with his preacherly counterparts, the "wise read" the Hermit offers is not, however, the Bible.[33] Nor, in a similar pun, will Scripture prove an "outward salue." Although, like his Reformation contemporaries, he is called upon to save his listener from despair ("What hope of helpe doth then for vs remaine[?]"), his sustaining counsel will not be the good news of Christian redemption. The salve he imparts is a series of non-theological exhortations, including that his listeners "restraine [their] will" (6.14). All his recommendations—abstaining from pleasure, subduing desire, and other curbs and leashes from the fund of Western asceticism—are available to human volition, without necessary recourse to supernatural agency. He promises that human effort will obtain the desired cure, that "shall you soone repair your present euill plight" (6.14). The needed results appear in short order. In the next stanza the afflicted couple "gladly hearken to his graue beheast" and are "throughly heal'd" (6.15).[34] By their "owne will" (6.7) they have repaired their evil plight. Immediately following their recovery, they perform acts of charity ("each the other vow'd t'accompany" Timias because he "Would not her leaue alone in her great need" [6.16])—a sequencing of cause-and-effect homologous to, if not actually a parody of, the Protestant relation between grace and works.

What is the larger meaning of this pivotal episode, toward which many of the preceding have been leading and out of which subsequent ones develop? On the one hand, the Hermit's function in the rehabilitation of Serena and Timias seems consonant with the book's first episode: the fallen agent through an effort of will participates in its own recovery. On the other hand, the Hermit's role in the cure of Serena and Timias seems defiantly indirect. Unlike Calidore in the first episode, the Hermit is less a savior than a channel of their self-induced deliverance. And yet their cure, from a wound emphatically aligned with original sin, is effected explicitly without recourse to the supernatural or its scriptural manifestations. God is not acknowledged, even obliquely, as the source of healing or the salve of the characters' mortal wounds. The Hermit offers a view of human self-sufficiency at odds with contemporary religious understandings on the relation of the will to salvation. No contemporary religious writer, Protestant or Roman Catholic, would assent to the Hermit's dictum that the source of salvation is exclusively the creature's "owne will," implying as it does a Pelagian self-sufficiency contrary to the inheritance of Pauline-Augustinian Christianity. The three hermits of *The Faerie Queene*, each of whom lives in a hermitage hard by a chapel, represent three approaches to the supernatural. Archimago summons diabolical spirits to help corrupt Redcrosse; Contemplation looks heavenward to provide Redcrosse with a vision of his destiny; the Hermit of Book VI looks neither above or below but directs his charges to look within themselves to find their cure in their own will. His portrait is offered without apparent irony, and his cure is efficacious. By midpoint in Book VI, the poem has represented not only Reformed and moderate theologies of the will. The episode with the Hermit also posits a view of human freedom nowhere on the continuum of Reformation (or Roman Catholic or patristic) judgments about the relation of the individual will to providence.

The episode opposing Arthur to Turpine and Blandina, immediately following the interlude with the Hermit, develops the book's rich commentary on free will. It also forms yet another counterpart to the first episode pitting Calidore against Crudor and Briana. Both episodes allegorize, to quite different ends, the human capability of moral regeneration. By the time he confronts Arthur, Turpine has already been exposed as a shameful and wicked knight, the book's chief representative of human malice. In Book V, at his first appearance in *The Faerie Queene*, he has opined about the relation of individual will to fate. In disavowing his own moral responsibility in the earlier episode, he exemplifies a shoddy blame-shifting. Confronted by Artegall with his malfeasance, he "little had for his excuse to say" except this cynical shoulder-shrugging: "who can scape, what his owne fate had wrought? / The worke of heauens will surpasseth humaine thought" (V.4.27). His syntax is delightfully ambiguous: has the agent been the victim of fate, or has he wrought his own fate? Artegall's response captures the difficulty of segregating acts of free will from the impositions of higher powers—and the ease with which we conveniently conflate the two:

> Right true: but faulty men vse oftentimes
> > To attribute their folly vnto fate,
> > And lay on heauen the guilt of their owne crimes.
>
> > > > > (V.4.28)

In Book VI, this dialogue on free will and fate resumes, with Arthur assuming Artegall's earlier role. Arthur confronts Turpine directly twice. In the first encounter he chases Turpine within the walls of his castle but stops short of dispatching him and attends to the pleas of Blandina, "intreating him for grace" (6.31). "Rising vp at last . . . / Like troubled ghost" (6.32), Turpine faces Arthur, who tells him "I much repent, / That euer I this life vnto thee lent" (6.33), guilty as the villain is of "shame," "crime," "wicked custome," and "euill vse" (6.34). Implicitly demanding that Turpine plead for mercy, Arthur declares to have "suffred him this wretched life to liue" (6.36) only because of Blandina's blandishments ("his life he graunted for her loue" [6.37]).

Here Arthur is performing the office Calidore fulfills for Crudor and Briana: he magnanimously spares the life of a shameful wretch. The difference is that Turpine chooses not to repent of his crimes. He does not, that is, participate in his own rehabilitation. His will is shown to be thoroughly debased, despite his opportunity to cooperate in his regeneration. That is the moral point behind subsequent events. Unlike Crudor, who exits the narrative presumably to lead an upright life, Turpine chooses to magnify his turpitude by corrupting two naive young knights to help retaliate against Arthur. As the narrator says in the stanza of instruction separating the two halves of the episode, "the baser mind it selfe displayes / In cancred malice and reuengefull spight." He implies that the will of the "base kind"—one with a "vile donghill mind" (7.1)—is inherently corrupt and impervious even to the offer of life and salvation. Although Turpine has "of the Prince his life receiued late," he willfully ("in his mind") "gan deuize, to be aueng'd anew / For all that shame, which kindled inward hate" (7.3). His malice widens to enmesh his willing young dupes. One of them Arthur quickly dispatches, the other "Cryde aloude for mercie to him saue." This act instantly elicits from Arthur the saving response: "The Prince soon hearkened, and his life forgaue" (7.12). The young knight (we learn later his name is Enias, whom Arthur "did to life restore" [8.3]) shows his repentance by cooperating in the ruse to trap Turpine: "He glad of life, and willing eke to wreake / The guilt on him, which did this mischiefe breed" (7.13). His will now properly rehabilitated, Enias helps to see that Turpine is "deliuered to his punishment" (7.21). Even when Turpine tries to rekindle Enias's animosity against Arthur,

the gentle knight
Would not be tempted to such villenie,
Regarding more his faith, which he did plight.
(7.23)

Enias's is a case of an agent whose will collaborates fully in its rehabilitation and who proves his "faith" by his deeds. Arthur then does the duty of the justiciar, though a clement one: "holding vp his hands, with silence mercie pray[ing]" (7.25), Turpine is spared an execution in favor of a mere baffling.

The episode presents two instances of the fallen will, Enias and Turpine. Enias's restoration allegorizes a view of the will a moderate Protestant would smile on. Turpine, on the other hand, exemplifies a will unalterably debauched and impervious to salvific might. Even when given multiple opportunities to rehabilitate himself, he only deepens his perfidy, dragging others down with him. One foul deed leads inexorably to the next, and no amount of correction will save him from further spite. The best to be done is to render him harmless. But he is not, it is important to note, "damned"—if by that we mean killed. His punishment is mild, nearly unprecedentedly so, and though the most persistent (human) malefactor of this book, he receives a peculiarly lenient punishment. If we place this episode among Reformation discourses of salvation, as its lexical resources invite us to do, we do not find the universal emphasis on damnation and eternal punishment (presumably Turpine's bafflement is temporary). This book of the poem neither speculates on the afterlife of its characters nor judges them as unforgivingly as the previous books often do. It accepts the facts of human failure and yokes those facts to the will, as outlined in contemporary theological discourse. It does not, however, present human nature in terms identical to either the moderate or the Reformed positions. Rather it dramatizes those discourses in a way that gradually demonstrates the inadequacy of both in amply comprehending the subtleties of human character.

The episodes of Mirabella and Serena among the salvage nation develop the pattern even as they complicate it. The two episodes function as twin examples of the fallen will. They also dramatize how the will responds to the peculiarly gendered conditions each episode enacts. Both characters are presented according to highly charged gender assumptions: Mirabella as the proud fair, Serena as the object of literal male depredation. Both characters are constructed as objects of male desire, and both suffer as a result of their beauty. Their stories, then, raise thorny questions about the will and its relation to destruction and salvation.

More than a canto before the poet takes up Mirabella's story, he forecasts that hers will be a tale of "shame" (aligning her with Turpine) and speaks of "how thereof her selfe she did acquite" (6.17), hinting that, like others in this book, she will prove at least partly responsible for her own rescue. Like others, she seems to have fallen from a state of grace—in this case "beauties grace" (8.2). Hers is an "Ensample" of one who "from the high degree of happy state, / Fell into wretched woes, which she repented late" (8.2). Her self-acquit-tal, when it is fully revealed, is highly ambiguous and challenges earlier assertions of human self-sufficiency and the power of the will to do good. Mirabella's background is twice recounted, first by the narrator (7.27–38), later by Mirabella to Arthur (8.19–24). In the first version, we are told that "She was borne free" and "so would euer liue" (7.30) had not her "pride" (7.29,30,32,38, 8.1) in her beauty brought her to Cupid's court. The narrative is unclear about the exact nature of her malefaction and the degree to which she is responsible. Although she is condemned for her cruelty to men smitten by her beauty, the narrative gives little indication of the degree to which her will is complicitous in her "crymes" (7.35). Is she condemned for being beautiful? She is said to be "proud and insolent" (7.29). What does her pride consist in? At her trial witnesses claim that "they were all betrayd / And murdred cruelly by a rebellious Mayd" (7.34), but no evidence is given of her active vice. Although the text relies here upon Petrarchan *topoi* to insinuate her crimes rather than to name them, it is notable that, in a text as permeated as this book with the discourse of moral responsibility, Mirabella's failure remains not merely vague but unspecified. Her "pride," so relentlessly reiterated, has none of the concrete referents that term has elsewhere in the book. She is nonetheless condemned and sentenced to atone—exactly like other characters in the book who are given the chance to rehabilitate themselves. Mirabella consents to be punished by wandering with the Carle and the foole, "Till she had sau'd so many loues, as she did lose" (7.37). But far from being able to cooperate in her eventual regeneration, Mirabella, unlike previous characters, proves wholly unsuccessful in fulfilling her penance.[35] In fact, by the time she enters this book's action, she is inflicting even greater harm (again, through no discernible fault of her own) by her indirect responsibility for Timias's "fall" (7.50) at the hands of Disdaine. Allegorically, she can be said to be responsible for this adversity—Disdaine being an allegorized projection of Mirabella's treatment of her suitors—but Disdaine is her tormentor as well as Timias's (7.44). Mirabella brings suffering to others, for which she is held accountable, though the extent to which her will conspires in these disasters remains uncertain. Unlike previous episodes, the first half of her story has not clarified her moral culpability but rather has muddled its extent.

In detailing for Arthur her own story in the next canto, Mirabella more fully implicates herself. "I triumphed long in louers paine," she admits, and "Did laugh at those that did lament and plaine" (8.21). Although one may question the seriousness of this crime, Arthur pronounces her punishment just. Earlier examples in this book suggest that her regeneration may now begin, for she has admitted wrongdoing. Furthermore she is "touched with compassion entire" (8.3) at Disdaine's defeat of Timias—"That for her sake fell into misery" (8.3)—suggesting that her insolent pride has been broken. But neither of these mitigations appears sufficient to warrant her reprieve. Indeed she is given the chance to end her punishment by no less an authority than Arthur himself:

> Now Lady sith your fortunes thus dispose,
> That if ye list haue liberty, ye may,
> Vnto your selfe I freely leaue to chose,
> Whether I shall you leaue, or from these villaines lose.
>   (8.29)

She elects, though, to "fulfill / This penaunce" (8.30), a choice that taxes interpretation. On the one hand, she can be seen as freely choosing an atonement Cupid has earlier imposed, that is, freely participating in her own rehabilitation. By this reckoning, even Arthur's exoneration is insufficient for her full regeneration. On the other, the text could be seen, as Ann Shaver has suggested, as acting out the inequities of a patriarchal system that more amply punishes women for their failures, even when those failures seem relatively less serious than those of men.[36] In either event, Mirabella does not, as had been initially forecast, "her selfe . . . acquite" (6.17). Nor does Arthur, as the argument to this canto has promised, truly "Quite . . . Mirabell from dreed." She leaves the narrative as she entered it, enslaved to her chastisement despite her professions of remorse and her "compassion" for those who suffer—both signs elsewhere in this book of moral regeneration and signs of the agent's participation in his or her own restoration to wholeness. Mirabella's story may simply indicate the boundaries of patriarchy delimiting this text. It also serves to cast doubt on the autonomy of one's "owne will" and the availability of redemption to the agent herself.

Alternatively, Mirabella's refusal to accept Arthur's offer of freedom could paradoxically emphasize her freedom. Although she believes herself to be enslaved, she chooses her own imprisonment at the hands of her tormentors. The text is not entirely clear here. It does not give definitive judgments on whether Mirabella is choosing appropriately in refusing Arthur's proffered freedom. Is she demonstrating free will by accepting full penance for her "crymes"? Or is she demonstrating a psychic enslavement by mistakenly thinking herself doomed to eternal punishment? The answer may depend on how we take Mirabella's response to Arthur's offer of freedom:

> Ah nay Sir Knight (sayd she) it may not be,
>> But that I needes must by all meanes fulfill
>> This penaunce, which enioyned is to me,
>> Least vnto me betide a greater ill;
>> Yet no lesse thankes to you for your good will.
>>> (8.30)

Is this acknowledgment of Arthur's "good will" a denial of her own free will? What exactly is the "greater ill" she fears? Damnation? Or is her refusal rather a paradoxical demonstration of free will—she chooses to be in thrall—and an accurate recognition of deficiency and the need for recompense? We are not told.

Mirabella's story is paired in the same canto with that of Serena and the salvage nation.[37] If Mirabella's punishment outweighs her crime, Serena's suffering (it cannot be termed a punishment) seems altogether capricious. Her tale seems egregious in a book hitherto presenting examples of willful misdeeds and their aftermath. Serena is the wholly passive victim of violence so deep that it cannot be redeemed. The term *saluage* is painfully ironic. Unlike the salvage man, the salvage nation salvage no one and have nothing salvageable about them. They are presented rather as a brute and alien force worthy only of being extinguished. Their "diuelish ceremonies" (8.45) suggest an evil so abhorrent as to be irredeemable. Their raison d'être is to "eate the flesh of men" (8.36), a kind of destructiveness that repulsively parodies the salvaging held forth elsewhere in the book as virtuous. As they leer lasciviously at her nakedness, they debase Serena into a grotesque object of lust, one whose "dainty flesh" (8.38) becomes "like an Altar . . . / To offer sacrifice diuine thereon" (8.42). Furthermore, their stripping of Serena and their cataloging of her "goodly threasures" (8.41) hideously parody the Petrarchan blazon. Serena's role is to serve as sacrifice, to both lust and cannibalism simultaneously.

The text gives no indication of her malfeasance, and of course she is hardly deserving of the enormity visited upon her.[38] Yet she is linked with Mirabella by more than the proximity of their stories.

Serena is separated from Calepine upon their meeting with Mirabella. Indeed her flight has an intimate allegorical link to Mirabella, specifically to her tormentors, Scorne and Disdaine:

> When first the gentle Squire at variaunce fell
> With those two Carles, [Serena] fled fast away, afeard
> Of villany to be to her inferd.
>
> (8.31)

Serena's fear of inflicted villainy is not further specified, but there are several possibilities. She may fear accusation of Mirabella's "crimes," rightfully or not; she may fear Mirabella's punishment, warranted or not; she may fear becoming like Mirabella, justifiably or not. All three possibilities are those of her gender, and all three possibilities are independent of a woman's choice. Serena's victimhood on the cannibals' altar, then, may allegorically be justified independently of her will. Her will is irrelevant to her victimizing by "fortune blynde" (8.36).

Perhaps, then, her function in this book *is* similar to Mirabella's. Both are sacrifices in the name of authority. Neither thinks of herself as an agent able to accept freedom when it is offered. Serena, of course, is the unequivocal victim of organized violence (a "nation") wishing to devour her flesh. Mirabella is also victimized by a Petrarchan discourse that objectifies the flesh of women and then sacrifices their bodies on its altars. The salvage nation believe Serena "by grace of God . . . there was sent," and so they wish to sacrifice her "guiltlesse bloud" and "dainty flesh" (8.38). The altar of the salvage nation has its institutional counterpart in Cupid's court. Both institutions have the effect of robbing the female characters of their will and making them sacrificial victims of male appetite. Mirabella may or may not be complicitous in her punishment; Serena is emphatically not. In both cases they are freed by male liberators—and with ambiguous results. Arthur offers Mirabella a freedom she refuses: her collaboration with the sources of her torment continues after her exit from the poem. Serena is freed more radically by Calepine, who, acting as an apocalyptic figure with "wrathfull hand," sends "swarmes of damned soules to hell" (8.49). But like Mirabella, Serena continues to feel guilty. Her nakedness is a source of shame to her, as though an emblem of her own transgression:

> So inward shame of her vncomely case
> She did conceiue, through care of womanhood,

> That through the night did couer her disgrace,
> Yet she in so vnwomanly a mood,
> Would not bewray the state in which she stood.
>
> (8.51)

Her "womanhood" is here aligned with her "shame," and her "disgrace" (her naked flesh) an index of her "state."[39] Like Mirabella she feels responsible for her degradation, in both cases peculiarly associated with gender. Though faultless, Serena responds to her liberation as Mirabella has to hers: a deepening of guilt and moral responsibility, though understandable as the reaction of a modest virgin to a violent assault. In Serena's case we see both the objective falsity and psychological realism of her assuming her own guilt and "shame." The ambiguity of her mistake reflects on Mirabella's story—with what irony the reader is free to choose.

The pastoral episodes and their aftermath challenge earlier representations of the will and demand a stricter accounting of the various positions that have been dramatized. In the last four cantos fortune more powerfully determines the characters' lives. Indeed the book changes its complexion rather markedly. Pastoral romance seems to have encouraged a leisure somewhat at odds with the mood in most of the rest of the poem. Generic conventions and stock figures (e.g., rural games, the *senex*, the lost infant, marauders) seem to have invited the poet to change his customarily dense allegory and to employ the broad brush befitting pastoral romance. Hence the deepened insistence on the power of fortune, one of the genre's abiding *topoi*.[40] These episodes elaborate the book's interrogation of the will, only to accent more prominently external limitations on its freedom. Frederick Kiefer's observation about the anomalous relation of providence to fortune often seen in Spenser's work is keenly felt in the final cantos: fortune seems to be both the executrix of providence and a "force of wanton destruction" antithetical to providential purposes.[41] These episodes, then, interlace contemporary religious polemic more audaciously than earlier cantos and so consummate Spenser's engagement with the discourses of Reformation England.

   These issues find a locus in Calidore's conversation with Meliboe, the chief spokesman of pastoral values and a figure of considerable complexity and controversy. Their great dialogue centers on the relation of the will to fortune. As he begins, Calidore sets the terms of the discussion by confusing happiness with freedom, for he considers happiness as something given rather than chosen. He commends the happy state by which Meliboe can lead "a life so free and fortunate," a pairing suggesting his equation of the two terms. Calidore thinks that the pastoral life is somehow exempt from "warres, and wreckes, and wicked enmite" and so allows more freedom. (Events, of course, will prove him wrong.) Yet his wish that his "lot were plast in such felicitie" (9.19), implying a passive receptivity to fortune, implicitly denies the very freedom he praises. Meliboe tries to clarify the difference. He is happy, he explains, because of choices he makes:

> If happie, then it is in this intent,
> That hauing small, yet doe I not complaine
> Of want, nor wish for more it to augment,
> But doe my self, with that I haue, content.
> (9.20)

Through efforts of his will—his "intent" to "doe my self" and "not complaine"—Meliboe forges his own happiness, which he ascribes to internal self-sufficiency: "So taught of nature, which doth litle need / Of forreine helpes to lifes due nourishment" (9.20). The autonomy he extols is grounded in freedom, primarily from enslavement to the worldly success he had once sought in "roiall court," where "I did sell my selfe" (9.24). Freeing himself from those circumstances has led to his present happiness, but he carefully differentiates the two terms. With one eye upon Pastorella and one on the serenity of his surroundings, Calidore seems not to grasp the distinction Meliboe makes between happiness and freedom, but continues to praise the pastoral life as though it were an inherent condition. Meliboe's autobiography, of course, has made precisely the opposite point, namely that he has chosen pastoral contentment. But Calidore fails to grasp this detail and persists in regarding happiness as granted, not chosen:

> [I] wish the heauens so much had graced mee,
> As graunt me liue in like condition;
> Or that my fortunes might transposed bee
> From pitch of higher place, vnto this low degree.
> (9.28)

Against this determinism Meliboe again tries to make headway and so outlines his famous statement of autonomy. People mistakenly the "heauens of their fortunes fault accuse," for "each hath his fortune in his brest" (9.29):

It is the mynd, that maketh good or ill,
>   That maketh wretch or happie, rich or poore:
>   For some, that hath abundance at his will,
>   Hath not enough, but wants in greater store;
>   And other, that hath litle, askes no more.
>   (9.30)

Meliboe focuses the issue squarely on the will, much as the Hermit had earlier: "It is the mynd, that maketh good or ill." Happiness is available to each "at his will." Even if, as one commentator has re-marked,[42] Meliboe means merely that one must be satisfied with one's station in life ("all contented rest / With what they hold" [9.29]), Meliboe advances an argument for free will. One chooses contentment. It is in this sense that "each vnto himself his life may fortunize" (9.30).

Meliboe's words have occasioned considerable critical disagree-ment. Is he, in advocating an acceptance of one's station in life, a model of humility and self-sufficiency?[43] Is he a spokesman for Boethian transcendence of fortune by means of inner tranquility and indifference to outer hazard?[44] Or is he a deluded escapist?[45] Each of these positions has merit or at least plausibility. But none speaks cen-trally to Meliboe's role as a spokesman for free will. Some condemn Meliboe on the grounds that he is somehow responsible for Cal-idore's abandonment of his quest, although Meliboe gives the knight no advice on the issue, and leaves the matter for Calidore to decide on his own.[46] It is certainly possible, as William Nelson notes, that Calidore misinterprets Meliboe's advice and takes "his instruction as warrant for electing what 'fortune' he wishes."[47] That has not been Meliboe's point—he has suggested not that one can choose fortune but simply that one has choices. Happiness may or may not follow, but the sequelae do not diminish the initial freedom. The wise soul then stoically chooses how to respond to the events fortune sends. Furthermore, Meliboe's death at the hands of the Brigants, agents of fortune if ever there were, cannot be seen to undermine his position on human freedom. Meliboe does not claim that one can guarantee happiness; he simply makes a case for free will in response to vicissi-tude. His biography, like that of most of us, comprises a mixture of good fortune and bad, none of which contradicts his thesis that he has choices.

But let us for the moment grant that Meliboe's argument is weak-ened by his later calamities or even by Calidore's misuse of his instruction to justify abandoning his quest. Are not these instances exactly in keeping with the ways the issue of free will is presented elsewhere in this book? The text consistently refuses to take a stand in the debate between free will and determinism. The very existence of the multiple glosses on his statements would indicate that Meliboe is a deliberately ambiguous figure. Calidore, like other characters, speaks as though he believes his will is constrained. And to some extent, of course, these characters are correct in that notion: fortune does constrain human freedom—and freedom is, after all, a feeling as well as a fact. But if we take Mirabella and now Calidore himself in his debate with Meliboe as cases in point, we can say that the will is actually not as constricted as these characters seem to believe it is. External confinements hamper every human will. But inner constraints—in the form, that is, of an inescapable propensity for wickedness—may not permanently impair the will. The Reformed Protestant looks primarily at internal bondage, the human compulsion to sin. And the text provides trenchant examples of fallen, seemingly irredeemable characters, notably in Turpine and the salvage nation. The moderate Protestant finds characters capable of restoring themselves (with help from a hero). The text inscribes the issue of free will, but that fact does not mean the text endorses one or the other side in the controversy. The dialogue between Calidore and Meliboe opens up the issue further without necessarily advocating a partisan position or ready answers to the problem of the will.

Something similar may be said of the Graces on Mount Acidale. One reason critics have had difficulty in pinning down their nature and what they are said to "grant" is the inclusiveness and open-endedness of their iconography and other signification—what Isabel MacCaffrey has termed their "unconstrained giving and undeserved receiving."[48] They "*all* gifts of grace do graunt" (10.15; emphasis added), an adjectival accentuation suggesting the comprehensiveness of their gifts. Colin Clout's description of the epiphany the Graces offer hints at the elusive relation of the individual will to external forces, a relation limned in their fleeting appearance: "For being gone, none can them bring in place, / But whom they of them selues list so to grace" (10.20). Are the Graces the embodiment of providence? Fortune? Humphrey Tonkin states aptly what other critics imply, that the term *graces* embraces and does not exclude the theological meaning of the term.[49] Book VI resists restricted theologizing.

In previous episodes, grace, the theological concept, is not the explicit source of good works or rehabilitation, but explicitness may be beside the point in Book VI. Good works derive from within the mind, from somewhere within humanity, but that does not exclude their origin elsewhere as well.

The adventures immediately following the appearance of the Graces corroborate these points. Like the Beast or the salvage nation, the tiger that bursts upon the *locus amoenus* is figured as yet another source of evil: a "feend" (10.35) with jaws "wide gaping like hell gate" (10.34). Calidore's rescue of Pastorella—his "comming to her ayde" (10.35)—illustrates the human will bringing good into the world, just the role Calidore plays in the early cantos. But the will cannot fully overcome the turns of fortune now, after the vision of the Graces, anymore than earlier. Though Calidore bests the tiger, three stanzas later he is powerless against the Brigants, if only because "It fortuned" (10.39) that he is absent when they invade. Like Serena among the salvage nation, Pastorella is captive to the Brigants through no fault of her own and certainly not as a punishment for wrongdoing. Yet she thinks "herself in hell, / Where with such damned fiends she should in darknesse dwell" (10.43). Like Serena, she is rather a "lucklesse mayd" (10.40), a victim of "fortune fraught with malice, blind, and brute" (10.38). Book VI never denies the existence of evil, of course, and it does not hesitate to assign evil to the human heart. But it just as often and just as powerfully locates evil outside the human will in the amoral condition of "mortall wretchednesse" (11.1). As the final cantos demonstrate, this book is ruled by "worldly chaunces," for "here on earth is no sure happinesse" (11.1). The emphasis is on "sure," for happiness is available, often through efforts of the will and perhaps through the intervention of providence. That is part of Meliboe's point about fortunizing one's life, and the narrative has often testified to his accuracy.

But the episode of Pastorella among the Brigants also gainsays Meliboe's position on free will. The poet's change of focus to Pastorella ("Faire *Pastorell*, of whom is now my song" [11.2]) provides an excellent example of a will confronting forces beyond its control. In "hellish dens . . . / Wrapped in wretched cares and hearts vnrest," Pastorella (11.3) is subjugated both to fortune and to the will of the Brigant captain (she fears that "his lust [would] make his will his law" [11.6]). Her adroit exploitation of the captain's affections indirectly leads to her being spared by the merchants, but that seeming assertion of her will in turn leads only to a kind of second death. When the surviving Brigants "call the soule backe to her home againe" (11.22) by reviving Pastorella after the merchants' invasion of their camp, they have "saued her from dying, / Renew'd her death by timely death denying" (11.23)—a kind of eternal death, a "wretched thraldome" (11.24) that reiterates her loss of freedom and her loss of life. The text takes great effort to reinforce its saws about fortune's ability to exacerbate "mortall wretchednesse."

As long as the poet concentrates upon Pastorella, any advocacy of free will seems feeble. She differs from most earlier figures in the book by having no moral responsibility attached to her story. Like Serena among the salvage nation, she exemplifies victimhood and bears no liability for her suffering. The Hermit's advice to Serena and Timias about curing their wounds by means of "wise read and discipline" rather than "outwarde salues" (6.13) hardly applies to Pastorella's various mortal scrapes. In every case, she not only needs an "outward salue" but is quite bereft without one. External "thraldomes" enslave her will. To talk of free will in Pastorella's case is almost meaningless. She is trapped in a kind of carceral economy that reflects back upon other depictions of human freedom. Her misadventures may give the lie retrospectively to Meliboe's apothegm that "each vnto himselfe his life may fortunize" (9.30)—a dictum whose validity Meliboe's own miserable end may already have made problematic. Surely she cannot, as Meliboe had recommended,

> doe my self, with what I haue, content;
> So taught of nature, which doth litle need
> Of forreine helpes to lifes due nourishment.
> (9.20)

Her father's stoic wisdom now seems like smugness, for Pastorella is much in need of "forreine helpes." Pastorella's mishaps, then, force us yet again to recognize how this book consistently refuses to be pinned down on the contemporary debates it interrogates. Although she has manipulated the Brigant captain, she still languishes in want of whatever aid fortune—or providence, or human good will—may extend.

Calidore, too, undergoes a kind of death at the news of Pastorella's presumed death, for his "hart quite deaded was with anguish great" and "death it selfe vnto himselfe did threate" (11.33). But through an effort of will he determines to act: "in his mind with better reason cast, / How he might saue her life, if life did last" (11.34). Here Calidore exerts his rational and physical powers to overcome what seems inevitable, the power of fortune and human wretchedness. He pierces through Coridon's equivocating announcement of Pastorella's death ("I saw faire *Pastorella* dye" [11.29], says Coridon, and "needs mote she die at last" [11.31]). Calidore will not accept Coridon's fatalism. Instead he asserts his will to "saue her life." Hence he can search out Pastorella "with God before" (11.36)—an emblematic parenthesis that hints at the mystery (or is it uncertainty?) of the relation of the will to the supernatural. Does God's protection follow from the agent's assertion of free will? Or does God lead the agent? Certainly Calidore's choice serves the good. His will is not altogether enslaved to any malevolent force, within or without. He no longer confuses happiness and fortune but takes steps to overcome what seems inevitable, to exert his will and bring about his own happiness. Like Arthur harrowing Orgoglio's dungeon, Calidore invades the "hellish dens" (11.41) of the Brigants and "with huge resistlesse might, / The dores assayled, and the locks vpbrast" (11.43). He resuscitates Pastorella, giving her "life to feele, that long for death had sought" (11.45). Calidore's will overcomes fortune.

The final canto rehearses yet another of Pastorella's resurrections (two, in fact: her rescue as an infant and her return to her parents as an adult.) Here, as the opening of this chapter has suggested, the relation of human will to external forces is delineated one last time. What may we say now in the light of this chapter's argument? Melissa leaves the abandoned infant abroad and hides behind a bush "To weet what mortall hand, or heauens grace / Would for the wretched infants helpe prouyde" (12.8). The juxtaposition of the two terms is teasing. Is Pastorella saved here (and elsewhere) by the hand of human effort or "heauens grace"? She has needed one or both at various points in her biography, and she indeed may have been the happy recipient of one or both.

This is exactly the point, and it has been the point throughout the book. The text does not polemicize about the operations of providence or fortune and their relation to the human will. That relation remains mysterious, at the end as at the beginning. And so Pastorella's rescues are ascribed in the recognition scene to various sources: human will ("mortall hand"), providence ("heauens grace"), fortune. Hence Melissa can decree that "high God did saue" (11.17) Pastorella and can tell Claribell that "the heauens had her graste, / To saue her chylde," a child who had also been consigned to "misfortunes mouth" (11.16). These forces have been at work throughout the book, and their relation to the will remains as enigmatic at the end as at the beginning. The issue of free will is this book's inscription of the inscrutable relation of human effort to the workings of forces beyond human control, be they providential or fortunate. At times the book suggests that events are often entirely within the bounds of human volition. The text engages the debate about free will as a means of dramatizing the characters' consuming struggles. It interrogates contemporary debates about free will less as a means of advancing a view than one of allegorizing the complexities of the issues.

Certainly the book's ending hardly encourages a partisan position. The issue of free will is not to be found in Calidore's provisional conquest of the Beast. Hamilton notes that this is Calidore's third and final victory over the forces of hell (the first two being the tiger and the Brigants), and indeed the "hellish Beast" (12.32) is portrayed as a "feend" (12.31) and "hell-borne" (12.32). This last is also figured as an apocalyptic triumph, for the Beast has a "blasphemous tong" (12.34) and is responsible for unleashing all manner of evil into the world. Just as the book opens with a refashioning of the Fall, so it closes with a refashioning of apocalypse—and a refashioning of the apocalyptic features of the previous book. Michael-like, Calidore wields his "fatall hand" (12.25) to suppress the Beast. But as in Book V, the victory is temporary, and apocalypse is postponed. Responsibility for the Beast's enlargement is ambiguously assigned as the book closes: "whether wicked fate so framed, / Or fault of men, he broke his iron chaine" (12.38).[50] Is the willful "fault of men" the source of evil, or is that source some larger extrinsic force, our "wicked fate"? We are no more certain of the issue now than earlier.

Conclusion

"We are no more certain of the issue now than earlier." This cannot, I hope, be said of this study's argument, though it applies to much of what I have claimed about Reformation belief in *The Faerie Queene*. This book has maintained that to be fully understood for its cultural and literary significance "the Reformation" needs to be regarded not merely as a body of belief but also as an intertextual confederation. Its net was so expansive, its grasp upon the culture so secure, that to fathom the comprehensive role of the Reformation in early modern culture requires expanding our conception of the domain of religion. To see how widely one (admittedly capacious) literary text inscribes the Reformation is to witness how the period's religious discourses permeate works of art produced merely in their proximity. It is also to sense tangibly the tensions and contradictions of the Reformation. It may now be helpful to press some of the implications that the foregoing chapters have been working out. Doing so will serve as both a summation and a prolegomenon to further inquiry about the relation of other Renaissance English texts to the Reformation.

Current scholarly conversation is only beginning to appreciate the negotiations between religion and literary texts. It appears that we are launching on a new course in early modern studies as we reassess the discursive role of religion.[1] We will, I believe, have to reconceptualize the relations of religious and literary discourses as we comprehend both the rich diversity of religious textuality in the period and its presence, often submerged, in canonical literary texts. Such a reformulation will help avoid pitfalls of the two major approaches of literary scholarship to religion in the period. The polite, and sometimes not so polite, ignoring of religion by recent literary historicizing on the one hand is counterposed on the other by earlier generations' searches for religious sources.[2] This book has suggested a middle way. We need to stake out the sites of religion in Renaissance canonical texts, no longer by source-hunting, as scholarship has chiefly done, or by dismissing "belief" as outside the sphere of critical inquiry. As different as these two approaches are in methodology and philosophical supposition about textuality, they are alike in treating religion principally as doctrine, as a frame of belief needing assent or repudiation, whether by writer or reader. To see doctrine alone as manifesting religion overlooks some of the deepest structures and profoundest features of cultural discourse. It undervalues what social historians of religion have long recognized, namely that the Reformation must be understood as a broadly cultural phenomenon.[3] Hypothesizing how the author or the text supports or denies tenets of belief risks overlooking how religion saturates early modern literary discourse, even when the text seems far removed from concerns about sin, death, and salvation. This study has instead proposed that we examine the diversified and numinous intertextual presence of religious discourses within literary texts quite apart from any claims of truth those discourses might be making on either reader or writer. If we do so, we see religion not only as a body of belief to be accepted or disavowed but also as an interpretive structure playing its part among other intertextual structures, merging with them and helping to fashion the work of art. We may more readily explore how religion is integrated into canonical literature in ways not previously seen when we treated religion primarily as theology. We will more ably grasp religion's role in forming cultural identity as we recognize the penetration of religion into the seemingly discrete discursive domains of the period.

In one of those domains is Spenser's allegory. *The Faerie Queene* slowly accumulates and absorbs and restructures not one but a variety of beliefs, values, texts, and lexical usages—in short, discourses—that "the Reformation" made available to it. The poem slowly gathers a multiform discursive identity. We can more fully recover this identity by seeing that the lineaments of its Reformation intertextuality are not easily restricted to a single doctrinal position. That identity is not, then, fixed but instead generates evolving models and stages. To trace the presence of Reformed religion in *The Faerie Queene* helps to break down some of the boundaries long demarcating Spenser studies and Renaissance studies generally. To track the Reformation as an intertextual organization within the poem and to discern the poem within the intertextual web of the Reformation is further to dissolve the apparent autonomy of the text. Enlarging our view of the role of religion by seeing it as cultural material that, to use Greenblatt's phrase, "is transferred from one discursive sphere to another and becomes aesthetic property" sharpens our sense of the fragility of these boundaries.[4] To segregate discourses impedes our recovery of a text (and a period) in which religious and literary cultures remain raveled. This study has argued that we misread both *The Faerie Queene* and other early modern literary texts if we misprize these discursive overlaps. We cannot get at what religion means in Spenser's poem or in the period if we confine our understanding of religion to doctrine. Instead I have argued that the intertextual role of Reformation discourses—shifting, acquiring different meanings over the poem's long course—reveals a profound indeterminacy and cultural instability.

This study has also proceeded on the conviction that intertextuality, rather than filiation, reveals the poem's wonderful synthesizing of discourses. We have long celebrated Spenser's "syncretism," often without a developed understanding of what the concept means. To recognize more fully the intertextual position of *The Faerie Queene* within Reformation discourses expands our understanding of that syncretism and allows us to explore the poem's cultural inclusiveness. Embedding the poem in Reformation materials allows us to see that the poem's relation to the Reformation is more complex and vastly more interesting than negotiation with a body of doctrine. That is partly why this book does not argue "Spenser's" partisanship to a set of adherent beliefs. Asking, for example, "Was Spenser a Calvinist?" limits inquiry, at least as far as determining the full presence of religion in his texts is concerned. Like Shakespeare's plays, *The Faerie Queene* will not yield, without fundamentally eliding the presence of contradictory or complementary evidence, a single doctrinal partisanship.[5] More important, the text's relation to the Reformation is freighted with more significance—and signification—than partisan religious allegiance, signification that is part of its cultural identity.

Much of this identity early modern studies is starting to recognize as "nonauthorial," that is, as produced by a variety of hands or the result of multiple texts and circumstances. For example, the correspondences we have begun to see between "prayerful performances" and literary discourse, particularly the soliloquy and the lyric, can only extend our understanding of this identity.[6] So, too, the vast and underinvestigated relation of much Renaissance literary discourse, including *The Faerie Queene*, to the Bible and Reformation hermeneutics.[7] Or the application to literary texts of the discourse of martyrdom initiated by John Foxe's *Acts and Monuments*.[8] The most prominent of these nonauthorial discourses for the present study has been homily, whose place in early modern culture has been greatly neglected by literary scholars, despite its ubiquity.[9] Every English person living in the Reformation heard or read homilies regularly, indeed incessantly, throughout his or her lifetime. Homilies were prescribed and regularized. They were both nationally uniform and individualized by the preacher. They were written, collected, printed, and read; they were spoken, heard, and digested (or forgotten). Readers annotated them, and auditors memorized them. Commentators codified and classified them by subgenre, and rhetoricians dissected them for remodeling. They were the one art form—and the one form of learning—that every person in Reformation England, educated or not, witnessed. Fusing art, rhetoric, and religion, sermons were models of social discourse charged with aesthetic energies. As political discourse, furthermore, they helped cement the national church's claim to its authority, even when they were crafted by individual preachers, parish by parish. The place of the pulpit, then, in the textual formation of the period and its cultural self-identity was necessarily huge.[10] But homily remains underexplored in early modern studies, despite recent efforts to understand circulations among works of art and the institutions and practices of society. This book has begun to investigate the intersection of homily and one canonical text, although I am under no illusion that the homiletic reservoirs surrounding and nourishing that text have here been drained. The boundaries between homily and *The Faerie Queene* remain vacillating and permeable, as they are between homiletic and much literary discourse of the period. The vastness of sermon discourse alone makes it worth our attention, and its universal access within early modern culture makes opening this territory imperative. That much of this access was auditory—at least initially, almost all access was auditory, though ours must of course be exclusively written—makes assessment of its place in canonical literature challenging, all the more so given how much sermon discourse remains unavailable outside major library collections. But as our recovery of such non-authorial discourse grows, so too will our understanding of its sites in canonical texts.

A series of those sites, as this study has shown, is found in the various homilies enacted throughout *The Faerie Queene*. How often advice of a decidedly homiletic cast is dispensed in the course of the action, and how carefully that advice-giving conforms to the prescribed features of Reformation homily. Each book of the poem features a representative homilist, a figure whose homiletic speech distills that book's chief preoccupations. To trace sermon activity from book to book of *The Faerie Queene* reveals how homiletic collides with other discursive spheres. We can also see how the poem critiques its kidnapped discourses, to use Berger's provocative term yet again, and so encourages textual interrogation. Let us briefly single out one preacherly character from each book, one key figure who illustrates the role of homily in that book. To chart such figures over the six completed books reveals a pattern not merely of homily in the poem. It also reveals a developing pattern toward Reformation religion. In other words, if we look serially at homiletic figures from book to book, we can learn a good deal about *The Faerie Queene* as a cultural artifact. We see how religious discourse intermingles with other discourses and becomes the text's aesthetic property. And we see how religion changes in the poem—a change, I conclude, that is part of larger cultural transformations.

Contemplation acts as protopreacher for both Book I and the entire poem. His dark counterpart in Book II is Mammon. If Contemplation is the poem's supreme homilist, Mammon is its homiletic parodist par excellence. Together these two figures erect the chief homiletic pillars of *The Faerie Queene*. As paradigmatic preachers—one genuine, the other ironic—they activate several homiletic subgenres. By focusing their forensic energies so squarely on the hero's mission, they show how sermon discourse contours other discourses in the first two books of the poem. Each homilist encounters the hero at a pivotal point in his quest. Their chief persuasive mechanism is homily—or, in Mammon's case, parody of homily. Both reproduce several subgenres of sermon (doctrinal, redargutive, persuasible, and so forth), all focused on the hero's quest—in Contemplation's case, to assist; in Mammon's case, to subvert. Within their homilies are gathered a variety of discourses, all converging on the hero's mission.

Contemplation's homiletic assurance of Redcrosse's "blessed end" (I.10.61) brings together apocalypse and nationalistic propaganda, not to mention medieval mystical discourse, with its goal of perfection by stages, and Aristotelian emphasis on action.[11] Mammon's parodic homily to Guyon, in contrast, contaminates the discourses of epic (the hero's visit to the underworld), Scripture (Christ's temptation in the wilderness), and scriptural commentary.[12] Like the books of *The Faerie Queene* in which they appear, these principal homilists present religious discourses straightforwardly and recognizably. Even Mammon's distortions of preaching and hermeneutics leave no doubt that when these homilists preach, the text is sheltered by the aegis of religion.

Later books of *The Faerie Queene*, however, displace homily from the hero's quest and so inscribe homiletic discourse less visibly. The decentering of homily in these books corresponds to the changing role of the Reformation in the structure of the work as a whole. As the poem seems to shift ever more distantly from its Reformation bedrock, it stands in more puzzling and uncertain relation to that grounding. It assumes a more challenging affiliation with the Reformation. We may easily see these changes in the poem's treatment of religion by noting the role of homily first in the central books and then in the final books.

Glauce delivers an important homily in each of the central books, but they are homilies nearly drained of theology. In addition Glauce's gender helps disguise or disperse the sermon rhetoric she deploys. In the mouth of a female (and minor) character, homiletic discourse is barely audible. In Book III, enjoining Britomart to repress "filthy lust" (2.40), Glauce preaches a persuasible sermon, to forgo some course of action.[13] Her sermon taps Reformation discourses of marriage and sexuality, which are part of a larger cultural discourse of love, seen most notably in Petrarchan conventions. She also assures Britomart that "ioy . . . haue thou and eternall blis" (2.42), a statement that sounds like classic homiletic assurance. In the recognition scene between Britomart and Artegall in Book IV, Glauce again plays an authoritative advisory role: "she gan wisely all vpknit" (6.30). She urges Artegall to accept Britomart's chivalric victory and "Ne henceforth be rebellious vnto love" (6.31). Using religious metaphor, she exhorts Britomart to forgive Artegall: "Graunt him your grace" (6.33). Britomart follows her advice and abjures revenge. By urging forgiveness, Glauce imitates the healing offices of the Reformation divine and guides the principals toward the nuptial altar. In both central books, then, homily intermingles with romance conventions; sermon idiom transforms these conventions into a celebration of (projected) married love. In both books, though, homily and religion have become so transmuted as to be less easily recognized than earlier—and as distant from theology.

In the final books, homily takes a peculiar turn and abets the process of secularizing the poem. In Book V, Artegall demonstrates the inefficacy of mere pacific preaching in his sermonlike rebuke of Burbon's "breach of faith" (10.62). The text suggests that homily is remarkably feeble compared to Arthur's victorious purging by sword of Belge's lands. Intersecting with the discourses of foreign policy and contemporary political apocalypticism, homily here seems overshadowed by those worldlier discourses. Not only has homily greatly changed its features; religion itself has also been altered by this crossing of discourses. Much the same may be said of Book VI. To take but one prominent example, the Hermit's counsel to Timias and Serena (6.6–14) comes close to repudiating the religious basis of *The Faerie Queene*'s early presentations of homiletic speech acts. The salves he dispenses, like those of his Reformation counterparts, assist in salvation. But he does not acknowledge God, even indirectly, as the source of the characters' help. The Hermit offers a view of human self-sufficiency at odds with contemporary religious understandings of the source of salvation. The Hermit does not parody sermon discourse so much as he secularizes it.[14]

Although sermon rhetoric is a constant in the poem, by the second half it has become so thoroughly assimilated into other discourses, and so altered, as to be nearly unrecognized by Spenser scholarship. As with homiletic discourse, so with other religious activity: the second half of the completed poem seems to drift far from its Reformation origins. The poem begins by straightforwardly reproducing Reformation discourse—in this instance preaching, the quintessential Reformation activity. Early books of the poem, even when parody is in play, often exemplify Thomas M. Greene's view of Renaissance imitative intertextuality: the "relationship to the subtext is deliberately and lucidly written into the poem as a visible and acknowledged construct."[15] In the second half of the poem, though, the relationship to the Reformation is less visible. The text shifts emphasis from the supernatural to the natural, or at least less patently religious, endorsement of heroic action. The emphatic religious discourse of the first half is modified under the increasingly secular pressures of the work's second half. Furthermore the later books appear to authorize views not readily squared with the religious postures of the 1590 version. The violence of later books, to choose a ready example, has been a source of anxiety for many readers (although the first three books can hardly be said to celebrate Christian pacificism) and seems to mark the movement of the poem away from its presumptive religious substratum.

In keeping with these changes in the poem's presentation of religion, studies of *The Faerie Queene*'s religious filiations have been lopsided, paying disproportionate attention to the early books, where theological and doctrinal meanings seem regnant. The later books do pay less heed to overt religious claims and appear to be less informed by religious doctrine. But this study has argued that understanding Reformation religion is more than a matter of identifying doctrinal positions. It is also a matter of determining how religious discourses have been rooted subterraneously in the text and of identifying subtle negotiations, often in distinct lexical and tropical usages, between literary and religious discourses. Doing so demonstrates how religious authority becomes transmuted in later books of *The Faerie Queene*, so that sermon idiom, for example, is deployed to endorse secular independence from the supernatural.

Some commentators have implicitly identified these changes with Spenser's putative growing disillusionment.[16] It has become a commonplace of even the most acute Spenser criticism that the poem's vision darkens and that the 1596 *Faerie Queene* becomes less optimistic in its final stages. Although the second half of the poem may reveal "Spenser's" disenchantment, it seems more productive to identify the poem's intertextual changes and to avoid the polarity of optimism versus pessimism. To do so enriches our understanding of the poem's play of reticulating discourses. It also helps us to avoid equating religion with doctrine. And it certainly avoids the trap of identifying religion with optimism. Finally, it helps us recognize that changes in religious discourse over the course of *The Faerie Queene* do not so clearly indicate disillusionment but instead comprise a facet of larger cultural shifts in the period.

We have seen that the evolving role of homiletic discourse is an aspect of a large transmutation in *The Faerie Queene*. Although homily greatly varies its colorations as the poem proceeds, and by its final books is only distantly related to the straightforward early renditions of religious discourse, it does not follow that the poem has become less "religious" or less "optimistic." Darryl Gless has recently argued a more temperate view: "as readers move beyond the boundaries of the 1590 *Faerie Queene*, they will need to expend still greater energy if they are to sustain doctrinally determined meanings. The text often seems to invite such readings, then to subvert or at least to test them with extraordinary rigor."[17] The text also invests religion, as we have seen, with more than doctrinally determined meanings. The presence of religion in the allegory suggests that the poem is as enthralled to religious discourse at the end as at the beginning. But the reproduction of those discourses is not as direct and usually not as readily perceptible in the surface narrative. The second half of the poem rarely advances "doctrinally determined meanings." As we have seen, however, the text has instead seized religious discourses and incorporated them into its structure, indeed into its very lexical fabric. The resulting role of religion in the poem is neither simple nor direct. This study has maintained that the poem's display of Reformed religion, especially in the later books, often questions or undermines religious ideas prevailing in the culture.

Changes in religious discourse also reveal how distant *The Faerie Queene* often is from doctrinalism and how far its author is from exercising a strong author-ity over the text. Spenser's readers rarely feel—as readers have felt, say, confronting *Paradise Lost*—that they stand before an intractable authorial presence demanding assent to his views. The only religious constant the poem advances is anti-Catholicism, an underinvestigated subject in contemporary early modern studies, awaiting the methodology of cultural poetics. This study has accordingly hypothesized that there is no "key" to the religious affiliations of *The Faerie Queene*. No single doctrinal stance, no label such as "Puritan" or "Anglican" and certainly not "Christian humanist," no adherent set of beliefs, no polemical stance motivates the poem—or motivates it for very long. As our thumbnail survey of chief homiletic figures suggests, the contradictions, the shifts, the changing allegiances identifiable in the poem mark a site—many sites—not easily characterized by polemical or doctrinal stability. These discursive variations also pertain to dichotomizing the poem into an "optimistic" first half and a "pessimistic" second half. To see the poem in its Reformation embeddedness is to cast a suspicious eye upon this dichotomy. The first books of the poem are too painfully aware of human frailty to be categorized as optimistic; the second half of the poem too hardheaded in professing human independence, or the benefits of supervising human weakness, to be labeled pessimistic.

The changes this study has registered in the poem's relation to the Reformation may instead be seen as part of wider changes in early modern culture's attitudes toward religion. C. John Sommerville has forcefully argued that early modern England marks a shift from religious culture to religious belief, that is, a "separation of almost all aspects of life and thought from religious associations or ecclesiastical direction."[18] The origins of the long process of secularizing English culture can be located in the various changes brought about by the Reformation, such as the separation of religious from secular institutions or the definite marking off of the sacred as something out of the ordinary. Patrick Collinson has traced the date of these changes "quite precisely to 1580" and sees in this phase of Reformation culture "an advanced state of separation of the secular from the sacred, something without precedent in English cultural history."[19] Such a shift comprehends both a defense of religion and a disregard of religion, and it includes a self-conscious appraisal of religion. This divided focus is part of the recasting of religion, the making of religion into an activity distinct from other cultural forms. Sommerville argues that this "change in religion's placement" reconstructs the "cultural grammar" of early modern England.[20]

The emergence of belief as an activity separable from religious culture is dramatized over the course of *The Faerie Queene*, making the poem part of that larger cultural reconstruction. As the poem progresses, it alters its religious placement. The text differentiates itself from a religious culture, that is, a culture in which religion cannot be easily segregated as a discursive activity. As it moves from its first to its second half, *The Faerie Queene* participates in contemporary cultural change. The 1590 poem exhibits the hallmarks of religious culture. The first two books in particular are almost impossible to analyze without recourse to religious discourses, so firmly rooted in religious culture is the poem's meaning. The second half of the poem, on the other hand, depends for much of its meaning on religious belief. In these books religion is an activity more disconnected

from religious culture than in the first half. The poem's later books inspire a nervous assessment of religious discourses and are difficult to categorize for "doctrinally determined meanings." As we have seen, religion in the later books is defended and doubted and again defended in turn. The work as a completed whole marks and indeed partakes of a cultural shift in relation to its religious materials. This shift includes, but is not confined to or even dominated by, active doubt and ignoring of religion. Over the course of the poem, religion becomes more problematically integrated into the structure.

But none of that makes the poem any the less "religious." Instead the changes in religious discourses help to reconstitute the poem's religious economy. In later books, as we have seen, religion as a discursive activity continues to be deeply structured into the text. But religion is reformulated and collides more violently with other discourses. It seems, but only upon determined critical inquiry, separable from them. *The Faerie Queene*'s treatment of the Reformation, and the changes visible in the movement from the versions of 1590 to 1596, exemplify Cassirer's view that the presence of a particular idea at any cultural moment counts less in itself than the intensity of dynamic interplay it achieves with other ideas and forces.[21] In tracing that interplay in Spenser's majestic text, the critic is made keenly aware of the vitality of that dynamic and of the complex interworkings of the period's discourses within it that we have yet to recover.

Notes

Introduction

1. William Perkins, "A Reformed Catholike," in *The Workes of That Famous and Worthy Minister of Christ in the Vniuersitie of Cambridge, Mr William Perkins*, 3 vols. (Cambridge, 1608–13), 1:559.

2. Plato represents the body as a prison in the *Phaedo*, secs. 7–8, 31–34; and in the *Cratylus*, sec. 18. For Pauline figurations, see Col. 4:3, Heb. 13:3, 1 Pet. 3:19. For a sample of Calvin's use of the trope, see *The Institution of Christian Religion*, trans. Thomas Norton (London, 1587), 1.15.2 (fol. 52ᵛ), 2.9.4 (fol. 182ʳ), 3.2.19 (fol. 234ʳ), 4.17.30 (fol. 469ᵛ). All subsequent quotations from Calvin are from this edition and are noted parenthetically in the text by section and folio numbers.

3. Alister E. McGrath, *From 1500 to the Present Day*, vol. 2 of *Iusitia Dei: A History of the Christian Doctrine of Justification* (Cambridge: Cambridge University Press, 1986), 98–105, pronounces on the theological mediocrity of the English Reformers.

4. The sinner-as-prisoner concept raises post-Foucauldian questions about the relation of prisons in *The Faerie Queene* to the "carceral system," which, for Foucault, represents "domination characteristic of a particular type of power" (231). See Michel Foucault, *Discipline and Punish: The Birth of the Prison*, trans. Alan Sheridan (New York: Pantheon, 1977), esp. pt. 4 (231–308). Foucault's analysis of prison as "a sort of artificial and coercive theatre in which [the prisoner's] life will be examined from top to bottom" (251) offers a social and secular homology to the intersections of romance and religious discourses I am here describing. For Perkins, the power to incarcerate is located in the fallen will; the power to liberate is God's. When Foucault claims that the most important effect of the carceral system "is that it succeeds in making the power to punish natural and legitimate" (301), he redefines in terms of the power of the state what Reformation culture defines as the power of God acting upon the sinner, whether to punish or to revive.

5. Edmund Spenser, *The Faerie Queene*, ed. A. C. Hamilton (New York: Longman, 1977). All quotations from the poem are from this edition and are cited parenthetically in the text by canto and stanza numbers; in citations from the notes and introductions, this volume is referred to as Hamilton's edition.

6. See Harry Berger Jr., "'Kidnapped Romance': Discourse in *The Faerie Queene*," in *Unfolded Tales: Essays on Renaissance Romance*, ed. George M. Logan and Gordon Teskey (Ithaca NY: Cornell University Press, 1989), 236–38. Berger quotes the following from Northrop Frye, *The Secular Scripture: A Study of the Structure of Romance* (Cambridge: Harvard University Press, 1976), 29–30: "In every period of history certain ascendant values are accepted by society and are embodied in its serious literature. Usually the process includes some form of kidnapped romance, that is, romance formulas used to reflect certain ascendant religious or social ideals." Berger expands Frye's point: "For me, to think of *The Faerie Queene* as a kidnapper of romances is . . . to think of it as always in some measure a critique of its victims." This leads Berger to postulate the concept of *discourse*: "The most important aspect of this notion is that it drives a wedge between our naive reception of the story as a first-order fiction and our more suspicious response to the story as a pastiche of parodied forms we are encouraged to scrutinize with a squint eye" (237). I trust the present study bears out Berger's remarks.

7. On intertextual formulations, see Jay Clayton and Eric Rothstein, "Figures in the Corpus: Theories of Influence and Intertextuality," in *Influence and Intertextuality in Literary History*, ed. Clayton and Rothstein (Madison: University of Wisconsin Press, 1991), 3–36; Michael Baxandall, *Patterns of Intention: On the Historical Explanation of Pictures* (New Haven: Yale University Press, 1985), 58–59; Thomas M. Greene, *The Light in Troy: Imitation and Discovery in Renaissance Poetry* (New Haven: Yale University Press, 1982), 16–53; John Frow, "Intertextuality and Ontology," in *Intertextuality: Theories and Practices*, ed. Michael Worton and Judith Still (New York: Manchester University Press, 1990), 45–55; and Michael Riffaterre, "Compulsory Reader Response: The Intertextual Drive," in *Intertextuality: Theories and Practices*, 56–78.

8. Clayton and Rothstein, "Figures in the Corpus," 3. In pointing out that the form of representation of intertextual structures ranges from the explicit to the implicit, John Frow states that "Since intertextuality may function as trace or as representation, this thematisation [of the text's relation to the structure of discursive authority] need not depend upon conscious authorial intention" ("Intertextuality and Ontology," 46).

9. Jonathan Culler, *The Pursuit of Signs: Semiotics, Literature, Deconstruction* (Ithaca NY: Cornell University Press, 1981), 114.

10. For an overview of some of the vexing problems of classification, see Borden W. Painter, "Anglican Terminology in Recent Tudor and Stuart Historiography," *Anglican and Episcopal History* 56 (1987): 237–49. I have generally preferred the term *Reformed* to *Calvinist*, reflecting the current view that Calvin was but one among a group of Continental Reformers popular with the English and that the term *Calvinism* shifted considerably over the course of the period. John New, *Anglican and Puritan: The Basis of Their Opposition, 1558–1640* (Stanford: Stanford University Press, 1964), finds differences throughout the period between the two major factions; see 12, 22, 71. Dewey D. Wallace Jr., *Puritans and Predestination: Grace in English Protestant Theology, 1525–1695* (Chapel Hill: University of North Carolina Press, 1982), on the other hand, focuses on the consistency of the doctrine of grace to English Protestantism and the agreement between conformist and nonconformist Elizabethan Protestants on the doctrines of election, sanctification, and assurance; see esp. vii, xii, 36–42. Peter Lake, *Moderate Puritans and the Elizabethan Church* (Cambridge: Cambridge University Press, 1982), argues that nonconformist divines successfully negotiated between rejecting conformist features of the church and remaining practitioners within it; see esp. 201–27 on the "Calvinism" of the 1590s.

11. In addition to the studies by Debora Kuller Shuger and Darryl J. Gless (see n.31 and n.32 below), Richard Helgerson's *Forms of Nationhood: The Elizabethan Writing of England* (Chicago: University of Chicago Press, 1992), 249–83, considers Reformation discursive practices in John Foxe and Richard Hooker as features of English political self-definition. Following upon his remark that "in sixteenth-century England, there was very little to which religion was irrelevant" (251), Helgerson demonstrates how apocalyptic and apologetic discourses clash and divide in their representations of national religious community. Chapters 1–3 of Stephen Greenblatt's *Renaissance Self-Fashioning: From More to Shakespeare* (Chicago: University of Chicago Press, 1980) are well-known and influential enough to need only a brief mention in a note about the interpenetration of religious and political discourses.

12. Christopher Haigh, ed., *The English Reformation Revised* (Cambridge: Cambridge University Press, 1987), 6. Haigh's essay in this volume, "The Recent Historiography of the Reformation" (19–33), summarizes from his revisionist perspective. For a fuller exposition of Haigh's project see his *English Reformations: Religion, Politics, and Society under the Tudors*

(Oxford: Clarendon, 1993), 12–14. For a detailed treatment of historiography between 1960 and 1985, see Rosemary O'Day, *The Debate on the English Reformation* (New York: Methuen, 1986), 102–33.

13. Patrick Collinson, "The Elizabethan Church and the New Religion," in *The Reign of Elizabeth I*, ed. Christopher Haigh (Athens: University of Georgia Press, 1985), 174. Collinson's essay (169–94) distills his vast knowledge of the subject and is surely one of the ablest expositions of the second phase of the Reformation.

14. See Wallace, *Puritans and Predestination*, 30–32. On Nowell's catechism see William P. Haugaard, "John Calvin and the Catechism of Alexander Nowell," *Archiv fur Reformationgeschichte* 61 (1970): 50–66.

15. See Wallace, *Puritans and Predestination*, 29–111; and Nicholas Tyacke, "Puritanism, Arminianism and Counter-Revolution," in *The Origins of the English Civil War*, ed. Conrad Russell (London: Macmillan, 1973), 119–43, esp. 120, 128. In *Anti-Calvinists: The Rise of English Arminianism c. 1590–1640* (Oxford: Clarendon, 1987), Tyacke elaborates the claim "that by the end of the sixteenth century the Church of England was largely Calvinist in doctrine" (see 3–8) and considers the Paul's Cross sermons of the 1590s (see 248–53). Patrick Collinson affirms this view in *The Religion of Protestants: The Church in English Society 1559–1625* (Oxford: Clarendon, 1982), 81–83. R. T. Kendall, *Calvin and English Calvinism to 1649* (Oxford: Oxford University Press, 1979), examines some of the English followers of Calvin, including William Perkins (see 51–78), on issues of soteriology.

16. See Wallace, *Puritans and Predestination*, 30–33.

17. See Kevin Sharpe, "Archbishop Laud," *History Today* 34 (1984): 57; and Peter White, "The Rise of Arminianism Reconsidered," *Past and Present* 101 (1983): 34–54. The subsequent debate between Tyacke and White sets forth the historiographic conflict later in the period, but their disagreements are illuminating, particularly Tyacke's claim that "anti-Calvinism was suppressed in the 1590s" and White's rejoinder that the church embraced a plurality of views on predestination. See "Debate: The Rise of Arminianism Reconsidered," *Past and Present* 115 (1987): 201–29.

18. Peter White's statement in "The Rise of Arminianism Reconsidered" sums up his and other revisionist views: "Within the Elizabethan church there was a spectrum of views on the doctrine of predestination" (54). See also D. M. Palliser, "Popular Reactions to the Reformation during the Years of Uncertainty, 1530–70," in Haigh, ed., *The English Reformation Revised*, 94–113. A capsule summary of the challenge to the view of Calvinist unifor-

mity is provided in Diarmaid MacCulloch, *The Later Reformation in England 1547–1603* (New York: St. Martin's, 1990), 70–77.

19. *The Book of Common Prayer, 1559: The Elizabethan Prayer Book,* ed. John E. Booty (Charlottesville: University Press of Virginia, 1976), 6–13; references hereafter are noted parenthetically in the text. See also *Certain sermons or homilies (1547); and, A homily against disobedience and wilful rebellion (1570): A Critical Edition,* ed. Ronald B. Bond (Buffalo NY: University of Toronto Press, 1987), 4–11, 55–58; unless otherwise noted, references to the homilies are from this edition, which is hereafter called *The Book of Homilies,* and are cited parenthetically in the text. A second edition, *Certain Sermons or Homilies,* was published in 1563 and contains an additional twenty-one sermons; I cite from this edition in subsequent chapters. Examining the potential effect of the fines in "The Elizabethan Church and the New Religion," Collinson notes that it is "hardly an exaggeration to say that the historian of Elizabethan religion knows little about the true nature of popular belief, since such belief was only rarely and sporadically a matter of official concern and searching inquiry" (178–79). O'Day, *The Debate on the English Reformation,* 159–61, summarizes the state of research on church attendance and, in particular, laxness among the poor.

20. Philip Schaff, *The History of Creeds,* vol. 1 of *The Creeds of Christendom* (New York: Harper, 1877), 633–38, sets forth article 17 in its original form with the later amendments, showing how the knotty points of a stronger Calvinism were later added. On the omission of the decree of reprobation in the Elizabethan version, see H. C. Porter, *Reformation and Reaction in Tudor England* (Cambridge: Cambridge University Press, 1958), 336–41; and William P. Haugaard, *Elizabeth and the English Reformation: The Struggle for a Stable Settlement of Religion* (London: Cambridge University Press, 1968), 250, 284. Charles Hardwick, *A History of the Articles of Religion: To Which Is Added a Series of Documents, from A.D. 1536 to A.D. 1615; Together with Illustrations from Contemporary Sources* (London: Charles Bell & Sons, 1895), 312, provides versions of article 17 from 1553, 1563, and 1571.

21. Peter Lake, "Calvinism and the English Church 1570–1635," *Past and Present* 114 (1987): 34. Lake affirms, however, the Calvinist dominance of the universities and printed culture.

22. See the debate between Tyake and White in *Past and Present* (n.17 above). Susan Doran and Christopher Durston's *Princes, Pastors and People: The Church and Religion in England 1529–1689* (New York: Routledge, 1991), 22–28, sketches some of the terms of this debate.

23. See J. J. Scarisbrick, *The Reformation and the English People* (Oxford: Basil Blackwell, 1984), 1–2, 41–44, 110–12. For a revisionist view of the continued prestige of Catholic clergy well into midcentury, see Peter Marshall, *The Catholic Priesthood and the English Reformation* (Oxford: Clarendon, 1994), esp. 211–32.

24. Haigh, ed., *The English Reformation Revised*, 9. Norman L. Jones, *Faith by Statute: Parliament and the Settlement of Religion, 1559* (London: Royal Historical Society, 1982), demonstrates the accommodations made in the Settlement to various factions. In *The Birthpangs of Protestant England: Religious and Cultural Change in the Sixteenth and Seventeenth Centuries* (London: Macmillan, 1988), Patrick Collinson says that if he "were to be asked when Protestant England was born I would answer, with greater conviction than I could have mustered even a few years ago: after the accession of Elizabeth I, some considerable time after. It is only with the 1570s that the historically minded insomniac goes to sleep counting Catholics rather than Protestants, since only then did they find themselves in a minority situation. I would even be prepared to assert, crudely and flatly, that the Reformation was something which happened in the reigns of Elizabeth and James I. Before that everything was preparative, embryonic. Protestantism was present, but as a kind of sub-culture, like Catholicism later" (ix). Christopher Haigh, on the other hand, claims that in the *second* half of the reign there was "a small Protestant minority rather than a thoroughly Protestant nation" (202). See Haigh, "The Church of England, the Catholics and the People," in *The Reign of Elizabeth I*, ed. Haigh (Athens: University of Georgia Press, 1985), 195–219.

25. A. G. Dickens, *The English Reformation* (London: Batsford, 1964). Dickens's monumental study cannot be readily summarized, but this statement about England on the eve of the Reformation is not uncharacteristic: "English Catholicism, despite its gilded decorations, was an old, unseaworthy and ill-commanded galleon, scarcely able to continue its voyage without the new seamen and shipwrights produced (but produced far too late in the day) by the Counter-Reformation" (108).

26. See G. R. Elton, *Reform and Reformation: England 1509–1558* (Cambridge: Harvard University Press, 1977), esp. 157–200.

27. See Christopher Haigh, "Puritan Evangelism in the Reign of Elizabeth I," *English Historical Review* 92 (1977): 30–58; Collinson, *The Religion of Protestants*, 203–5; and Ronald Hutton, "The Local Impact of the Tudor Reformations," in Haigh, ed., *The English Reformation Revised*, 114–38.

28. Collinson, "The Elizabethan Church and the New Religion," 177, challenges the distinction as one that constantly breaks down in view of the dependence of preachers on political support and that of policy on cooperation from preachers.

29. See Collinson, *The Religion of Protestants*, 189–241.

30. White, "The Rise of Arminianism Reconsidered," 35 n.5, cites historians of religion who support this claim.

31. Debora Kuller Shuger, *Habits of Thought in the English Renaissance: Religion, Politics, and the Dominant Culture* (Berkeley and Los Angeles: University of California Press, 1990), 2–3; see also 44–47, 63–65, 254–57. Shuger's comments deserve quotation: "the relation between religion and culture needs careful explication if religion is not to be confused with society itself or narrowed into theology." In the Renaissance "religious discourse enfolds more than . . . specifically theological concerns" for "it is the cultural matrix for explorations of virtually every topic: kingship, selfhood, rationality, language, marriage, ethics, and so forth" (6–7). In *The Renaissance Bible: Scholarship, Sacrifice, and Subjectivity* (Berkeley and Los Angeles: University of California Press, 1994), Shuger extends these interests to situate Renaissance exegetical practice within the larger intellectual culture.

32. Darryl J. Gless, *Interpretation and Theology in Spenser* (Cambridge: Cambridge University Press, 1994). Gless adapts the view that "Elizabethan Reformed Christianity spoke with more than one voice" (15) to a reader-oriented interpretation of what those voices "might mean to an attentive reader of Spenser's *Faerie Queene* who might also be an attentive reader of sixteenth-century theology" (17).

33. See Kevin Sharpe and Steven N. Zwicker, "Politics of Discourse: Introduction," in *Politics of Discourse: The Literature and History of Seventeenth-Century England*, ed. Sharpe and Zwicker (Berkeley and Los Angeles: University of California Press, 1987), 1–20.

34. Wallace, *Puritans and Predestination*, 43, 55. On literacy see David Cressy, *Literacy and the Social Order: Reading and Writing in Tudor and Stuart England* (New York: Cambridge University Press, 1980), 146, 152. For the fullest recent account, with statistical evidence, of the evangelists in action see Haigh, *English Reformations*, 268–84: "The hierarchical and parochial Church of England was being restructured in missionary fashion. Borough lectureships provided evangelical platforms for leading preachers, who became civic apostles with fervent followings" (275).

35. Rom. 10:14–17, *The Geneva Bible: A Facsimile of the 1560 Edition*, intro. Lloyd E. Berry (Madison: University of Wisconsin Press, 1969). Subse-

quent quotations from Scripture are from this edition and are noted parenthetically in the text, as are references to the Geneva glosses.

36. Collinson, *The Religion of Protestants*, 232–34; Wallace, *Puritans and Predestination*, 32. Ian Green surveys genres, purposes, authors, and audiences of catechisms and shows how they supplemented preaching as an evangelical aid in " 'For Children in Yeeres and Children in Understanding': The Emergence of the English Catechism under Elizabeth and the Early Stuarts," *Journal of Ecclesiastical History* 37 (1986): 397–425.

37. See Anthea Hume, *Edmund Spenser: Protestant Poet* (Cambridge: Cambridge University Press, 1984). Hume argues that "Spenser's Protestantism was of the militant variety . . . requir[ing] the label 'Puritanism' " (2–3). She also avers that Spenser's writing reflects the "religion to which he adhered throughout his life . . . [,] a fervent Protestantism which requires the label 'Puritan' during a specific period" (9). Hume lists (3–4) her predecessors in this century who have identified Spenser with one or another partisan position—a list expanded by James Schiavone in "Predestination and Free Will: The Crux of Canto Ten," *Spenser Studies* 10 (1992): 192–93 nn.10–17. In *The Birthpangs of Protestant England*, Collinson characterizes the "long-running dispute about Spenser, whether he should be classed as a Protestant or a Puritan" as "sterile, since it rests on a distinction which cannot in fact be made" (94).

38. John N. King, for example, in *Spenser's Poetry and the Reformation Tradition* (Princeton: Princeton University Press, 1990) contends that Spenser adheres to the "normative sources for Elizabethan theology" (11); see also 9, 237–38.

39. Barbara Lewalski, *Protestant Poetics and the Seventeenth-Century Religious Lyric* (Princeton: Princeton University Press, 1979), 14. The opposite (though vastly more simplistic) perspective is offered by Alan Sinfield in *Literature in Protestant England 1560–1660* (London: Croom Helm, 1983). Sinfield finds "the internal contradictions of protestant religious orthodoxy" (4) a source of anxiety and cultural dislocation for Renaissance writers, for Calvinist theology "insisted on the need for grace whilst denying any means to obtain it" (11). David Mikics, *The Limits of Moralizing: Pathos and Subjectivity in Spenser and Milton* (Lewisburg PA: Bucknell University Press, 1994), advances an interpretation of the 1596 *Faerie Queene* based on an understanding of the "Reformation's emphasis on the individual human subject" (3). The poem, Mikics argues, dramatizes a gap "between rigid or archaic doctrinal patterns," which he associates with Calvinist predestination, and the "pathos" of Protestant subjectivity (8). Hence the movement from

Book I to its successors entails a shift from "the plot of sacred history" to an emphasis on "subjective sensitivity to pathos" (40) characteristic of Protestant inwardness.

40. King, *Spenser's Poetry*, 5. King's study "presupposes a concept of literary tradition based upon topoi, conventions, genres, countergenres, inversions, and parodies rather than the interplay of sources, analogues, and influences" (13). Its greatest strength is to embed Spenser's work in native literary and iconographic Reformation types from earlier in the century.

41. Linda Gregerson, *The Reformation of the Subject: Spenser, Milton, and the English Protestant Epic* (Cambridge: Cambridge University Press, 1995), considers idolatry and iconoclasm as aspects of subjectivity and identity formation; see 58–61, 67–69, 143–45. Kenneth Gross, *Spenserian Poetics: Idolatry, Iconoclasm, and Magic* (Ithaca NY: Cornell University Press, 1986), traces the reciprocity and mutuality of idolatry and iconoclasm. Ernest B. Gilman, *Iconoclasm and Poetry in the English Reformation: Down Went Dagon* (Chicago: University of Chicago Press, 1986), considers the "deeper debate between pictorialism and iconoclasm in *The Faerie Queene*" (61); see 61–84.

42. John N. Wall Jr., *Transformations of the Word: Spenser, Herbert, Vaughan* (Athens: University of Georgia Press, 1988), 3. Wall's "thesis in this study is that Spenser, Herbert, and Vaughan set out to promote the social agenda of the Church of England, both its assuring-giving worship and its transformation-promoting goal of realizing the true Christian commonwealth in England" (6).

43. In *Interpretation and Theology in Spenser* Gless reconstructs Elizabethan doctrinal history as a way of showing how the "poem's theological content and meanings can be realized only by readers, who themselves must provide much of the doctrinal material this enactment requires" (47). His aim is to reveal the interplay between doctrine and poetry. The result is a rich amalgam of theological and critical insight, especially into Book I, his chief concern. Although our treatments are as different as those between theology and religious discourse, I have profited in this introduction and the next chapter from Gless's theological perspicuity and its application to the verse.

44. The absence from these pages of the Mutabilitie Cantos is perhaps especially pronounced. Uncertainly related to the poem as a whole, these cantos have been subjected to a variety of interpretive claims. Recently and not implausibly, Harold L. Weatherby, *Mirrors of Celestial Grace: Patristic Theology in Spenser's Allegory* (Toronto: University of Toronto Press, 1994), 76–94, has argued that they derive from the Greek patristic concep-

tion of *theosis* and its bearing on the Transfiguration, and hence are quite distant from Reformation discourses. Like the Mutabilitie Cantos, most of the prominent episodes absent from this study are in the nature of set pieces and have in common a specialness that to some readers epitomizes the books of the poem that they are found in and to others makes these episodes inherently different from these books. Be that as it may, this study omits such episodes in the interest not so much of synecdoche as of accuracy: the purpose here is to show how the poem responds to the discourses of the Reformation, and I do not venture where I do not find such discourse applicable.

45. Charles H. George and Katherine George, *The Protestant Mind of the English Reformation 1570–1640* (Princeton: Princeton University Press, 1961), 23. The major themes of the Georges' study, sometimes reductive, have been refined by the abundance of scholarship since, but it remains monumental and a fount of insight and refreshment for the literary scholar. For purposes of this introduction I find this statement noteworthy, for it has guided much subsequent scholarship, including the present book: "orthodox Christian argumentation tends to be a complex of contradictions. English Protestantism certainly contains its full share of such ambivalences" (37).

46. Wallace, *Puritans and Predestination*, 61–65.

47. Lewalski, *Protestant Poetics*, 16–24, offers an incisively sketched treatment of the *ordo*.

48. Greene, *The Light in Troy*, 20–21. Greene sets forth a typology of humanist imitation (38–48) that I find especially productive and adaptable to relations among other discourses: reproductive or sacramental, eclectic, heuristic, and dialectical.

Discourses of Preaching

1. See Hamilton's edition, 104.

2. Perkins, "The Whole Treatise of Cases of Conscience," *Workes* 2:70.

3. Anne D. Ferry, *The "Inward" Language: Sonnets of Wyatt, Sidney, Shakespeare, Donne* (Chicago: University of Chicago Press, 1983), investigates the difference between "inward" states and outward expression in the sixteenth century. The scene between Arthur and Una, as well as many others in Spenser, needs to be interrogated with the resources Ferry brings to her study. See esp. 1–30; e.g., "Hamlet shows a sense of inward experience and the difficulty of denoting it truly which makes him a new kind of figure in English literature, and distinguishes him from the speakers in virtually all sixteenth-century verse, except the poet-lovers in the sonnet sequences of Sidney and Shakespeare" (29).

4. Richard Hooker, *Tractates and Sermons*, vol. 5 of *The Folger Library Edition of the Works of Richard Hooker*, ed. W. Speed Hill (Cambridge: Harvard University Press, 1990), 30. Perkins, "A Godly and Learned Exposition Vpon the whole Epistle of Iude," *Workes* 3:520.

5. The subject has been much debated in contemporary Protestant studies. See, for example, Wallace, *Puritans and Predestination*, 45–52; Tyacke, *Anti-Calvinists*, 17–19, 249–52; Kendall, *Calvin and English Calvinism*, 3–5, 25, 61–62, 67–76; Gless, *Interpretation and Theology in Spenser*, 41–44, 151–52; and Shuger, *Habits of Thought in the English Renaissance*, 7–8, 78–83.

6. John Downame, *The Christian Warfare* (London, 1612), 191. Kendall, *Calvin and English Calvinism*, 8 9, demonstrates how Perkins uses 2 Pet 1:10 as prooftext for the doctrine of assurance: "Wherefore, brethren, giue rather diligence to make your calling & election sure: for if ye do these things, ye shal neuer fail"—which is glossed in the Geneva version with the words "For God will vpholde you."

7. Perkins, in "A Treatise . . . Whether a Man Be in the Estate of Damnation, or . . . Grace," fabricates a dialogue between Minister and Christian: "*Christian*. I will hereafter doe my endeauor to practice this your counsell . . . [but] I doe not feele the assurance of the forgiuenesse of my sinnes . . . *Minister*. But do you desire with all your heart to feele [assurance of God's mercy]? *Christian*. I doe indeede. *Minister*. Then doubt not, you shall feele it. . . . *Christian*. I haue now opened vnto you the chiefe things that troubled me: & your comfortable answers haue much refreshed my troubled mind" (*Workes* 1:411–13).

8. See Wallace, *Puritans and Predestination*, 45–46, 75. See also Ian Breward, "The Significance of William Perkins," *Journal of Religious History* 4 (1966): 122; and Gordon Wakefield, *Puritan Devotion: Its Place in the Development of Christian Piety* (London: Epwort, 1957), 111.

9. Porter, *Reformation and Reaction*, 217. See also William Haller, *The Rise of Puritanism* (New York: Columbia University Press, 1938), 26–28. Richard Greenham gives a third-person account of his ministry in "Grave Counsels, and Godly Observations . . . applyed to instruct, and comfort all afflicted consciences," in *The Workes of the Reverend and Faithfvll Servant of Iesus Christ M. Richard Greenham* (London, 1612), 1–43. Peter Iver Kaufman, *Prayer, Despair, and Drama: Elizabethan Introspection* (Urbana: University of Illinois Press, 1996), 52–58, provides ample description of Greenham's work of "therapeutic despair" as a religious antidote against complacence and arrogance. In his treatment of Book I of *The Faerie*

Queene, Kaufman focuses on the Despaire episode (see 71–79) and concludes that this book of the poem invites the reader "to fix on the protagonist's diehard vulnerability and on a dialectic between despair and assurance" (78).

10. The opposition of faith and despair is commonplace. In "A Sermon Preached at Pauls Crosse" (1591), Gervase Babington answers concerning the question of how the "use of holy Doctrine" is manifest: "by confirming most strongly this feeble faith of ours against Despaire, when troubles and crosses do euery way beset us, and as it were ouerwhelm us" (*The workes of the Right Reverend Father in God Gervase Babington* [London, 1637], 275).

11. Perkins, "An Exposition of the Symbole, or Creed of the Apostles," in *Workes* 1:200; subsequent quotations from Perkins's works in the present chapter are noted parenthetically in the text by volume and page numbers only.

12. A wide variety of scholarship documents this fact. Notable examples include Horton Davies, *Worship and Theology in England from Cranmer to Hooker 1534–1603* (Princeton: Princeton University Press, 1970), 227–54, 294–324; George and George, *The Protestant Mind of the English Reformation*, 335–43; and Haller, *The Rise of Puritanism*. An incisive sketch is offered by Collinson in "The Church and the New Religion," where he sets the role of preaching against the backdrop of controversies over ecclesiastical policies and outlines the gradual institution of a preaching ministry in the second half of the century (see 182–93).

13. Richard Hooker, *Of the Laws of Ecclesiastical Polity: Book V*, vol. 2 of *The Folger Library Edition of the Works of Richard Hooker*, ed. W. Speed Hill (Cambridge: Harvard University Press, 1977), 87; see also 97–99, 106–8. Hooker's praise is qualified by his redefining of preaching to include the reading of Scripture and, in the absence of preaching, of homily; in addition, he worries that the Reformed privileging of preaching in fact exalts the preacher over the Word.

14. Greenham, "Of hearing Gods Word," in *Workes*, 708.

15. Heiko Obermann, "Preaching and the Word in the Reformation," *Theology Today* 18 (1961): 26, notes the adage and its centrality to Reformation hermeneutics.

16. The terms *homily* and *sermon* are often used interchangeably in the Reformation, as the very title *Certain sermons or homilies* suggests. Bond points out in his edition (18–19 n.4) that "in the Middle Ages a sermon tended to be a piece of moral exhortation, whereas a homily was a piece of expository exegesis." The fluidity of genre speaks to the penetration of Scripture into all areas of religious discourse in the period.

17. See Bond's introduction to *The Book of Homilies,* 4–5, 10–11, 55–58. See also "An Act for the Uniformity of Common Prayer," in *The Book of Common Prayer 1559,* which proclaims that "all and singular ministers in any cathedral or parish church or other place within this realm of England . . . shall . . . be bounden to use [*The Book of Common Prayer*] . . . in such order and form as is mentioned in the said book so authorized by Parliament" (6).

18. See T. H. L. Parker, ed., *English Reformers,* Library of Christian Classics, vol. 26 (Philadelphia: Westminster, 1966), 221–26.

19. Haller, *The Rise of Puritanism,* 258.

20. See esp. Christopher Hill, *Society and Puritanism in Pre-Revolutionary England* (New York: Schocken Books, 1964), 30–79; Collinson, *The Religion of Protestants,* 232, 257–59; and Irvonwy Morgan, *The Godly Preachers of the Elizabethan Church* (London: Epworth, 1965).

21. Haller, *The Rise of Puritanism,* 21. See also Alan Fager Herr, *The Elizabethan Sermon: A Survey and a Bibliography* (Philadelphia: University of Pennsylvania Press, 1940); and Millar Maclure, *The Paul's Cross Sermons 1534–1642* (Toronto: University of Toronto Press, 1958). An authoritative study redressing this neglect is John N. King's *English Reformation Literature: The Tudor Origins of the Protestant Tradition* (Princeton: Princeton University Press, 1982). Sean Kane's *Spenser's Moral Allegory* (Buffalo NY: University of Toronto Press, 1989) begins its treatment of Book I of *The Faerie Queene* by noting that the "official sermons and homilies fell on Spenser's generation like the English rain" (32). Kane sees the *Homilies* as a "frame" of faith and finds several provocative passages motivating Redcrosse's early adventures (see 33–40).

22. See Joachim Dyck, "The First German Treatise on Homiletics: Erasmus Sarcer's *Pastorale* and Classical Rhetoric," in *Renaissance Eloquence: Studies in the Theory and Practice of Renaissance Rhetoric,* ed. James J. Murphy (Berkeley and Los Angeles: University of California Press, 1983), 221–37; and J. W. Blench, *Preaching in England in the Late Fifteenth and Sixteenth Centuries* (Oxford: Basil Blackwell, 1964), 228–320.

23. Obermann, "Preaching and the Word," 17, speculates that the Protestant sermon substitutes for the pre-Reformation sacrament of penance.

24. Greenham, "Of Prophecie and Preaching," in *Workes,* 772. See also "The Readyng and Knowledge of Holy Scripture" in *The Book of Homilies*: "If it shal require to teach any truth or reprove false doctrine, to rebuke any vice, to commend any vertue, to geve good counsail, to comfort, or to exhort, or to do any other thyng requisite for our salvacion, all those thinges . . . we maye learne plentifully of the Scripture" (62).

25. Richard Rogers, "Of the Meanes whereby a godly life is holpen and continued," in *Seven Treatises* (London, 1630), 283.

26. See John N. Wall Jr., "Goodly and Fruitful lessons: The English Bible, Erasmus' Paraphrases and the Book of Homilies," in *The Godly Kingdom of Tudor England: Great Books of the English Reformation*, ed. John E. Booty (Wilton CT: Morehouse-Barlow, 1981), 47–138.

27. Edwin Sandys, "The fourteenth sermon. . . . Then Peter opened his mouth," in *Sermons* (London, 1585), sig. R1^r. Sandys continues: "We must beseech God . . . to print into our hearts that which we heare with our eares." Cf. Perkins in "The Art of Prophesying": "whenas the Minister of the word doth in the time of preaching so behaue himselfe, that all, euen ignorant and idle persons & vnbeleeuers may iudge, that it is not so much hee that speaketh, as the Spirit of God in him and by him" (*Workes* 2:671). Cf. Thomas Becon, "The Syckmans Salue," in *The worckes of Thomas Becon* (London, 1646), fol. cclxxii^r: "I at all times bene glad to repaire unto those places, where the word of God hath bene preached, and the doctrine hath bene taught. I marked diligently, kept it in memorye, and to the uttermost of my power I laboured to frame my life according to the same, that I might be no forgetfull hearer, but a diligent doer of those words, which I learned of the holy Scriptures . . . Phi. Is there not a more euident testimony and a surer argument, that that man is in a state of euerlasting damnation, which hath no mynde to heare the word of God, nor to trayne his life according to the doctrine therof: so likewise is there not a more certayne signe, that any man is predestined to be saued, then when he hath a mynd to heare the word of God. . . . He that is of God heareth gods wordes. . . . They that are the children of the deuil, haue no mynde to heare the worde of God. But they that are the sonnes of God, haue a feruent delite and singulare great pleasure to heare goddes worde, yea and as the Prophete sayeth, to exercise the selues in it day and nyght."

28. Anne D. Ferry, *The Art of Naming* (Chicago: University of Chicago Press, 1988), 10, 14. Ferry's chapter on sixteenth-century uses of the verb *to read* (9–48) bears especially closely on Book I and its concern with "the difficulties of interpreting the appearances of things" (47) for characters, narrator, and reader. Patricia Parker, *Inescapable Romance: Studies in the Poetics of a Mode* (Princeton: Princeton University Press, 1979), 66–68, notes the usage of reading as advice and suggests some of the difficulties the moral landscape possesses for the characters.

29. Greenham, "Of hearing Gods Word," 709. Cf. the preface to *The Book of Common Prayer*: "whereas Saint Paul would have such language

[as the Scriptures] spoken to the people in the Church as they might understand and have profit by the same hearing, the service in this Church of England these many years hath been read in Latin to the people, which they understood not, so that they have heard with their ears only, and their hearts, spirit, and mind have not been edified thereby" (15). Perkins claims that "there be two kindes of hearers: one, which heareth onely the outward sound of the word with his bodily eares, and he hauing eares doth not heare: the second, is he that doth not onely receiue the doctrine that is taught with his eares, but also hath his heart opened to feele the power of it, and to obey the same in the course of his life" ("An Exposition of the Symbole, or Creed of the Apostles," 200). The scriptural subtext is Matt. 13:9: "He that hath eares to heare, let him heare." Redcrosse, too, cannot hear Una's words fully, perhaps because she reads at least one in Latin (*cave*).

30. Greenham, "Of hearing Gods Word," 710.

31. Cf. *The Book of Common Prayer*: "Blessed Lord, which hast caused all Holy Scriptures to be written for our learning: Grant us that we may in such wise hear them, read, mark, learn, and inwardly digest them" (79).

32. John N. King, *Spenser's Poetry*, 195–99, traces Redcrosse's use of (or failure to use) his sword throughout the book as exfoliating Ephesians 6:17: "the sworde of the Spirit, which is the worde of God." Ignorance of the Scriptures, says King, "renders Redcrosse incapable of winning victory" (195) against Errour and other antagonists. But it is "the blade personifying the power of the Word that slays the beast" (199) in canto 11, a blade that King says refers to the "sharpe sworde" from the mouth of Christ in Rev. 19:11–15. Kane, *Spenser's Moral Allegory*, notes that "The Third Part of the Sermon of Faith" from *The Book of Homilies* lists "errours" as among the sequential steps into sin (37).

33. See the table "Howe to take profite by reading of the holy Scriptures," from the 1599 edition of the Geneva Bible, facing 1ʳ, item 7, reproduced in Rivkah Zim, "The Reformation: The Trial of God's Word," in *Reading the Text: Biblical Criticism and Literary Theory* (Cambridge MA: Basil Blackwell, 1991), 72.

34. John Hooper, "How Man is Broughte to the Knowledge of Life and Saluation," in *Certeine Comfortable Expositions* (London, 1580), fol. 23ʳ.

35. Perkins, for example, declares in "A Treatise of Gods Free-Grace, and Mans Free-Will" that "nature corrupted wants ability so much as to thinke a good thought: much lesse to will that which is good. . . . There is not only an impotencie to good, but such a forcible pronenes and disposition to euil, as that we can do nothing but sinne" (*Workes* 2:730).

36. The majority of commentators argue that Spenser advances an Augustinian-Calvinist understanding of the fallen will as in bondage to sin. These positions are classified and summarized in Schiavone, "Predestination and Free Will"; see esp. nn.10–17. To Schiavone's list may be added Gless, *Interpretation and Theology*, whose measured exegesis of Book I sets this study above all previous ones by its comprehending a variety of interpretations available to the theologically knowledgeable sixteenth-century reader.

37. See Gless, *Interpretation and Theology*, 2.

38. Douglas Brooks-Davies, "*The Faerie Queene*, Book I," in *The Spenser Encyclopedia*, ed. A. C. Hamilton et al. (Toronto: University of Toronto Press, 1990), treats holiness as "at once private . . . and public" (259), but he notes that the public and national dimension "was probably Book I's main meaning for contemporaries" (260).

39. See Gless, *Interpretation and Theology*, 29–33, 148–49. The chapter "Providence, Fortune, and Free Will in Book VI," below, explores this issue more fully.

40. "The Readyng and Knowledge of Holy Scripture," 64.

41. John Jewel, "Sermons Preached by Bishop Jewel," in *The Workes of the Very Learned and Reuerend Father in God John Jewel*, 2 vols. (London, 1621), 2:221.

42. Horton Davies, *Worship and Theology*, 237.

43. Calvin calls reliance on the sacraments "diuelish": "affiance of saluation hangeth not vpon the partaking of the Sacrament, as though Iustification consisted therein: which we know to be reposed in Christe onely, and to be communicated vnto vs no lesse by the preaching of the Gospel" (4.14.14; fol. 431ᵛ).

44. Blench, *Preaching in England*, 131–32; see also 171–72.

45. But Fradubio claims a "living well" will "vnbynd" and "restore" them to "former kynd" (I.2.43). He does not, in other words, define any more certainly the issue of the will to effect or cooperate in its restoration. Will "living well" (i.e., by freely chosen good works, perhaps even a sacrament such as baptism) help restore him to unfallen health, or is the "living well" an effect (i.e., sanctification) of the unmerited grace that may be his?

46. For a discussion of Spenser's reliance on medieval homiletic discourse in this episode, see Joan Heiges Blythe, "Spenser and the Seven Deadly Sins: Book I, Cantos IV and V," *ELH* 39 (1972): 342–52. From the perspective of the Reformation preoccupation with sin, it should be noted that a number of figures in the procession are said to choose their sins: Idleness "Upon a slouthfull Asse . . . chose to ryde" (4.18); Lechery is "fraught with fick-

lenesse" (4.25). All these forms of freely willed enthrallment are mirrored in the "wretched thralles" beneath Lucifera's house. They, too, have freely enslaved themselves, for they have "throwne themselues into these heauy stowres" (5.51).

47. Henry Bullinger, "Of the ministerie, and the ministers of Gods worde," in *Fiftie Godlie and Learned Sermons* (London, 1577), 831.

48. Richard Taverner, *Postils on the Epistles and Gospels*, ed. Edward Cardwell (Oxford: Oxford University Press, 1841), 293.

49. John M. Steadman, "Una and the Clergy: The Ass Symbol in *The Faerie Queene*," *Journal of the Warburg and Courteauld Institutes* 21 (1958): 134–37, identifies the ass whom the satyrs worship as *pura verbi praedicatio* of the Reformed visible church.

50. Taverner, *Postils*, 375.

51. Becon, "The inuectiue against swearinge," in *The worckes*, fol. ccxvi^r.

52. Perkins's table of the *ordo salutis* is reproduced in *The Work of William Perkins*, ed. Ian Breward (Abingdon, Berkshire: Sutton Courtenay, 1970), 169. It is cogently discussed in Andrew D. Weiner, "'Fierce Warres and Faithful Loues': Pattern as Structure in Book I of *The Faerie Queene*," *Huntington Library Quarterly* 37 (1973): 33–58.

53. Niels Hemmingsen, *The Preacher, or Methode of Preaching*, trans. John Horsfall (London, 1574), fols. 64^r, 53^r.

54. See especially Ernest Sirluck, "A Note on the Rhetoric of Spenser's 'Despair,'" *Modern Philology* 47 (1949): 8–11; Katherine Koller, "Art, Rhetoric, and Holy Dying in the *Faerie Queene* with Special Reference to the Despair Canto," *Studies in Philology* 61 (1964): 128–39; James Nohrnberg, *The Analogy of "The Faerie Queene"* (Princeton: Princeton University Press, 1976), 152–55; and Harold Skulsky, "Spenser's Despair Episode and the Theology of Doubt," *Modern Philology* 78 (1981): 227–42. Skulsky is especially acute in arguing that the episode reveals fissures in the professed theology of assurance Una advances. Skulsky's article "Despair" in *The Spenser Encyclopedia*, 213–14, summarizes many earlier investigations and skillfully contextualizes the episode in canto 10.

55. Patrick Cullen, *Infernal Triad: The Flesh, the World, and the Devil in Spenser and Milton* (Princeton: Princeton University Press, 1974), 59–61.

56. Ann E. Imbrie, "'Playing Legerdemaine with the Scripture': Parodic Sermons in *The Faerie Queene*," *English Literary Renaissance* 17 (1987): 147.

57. Dyck, "First German Treatise," 234.

58. See, for example, Greenham, "Of Prophecie and Preaching," on what is to be learned from the Word: "First, to know and to be perswaded of the

greatnes of our sinnes, and the miserie due to the same. . . . Secondly, to know and be perswaded, how we may be deliuered from them. . . . Thirdly, to know and bee perswaded what thankes wee owe to God for our deliuerance" (772).

59. Hemmingsen, *The Preacher*, fols. 64ʳ–65ʳ.

60. Henry Smith, "The Calling of Ionah," in *Twelve Sermons* (London, 1632), sigs. G6ʳ–ᵛ. See also sig. M7ʳ, "Trumpet, of the Soule sounding to Judgement," where Smith preaches on this text: "Rejoyce, O young man, in thy youth, and let thy heart bee merry in they young day, follow the ways of thine owne heart and lusts of thine eyes. But remember for all these things then must come to judgement (Eccles. 1.9)."

61. Greenham, "Of hearing Gods Word," 708. Cf. Matt. 7:15; 2 Cor. 11:13 and gloss; 2 Pet. 2:1; 1 John 4:1 and gloss. This last seems to have had particular claims on English Reformers: "Derely beloued, beleue not euerie spirit, but trye the spirits whether they are of God: for many false Prophets are gone out into the worlde. [Geneva gloss:] They which boast that thei haue the Spirit to preache or prophecie." See also William Tyndale, "Exposition of the First Epistle of Saint John," in *Expositions of Scripture and Practice of Prelates*, ed. Henry Walker (Cambridge: Cambridge University Press for the Parker Society, 1869): "there be many false prophets abroad already. We told you before that antichrist should come: but now I certify you that antichrist's kingdom is begun already; and his disciple are gone out to preach" (195). This treatise is not included in Tyndale's *The Whole workes*, the edition cited in n.18 of the next chapter.

62. Archimago has been associated with the False Prophet in commentary on this book of the poem. See, for example, John Hankins, *Source and Meaning in Spenser's Allegory: A Study of "The Faerie Queene"* (Oxford: Clarendon, 1971), 67. Nohrnberg, *The Analogy of "The Faerie Queene,"* 128–29, links Archimago with "the Antichrist complex of the New Testament" and cites scriptural passages "concerning the success of the false teacher."

63. See n.9 of the following chapter, "Sermon Parody and Discourses of the Flesh," for a fuller description of the five subgenres of the sermon.

64. Skulsky, "Despair," 214, and Hamilton's edition, 129, point out that this assurance is but temporary (and adds to the burden of Redcrosse's conscience in the house of Holinesse); furthermore, as the divines' practical experience verifies, it must be reiterated each time Redcrosse loses sight of it (see *The Faerie Queene* I.10.22).

65. For summaries of most of the previous accounts of this stanza and its relation to canto 10, see Schiavone, "Predestination and Free Will," 192–93;

and Gless, *Interpretation and Theology*, 146–63. Gless's delicate exegetical method serves him exceptionally well in finding theological richness in this canto. After demonstrating how Reformed theology, like that of Roman Catholicism, grants to the will "a role in the performance of good works," Gless suggests that the Protestant idea of "holiness" involves "both the cooperative achievement and the sinful corruption of works that nonetheless remain 'holy'" and thereby "suggests a way to reconcile features of the canto readers have found incongruous" (150).

66. Cf. Perkins: "Then let the Gospell be preached, in the preaching whereof, the holy Spirit worketh effectually vnto saluation. For whilest he reneweth men, that they may begin to will and worke those things that are pleasing to God, he doth truly and properly bring forth in them that sorrow which is according to God, and repentance vnto saluation" ("The Art of Prophesying," 2:666). John N. King, *Spenser's Poetry*, calls Fidelia a "religious advisor" whose "function as a wise tutor conforms to the Protestant doctrine of the priesthood of all believers" (64).

67. Greenham, "Of hearing Gods Word," 709.

68. Rogers, "Of the Meanes," 285.

69. Hemmingsen, *The Preacher*, fol. 53ᵛ.

70. See below, the chapter "Post-Armada Apocalyptic Discourse."

71. See Bernard Capp, "The Political Dimension of Apocalyptic Thought," in *The Apocalypse in English Renaissance Thought and Literature: Patterns, Antecedents, and Repercussions*, ed. C. A. Patrides and Joseph A. Wittreich Jr. (Ithaca NY: Cornell University Press, 1984), 93–124.

72. Earlier treatments are summarized in vol. 1 of *The Works of Edmund Spenser, a Variorum Edition*, ed. Edwin A. Greenlaw et al., 11 vols. (Baltimore: Johns Hopkins University Press, 1932–49); this edition of Spenser's works is referred to hereafter as *Variorum*. More recent modern studies include Josephine Waters Bennett, *The Evolution of "The Faerie Queene"* (Chicago: University of Chicago Press, 1942), 110–22; Hankins, *Source and Meaning in Spenser's Allegory*, 99–127; Joseph A. Wittreich Jr., *Visionary Poetics: Milton's Tradition and His Legacy* (San Marino CA: Huntington Library, 1979), 59–78; Florence Sandler, "*The Faerie Queene*: An Elizabethan Apocalypse," in *The Apocalypse in English Renaissance Thought and Literature: Patterns, Antecedents, and Repercussions*, ed. C. A. Patrides and Joseph A. Wittreich Jr. (Ithaca NY: Cornell University Press, 1984), 148–74; and John N. King, *Spenser's Poetry*, 72–75, 82–98.

73. The role of preaching in Tudor apocalypse is discussed by Paul Christianson, *Reformers and Babylon: English Apocalyptic Visions from the Ref-*

ormation to the Eve of the Civil War (Toronto: University of Toronto Press, 1978), 11; and Richard Bauckham, *Tudor Apocalypse* (Abingdon, Berkshire: Sutton Courtenay, 1978), 129–30.

74. Sandys, "The twentieth sermon. . . . The end of al things is at hand," in *Sermons*, sigs. Aa1ᵛ–Aa2ʳ. Cf. Becon in the preface to "The Castel of Comfort": "Agaynst these [papists] ought all men to fyghte, that tender the glorye of God. To confounde these Antichristes, ought we to sel walet, scrippe, cote, with all that euer we haue, and to bye us a swerde. I meane that swerde of the spirit, whiche is the worde of God. . . . And to this ende that I maye prouoke other valeauntlye, and boldelye to fyghte agaynst these aforesayd Antichristes: I according to the talent geuen me, haue taken upon me to wrastle with those wycked Papysts" (*The worckes*, fol. cᵛ). See also Bullinger, "Of the ministerie, and the ministers": "He shall consume Antichriste, sayth the Apostle, with the spirite of his mouth, and shall abolishe him with the brightnesse of his comming vnto iudgement. There shall be therefore ministers in the Churche and preachers, yea, in despite of the gates of hell, rage they neuer so horribly, euen vnto the ende of the world" (913).

Sermon Parody and Discourses of the Flesh

1. Maurice Evans, *Spenser's Anatomy of Heroism: A Commentary on "The Faerie Queene"* (Cambridge: Cambridge University Press, 1970), notices Guyon's erotic response, but it remains underinvestigated: "The salacious tale of the maiden's rape told, inevitably, by Archimago, moves him as it could only move a repressed personality" (112). Madelon S. Gohlke, "Embattled Allegory: Book II of *The Faerie Queene*," *English Literary Renaissance* 8 (1978): 123–40, also finds Guyon to be "repressed" (128) and takes up the issue of the human body in this book of the poem, though in a different context and with different conclusions from mine in this chapter. I find many of her insights rewarding. For example, she notes that "sexuality throughout the Book is associated with death" (137) and that "Book II is about the intransigence of matter, about the residue of what is savage, bestial, and uncivilized in human nature, specifically in the life of the flesh." Although Gohlke recognizes the "daemonic energies which rage beneath its cool rhetorical surface," she does not situate Book II in contemporary discourses to help account for how "Spenser forces the Book into conflict with itself" (139).

2. Becon, "A fruitful treatise of Fasting," in *The worckes*, fol. xciiiᵛ.

3. Many critics have sought connections between Books I and II, as summarized in Hamilton's edition, 163. More recent is the work of Norman K. Farmer Jr., "The World's New Body: Spenser's *Faerie Queene* Book II, St

Paul's Epistles, and Reformation England," in *Renaissance Culture in Context: Theory and Practice*, ed. Jean R. Brink and William F. Gentrup (Brookfield VT: Ashgate, 1993), 75–85. Farmer claims that "where Spenser's chief concern in Book I is with the nature of the spirit, his concern [in Book II] is the collateral nature of the corporeal" (77); he finds Book II allegorizing "neatly and without procrustean distortion" (79) the Pauline distinction between *sarks* and *soma*. The present chapter makes clear that I too find the Pauline understanding of the flesh to be crucial to this book of the poem. But I do not see Paul's definitions of the body as normative, nor do I find Paul an adequate gloss on the allegory (Farmer finds Book II divided "into three equal parts" [79] according to the Pauline distinctions).

4. A. S. P. Woodhouse, "Nature and Grace in the *Faerie Queene*," ELH 16 (1949): 194–228. Hamilton's edition, 163, summarizes links other scholars have found.

5. Earlier treatments according to "classical" and "Christian" standards are classified in Hamilton's edition, 163–65, and in Richard Mallette, "The Protestant Ethics of Love in Book II of *The Faerie Queene*," *Christianity and Literature* 3, no. 4 (1989): 62–63.

6. For the Reformation, Heb. 4:12 ("For the worde of God is liulie and mightie in operation, and sharper than anie two edged sworde, & entreth through, euen vnto the diuiding a sonder of the soule & the spirit, and of the ioynts, and the marie, and is a discerner of the thoughts and the intentes of the heart") joins sermon theory and the body, as the Geneva gloss suggests: "For [the Word] mortalie woundeth the rebellions, and in the elect it killeth the olde man that they shulde liue vnto God."

7. While the role of sermon discourse has remained largely unexplored by critics of Book II, it has been recently touched upon by Lauren Silberman, who notes in "*The Faerie Queene*, Book II and the Limitations of Temperance," *Modern Language Studies* 17 (1987): 9–22, that the Palmer "is the model of the simple-minded exegete who directs Guyon away from the stuff of human experience" (12). She cites two examples: the Palmer's misreading of the blood-stained hands of Ruddymane (he rejects the Christian interpretation and "instead provides a doubtful epyllion about a nymph who is turned into a fountain to avoid rape" [11]), and his interpretation of Acrasia's beasts (12.85), which she sees as a simplistic and "perfect synopsis of his characteristic exegetical method" (13). I find both examples telling, although I hesitate to conclude they constitute proof that Book II advances a critique of temperance "as a ready-made theoretical framework for acting in the fallen world" (9). Silberman suggests temperance proves inadequate because

it attempts to function as "revealed truth" and an adaptation of "Christian modes of allegory to secular uses" (10).

8. Ann E. Imbrie in "'Playing Legerdemaine with the Scripture'" appears to be the first to investigate sermon parody in the poem. A provocative historical context for sermon parody is offered by Haigh in "The Church of England, the Catholics and the People" (214–16), where he records widespread hostility toward Protestant preachers, often the butt of jokes among a recalcitrant lay audience.

9. The five sermon genres identified in this chapter are variously named by Reformation theorists. I have modified those named in Perkins, "The Art of Prophesying," 668–69; in Andreas Hyperius [Gerardus], *The Practis of Preaching*, trans. John Ludham (London, 1577), fols. 17^v–20^v; and in Hemmingsen, *The Preacher*, fols. 17^v–18^v. In "Of Prophecie and Preaching," Greenham summarizes how the preacher is to "apply" his wisdom: "All application of doctrine must be referred to one of these heads: 1. To teach and establish true opinions; 2. Or to confute false opinion; 3. Or to correct evil manners; 4. Or to frame good manners; 5. Or to comfort the will" (772). Jerome Dees's article "homiletics" in *The Spenser Encyclopedia*, 376–77, offers a useful outline of Reformation sermon theory, which he sees applied throughout the poem.

10. Greene, *The Light in Troy*, 46.

11. See Hugh MacLachlan, "The 'careless heauens': A Study of Revenge and Atonement in *The Faerie Queene*," *Spenser Studies* 1 (1980): 135–62.

12. See Carol V. Kaske, "hair," in *The Spenser Encyclopedia*, 344–45.

13. Alastair Fowler, "The Image of Mortalitie: *The Faerie Queene* II i-ii," *Huntington Library Quarterly* 24 (1961): 91–110, identifies the washing as baptism, but this interpretation has inspired no consensus, as Hamilton's edition notes (165). For example, Hume, *Edmund Spenser*, refutes the idea as defying "linguistic, thematic, and narrative effects" (173).

14. Scholarly attention to the human body has increased enormously since Elaine Scarry's *The Body in Pain: The Making and Unmaking of the World* (New York: Oxford University Press, 1985). Most relevant to this chapter—besides Scarry, 1–47—are Theresa M. Krier, *Gazing on Secret Sights: Spenser, Classical Imitation, and the Decorums of Vision* (Ithaca NY: Cornell University Press, 1990), 113–47, which explores the condition of the body in *The Faerie Queene* as having "a hallowed interior space and an eloquent, if vulnerable, exterior" (125); and Elizabeth Bellamy, "Em(body)ments of Power: Versions of the Body in Pain in Spenser," *Lit: Literature-Interpretation-Theory* 2 (1991): 303–21, which focuses on the

maimed bodies of Malfont and Timias. I have also profited from the following: Francis Barker, *The Tremulous Body Private: Essays on Subjection* (New York: Methuen, 1984), 3–41; John Hunt, "A Thing of Nothing: The Catastrophic Body in *Hamlet*," *Shakespeare Quarterly* 39 (1988): 27–42; Harry Berger Jr., "Bodies and Texts," *Representations* 17 (1987): 144–66; Bryan S. Turner, "Recent Developments in the Theory of the Body," in *The Body: Social Process and Cultural Theory* (Newbury Park CA: Sage, 1991), 1–35; Gail Kern Paster, *The Body Embarrassed: Drama and the Disciplines of Shame in Early Modern England* (Ithaca NY: Cornell University Press, 1993); and Patrick J. Gallagher, "Chaucer and the Rhetoric of the Body," *Chaucer Review* 28 (1994): 216–36.

15. Carol V. Kaske, "Amavia, Mortdant, Ruddymane," in *The Spenser Encyclopedia*, 25–27, trenchantly treats the episode by noting Pauline and other scriptural subtexts. Kaske points out that because Mortdant does not, despite his name, give death to anyone, he must suggest Adam's fall. She also identifies Amavia as reason—but as mere reason, not the right or divinely illuminated reason embodied in the Palmer. Hume, another Christianizing critic, disputes this reading by claiming Amavia has nothing to do with inward man nor Mortdant with flesh; instead she is irascible, he concupiscible (see *Edmund Spenser*, 171). I cite both critics as indicative of the power of an influential reading, namely Fowler's "The Image of Mortality."

16. Perkins, "The Combat of the Flesh and the Spirit," in *Workes* 1:470.

17. Becon, "The demaundes of holy scripture," in *The worckes*, fol. 454[r].

18. William Tyndale, "A Prologue vpon the Epistle of S. Paule to the Romaines," in *The Whole workes of W. Tyndall* (London, 1573), 43.

19. Cited in Philip Schaff, *The Evangelical Protestant Creeds*, vol. 3 of *The Creeds of Christendom* (New York: Harper, 1877), 493.

20. Weatherby, *Mirrors of Celestial Grace*, 97–107, argues Greek patristic texts that urge utter mortification of the passions as one of Spenser's sources in Book II.

21. Sandys, "The ninth sermon. . . . All the daies of my warrefare," in *Sermons*, sig. I8[r].

22. Tyndale, "A Prologue vpon . . . Romaines," 42, 46, 48.

23. Tyndale, "An exposition vpon the v. vi. vii. chapters of Mathew," in *The Whole workes*, 186.

24. Becon, "A fruitful treatise of Fasting," fol. xciiii[r]. Becon claims in "The Catechisme" that the flesh is "an aduersarye so muche the more to be feared, because she is domesticall, and one of the household, yea nourisshed and brought up euen in our own breaste" (*The worckes*, fol. ccccx[r]; see also fol. cccxci[r]).

25. Becon, "A Dialogue betweene the Christian knyght and Satan," in *The worckes*, fols. cl^{r–v}.

26. Tyndale, "A Prologue vpon . . . Romaines," 42, 46.

27. *Variorum* 2:415–23 summarizes earlier critical positions on the relation of Book II of *The Faerie Queene* to Aristotelian continence and temperance. For recent considerations of Aristotle's virtues in Book II, see J. Carscallen, "temperance," in *The Spenser Encyclopedia*, 680–82; and Weatherby, *Mirrors of Celestial Grace*, 108–13. Most scholars consider Spenserian temperance close to Aristotelian continence as it is mapped out in the *Nicomachean Ethics*, bk. 2, sec. 7; bk. 3, secs. 10–12; and all of bk. 7. See Cicero, *Tusculan Disputations*, bk. 4, secs. 6–7, sec. 31.

28. Hamilton's edition illuminates these lines with the Geneva gloss to 2 Cor. 5:1: "After this bodie shalbe dissolved, it shalbe made incorruptible and immortal" (277).

29. Leonard Barkan, *Nature's Work of Art: The Human Body as an Image of the World* (New Haven: Yale University Press, 1975), speaks for other commentators who accept (too readily) the surface details of the blazon: "Belphoebe's [body] is viewed and iconographically interpreted on a cosmic plan. Because she is chaste and beautiful, her body is a microcosm of heaven. . . . This description . . . serves to inscribe the perfect human body in a figurative circle of the cosmos" (216).

30. See Mikhail Bakhtin, *Rabelais and His World*, trans. Helene Iswolsky (Bloomington: Indiana University Press, 1984), 24–29. Peter Stallybrass argues that bodily definitions are important in mapping out both gender and class in the early modern period. His citing of the Bakhtinian contrasts in the constructions of female bodies, especially in his treatment of the queen's body, has intriguing applications to the contrasts between Amavia and Belphoebe. See Stallybrass, "Patriarchal Territories: The Body Enclosed," in *Rewriting the Renaissance: The Discourse of Sexual Difference in Early Modern Europe*, ed. Maureen Quilligan, Nancy J. Vickers, and Catherine Stimpson (Chicago: University of Chicago Press, 1986), 123–42.

31. Nancy J. Vickers, "Diana Described: Scattered Woman and Scattered Rhyme," in *Writing and Sexual Difference*, ed. Elizabeth Abel (Brighton: Harvester, 1982), 96, 103. Maureen Quilligan regards the dismemberment of the blazon as neutralizing Elizabethan anxieties about female public authority; see "The Comedy of Female Authority in *The Faerie Queene*," *English Literary Renaissance* 17 (1987): 162–65. Mary Villeponteaux considers the blazon as part of the critique of Elizabeth's virginity, neither allowing nor admitting sexual desire; see "*Semper Eadem*: Belphoebe's De-

nial of Desire," in *Renaissance Discourses of Desire*, ed. Claude Summers and Ted-Larry Pebworth (Columbia: University of Missouri Press, 1993), 29–45, esp. 33. Krier, *Gazing on Secret Sights*, 66–79, considers the encounter between Belphoebe and Braggadochio at length, focusing on the "therapeutic, beneficial effects" of Belphoebe on the viewer; Krier sees the episode as a "salute to Elizabeth's wonderful presence" (74–75).

32. Based on such descriptions as these, an earlier generation of scholars holds a more idealist view of Belphoebe. For example, A. C. Hamilton, *The Structure of Allegory in "The Faerie Queene"* (Oxford: Clarendon, 1961), considers her the "unfallen Eden watered and nourished by the Well and Tree of Life" (136–37); and Harry Berger Jr., *The Allegorical Temper: Vision and Reality in the "Faerie Queene" II* (New Haven: Yale University Press, 1958) regards her as "prelapsarian" and untouched by sin; see 144–49.

33. See Hemmingsen, *The Preacher*, fols. 64ʳ–66ᵛ.

34. Hamilton's edition glosses II.5.22 with this verse from James, but it strikes me as more appropriate here.

35. Weatherby, *Mirrors of Celestial Grace*, sees in the Palmer's advice a call for Saint Basil's version of fleshly mortification: "to wipe [the passions] 'cleane away' seems requisite for salvation" (127–28). Perhaps so, but the Palmer's is not Book II's sole admonition; nor is it indisputably normative; nor is it consistent with advice the Palmer offers elsewhere. John Webster analyses the Palmer's stanzas (4.34–35) and rightly notes their inadequacy as a guide to human behavior: "one would hope that no one would willingly give up grief and especially love, as if they, too, were merely ghastly specters." Webster notes that Atin's subsequent appearance and his active seeking out of Occasion also undermines the Palmer's certainties about merely avoiding her. In this fashion the reader is forced, says Webster, to revise "relatively simple allegorical schemes [that] teach directly." See Webster, "'The Methode of a Poete': An Inquiry into Tudor Conceptions of Poetic Sequence," *English Literary Renaissance* 11 (1981): 40. I would add that Atin's seeking of Occasion also suggests that Book II's representation of sermon discourse is likewise undermined by such means, often bringing it closer to parody.

36. See, for example, Perkins, "A Godly and Learned Exposition of Christ's Sermon on the Mount," in *Workes* 3:1.

37. Imbrie, "'Playing Legerdemaine with the Scripture,'" 150. Imbrie cites the Geneva gloss: "If the concupiscence & wicked affections ouercome reason, we must not marueile though men be blinded, and be like unto beasts." See also Virgil Whitaker, *The Religious Basis of Spenser's Thought* (Stanford: Stanford University Press, 1950), 25–26.

38. Anne Lake Prescott, "Mammon," in *The Spenser Encyclopedia*, 451–52. This essay is admirably lucid, not only encompassing most readings of the episode but also adding to the fund of knowledge about it. Later references to Prescott's views of Mammon are from this essay.

39. Cullen, *Infernal Triad*, 68–70, reviews scholarly investigations of biblical parody in the Mammon episode.

40. Imbrie, "'Playing Legerdemaine with the Scripture,'" 143–44, outlines uses made of Matthew 4 by sixteenth-century hermeneuts to comment on preaching. Satan, Imbrie notes, is consistently seen as the prototype of the false preacher.

41. But *before* they enter the house of Richesse, in debating Mammon (7.12–17) Guyon replicates homiletic commonplace. Here Guyon replays his earlier preacherly role, expanding his sweep to comment on the human condition in the corrective fashion: riches are "roote of all disquietnesse" and "Infinite mischiefes of them do arize" (7.12); "Frayle men are oft captiu'd to couetise" (7.15); and so forth. Only after he has entered the house of Richesse does his sermonizing cease.

42. See Frank Kermode, *Shakespeare, Spenser, Donne: Renaissance Essays* (New York: Viking, 1971), 70.

43. Berger, *The Allegorical Temper*, claims that Guyon is "the megalopsychos relying on himself" (16) and in need of Christian grace. Berger's view prompts later critical variations on the theme that Guyon (or the temperance he defends) is wanting Christian supplementary grace, provided by Arthur's rescue. These positions are summarized in Hamilton's edition, 165–66, and in Weatherby, *Mirrors of Celestial Grace*, 132–39. Most critics have approached the faint as a portentous affair. In an influential and compelling discussion in *Infernal Triad*, 88–94, Cullen sees in the faint Guyon's inheritance as an Adamic being: "the image of Guyon prostrate on the earth is an image of man's bondage to the flesh, to the old Adam within who is 'of the earth, earthly' (I Corinthians 15:47)" (89). Guyon faints because, says Cullen, he tries to defeat the devil—to play Christ—without access to grace. So Cullen separates Christ's two natures: in his faint, Guyon approximates Christ as a man, "but without the direct assistance of grace, Guyon cannot as *homo* imitate the total triumph of the *deus homo* over the original taint of the flesh and over the devil" (90). Modeled as it is on a Pauline-Augustinian paradigm, Cullen's insistence on Guyon's *imitatio Adamis* is sympathetic to Reformation discourses of the flesh.

44. See Hamilton's edition, 166. Cullen, *Infernal Triad*, 88–89, sketches critical positions of previous commentators on the faint, including those

who ascribe it to physical causes. Two other commentators treat the faint as primarily physical, with other ramifications: the position of Lewis H. Miller Jr., in "A Secular Reading of *The Faerie Queene*, Book II," *ELH* 33 (1966): 154–69, is confirmed by Gohlke, who asserts in "Embattled Allegory" that Guyon faints "not only because he has ignored bodily needs but also because he has assumed a psychological stance which abhors the body and any pleasures which may be derived from it" (129). Silberman, "The Limitations of Temperance," sees the faint as indicative of Guyon's "neglect of his grosser sensual needs" (12) and of the limitations of the titular virtue. Evans, *Spenser's Anatomy of Heroism*, suggests a pun on "vittles" and "vital" (131).

45. See, for example, Hugh MacLachlan, "The Death of Guyon and the *Elizabethan Book of Homilies*," *Spenser Studies* 4 (1983): 93–114; and Weatherby, *Mirrors of Celestial Grace*, 145–51.

46. Hume, *Edmund Spenser*, notes the resemblance to "sermon idiom . . . heightened by the impassioned sequence of questions and exclamations" (119).

47. Kathleen Williams, *Spenser's World of Glass: A Reading of the "Faerie Queene"* (Berkeley and Los Angeles: University of California Press, 1966), 63, reads this episode as a battle within Guyon, between his regenerate and unregenerate parts. See John Hankins, "psychomachia," in *The Spenser Encyclopedia*, 570, on the origins of the form as a battle.

48. Peter Stambler, "The Development of Guyon's Christian Temperance," *English Literary Renaissance* 7 (1977): 51–89, claims that when Guyon emerges from Mammon's house, "he seems to have undergone the kind of baptism . . . described by Romans 6 and Article 27" (73). In general, Christianizing critics are eager to see in Guyon's adventures those of Redcrosse.

49. David Lee Miller, *The Poem's Two Bodies: The Poetics of the 1590 "Faerie Queene"* (Princeton: Princeton University Press, 1988), argues that this stanza "sets forth a politics of bodily form" that "naturalizes an authoritarian image of restraint, fulfilling one of the classic functions of ideology: to derive political structures from nature or God" (154–55). I would argue something like the converse: that this stanza, when seen in the context of Book II's preoccupation with the body, ideologizes the body, that it derives bodily images of restraint from ideology—hence the book's focus on temperance as a bodily phenomenon, shored up by a complex intertextual network of political and religious discourses.

50. Evans, *Spenser's Anatomy of Heroism*, 141, seems to be the first to record the absence of sexual organs. This omission is closely investigated by

David Lee Miller, who ponders in *The Poem's Two Bodies* the "cultural ta-
boo against naming [the penis]" and sees the elision of the genitals as an aspect of the ideological transformation of the body for political purposes: the
female organ disappears, and the head is privileged as the source of masculine authority (see 164–68, 182–83). More persuasively, he finds that
"genital eros" is displaced in Alma's house by "framing" sexuality in the encounters with Shamefastnesse and Prays-desire (see 169–80). The tour of the
house "turns aside from the instruments of copulation to discover an allegorical coupling in the heart" (180). In keeping with his view that Book II ideologizes Tudor monarchy, Miller finds that the "phallic completion of the
temperate body is displaced into canto 10 and our reading of the two histo-
ries" (213). Reviewing Miller's book in *Spenser Newsletter* 20, no. 1 (1989):
7, Donald Cheney notes that "Even the conspicuously ungendered house of
Alma may owe its elided genitalia to the fact that it is figuring the human
body and not just the male or female body." Harry Berger Jr., "Narrative as
Rhetoric in *The Faerie Queene*," *English Literary Renaissance* 21 (1991): 3–
48, observes wisely that the house figures a gendered body throughout, not
merely in the heart's parlor but also in the ways power and potential conflict
are organized (33). None of these commentators notes the lead of Gohlke,
who, however erring in her conclusions, contextualizes in "Embattled Allegory" the episode in Book II's preoccupation with the body: as allegorized in
Alma's house the body is "disorganized in two out of three of its brain cham-
bers and built on slime. . . . The body has virtually no positive functions, ex-
isting primarily as a threat to the embattled soul" (130).

51. See Hamilton's edition, 280, the note to stanzas 45–46.

52. In "Nature and Grace," Woodhouse influentially identifies Maleger
as original sin. Hume, *Edmund Spenser*, finds a more apt gloss for the character in article 9 of the Thirty-nine Articles: "the infection of nature [that]
doth remain, yea in them that are regenerated" (see 125). Stambler, "The Development of Guyon's Christian Temperance," sees Maleger as standing for
"mortality—all those ills, pains, diseases, sins, and results of sin which stem
from the ineradicable original sin. He is a composite portrait of all that mortality entails" (87). Hamilton's edition finds in Maleger "the old Adam in us,
against whom Paul laments: 'O wretched man that I am, who shal deliver me
from the bodie of this death?' (Rom. 7:24)" (167). I am more persuaded by
Philip Rollinson in "Arthur, Maleger, and the Interpretation of *The Faerie
Queene*," *Spenser Studies* 7 (1987): 103–20. Rollinson sees Maleger as "Dis-
tempered through misrule and passions bace" (9.1) and grown a monster:
"in the moral framework, then, Maleger is 'misrule,' his army the army of

the base passions, and together they assault the castle of temperance, the so-ber, well-governed body" (107).

53. See Sol. 4:12. See Stanley Stewart, *The Enclosed Garden: The Tradition and the Image in Seventeenth-Century Poetry* (Madison: University of Wisconsin Press, 1966), 171–76.

54. Greenblatt, *Renaissance Self-Fashioning*, 172–73.

55. See Imbrie, " 'Playing Legerdemaine with the Scripture,' " 152. Hamilton's edition, 295, lists other sources and commentary in Spenser criticism.

Reformation Continence and Chastity

1. J. S. Weld, "The Complaint of Britomart: Word-Play and Symbolism," *PMLA* 66 (1951): 548–51, first called attention to Britomart's wordplay, although Weld does not treat its intertextual implications in Reformation discourse. The episode is explored for its Petrarchan subtext by Susanne Lindgren Wofford, "Britomart's Petrarchan Lament: Allegory and Narrative in *The Faerie Queene* III, iv," *Comparative Literature* 39 (1987): 28–57. Wofford demonstrates convincingly how the Petrarchan subtext, by calling attention to the difficulty of distinguishing inner state from outer setting, has implications for the Spenserian difficulty of representing truth through allegory. Wofford sees the pun as reinforcing the in-between nature of both Britomart's state (at once continent and incontinent) and Spenserian allegory, where inner and outer, mortal and mythic, story and meaning are brought together (52–53).

2. *Variorum* 3:400–402 lists sources and analogues. Berger, " 'Kidnapped Romance,' " 212–35, examines the interplay of erotic discourses in the book, particularly Ovidian, Petrarchan, and Ariostan in the Florimell episodes.

3. C. S. Lewis, *The Allegory of Love: A Study in Medieval Tradition* (Oxford: Oxford University Press, 1936), 340–45, maintains that "Chastity for [Spenser] means Britomart, married love" (340) and that Book III of *The Faerie Queene* explores a conflict between "courtly love" and marriage, but he does not investigate this idea in a Protestant context. Mark Rose, *Heroic Love: Studies in Sidney and Spenser* (Cambridge: Harvard University Press, 1968), interprets Book III as endorsing Protestant attitudes toward marriage; see esp. 98, 111, 117, 126–27. Rose's conclusions differ considerably from mine. John N. King, *Spenser's Poetry*, 148–51, treats the virginity of Britomart and Belphoebe in the context of the unmarried state of Elizabeth I. Lisa Klein, " 'Let us love, dear love, lyke as we ought': Protestant Marriage and the Revision of Petrarchan Loving in Spenser's *Amoretti*," *Spenser Studies* 10 (1992): 109–37, argues persuasively in terms bearing also on

Book III that the *Amoretti* uses a Petrarchan representation of the woman to renounce Petrarchanism and to present her anew in Protestant terms: "A humble companion of a wife is formed from and supplants a proud tyrant of a mistress, and the concord of marriage is ensured only after the possibility of discord is eliminated" (116).

4. See H. S. V. Jones, *A Spenser Handbook* (New York: Appleton-Century-Crofts, 1930), 213–15; William Nelson, *The Poetry of Spenser: A Study* (New York: Columbia University Press, 1963), 228–29; John C. Bean, "Cosmic Order in *The Faerie Queene*: From Temperance to Chastity," *SEL* 17 (1977): 67–79; and Mark Rose, *Heroic Love*, 117, 124, 128. The notes to Book III in Hamilton's edition provide the most extensive treatment of the connections between the second and third books of the poem.

5. On the subject of virginity, see John Bugge, *Virginitas: An Essay in the History of a Medieval Ideal* (The Hague: Nijhoff, 1975). As the following notes demonstrate, the Reformation undoing of celibacy is commonplace and the subject of wide investigation by modern scholarship. Two notable discussions from an earlier generation of students of the Reformation are George and George, *The Protestant Mind of the English Reformation*, 265–75; and Christopher Hill, *Society and Puritanism in Pre-Revolutionary England* (London: Macmillan, 1964), 443–81.

6. Perkins, "Oeconomie or, Household-government," in *Workes* 3:671. Calvin phrases the issue similarly: "If strengthe faile him to tame his lust, let him learne that the Lorde hathe now layde vpon him a necessitie to marrie" (2.8.42; fol. 127ʳ).

7. Thomas Pritchard, *A Pithie Epistle and learned Discourse . . . of honourable Wedlocke* (London, 1579), 48.

8. Krier, *Gazing on Secret Sights*, argues Spenser's "conflicted sense that virginity is atavistic as well as beautiful" (164; see also 170, 224).

9. The classic statement of this position is that of William and Malleville Haller, "The Puritan Art of Love," *Huntington Library Quarterly* 5 (1942): 235–72. See also Carroll Camden, *The Elizabethan Woman* (New York: Elsevier, 1952), 109–49; Roland Mushat Frye, "The Teachings of Classical Puritanism on Conjugal Love," *Studies in the Renaissance* 2 (1955): 148–59; John K. Yost, "The Value of Married Life for the Social Order in the Early English Renaissance," *Societas* 6 (1976): 25–37; Lawrence Stone, *The Family, Sex, and Marriage in England 1500–1800* (New York: Harper & Row, 1977), 135–38; and Mary Beth Rose, *The Expense of Spirit: Love and Sexuality in English Renaissance Drama* (Ithaca NY: Cornell University Press, 1988), 12–21, 29–32, 119–31. I have benefitted throughout this chapter from Rose's insights.

10. Stone is the also the most notable proponent of the paradigm of "restrictive patriarchy"; see *The Family, Sex, and Marriage*, 151–218. See also Catherine M. Dunn, "The Changing Image of Woman in Renaissance Society and Literature," in *What Manner of Woman: Essays in English and American Literature*, ed. Marlene Springer (New York: New York University Press, 1977), 15–38; and Steven Ozment, *When Fathers Ruled: Family Life in Reformation Europe* (Cambridge: Harvard University Press, 1983), 55, 70. In contrast, Margaret J. M. Ezell, *The Patriarch's Wife: Literary Evidence and the History of the Family* (Chapel Hill: University of North Carolina Press, 1987), 1–35, challenges the idea of continued patriarchy in the period by reclaiming women's voices in various contexts. The most convincing short treatment of the subject, which confirms Stone's thesis (with qualifications), is Kathleen M. Davies, "Continuity and Change in Literary Advice on Marriage," in *Marriage and Society: Studies in the Social History of Marriage*, ed. R. B. Outhwaite (London: Europa, 1981), 58–80. Davies stresses continuities between pre-Reformation and Protestant texts on marriage and concludes that women are granted no greater "liberty than that described by pre-Reformation writers who discussed the same problems" (70). This position is confirmed by Linda T. Fitz, "'What Says the Married Woman?': Marriage Theory and Feminism in the English Renaissance," *Mosaic* 13 (1980): 1–22. Four notable studies provide balanced views: Linda Woodbridge, *Women and the English Renaissance: Literature and the Nature of Womankind, 1540–1620* (Urbana: University of Illinois Press, 1984); Katherine Usher Henderson and Barbara F. McManus, *Half Humankind: Contexts and Texts of the Controversy about Women in England 1540–1640* (Urbana: University of Illinois Press, 1985), esp. 11–20, 47–81; Elaine V. Beilin, *Redeeming Eve: Women Writers of the English Renaissance* (Princeton: Princeton University Press, 1987); and Guido Ruggiero, "Marriage, Love, Sex, and Renaissance Civic Morality," in *Sexuality and Gender in Early Modern Europe: Institutions, Texts, Images*, ed. James Grantham Turner (Cambridge: Cambridge University Press, 1993), esp. 11–13.

11. Heather Dubrow, *A Happier Eden: The Politics of Marriage in the Stuart Epithalamium* (Ithaca NY: Cornell University Press, 1990), 13. I have found Dubrow's study, esp. 6–26, a model of useful scholarship. In *The Birthpangs of Protestant England*, 60–93, Collinson explores whether the Reformation "rivetted home patriarchy" (62) and presents evidence for several positions on the question. He concludes that the Reformation family as a concept is not a novelty but longstanding and part of a historical continuum (93).

12. Greenblatt, *Renaissance Self-Fashioning*, 247–50. Greenblatt's paragraphs on Reformation cautions against sexual "excess" in marriage, which he offers in his analysis of *Othello*, have not had the scholarly impact that nearly every other section of this book has.

13. John Dod and Robert Cleaver, *A Godlie Forme of Householde Government* (London, 1598), 138.

14. William Gouge, *Of Domesticall Duties* (London, 1622), 15.

15. "Of the State of Matrimony," in *Certain Sermons or Homilies* (London, 1563), sig. Gg4ᵛ.

16. Gouge, *Of Domesticall Duties*, 216.

17. Perkins, "A Reformed Catholike," 586. See also William Whately, *A Bride-bush: or, A Direction for Married Persons* (London, 1619): "Now God hath ordained matrimony to preuent whoedom, euen in those that want the gift of continency; that is, of restraining their passions in this kind" (13).

18. Dod and Cleaver, *A Godlie Forme*, 98. Cf. Henry Bullinger, *The Golden Boke of Christen Matrimonye*, trans. Miles Coverdale, with a preface by Thomas Becon (London, 1543), sig. Cviʳ: "In the loue and consenting of harlots ther is also an ernest fauour of the one louer toward the other, but that is carnal and wycked, therfore doth the deuyl knit that whorish and unthriftie knot."

19. Edmund Tilney, *A briefe and pleasaunt discourse of duties in Mariage, called the Flower of Friendship* (London, 1587), sig. Biiiiʳ. Tilney's is not a Protestant tract, but he is contemporary with Reformation efflorescence of marriage discourse and exhibits many structural features of that discourse. In the introduction to her volume *"The Flower of Friendship": A Renaissance Dialogue Contesting Marriage* (Ithaca NY: Cornell University Press, 1992), Valerie Wayne places Tilney's tract within "residual, dominant, and emerging ideologies of marriage" (3). For the Reformation views and continuity with humanist approaches, see 24–36, 89–93, especially for the idea that companionship did not lead to equality in marriage.

20. Thomas Gataker, *Marriage Duties Briefely Couched Togither* (London, 1620), 37.

21. The *Oxford English Dictionary* also lists "self-restraint in sexual appetite, either by moderation or abstinence" as one of the primary meanings of "continence." "Continent" has "sexual self-restraint" as a primary meaning. In discussing the role of the queen as both Venus and Diana, Krier, *Gazing on Secret Sights*, notes that "if virginity is a state in which something is contained and hidden within, inviolate, then the contained is to become the abundance of eros, . . . sanctioned by propinquity to Christian images of love" (131).

22. Bullinger, *The Golden Boke*, sig. Div^r.

23. Pritchard, *A Pithie Epistle*, 84.

24. Bullinger, *The Golden Boke*, sig. Dii^r.

25. Whately, *A Bride-bush*, 6.

26. Dod and Cleaver, *A Godlie Forme*, 158.

27. Pritchard says: "the [sexual] acte in marriage is no sinne . . . yet if yee take excesse or use it beastly, vilely, or inordinately, your mistemperance make that yll which is good" (*A Pithie Epistle*, 84). Perkins: "For euen in wedlocke excesse in lusts is no better then plaine adulterie before God. This is the iudgement of the ancient Church, that Intemperance, that is immoderate desire euen betweene man and wife, is fornication" ("Oeconomie," 691). And Whately: "in a word, marriage must bee vsed . . . seldome and sparingly. . . . Excessiuenesse inflameth lust, and disposeth the persons so offending to adultery. Moderation kills lust, and is a great furtherance to purity. . . . But to satisfie the naturall desires, when vnprovoked, they tend to vnrulinesse" (*A Bride-bush*, 19–20). See also Gouge, *Of Domesticall Duties*, 223, and Greenblatt, *Renaissance Self-Fashioning*, 247–50.

28. Augustine, "The Good of Marriage," trans. Charles T. Wilcox, in *On Marriage and Other Subjects*, ed. Roy J. Deferrari (Washington DC: Catholic University of America Press, 1955), 13.

29. On the humanist positions on marriage see Margo Todd, *Christian Humanism and the Puritan Social Order* (Cambridge: Cambridge University Press, 1987), 96–117; and Wayne, ed., *"The Flower of Friendship,"* 13–38.

30. Erasmus, "An Epistle to persuade a yong Gentleman to mariage," in Thomas Wilson, *The Arte of Rhetorique* (London, 1580), 56. See also Erasmus's colloquy "A mery Dialogue, declaring the propertyes of shrowde shrewes, and honest wyues," in *Tudor Translations of the Colloquies of Erasmus (1536–1584)*, ed. Dickie Spurgeon (Delmar NY: Scholars' Facsimiles and Reprints, 1972), 245–84. Other colloquies by Erasmus on marriage and related topics are relevant; see *The Colloquies of Erasmus*, trans. Craig R. Thompson (Chicago: University of Chicago Press, 1965), 86–127.

31. Reformation commentators do, of course, commend married sexual relations, usually with the Pauline euphemism "due beneuolence" (1 Cor. 7:3). Perkins calls married relations "a holie and undefiled action" ("Oeconomie," 691). See Anthony Fletcher, "The Protestant Idea of Marriage in Early Modern England," in *Religion, Culture and Society in Early Modern Britain: Essays in Honour of Patrick Collinson*, ed. Anthony Fletcher and Peter Roberts (Cambridge: Cambridge University Press, 1994),

161–81. Fletcher asserts that the Reformation writers of conduct books on marriage "valued the physical and intimate aspect of marriage very highly indeed. . . . The Puritan writers gave an account of sex that was entirely positive" (175–76). Such statements seem to me based on a reading of texts that simply ignores the severe qualifications these writers place upon sexuality.

32. Dod and Cleaver, *A Godlie Forme*, 184.

33. Nona Fienberg has pointed out to me that there are at least three puns here, one playing on Britomart's role as Elizabeth I, who will "raign" indeed, if not on the continent. The wordplay continues in this episode as Britomart is said to "powre" her cares into vengeance (3.13), "for all was in her powre" (3.18). The play of double (and more) senses asks that Britomart be seen not only as hero of chastity but also as the queen herself. Philippa Berry, *Of Chastity and Power: Elizabethan Literature and the Unmarried Queen* (New York: Routledge, 1989), 65–66, considers the queen's role as a chaste Protestant ruler. Julia Walker, "Spenser's Elizabeth Portrait and the Fiction of Dynastic Epic," *Modern Philology* 90 (1992): 172–99, sees Britomart as a "secret depiction of Elizabeth" (177). I disagree with her conclusion that Britomart is not presented "primarily as a future wife and mother" (189), but Walker makes a convincing case that Britomart gradually becomes a "chiastic portrait of public female power" (189), especially in later books of *The Faerie Queene*. See also Margaret Thickstun, *Fictions of the Feminine: Puritan Doctrine and the Representation of Women* (Ithaca NY: Cornell University Press, 1988): "Protestant companionate marriage—the telos of Britomart's quest—effectively channels and controls female power" (44). Britomart demonstrates this herself in Book IV when she voluntarily cedes her power to Artegall, whom she has shown herself capable of unhorsing: "she yeelded her consent / To be his loue, and take him for her Lord" (IV.6.41). Gregerson, *The Reformation of the Subject*, 9–47, treats Britomart as a positive example of the erotic construction of subjectivity: "In Britomart's addendum to the genre of chivalric romance, the reciprocal unfolding of errancy and linear purpose is further complicated by the differential interplay between ostensible and occluded intentions, initiating and interpolated quests; the inevitable contingencies of martial and moral example are aggravated by the problematics of surrogacy and erotic 'invention'" (9).

34. Britomart's androgyny has been plentifully discussed. Richard A. Lanham, "The Literal Britomart," *Modern Language Quarterly* 28 (1967): 426–45, summarizes earlier critics' observations of Britomart's "unique mixture of masculine and feminine traits" (427) and notes that her Petrarchan clichés "are for a man" (437). Sheila T. Cavanagh, *Wanton Eyes*

and Chaste Desires: Female Sexuality in "The Faerie Queene" (Bloomington: Indiana University Press, 1994), 139–72, considers Britomart's gender transgressions in a variety of contexts, including the necessity of "becoming more male than female" (150). Cavanagh argues that Britomart is forced into dull-wittedness and other compromises because "the text implicitly supports the culture's systematic denial of women" (171).

35. See Robert Ellrodt, *Neoplatonism in the Poetry of Spenser* (Geneva: E. Droz, 1960), 34; John Charles Nelson, *The Renaissance Theory of Love* (New York: Columbia University Press, 1958), 67.

36. Merritt Y. Hughes, in *Variorum* 3:334–35, traces how this episode imitates the *Ciris*. Of stanza 32 he notes, "Britomart's talk of reason as the bridle of love has no justification in the *Ciris*."

37. Hamilton's edition at stanza 39 is relevant: "the Castle of Alma treats the body from the waist up, in accord with Temperance's control over the passions. Book III treats the body's lower half" (323). I suggest that Reformation erotic discourse, mediating between these two books of the poem, makes this shift more likely. Henderson and McManus, *Half Humankind*, claim that "the chastity of the Renaissance woman, unlike that of the Victorian woman, was not attributed to a low level of sexual desire; rather it was seen as the product of conscious and virtuous self-control" (59).

38. Thickstun, *Fictions of the Feminine*, claims that after the defeat of Radigund (V.7.37–42) Britomart yields her authority to Artegall and thus "uses her political power to reinforce patriarchal order" by repealing the "liberty of women" (V.7.42). In this way, says Thickstun, "the most aggressive, active good woman in the poem articulates [a] doctrine of female subordination" (57). Harry Berger Jr., *Revisionary Play: Studies in the Spenserian Dynamics* (Berkeley and Los Angeles: University of California Press, 1988), notes of Britomart's chastity: "whether erotic or anti-erotic, it is a virtue prized by and necessary to male control of the institutional cornerstone, marriage, on which the preservation and continuity of patriarchal order are founded" (464).

39. See Paul J. Alpers, *The Poetry of "The Faerie Queene"* (Princeton: Princeton University Press, 1967), 363. Hugh MacLachlan, "The 'carelesse heauens': A Study of Revenge and Atonement in *The Faerie Queene*," *Spenser Studies* 1 (1980): 135–61, thoroughly treats the motif of vengeance and wrath in Book II, and I have profited by applying his insights to Book III. Berger, *Revisionary Play*, notes that Britomart "protects herself against aggressive male warfare by wearing armor, against aggressive male passion by wearing disguise, and against the assaults of eros within by using the forms of male aggressiveness as an outlet" (107).

40. Hamilton's edition, 338, points out that Natalis Comes, *Mythologiae* (Venice, 1567), identifies Aeolus with reason.

41. Camille Paglia, "sex," in *The Spenser Encyclopedia*, 638–41, claims that "Spenser is the anatomist of an economy of sex, of physiological laws of pressure and control, which he embodies in frequent images of binding and loosing" (639). Paglia's article is trenchant, but her claim that the "premiere principle of *The Faerie Queene* is marriage" (638) is simply false.

42. See, for example, *The Faerie Queene* II.5.1, 7.1, 12.51; III.1.19, 12.2, 12.31, 12.37.

43. See, for example, *Variorum* 3:323–24; and Hankins, *Source and Meaning in Spenser's Allegory*, 151.

44. A typical example is Guyon's reaction to the temptations of the Bowre:

> Much wondred *Guyon* at the faire aspect
> Of that sweet place, yet suffred no delight
> To sincke into his sence, nor minde affect,
> But passed forth, and lookt still forward right,
> Bridling his will, and maistering his might.
>   (II.12.53)

Unlike the characteristic uses of the metaphor in Book III, those describing Guyon's bridling suggest his ease with self-control.

45. Julia Walker, "Spenser's Elizabeth Portrait," makes a clever case for Britomart as a "conflation of Dido and Aeneas" (188).

46. Lesley W. Brill, "Chastity as Ideal Sexuality in the Third Book of *The Faerie Queene*," *SEL* 11 (1971): 15–18, sees chastity as heroism.

47. See Aristotle, *Nicomachean Ethics*, bk. 3, secs. 10–12, and bk. 7, trans. H. Rackham, Loeb Classical Library (Cambridge: Harvard University Press, 1956), 173–87, 374–449.

48. "Temperance is the virtue which makes for moderation through right reason in eating and drinking," Melanchthon writes in *Enarrationes*; "In Latin, temperance properly has meaning only in these things [eating and drinking], but Aristotle adds to them moderation in sexual matters, which is usually described with the word continence [*continentia*]." Melanchthon then ties these virtues to "apostolic writings," citing the Epistles: "In these places, scripture speaks properly of chastity [*pudicitas*] or chasteness [*castitas*]." (Unpublished translations by Paul F. Gehl.) For Melanchthon's full statement in Latin, see *Variorum* 3:322–23.

49. See H. S. V. Jones, "The *Faerie Queene* and the Medieval Aristotelian Tradition," *JEGP* 25 (1926): 283–98; and F. M. Padelford, "The Allegory of Chastity in The Faerie Queene," in *Variorum* 3:322–23. Jones asserts that

"What we have in Melanchthon's commentary upon Aristotle is . . . Continence and Chastity enjoined in the seventh commandment and celebrated in *F.Q.* books 2, 3" (296). See also Ernest Sirluck, "*The Faerie Queene*, Book II, and the *Nicomachean Ethics*," *Modern Philology* 49 (1952): 73–100. Thomas Elyot, *The Boke Named the Governor* (London, 1531), opines that "Continence is a vertue which keepeth the pleasaunt appetite of man under the yoke of reason. Aristotle making them both but one, describeth them under the name of Continence, saying: He that is continent, forasmuch as he knoweth that couetous desires be euil, doth abandon them, reason perswading him . . . Continence, the only forbearing the unlawfull company of women" (fol. 179ʳ). Elyot goes on to aver that "to imbrace Continence, I meane not to liue euer chast; but to honour matrimonye" (fol. 184ʳ).

50. See Humphrey Tonkin, *The Faerie Queene* (London: Unwin Hyman, 1989), 115–16; and Brill, "Chastity as Ideal Sexuality," 20.

51. For a summary of interpretations of the wound, see Lesley W. Brill, "'Battles That Need Not Be Fought': *The Faerie Queene* III i," *English Literary Renaissance* 5 (1975): 15–26. Thomas P. Roche Jr., *The Kindly Flame: A Study of the Third and Fourth Books of Spenser's "Faerie Queene"* (Princeton: Princeton University Press, 1964), 70, treats the wound as Britomart's initiation into love and sexuality.

52. See J. Carscallen, "temperance," in *The Spenser Encyclopedia*, 681–82.

53. See George and George, *The Protestant Mind of the English Reformation*, 266; and Dubrow, *A Happier Eden*, 17. Carol Kaske, "chastity," in *The Spenser Encyclopedia*, 142–44, writes discerningly about Spenser's evident approval of celibacy elsewhere in his oeuvre: "This stand is conservative, though by no means unique for [Spenser's] time" (143).

54. Hooker, *Of the Laws of Ecclesiastical Polity: Book V*, 402.

55. Erasmus, while commending wedlock, nonetheless grants that "virginitie forsothe is an heauenly thing" ("An Epistle to persuade a yong Gentleman," 52). See also Bullinger, *The Golden Boke*, sig. Divᵛ.

56. Maureen Quilligan, *The Language of Allegory* (Ithaca NY: Cornell University Press, 1979), 80–84, treats the relationship between some of the metaphorical and literal meanings of words in the Marinell episode.

57. A. Kent Hieatt, *Chaucer, Spenser, Milton: Mythopoeic Continuities and Transformations* (Montreal: McGill-Queen's University Press, 1975), 94.

58. See Hamilton's edition, 340. On the connection between Marinell and Mammon, see also Evans, *Spenser's Anatomy of Heroism*, 176.

59. A. Leigh Deneef, "Timias," in *The Spenser Encyclopedia*, 690–91, summarizes the historical interpretations. Roche, *The Kindly Flame*, 142–45, offers objections to a historical reading.

60. See Isabel G. MacCaffrey, *Spenser's Allegory: The Anatomy of Imagination* (Princeton: Princeton University Press, 1976), 277–78.

61. Lauren Silberman, *Transforming Desire: Erotic Knowledge in Books III and IV of "The Faerie Queene"* (Berkeley and Los Angeles: University of California Press, 1995), 33–40, also examines this episode as a critique of Petrarchan discourses. Timias "loses control of his discourse" and is "feminized" (40) for taking ideals seriously and so undermining what Silberman defends as the project of this book of the poem, an education in reading as "paradigmatic, morally charged, heroic activity" (71).

62. Villeponteaux argues in "*Semper Eadem*" that Belphoebe is a negative figure embodying Spenser's censure of the queen's virginity: "Belphoebe, and Elizabeth by implication, forbids desire not only for herself but for others as well" (44). Villeponteaux does not, however, account for the attractions of chastity, both culturally and to individual writers such as Spenser. See also Judith Anderson, "'In liuing colours and right hew': The Queen of Spenser's Central Books," in *Poetic Traditions of the English Renaissance*, ed. Maynard Mack and George de Lord (New Haven: Yale University Press, 1982), 47–66. Anderson sees in Belphoebe a warning to the queen about the dangers and costs of power.

63. Hamilton's edition, 371.

64. See William Nelson, *The Poetry of Spenser*, 229. One of the difficulties with the text in these episodes is the distinction between the kindly flame of "virtuous" longing and the fires of destructive lust. They often seem to be akin.

65. Laurence Lerner, "marriage," in *The Spenser Encyclopedia*, 454–55, asserts that "The married state is not directly treated in *The Faerie Queene*." This is not true.

66. For example, Bullinger, *The Golden Boke*: "Neither would I haue [women] euer shut up as it were in a Cage, neuer to speake nor to come forth, but some tymes to see the good fashions and honest behauiour of others" (sig. Mviʳ).

67. Linda Gregerson, *The Reformation of the Subject*, 48–79, sees Malbecco's hoarding and impotence in Augustinian terms: "when Concupiscence comes face to face with the accomplished fact of his own cuckoldry, narrative dilation contends with allegory for control of a destabilized and modulating tone" (71).

68. Hamilton's edition notes that "Malbecco stands between beauty and money. . . . In Book II these temptations, displayed in Acrasia and Mammon, confront the Knight of Temperance" (394).

69. Hamilton's edition, 399. John D. Bernard, *Ceremonies of Innocence: Pastoralism in the Poetry of Edmund Spenser* (Cambridge: Cambridge University Press, 1989), 99–103, demonstrates how the episode elicits our sympathies for Malbecco as well as our "attraction to the dream of pleasure" (101) in Hellenore's erotic freedom.

70. See, for example, Perkins, "Oeconomie," 683.

71. For example, Silberman, *Transforming Desire*, 62–67, sees Scudamour as a Petrarchan poet and Britomart as an anti-Petrarchan heroine.

72. Maureen Quilligan, *Milton's Spenser: The Politics of Reading* (Ithaca NY: Cornell University Press, 1983), 197, sees Busirane as a sadistic sonneteer who has punningly penned Amoret in his art. Silberman, *Transforming Desire*, sees "Busirane as a poet figure and Britomart as an exegete . . . the resisting reader" in a Petrarchan dialectic (61).

73. Judith Anderson, "Britomart," in *The Spenser Encyclopedia*, 113–15.

74. The classic formulation is by Rosemond Tuve, *Allegorical Imagery: Some Medieval Books and Their Posterity* (Princeton: Princeton University Press, 1966), 363.

75. Evans, *Spenser's Anatomy of Heroism*, believes that Scudamour "personifies the stirring of sexual temptation in man or woman, and marks in Britomart the fact that sexual nature is now awake. . . . His lament for Amoret shut away and tortured by Busirane is Britomart's own dawning realisation of the physical instinct which is imprisoned within herself and in need of release" (159). Roche, *The Kindly Flame*, 83, sees Busirane as signifying, among other things, "abuse of marriage."

76. Silberman, *Transforming Desire*, 69–70.

77. See, for example, Lesley W. Brill, "Scudamour," in *The Spenser Encyclopedia*, 635. Berger, *Revisionary Play*, notes that "As the goal of a human lover this happy ending is incomplete and illusory, and it is an example of too violent an oscillation; completely separated from and alien to each other in the Busirane experience, they close as if the otherness separating them could be entirely dissolved by the mere act of *physical* embrace" (90).

Revenge and Companionate Marriage

1. Tilney, *A briefe and pleasaunt discourse*, sig. Biiii^r.

2. Bullinger, *The Golden Boke*, sig. Avi^v.

3. Two studies come close to considering Reformation discourses of matrimony in Book IV: Roche, *The Kindly Flame*, 114–33, treats Amoret as a

figure of "Christian marriage" and the uniting of Scudamour and Amoret in the Temple of Venus as an idealized "vision of the relation of the sexes" (129); and Mark Heberle, "The Limitations of Friendship," in *Spenser Studies* 8 (1987): 101–18, distinguishes between marriages formed in the "background" narratives (unions he finds generally harmonious but variously "separated from the rest of Book IV" [103]) and friendship between men and women in the "foreground" narratives (unions he finds limited and imperfect). Although I regard evidence of the distinctions Heberle draws too often strained to convince fully—and, as this chapter makes clear, I see all the unions as problematic—I indicate in later notes my agreement with his perceptions. Jonathan Goldberg, *Endlesse Worke: Spenser and the Structures of Discourse* (Baltimore: Johns Hopkins University Press, 1981), finds the projected unions of this book of the poem unsatisfactory or illusory and sees their deferrals as symptomatic of the problematic nature of narration (see 29). He does, however, consider marriage as a "sociopolitical fact" (134) and treats the marriage of the Thames and the Medway as a "fantasy of power" (135) related to the mythology of Elizabethan veneration (see 140–65).

4. "Of the State of Matrimony," sigs. Gg3^v, Gg4^v.

5. There are dissenting views: C. S. Lewis, *Spenser's Images of Life*, ed. Alastair Fowler (Cambridge: Cambridge University Press, 1967), sees the statue of Venus in canto 10 as a "symbol of God" (16); Evans, *Spenser's Anatomy of Heroism*, claims that "of all the books of the poem, that of Friendship is the most metaphysical" (179) and that Book IV portrays an extended conflict between the physical and the spiritual (see 179–96); and Alan MacColl, "The Temple of Venus, the Wedding of the Thames and the Medway, and the End of *The Faerie Queene*, Book IV," *Review of English Studies* n.s. 40 (1989): 26–47, sees a "religious as well as an erotic vision" (29) in the Temple of Venus.

6. Throughout this chapter, for the sake of stylistic convenience, I refer to the characters as men and women, irrespective of their problematic ontological status.

7. The already-classic account of homosociality is that of Eve Kosovsky Sedgwick, *Between Men: English Literature and Male Homosocial Desire* (New York: Columbia University Press, 1985), esp. 1–27. In chapter 1, Sedgwick examines male homosocial desire, as outlined by René Girard, within the context of heterosexual desire, a structure pertinent to Book IV: "the bond that links the two rivals is as intense and potent as the bond that links either of the two rivals to the beloved; . . . the bonds of 'rivalry' and 'love,'

differently as they are experienced, are equally powerful and in many senses equivalent" (21). Richard Rambuss, *Spenser's Secret Career* (Cambridge: Cambridge University Press, 1993), 103–5, touches briefly on the homosociality of Book IV when he points out that male ties are "more highly valued" in this book, which valorizes the masculine more than other books do. Cavanagh, *Wanton Eyes and Chaste Desires*, 77–109, sees homosocial bonding as governing "female circulation in Faeryland's marital economy" (76) and notes how this bonding operates throughout the second half of the poem, especially in Book IV (e.g., "Female characters typically only figure as booty in these tournaments" [81]). Silberman, *Transforming Desire*, 94–98, examines the Cambell-Canacee episode in terms of homosocial rivalry and suggests that the opening episodes of Book IV present a series of fights between men over a woman as a way of examining issues of textuality.

8. The subject of revenge proved especially interesting to scholars of English Renaissance drama a generation or more ago. Among the most important discussions are Lily B. Campbell, "Theories of Revenge in Elizabethan England," *Modern Philology* 28 (1931): 281–96; Fredson Bowers, *Elizabethan Revenge Tragedy: 1587–1642* (Princeton: Princeton University Press, 1940), 3–61; Robert Ornstein, *The Moral Vision of Jacobean Tragedy* (Madison: University of Wisconsin Press, 1960), 1–27; Elinor Bevan, "Revenge, Forgiveness, and the Gentleman," *Review of English Literature* 8 (1967): 55–69; John Sibly, "The Duty of Revenge in Tudor and Stuart Drama," *Review of English Literature* 8 (1967): 46–54; Eleanor Prosser, *Hamlet and Revenge* (Stanford: Stanford University Press, 1967), 3–94; Harold Skulsky, "Revenge, Honor and Conscience in *Hamlet*," *PMLA* 85 (1970): 78–87; and Philip Ayres, "Degrees of Heresy: Justified Revenge and Elizabethan Narratives," *Studies in Philology* 69 (1972): 461–74.

9. Maurice Keen, *Chivalry* (New Haven: Yale University Press, 1984), 247–53, provides an overview of the last throes of European chivalry in the sixteenth century. See also Frank Whigham, *Ambition and Privilege: The Social Tropes of Elizabethan Courtesy Theory* (Berkeley and Los Angeles: University of California Press, 1984), 13–31. Richard C. McCoy, *The Rites of Knighthood: The Literature and Politics of Elizabethan Chivalry* (Berkeley and Los Angeles: University of California Press, 1989), argues that Spenser offers a "detached perspective" on chivalry: "Spenser's treatment of Elizabethan chivalry is typically more ambiguous than celebratory" (143).

10. As this chapter makes clear, Book IV is permeated with situations and formulations about women as spoil or prizes. While Spenser criticism has been slow to investigate how the book presents the motif, it is noted in Ham-

ilton's edition, 428, and in Hieatt, *Chaucer, Spenser, Milton*, 92. Goldberg, *Endlesse Worke*, 104–19, investigates the motif in terms of the construction of self and other. Cavanagh, *Wanton Eyes and Chaste Desires*, 74–108, considers the problem in greater variety and detail than earlier commentary.

11. Cf. the parallel homoerotic scene with Malecasta in III.1.59–67, where Britomart, surprised to find the wanton Malecasta sharing her bed, resists the intrusion. In the episode with Amoret the text heightens the homoeroticism by its confusion of pronouns, as in these lines:

For *Amoret* right fearefull was and faint,
Lest she with blame her honor should attaint,
That euerie word did tremble as she spake,
And euerie looke was coy, and wondrous quaint,
And euerie limbe [whose?] that touched her [whom?] did quake.
Yet could she [which?] not but curteous countenance to her [?] make.

(1.5)

Evans, *Spenser's Anatomy of Heroism*, 179–81, draws attention to these ambiguities without recognizing the homoerotic implications. He says, for example, that when the two women share the same bed, they "now openly admit their sexual longings to each other, safe in their determination to remain chaste" (181). The homoerotic nature of the passage seems to have been first pointed out by Camille Paglia, "The Apollonian Androgyne and *The Faerie Queene*," *English Literary Renaissance* 9 (1979): 51–52. I use the problematic term *homoerotic* here and elsewhere as one of the most neutral we currently have to designate erotic bonds, whether or not they are conscious or acted upon, between members of the same sex.

12. Dorothy Stephens, "Into Other Arms: Amoret's Evasions," in *Queering the Renaissance*, ed. Jonathan Goldberg (Durham: Duke University Press, 1994), 190–217. Stephens's essay is a model of tact and persuasion. Of the stanzas describing the bedding of Amoret and Britomart she notes, for example, that "the double entendres of 'passion,' 'bemone,' and 'hard aduentures' reinforce one's initial sense that the phrase 'their loues' not only points outward to male objects but encloses a more private exchange between the two women. They speak 'twixt themselues alone' of their previous 'hard aduentures,' while at the same time, they speak of 'hard aduentures' that happen 'twixt themselues alone'" (202).

13. Valerie Traub, *Desire and Anxiety: Circulations of Sexuality in Shakespearean Drama* (London: Routledge, 1992), makes a convincing case against confusing gender and sexuality; see esp. 19–22 and 98–102. Her analysis of homoerotic significations in the bonds between Rosalind and Celia in *As You Like It* is especially pertinent here (see 122–30).

14. In "An exposition vppon . . . Mathew," Tyndale provocatively brings together the discourses of marriage and revenge: "Christe here [Matt. 5:38–42] entendeth not to disannul the temporall regiment, and to forbid rulers to punyshe euil doers, no more then he meant to destroye matrimonie when he forbade to lust and to covet another mans wife in the herte. But as he there forbade that which defileth matrimonie even so he forbiddeth here that which troubleth unquieteth and destroieth the temporall regiment, and that thynge whych to forbidde the temporall regiment was ordayned which is that no man aveng himselfe" (184).

15. Paul's text is buttressed by Exod. 21:23–25; Deut. 32:35; Jer. 15:15, 20:12; Heb. 10:26–31; and (of course) Matt. 5:38–39.

16. Tyndale, "An exposition vppon . . . Mathew," 189.

17. Becon, "The Catechisme," fol. ccclxxxv^r.

18. See Campbell, "Theories of Revenge"; Bowers, *Elizabethan Revenge Tragedy*, 3–61; and Prosser, *Hamlet and Revenge*, 3–94.

19. See Skulsky, "Revenge, Honor, and Conscience in *Hamlet*."

20. See Ornstein, *The Moral Vision*, 15–16. See also Lawrence Stone, *The Crisis of the Aristocracy: 1558–1641* (Oxford: Clarendon, 1965), 199–270, on the prevalence of violence in sixteenth- and seventeenth-century English society.

21. Hugh Latimer, "The Second Sermon of Maister Latimer. 1552. Math. 5," in *Fruitfull Sermons* (London, 1596), fol. 190^v.

22. Tyndale, "An exposition vppon . . . Mathew," 191.

23. "An exposition vppon . . . Mathew," 188.

24. Bullinger, "Of the patient bearing and abiding of sundrie calamities and miseries," in *Fiftie Godlie and learned Sermons*, 316.

25. See MacLachlan, "The 'careless heauens.'"

26. Judith Anderson, "Cambell, Canacee, Cambina," in *The Spenser Encyclopedia*, expertly outlines the main critical issues in this episode. She is especially adept at demonstrating how Spenser makes use of Chaucer: "Spenser did not merely replicate Chaucer's parodies of romance, and still less did he insensitively moralize their comedy out of existence. Instead, he both assimilated and transformed them, much as Triamond's spirit revives and transforms those of his dead brothers" (129–30).

27. Patrick Cheney, "Spenser's Completion of *The Squire's Tale*: Love, Magic, and Heroic Action in the Legend of Cambell and Triamond," *Journal of Medieval and Renaissance Studies* 15 (1985): 135–55, sees a "potentially incestuous relationship" (150) between brother and sister (noted in Hamilton's edition, 445) but finds that Cambina's magic, which "figures the power of cosmic love" (152), frees them from incestuous possibilities.

28. Alastair Fowler, *Spenser and the Numbers of Time* (London: Routledge, 1964), explains: "The intervention of Cambina as a second mean [the first being Canacee] . . . leads to immediate reconciliation, and to a system of interlocking relationships linking all four characters permanently together . . . a resolution that Canacee herself finds impossible" (27).

29. Hamilton's edition, 453, notes the connection between beauty and arms: "In both [contests], masculine strength and feminine beauty are simply physical: the former is not concerned with force as the instrument of right nor the latter with beauty as the expression of virtue."

30. Alternatively, depending on how seriously one wishes to take the homoerotic signification of their relation, Britomart departs with "her owne *Amoret*" (5.20) as a means of strategically removing the two of them from the transactions and cementing their bonds.

31. See n.9 of the previous chapter. More recently Anthony Fletcher has argued in "The Protestant Idea of Marriage in Early Modern England" a modified return to the Hallers' position, which "has been too much neglected" (180). Within the expected constrictions of biblical patriarchy, Fletcher sees a new pattern of love and marriage advanced in the conduct books.

32. See Stone, *The Family, Sex, and Marriage*, 151–218; Dunn, "The Changing Image of Woman," 15–38; and Ozment, *When Fathers Ruled*, 55, 70.

33. Stone, *The Family, Sex, and Marriage*, 195.

34. See Kathleen M. Davies, "Continuity and Change in Literary Advice," 59–80; Fitz, " 'What Says the Married Woman?' "; Todd, *Christian Humanism*, 96–117; Keith Wrightson, *English Society, 1580–1680* (New Brunswick: Rutgers University Press, 1982), 100–105; Wayne, ed., *"The Flower of Friendship,"* 1–93; and James Grantham Turner, *One Flesh: Paradisal Marriage and Sexual Relations in the Age of Milton* (Oxford: Clarendon, 1987), 24–123. An overview is provided by Barbara B. Diefendorf, "Family Culture, Renaissance Culture," in *Renaissance Quarterly* 40 (1987): 661–81. Collinson, *The Birthpangs of Protestant England*, hypothesizes that when the marriage homily stressed "perpetual friendship" between husband and wife, "this was to express not a novel but a very traditional sentiment" (88).

35. Perkins, "Oeconomie," 691–92.

36. For a similar paradox in describing the classical-Renaissance analogy of marriage and the state, see Constance Jordan, "The Household and the State," *Modern Language Quarterly* 54 (1993): 307–26. Anthony Fletcher,

"The Protestant Idea of Marriage," 167–75, arrays quotations from Puritan conduct books on marriage to demonstrate the paradoxes of hierarchy within mutuality and concludes that the divines resisted mutuality: "The sticking point, which prevented them opening their minds to a proper mutuality, was their conviction that women were inferior" (175).

37. Bullinger, *The Golden Boke*, sig. Aiiiʳ̣-v. He also puts it this way: "Wedloke is the yoking together of one man and one woman, whom God hath coupled according to his word . . . thenceforth to dwel together, and spend their lyfe in the equal partakyng of all suche thinge as God sendethe" (sig. Aviᵛ). And yet, he says, following Paul, "ye wiues, submit yourselues unto your husbandes, as unto the Lorde" (sig. Hvᵛ).

38. Whately, *A Bride-bush*, sigs. I2ʳ, Bb3ʳ. Whately continues: "Nature hath framed the lineament of his body to superioritie, and set the print of gouernment in his very face, which is the more sterne, and lesse delicate than the womens; he must not suffer this order of nature to be inuerted" (sigs. O1ʳ̣-v).

39. Gouge, *Of Domesticall Duties*, 356–57. Gouge goes on to provide and refute an objection to this position: "Obiect: Fellowship betwixt man and wife cannot stand with a wiues inferiority and subiection. Ans: . . . Is there not a fellowship betwixt superiour and inferiour magistrates?" *The Book of Common Prayer* echoes these prescriptions on women's subjugation: "let the wiues also be in subjection unto their husbands in all things. . . . Saint Paul giveth you this short lesson, Ye wives submit yourselves unto your husbands, as it is convenient in the Lord [Col. 3]. Saint Peter also doth instruct you very godly, thus saying, Let wives be subject to their own husbands" (298).

40. Rosemary Freeman, *"The Faerie Queene"*: *A Companion for Readers* (Berkeley and Los Angeles: University of California Press, 1970), 235, points to forgiveness as a motif in the central episodes.

41. Two critics of Book IV have drawn attention to its Shakespearean features. MacCaffrey, *Spenser's Allegory*, sees its resolutions as a Shakespearean pattern of "concords emerging from discords" (328). MacColl, "The Temple of Venus," claims that "the book comes nearest in subject-matter and spirit to the comedies of Shakespeare" (see 26 ff.).

42. Perkins, "Oeconomie," 670.

43. Heberle, "The Limitations of Friendship," finds the reconciliation between Belphoebe and Timias problematic because they "realize the titular virtue only by denying other human relationships and removing themselves from the continuing narrative" (106). The latter point is true, but we never

hear of their life together. Timias's reappearance in Book VI recounts, however feebly, their reconciliation. Timias "of her grace did stand againe assured," and "in her soueraine lyking he dwelt euermore" (VI.5.12)—apparently happily ever after.

44. Two earlier studies, in addition to the sources listed in *Variorum* 4, treat the medieval and classical conceptions of friendship: Charles G. Smith, *Spenser's Theory of Friendship* (Baltimore: Johns Hopkins University Press, 1935); and Laurens J. Mills, *One Soul in Bodies Twain: Friendship in Tudor Literature and Stuart Drama* (Bloomington: Principia, 1937).

45. The text gives rise to confusion about the marital unions, but the evidence is strong that Amyas weds Æmylia and Placidas Poeana. The matter is examined in Walter F. Staton Jr., "Ralegh and the Amyas-Aemylia Episode," *SEL* 5 (1965): 105–14. Staton calls the union between Placidas and Poeana a "Gilbert-and-Sullivan-like marriage" (112).

46. Fowler, *Spenser and the Numbers of Time*, sees Arthur's role here as that of the "mean," not unlike that of Cambina in the earlier marriage tetrad: "Friendship by itself is not enough: only with reconciliation, forgiveness, and mutual adaptation can there be any stable and peaceful relationship" (29–30).

47. Silberman, *Transforming Desire*, 77–86, examines Scudamour's winning of Amoret and notes puns at 10.4 on *prize/emprize* that reduce Amoret's presence to "marginal at best because the woman's role in the economy of winning and losing is at a categorical remove from the man's" (79). Silberman also notes that when Scudamour substitutes for Spenser's narrator, he substitutes "self-pity for the pity Spenser's narrator expresses for Amoret" (84).

48. MacColl, "The Temple of Venus," points out that the "male and female in the episode are those traditionally identified as primal—Scudamour all ruthless masculinity . . . and Amoret all maidenly passivity and fearfulness. They form part of the conception of the adventure as an archetypal courtship conducted, appropriately, in a manner of high chivalry" (30). Scudamour's aggressiveness has been noted by several other critics, including Hieatt, *Chaucer, Spenser, Milton*, 112–13; and Heberle, "The Limitations of Friendship," 107.

49. John Manning, "Venus," in *The Spenser Encyclopedia*, 709, traces the iconography and ties it to Renaissance symbols of marriage. Fowler, *Spenser and the Numbers of Time*, identifies Venus as "ideal union" (163). Dissenters are Berger and Goldberg: Berger sees the devotees of the statue-goddess as isolating "her visible form with its self-contained 'life' from the

oceanic reality behind the appearance; they isolate love as a game from love as a function, love as a state of mind and a way of life from love as a natural process (*Revisionary Play*, 198); Goldberg sees the Temple as a "place of fragmentation and deformation, of genital tyranny in which love is a game" (*Endlesse Worke*, 64).

50. Linda Woodbridge, "Womanhood," in *The Spenser Encyclopedia*, 731, carefully explicates the figures in this scene in terms of maidenhood and marriage.

51. Cavanagh, *Wanton Eyes and Chaste Desires*, 96–102, argues the similarity of Scudamore's and Busirane's abductions and treatments of Amoret and suggests that many male characters are "most interested in sexual alliances because of the stories they create" (101). Cavanagh reviews critics' insensitivity to Amoret's plight.

52. Upton first suggested Spenser planned to reunite the couple here; see *Variorum* 4:215–16. Hieatt, *Spenser, Chaucer, Milton*, 85–86, claims the text cries out for Arthur to produce Amoret at the end of canto 9, when she seems to be in Scudamour's presence. In *The Spenser Encyclopedia* Brill reproves Spenser for his "failure" (635) to bring together Scudamour and Amoret at this point. Both Hieatt and Brill, however, fail to see that the silence of the text turns out to be exactly correct in showing the failures, not of Spenser but of Scudamour in canto 10.

53. W. H. Herendeen, "rivers," in *The Spenser Encyclopedia*, finds that "the episode is unique in *The Faerie Queene*: though only a wedding procession, it is the closest thing to a wedding in the poem. . . . Structurally, the episode functions in the Book as a narrative surrogate for these couples, and is a framing device for the reconciliation of two symbolic figures, Marinell and Florimell, whose names suggest the fruitful union of opposites, earth and water" (608). I would add that it stands in contrast to the union of Scudamour and Amoret in the previous canto. MacColl, "The Temple of Venus," finds this episode to be the "climax to the love-comedy of the book" and "an archetypal wedding" (37). I also find persuasive his analysis of canto 11 as "an extended image of the whole earth in terms of rivers" (38) and Spenser's presentation of the "'idea' of the earth" in the Sidneian sense of the term (46). Roche, *The Kindly Flame*, finds that the "essential purpose of this procession is to show the unity underlying the multiplicity of life, as symbolized by the world of the sea" (181).

54. The union of England and Ireland is allegorized, according to A. M. Buchan, "The Political Allegory of Book IV of *The Faerie Queene*," *ELH* 11 (1944): 237–48. Fowler, *Spenser and the Numbers of Time*, suggests that

the river-bride is to be identified with the queen, and that the episode celebrates a "visionary England—and Ireland—united in friendly alliance and
married to [their] sovereign" (175).

55. Hamilton's edition, 508, notes that Marinell too is imprisoned—by
his mother: he is "her thrall; / Who sore against his will did him retaine"
(11.7).

56. Williams, *Spenser's World of Glass*, makes a similar point: "in this episode, goodness will find grace through the agency of the characters, not the
gods they cry out to in their various laments" (136).

Post-Armada Apocalyptic Discourse

1. Perkins, "A Fruitfull Dialogue concerning the End of the World," in
Workes 3:467. Katherine R. Firth, *The Apocalyptic Tradition in Reformation Britain 1530–1645* (Oxford: Oxford University Press, 1979), 151–53,
discusses the apocalyptic significance of the year 1588.

2. See Bauckham, *Tudor Apocalypse*; Paul Christianson, *Reformers and
Babylon: English Apocalyptic Visions from the Reformation to the Eve of
the Civil War* (Buffalo NY: University of Toronto Press, 1978); Bryan W. Ball,
*A Great Expectation: Eschatological Thought in English Protestantism to
1660* (Leiden: Brill, 1975); Firth, *The Apocalyptic Tradition*; and Capp,
"The Political Dimension," 93–124. Although (or perhaps because) it is a literary study, Wittreich's *Visionary Poetics: Milton's Tradition and His Legacy* (San Marino CA: Huntington Library, 1979) illuminates the whole tradition of apocalyptic and its exegesis. For an incisive sketch of the peculiarly
English "strains" of sixteenth-century apocalypse, see Janel Mueller, "Embodying Glory: The Apocalyptic Strain in Milton's *Of Reformation*," in *Politics, Poetics, and Hermeneutics in Milton's Prose*, ed. David Loewenstein
and James Grantham Turner (Cambridge: Cambridge University Press,
1990), 9–17.

3. For example, see Michael O'Connell, *Mirror and Veil: The Historical
Dimension of Spenser's "Faerie Queene"* (Chapel Hill: University of North
Carolina Press, 1977), 147–60. "The Legend of Justice," O'Connell asserts,
"fails finally to be prophetic poetry" (156).

4. Two recent historicist treatments are especially provocative: Jonathan
Goldberg, *James I and the Politics of Literature: Jonson, Shakespeare,
Donne, and Their Contemporaries* (Baltimore: Johns Hopkins University
Press, 1983), 2–11; and Clark Hulse, "Spenser, Bacon, and the Myth of
Power," in *The Historical Renaissance: New Essays on Tudor and Stuart
Culture*, ed. Heather Dubrow and Richard Strier (Chicago: University of
Chicago Press, 1988), 316–46.

5. See, for example, David Norbrook, *Poetry and Politics in the English Renaissance* (London: Routledge & Kegan Paul, 1984), 133–36; and John N. King, *Spenser's Poetry*, 106–9, 227–29.

6. Kenneth Borris, *Spenser's Poetics of Prophecy in "The Faerie Queene" V* (Victoria BC: English Literary Studies, University of Victoria, 1991). Borris's monograph is a model of careful scholarship. He performs the rare feat of reorienting critical understanding of a major work. I have benefitted throughout this chapter from his study, although I disagree at various points. Borris makes no reference to the exegesis of the post-Armada apocalypticists and does not place the poem among other exegetical texts of the late Elizabethan era. Nor does he account for the apocalyptic features of Book V before the tenth canto. In notes to the following pages I merely touch upon my chief debts to his work as well as our divergences.

7. Angus Fletcher, *The Prophetic Moment: An Essay on Spenser* (Chicago: University of Chicago Press, 1971), notes that Spenser "looks not to the future as a prophet but to the past, and even more, to the present" (4). Fletcher's work illuminates many features of Spenser's archetypes and their relation to prophecy, though he is not concerned with apocalypticism in detail.

8. See Jan van der Noot, *A Theatre for Voluptuous Worldlings* (London, 1569), sigs. D3^v–D6^r. For useful commentary on the place of *A Theatre* in the Reformation see J. A. van Dorsten, *The Radical Arts: First Decade of an Elizabethan Renaissance* (Leiden: University Press, 1970), 75–85; and Carl Rasmussen, "'Quietnesse of Minde': *A Theatre for Worldlings* as a Protestant Poetics," *Spenser Studies* 1 (1980): 3–27.

9. For a comprehensive survey of Spenser's references to apocalyptic writings, see Joseph A. Wittreich Jr., "Apocalypse," in *The Spenser Encyclopedia*, 46–48, which distills Spenser's copious knowledge of the subject.

10. There are three chief studies of the relation of Book I of *The Faerie Queene* to Revelation: Bennett, *The Evolution of "The Faerie Queene,"* 110–22; Hankins, *Source and Meaning in Spenser's Allegory*, 99–127; and Wittreich, *Visionary Poetics*, 59–78.

11. See Firth, *The Apocalyptic Tradition*, 23–26.

12. Bernard McGinn, "Revelation," in *The Literary Guide to the Bible*, ed. Robert Alter and Frank Kermode (Cambridge: Harvard University Press, 1987), 529.

13. Bauckham, *Tudor Apocalypse*, 13. Bauckham's exposition is definitive; he is especially lucid on the early-sixteenth-century exegetes; see 68–90, 113–144.

14. John Bale, *The Ymage of Both Churches* (London, 1550), sig. A3ᵛ. See also Leslie P. Fairfield, *John Bale: Mythmaker for the English Reformation* (West Lafayette: Purdue University Press, 1976), 50–85.

15. See Bauckham, *Tudor Apocalypse*, 13, 125. See also V. Norskov Olsen, *John Foxe and the Elizabethan Church* (Berkeley and Los Angeles: University of California Press, 1973); and Firth, *The Apocalyptic Tradition*, 69–110.

16. William Fulke, *A Sermon Preached at Hampton Court* (London, 1570), sig. Aivʳ. See Peter Lake, "The Significance of the Elizabethan Identification of the Pope as Antichrist," *Journal of Ecclesiastical History* 31 (1980): 161–78; and Bauckham, *Tudor Apocalypse*, 91–112.

17. Capp, "The Political Dimension," 94.

18. See John N. King, *Tudor Royal Iconography: Literature and Art in an Age of Religious Crisis* (Princeton: Princeton University Press, 1989), 154–57; and Borris, *Spenser's Poetics of Prophecy*, 29–30. Both of these works reproduce and discuss the frontispiece.

19. John Aylmer, *An Harborwe For Faithfull and Truwe Subiectes* (London, 1559), sig. R3ʳ.

20. John Foxe, *Acts and Monuments*, ed. Josiah Pratt, 8 vols. (London: Religious Tract Society, 1931), 8:673–79. These pages reward the student of apocalypse, not least for the intimate connections Foxe avers among the accession of the queen, the downfall of papal tyranny, and the triumph of justice.

21. See McGinn, "Revelation," 535; and Bauckham, *Tudor Apocalypse*, 129–30.

22. John Jewel, *Upon the Second Epistle to the Thessalonians* (London, 1583), 362–63. Jewel died in 1579.

23. Arthur Dent, *The Ruine of Rome* (London, 1603), 254.

24. George Gifford, "Epistle Dedicatory," *Sermons Vpon the Whole Booke of the Revelation* (London, 1596), sig. A3ᵛ.

25. Gifford, *Sermons*, 380. In I. L., *The Birth, Purpose, and Mortall Wound of the Romish Holie League* (London, 1589), where the pope is identified as "that purple Whore" and it is observed that "the most part of Christian Princes with their people haue imbraced the free libertie of the Gospel, and freed themselues from her Antichristian yoake" (sig. A3ᵛ).

26. Laurence Deios, *That the Pope is That Antichrist* (London, 1590), 181. Deios begins his treatise by claiming that Revelation sets forth the "persecutions and rewardes of those that with true faith cleaue onely to Christ; secondly, the assaults and wicked attempts of the enemies of the truth against the Church, together with their punishments and ouerthrowe" (1).

27. Anthony Marten, *An Exhortation, to stirre vp the mindes of all her Maiesties Faithfull Subiects* (London, 1588), sig. E5ᵛ. Marten's riproaring tract is not a proper apocalyptic commentary, but it gives a vivid sense of how the Armada event kindled apocalyptic passion: "For though the Spanish King lately approached to the kingdome with wonderfull force and preparation to haue conquered the same, yet he was but a deputie therein to the Pope, and should haue taken possession but of that which he gaue vnto him" (sig. B1ᵛ). He exhorts the queen's subjects to strengthen themselves against "that horrible beast [Spain], who hath receiued power from the Dragon [the papacy]" (sig. A2ᵛ).

28. John Napier, *A Plaine Discouery of the Whole Reuelation of Saint John* (London, 1593), sig. A3ʳ.

29. James I, "A Fruitfvll Meditation, Containing A Plaine and Easie Exposition . . . of the 20. Chapter of the Revelation" (1588), in *The Workes of the Most High and Mighty Prince, Iames* (London, 1616), 78.

30. See Bauckham, *Tudor Apocalypse,* 173–77.

31. See Capp, "The Political Dimension," 100.

32. Napier, *A Plaine Discouery,* sig. A3ʳ. Wittreich, *Visionary Poetics,* maintains that for Napier "such wars represent the way of Rome and Antichrist" (243), but Napier's tone and diction at times are expressly militant. For example: "God hath shewed mervellous indices, that the Empire of Rome & Papistical Kingdom, shal shortly fal: the Antichristian and Spanish flote is destroyed: the late King of France, Duke of Guize, & his brother Papists, and committers of the Parisian massacre, al murthered by other: a Protestant nowe made King of France [Napier is writing on the eve of Henry IV's conversion to Roman Catholicism]: So that before the ende of this Iubelie (God willing) Rome and the whole Papistical kingdome thereof, shal be ruined" (*A Plaine Discouery,* 179). Wittreich says that "Spenser and Milton would clearly place themselves among those who extract from the Apocalypse the message that man must learn 'to War no more'" (244). As this chapter makes clear, in the case of Spenser in Book V, I disagree.

33. Deios, *That the Pope,* 27.

34. Marten, *An Exhortation,* sigs. E4ᵛ, F3ᵛ.

35. On Elizabethan foreign policy, see Charles Wilson, *Queen Elizabeth and the Revolt of the Netherlands* (London: Macmillan, 1970); P. S. Crowson, *Tudor Foreign Policy* (London: Adam & Charles Black, 1973), 158–236; and John Guy, *Tudor England* (Oxford: Oxford University Press, 1988), 309–51.

36. Gifford, "Epistle Dedicatory," sig. A4ʳ.

37. A typical opposition, such as that between Mercilla and the Souldan, is drawn by I. L., *The Birth, Purpose, and Mortall Wound*, sig. A3ᵛ: "*England* happie through her *Elizabeth*, fate crowned with a wreath of peace (making Christ her hope). . . . *Philip* king of *Spaine* made drunke and deceiued with the superstitious cup of Romish abhomination." I am grateful to Anne Prescott for bringing this text to my attention.

38. See *Variorum* 5:299–302.

39. Cited in Schaff, *The Evangelical Protestant Creeds*, 494. Dent, for example, speaks in *The Ruine of Rome* of the "surpassing blasphemies of the Popes against God, and all goodnesse" (172). Deios claims in *That the Pope* that the Roman Catholic Mass and other practices are "vile and horrible blasphemies" (33).

40. An officially sanctioned example comes from "An Homelie against perill of Idolatrie and superfluous decking of Churches," in *Certain Sermons or Homilies* (London, 1563): "the corruption of these latter dayes [i.e., under the papacy] . . . hath brought into the Church infinite multitude of images . . . occasioning [Christians] to commit most horible idolatrie" (sig. B6ᵛ). Cf. Gifford: "If we follow the decrees of Popes and Emperours, setting vp Idolatrie and superstition, then as we worship diuels, so we worship the beast" (*Sermons*, 380). In *That the Pope* Deios refers to the "whorish and idolatrous Religion" of Rome (32).

41. In *The Ruine of Rome* Dent speaks of the "tyrannie" of the papacy (170). It is, however, an almost official term of abuse, as evinced in "A Homily against Disobedience & Wilful Rebellion" in *The Book of Homilies*: the "Byshop of Rome" is "spoyler and destroyer both of the church . . . and all Christian kingdomes, as an universall tyraunt over all" (238–39). The term *tyrant*, rarely used in other books of *The Faerie Queene*, is employed in its various forms nearly thirty times in the second half of Book V.

42. Dent, *The Ruine of Rome*, 238.

43. Greenlaw, *Variorum* 5:306; H. S. V. Jones, *A Spenser Handbook*, 316.

44. See Helgerson, *The Forms of Nationhood*. Helgerson's discussion of Foxe (249–68) is especially pertinent in this connection. He notes, for example, Foxe's assertion that Elizabeth I was sent to triumph over Antichrist by means of the Word.

45. Aylmer, *An Harborwe*, sig. P4ᵛ.

46. Dent, *The Ruine of Rome*, 217. Cf. I. L., *The Birth, Purpose, and Mortall Wound*:

To them [i.e., the Spanish] a certaine signe of Heauens heauie rod,
To vs a shewe of loue; let vs be thankfull then,

And praise that Lord, which is the Lord of hoast,
That doth defend and shield our English Coast.
(sig. B2ᵛ)

47. Alfred B. Gough, *Variorum* 5:312.

48. Borris, *Spenser's Poetics of Prophecy*, notes that "Protestant historiography was ready-made for Spenser's endeavour to transform historical particulars into an epically appropriate paradigm of Justice in human history" (32).

49. Napier, *A Plaine Discouery*, sig. A3ᵛ.

50. Marten, *An Exhortation*, sig. E4ᵛ.

51. For an illuminating amplification of this point, see Hulse, "Spenser, Bacon, and the Myth of Power," 318–20.

52. Douglas A. Northrop, "Spenser's Defence of Elizabeth," *University of Toronto Quarterly* 38 (1969): 277–94, identifies Mercilla's court as the English Parliament (280). Northrop provides a wealth of detail to interpret the historical referents in Book V.

53. The point is confirmed in Bauckham, *Tudor Apocalypse*, 128–30, 173–80; and in Capp, "The Political Dimension," 95–100. See also Richard A. McCabe, *The Pillars of Eternity: Time and Providence in "The Faerie Queene"* (Dublin: Irish Academic Press, 1989), 123–25; and Wittreich, *Visionary Poetics*, 59. Edward Hellwis, *A Maruell Deciphered* (London, 1589), sigs. B2ᵛ⁻ʳ, identifies the queen as the woman "clothed with the Sunne."

54. Leonard Wright, *The Hunting of Antichrist* (London, 1589), 15.

55. Gifford, *Sermons*, sig. A3ʳ, 339.

56. Kermode, *Shakespeare, Spenser, Donne*, 33–59, was the first to give extensive treatment to these two books of the poem in tandem. He argues that Spenser advances a "Protestant imperialist eccleslastlcal history in Book I and . . . [a] Protestant imperialist equity in Book V" (58). John N. King, *Spenser's Poetry*, observes that Book V builds upon Book I as a "model for religious iconography" (227). Bennett, *The Evolution of "The Faerie Queene,"* comments that Book V "is, in a sense, a coda to the Book of Red Cross, bringing the English phase of the religious struggle up to date" (189). I hope this chapter illustrates the truth of her remark.

57. Sandler, *"The Faerie Queene:* An Elizabethan Apocalypse," 148.

58. John N. King, *Spenser's Poetry*, 229, makes a similar point.

59. See Richard A. McCabe, "The Masks of Duessa: Spenser, Mary Queen of Scots, and James VI," *English Literary Renaissance* 17 (1987): 224–42; and James E. Phillips, *Images of a Queen: Mary Stuart in Six-*

teenth-Century Literature (Berkeley and Los Angeles: University of California Press, 1964), 200–203.

60. Goldberg, *James I*, 4, focuses on Duessa's alleged crime of "lewd *Impietie*" (9.48) as evidence that she is still perceived in Book V as sexually duplicitous. It strikes me that the phrase points rather to her religious criminality, which was certainly a political crime as well.

61. Greenlaw, *Variorum* 5:303, notes that the execution of the Queen of Scots was a necessary step in repelling Spanish aggression.

62. See Bennett, *The Evolution of "The Faerie Queene,"* 188–89; and Northrop, "Spenser's Defence of Elizabeth," 281. Harold Skulsky, "Malengin," in *The Spenser Encyclopedia*, 450, provides Malengin's literary genealogy.

63. Dent, *The Ruine of Rome*, 217.

64. The first to outline how Book V develops force and fraud as enemies of justice is Jane Aptekar, *Icons of Justice: Iconography and Thematic Imagery in Book V of "The Faerie Queene"* (New York: Columbia University Press, 1969), 116–19.

65. Jewel, *Upon the Second Epistle*, 305.

66. For example, Dent, *The Ruine of Rome*: "notwithstanding al forces and armies cunningly contriued and raised up against the Church by Seminary Priests, Iesuites, Pope, Cardinall, and King of Spaine . . . [Rome] shall fall as Dagon before the presence of the Arke" (sig. B1ᵛ).

67. Gifford, "Epistle Dedicatory," sigs. A3ʳ, A4ʳ.

68. Deios asserts in *That the Pope* that the "*Spaniard*, not in any regard of his Religion, but in hope of a Monarchie vnder [Antichrist's] title, hath stepped forth as his champion in this age, to fight his warres for him. By him the armies are renewed and supplied in the Lowe countries: by him the warres are holden vp in *France*: through his meanes, *Geneva* hath bin besieged: and he hath sent his inuincible nauie to subdue vs: but God bee thanked, that hath drowned it in the seas" (75).

69. H. S. V. Jones, *Variorum* 5:211, identifies Dolon with Philip II. Nohrnberg, *The Analogy of "The Faerie Queene,"* 406, interprets the Samient incident as a reference to England's contest with Spain for the privilege of the seas.

70. Borris, *Spenser's Poetics of Prophecy*, 12, recognizes the analogy between Geryoneo's monster and the beast of the Whore of Babylon (Rev. 17:3–8).

71. *Spenser's Poetics of Prophecy*, 12; see also 25–26, 40.

72. *Spenser's Poetics of Prophecy*, 54.

73. Edmund Spenser, *The Faerie Queene, Book V: The Legend of Artegall or of Justice*, ed. Alfred B. Gough (Oxford: Clarendon, 1918), 108; John N. King, *Spenser's Poetry*, 107.

74. Borris, *Spenser's Poetics of Prophecy*, 53.

75. Anne Lake Prescott, "Burbon," in *The Spenser Encyclopedia*, 121. Prescott's article "Belge," also in the *Encyclopedia* (82–83), is equally incisive; here she points out, for example, that Spenser would have read glowing reports of the campaigns in the Netherlands in Holinshed. Here is a fact put to good apocalyptic use in the Belge episode and an application of Bale's maxim that the text gives light to the chronicles.

76. Bennett, *The Evolution of "The Faerie Queene,"* 188. Hamilton's edition, 603, cites the support.

77. Gifford, "Epistle Dedicatory," sig. A3ᵛ.

78. Richard A. McCabe, "The Fate of Irena: Spenser and Political Violence," in *Spenser and Ireland: An Interdisciplinary Perspective*, ed. Patricia Coughlan (Cork, Ireland: Cork University Press, 1989), 109–25. McCabe's Machiavellian reading of Book V and its relation to Spenser's *A View of the Present State of Ireland* is one of the most expert recent examinations of the two texts in tandem—grounded, as is all of McCabe's work on Book V, on a deep knowledge of history.

79. Dent, *The Ruine of Rome*, 240.

80. I have found the following most useful: Ciaran Brady, "Spenser's Irish Crisis: Humanism and Experience in the 1590's," *Past and Present* 111 (1986): 17–49; Sheila T. Cavanagh, "'Such Was Irena's Countenance': Ireland in Spenser's Prose and Poetry," *Texas Studies in Literature and Language* 28 (1986): 24–50; McCabe, "The Fate of Irena"; and Julia Reinhard Lupton, "Mapping Mutability: Or, Spenser's Irish Plot," in *Representing Ireland: Literature and the Origins of Conflict, 1534–1660*, ed. Brendan Bradshaw, Andrew Hadfield, and Willy Maley (Cambridge: Cambridge University Press, 1993), 93–115. Jean R. Brink, "Constructing the *View of the Present State of Ireland*," *Spenser Studies* 11 (1994): 203–28, questions Spenser's authorship of this work and cautions against interpretation of other Spenserian texts from its perspective. The parallels I draw between the *View* and Book V would certainly be inconvenienced by its being found that Spenser is not the author of both texts, but they would not be invalidated.

81. Spenser, *A View of the Present State of Ireland*, in *Variorum* 9:136–38, 147–48. See also Andrew Hadfield, "The 'sacred hunger of ambitious minds': Spenser's Savage Religion," in *Religion, Literature, and Politics in Post-Reformation England, 1540–1688*, ed. Donna B. Hamilton and Rich-

ard Strier (New York: Cambridge University Press, 1996), 27–45. Hadfield makes a case for connecting the religion of Ireland to the larger problem of "savages" throughout *The Faerie Queene*: "Eradicating savagery will, of necessity, require the use of savage violence" (39).

82. Angus Fletcher, *The Prophetic Moment*, observes that "the Beast's cruelty seems to have something essentially verbal about it; his 'blatting' is a deformed kind of speech, the blasphemous perversion of eloquence" (288).

83. On the tension between Spenserian dilation and a Sabbath ending in the Mutabilitie Cantos and elsewhere in the poem, see Parker, *Inescapable Romance*, 58–64. Susanne Wofford, "Britomart's Petrarchan Lament," *Comparative Literature* 39 (1987): 55, considers deferral as an "anti-apocalyptic position . . . fundamental to Spenser's poetic project." I would regard "anti-eschatological" a more accurate description.

84. In *The Spenser Encyclopedia*, Wittreich observes that "it is a definition of an apocalyptic poem that until history is complete the poem cannot be complete. . . . In the very act of postponing apocalypse, Spenser implies that the beast still rules history because it is still enthroned in man and so continues to manifest itself both there and in the world" ("Apocalypse," 48).

Providence, Fortune, and Free Will

1. Kenneth Borris, "Fortune, Occasion, and the Allegory of the Quest in Book Six of *The Faerie Queene*," *Spenser Studies* 7 (1987): 123–45, details his view that courtesy properly exercised prevents the depredations of fortune, which he sees allegorized in the Blattant Beast. The Beast, says Borris, "is as arbitrary as chance itself, for it attacks unpredictably 'without regard of person or of time' (VI.xii.40)." Borris builds on earlier investigations of the role of Fortune in Book VI: Dorothy Woodward Culp, "Courtesy and Fortune's Chance in Book 6 of *The Faerie Queene*," *Modern Philology* 68 (1971): 254–59; Humphrey Tonkin, *Spenser's Courteous Pastoral: Book VI of "The Faerie Queene"* (Oxford: Clarendon, 1972), 268–70; Judith Anderson, "'Come, Let's Away to Prison': Fortune and Freedom in *The Faerie Queene*, Book VI," *Journal of Narrative Technique* 2 (1972): 133–37; and MacCaffrey, *Spenser's Allegory*, 371–96. Frederick Kiefer, "fortune," in *The Spenser Encyclopedia*, 312–13, perceptively outlines the role of fortune in Spenser's work.

2. McCabe, *The Pillars of Eternity*, 154–93, considers the issue generally in the poem and in some of Spenser's other works. His sketch of the primary distinctions among fortune, fate, and providence in major Western thinkers is especially useful, but as this chapter makes clear, I disagree that the poem (at least in Book VI) endorses the Boethian view that fate is subject to provi-

dence. McCabe's views are summarized in his article "providence," in *The Spenser Encyclopedia*, 565.

3. For example, Peter Bayley, *Edmund Spenser: Prince of Poets* (London: Hutchinson University Library, 1971), finds in the fourth Graces on Mount Acidale "more than a suggestion of the Christian *agape*. Christ was a pattern of love and generosity, as he was also the vehicle and the vessel of God's love to man" (151). Williams, *Spenser's World of Glass*, 209–18, claims that the Graces "signify the circulation of blessings throughout a beneficent universe, and what they give to men must be passed on, to be given in greater store" (218). Evans, *Spenser's Anatomy of Heroism*, 209–28, believes that for "Spenser the Graces lent themselves . . . to a specifically Christian interpretation as a symbol of Grace—God's love of man through Christ raising him up, Man's love of God drawing Grace down upon himself" (214). MacCaffrey, *Spenser's Allegory*, 371–96, finds that courtesy "thus resembles the central Christian virtues of Charity and Mercy; it testifies that grace has touched those mortals who manifest it" (388). Two brief essays find quasi-theological significance in the term *grace*: Gerald Snare, "The Poetics of Vision: Patterns of Grace and Courtesy in *The Faerie Queene*, VI," *Renaissance Papers* 8 (1974): 1–8; and Lila Geller, "The Acidalian Vision: Spenser's Graces in Book VI of *The Faerie Queene*," *Review of English Studies* n.s. 23 (1972): 267–77. Two major studies see courtesy encompassing religious motifs, though neither finds theology central to Book VI: Tonkin, *Spenser's Courteous Pastoral*, considers Evans's view of grace too exclusive but sees a link between Spenserian courtesy and "God's New Dispensation to mankind" (257); and Nohrnberg, *The Analogy of "The Faerie Queene,"* asserts that "some meanings of grace in Book VI are . . . vaguely theological" and that "grace supplies the 'poetic theology' for this legend" (698).

4. Vol. 6 of the *Variorum* provides a wealth of instances in which critics fail to appreciate the intellectually serious nature of the book, and I cite but two favorites: "Possessed by the pure, strong love of a woman who was to him an ideal of beauty within and without, [Spenser] was living for a time in touch with both heaven and earth. His lady was a real woman, but he saw in her also the embodiment of all that he had dreamed of the fair woman of his imagination as he drew them in *The Faerie Queene*. . . . The Legend of Courtesy is simple because Spenser was happy in his love" (Kate Warren, 6:318); and "The pastoral world was deeply associated with Spenser's own personal experience; and as he turns to it again, though this story has still the character of naive impossible romance, its setting and its atmosphere grow at once more tender, more natural, more intimate" (E. de Selincourt, 6:328).

5. Berger, *Revisionary Play*, 219, traces the interruption motif.

6. Calvin speaks unequivocally on the role of fortune: "Fortune and chaunce are heathen mens wordes, with the signification whereof the mindes of the godly ought not to be occupied. For if euerie good successe be the blessing of God, and euerie calamitie and aduersitie be his curse, now there is in mens matters no place left for fortune or chaunce" (1.16.8; fol. 48ʳ).

7. Martin Luther, *The Chiefe and Pryncypall Articles of the Christian Faythe*, trans. Walter Lynne (London, 1558), sig. F1ʳ.

8. On the role of Augustine's theology in the Reformation, see Jaroslav Pelikan, *Reformation of Church and Dogma (1300–1700)*, vol. 4 of *The Christian Tradition: A History of the Development of Doctrine* (Chicago: University of Chicago Press, 1983), 13–22, 224–32, 375–85.

9. Sandys, "The seuenth sermon. . . . Drawe neere to God," in *Sermons*, sig. H1ᵛ. This one of the most frequently voiced themes in Sandys's sermons: "corruption is bred and setled within our bones; that we are both borne and begotten in it; that with it all the powers and faculties of our nature are infected; that still it cleaueth fast vnto our soules, and, although the deadly sting be taken from it, yet there it sticketh as long as life doth indure, so irksome and grievous" (12). In "The first sermon. . . . Ho euerie one that thirsteth," Sandys quotes Augustine: "free will hath in itself ability enough to euil, but not to good" (sig. A7ʳ).

10. Cited in Schaff, *The Evangelical Protestant Creeds*, 493–94.

11. Jewel, *The Defense of the Apologie of the Church of England*, in *Workes* 1:13.

12. Thomas Rogers, *The Faith, Doctrine, and religion, professed, and protected in the Realm of England* (Cambridge, 1607; first ed., 1586), 48.

13. Perkins, "A Golden Chaine: or, the Description of Theologie," in *Workes* 1:162.

14. See Martin Luther, *De servo arbitrio*, trans. and ed. Philip S. Watson; and Erasmus, *De libero arbitrio*, trans. and ed. E. Gordon Rupp; both in *Luther and Erasmus: Free Will and Salvation*, Library of Christian Classics, vol. 17 (Philadelphia: Westminster, 1959). "For although free choice is damaged by sin, it is nevertheless not extinguished by it" (51), says Erasmus here; his position is outlined at 89–91. Luther retorts, "there can be no such thing as free choice" (332); his position is outlined at 319–27.

15. Becon, "The demaundes of holy scripture," fol. ccclvʳ. Becon goes on to argue that grace is needed for the "will to loue God," but like many otherwise Calvinist writers of the period, he tacitly acknowledges the human ability to do good. See also Becon, "The Catechisme," fol. cccxciiiiʳ.

16. Richard Hooker, *Of the Laws of Ecclesiastical Polity: Book I*, vol. 1 of *The Folger Library Edition of the Works of Richard Hooker*, ed. W. Speed Hill (Cambridge: Harvard University Press, 1977), 78.

17. Hooker, "Attack and Response," in *Of the Laws of Ecclesiastical Polity: Attack and Response*, ed. John E. Booty, vol. 4 of *The Folger Library Edition of the Works of Richard Hooker*, ed. W. Speed Hill (Cambridge: Harvard University Press, 1982), 103–4, 108–9.

18. See Weatherby, *Mirrors of Celestial Grace*, 172–85. In glossing the poem with patristic theology, Weatherby demonstrates how "all the early and Eastern Fathers attribute to Adam—*mortality*" (158)—that is, Adam's progeny are responsible only for their own sins; and death, not guilt, is Adam's legacy. He notes that "Luther and Calvin (or an Englishman like William Perkins) are more Augustinian than Augustine in their insistence on man's congenital sinfulness and liability for Adam's trespass" (157). That pre-Augustinian concepts of the will continue to nettle Reformation discourses may be seen in John Whitgift, *The Defense of the Answere to the Admonition* (London, 1574): "Is this, thinke you, a sounde argument: Diuerse of the fathers of the Greek Churche, which were great patrones of free-will, are saued, holding the foundation of the fayth which is Christ: Ergo, The doctrine of free will is not a doctrine of saluation or damnation? You might as well say, that many in the popishe Church, which beleeued that the Pope was supreme head of the Church, that the Masse was a sacrifice for the quicke and the dead, and such like poynts of papistical Religion, be saued: Ergo, these are no matters of saluation or damnation" (83). See also Calvin, *Institution* 2.2.4.

19. Schiavone carefully outlines in "Predestination and Free Will" the chief differences between Roman Catholic and Reformed theologies and emphasizes how each position draws on different works of Augustine as support. He finds evidence of both in Book I of *The Faerie Queene*: "Spenser adheres to an Augustinianism not coextensive with that of any specific church" (178). Most valuable for the purposes of the present chapter is this statement: "Certain Anglican theologians (such as Jewel and Cranmer) tended toward the Protestant reading of Augustine, others (such as Hooker) toward the Roman Catholic" (178). Schiavone's sharp division between Reformed and Roman Catholic positions might be modified to recognize the intermingling of theological discourses in the period, notably in Hooker, as Schiavone in fact does in his reading of the first book—e.g., "Book I of *The Faerie Queene*, then, revolves around Spenser's reading of Augustinian theology, a pattern of free will operating paradoxically within the context of divine election and grace" (191).

20. See especially Kendall, *Calvin and English Calvinism*, 151–64; Lake, *Moderate Purtans*, 201–42; and Tyacke, *Anti-Calvinists*, 1–8, 248–65. Wallace, *Puritans and Predestination*, 65–78, provides an incisive sketch of the burgeoning opposition to Reformed theology in England after 1585 that gradually coalesced into "Anglicanism."

21. Michael Tratner, " 'The thing S. Paule ment by . . . the courteousness that he spake of': Religious Sources for Book VI of *The Faerie Queene*," *Spenser Studies* 8 (1990): 147–74, argues that several passages of both sixteenth-century Biblical translation and of Calvin's sermons serve as "sources" for Spenserian courtesy. Some of Tratner's assertions are dubious, if not distorted (e.g., "Elizabethan Protestants, following Calvin, believed that the human will is utterly corrupt, so humans cannot on their own treat each other courteously; relying on human judgment, humans would disdain to have anything to do with each other because each person can see that all others are worthless sinners" [150]), and he uses them freely to gloss the narrative. I disagree that Book VI, in accordance with Tratner's conception of Calvinist courtesy, shows its characters being brought into a "community of the faithful" (155). If anything, Book VI repeatedly dramatizes the explosion of communities. Tratner's essentialist and idealist reading is based on selected and sharply focused sources and doctrine (e.g., "courtesy can, by eliciting divine aid to awaken dormant graces in isolated sinners and savages, transform them into noble Christians" [160]).

22. The best treatment of connections between Book V and Book VI remains that of Donald Cheney, *Spenser's Image of Nature: Wild Man and Shepherd in "The Faerie Queene"* (New Haven: Yale University Press, 1966), 178–90. His observation that "Calidore tries to reform offenders whenever possible, while Artegall moves decisively and forcefully against injustice with little concern for the feelings of his victims" (186) bears closely on my view of this episode.

23. Evans, *Spenser's Anatomy of Heroism*, 212. "Spenser traces this aspect of human nature back to the guilt and shame which came with the loss of primal innocence" (210), says Evans.

24. *Variorum* 6:191 notes the instances of "malevolent pride" as the antithesis of courtesy.

25. As Harold Toliver puts it in his insightful article "Crudor" in *The Spenser Encyclopedia*: "The central question about Crudor is how his faults are to be curbed or cured. . . . Henceforth an internalized spiritual and chivalric discipline must keep him in check" (200–201).

26. Hamilton's edition, 631, quotes James 2:13: "For there shalbe judgement merciles to him that sheweth no mercie."

27. Kenneth Borris, "courtesy," in *The Spenser Encyclopedia*, points out that "medieval courtesy had theological implications, for its affinities with charitable love of one's neighbor opened it to religious treatment" (194).

28. Tonkin, *Spenser's Courteous Pastoral*, 254–57, examines the issue.

29. *Spenser's Courteous Pastoral*, 44.

30. Cf. *The Faerie Queene* I.10.25, 11.38.

31. Even Serena, so seemingly innocent, is wounded when the Blattant Beast "Caught her loosely wandring here and there" (3.24), a phrase elsewhere in the poem suggesting moral wandering (i.e., *errare*).

32. The word *grace* is used once, ironically. When Arthur first smites Turpine, Blandina "intreat[s] him for grace" (6.31). Arthur spares the wretch, only to be rewarded not with Turpine's gratitude or rehabilitation but with his subsequent betrayal.

33. See Ferry, *The Art of Naming*, 9–48, on the verb *to read*.

34. John D. Bernard, "hermits," in *The Spenser Encyclopedia*, 359–60, claims that the Hermit's "'cure' is too vague to be useful (and seems little more efficacious than that of Friar Lawrence in *Romeo and Juliet*)." While it is true, as Bernard points out, that Timias and Serena later have serious misadventures, they are nonetheless cured of a mortal wound in this episode. Surely the cure is neither vague nor useless.

35. Anne Shaver, "Rereading Mirabella," *Spenser Studies* 9 (1991): 209–25, provocatively treats this difficult episode. Of Mirabella's woes she writes, "the very nature of her punishment prevents its completion," for it demands the "painful absurdity" of constant wandering with the encumbrances of Disdaine and Scorne (221). In using this episode as a primary instance of the display of female power, Cavanagh, *Wanton Eyes and Chaste Desires*, 120, acutely notes how the text suppresses female agency at a cost to female bodies.

36. Shaver, "Rereading Mirabella," suggests that Mirabella's "meane parentage and kindred base" (7.28) also earn Spenser's disapproval: "Thus it would seem that her crime is legion; she claims power beyond her gender and beyond her class, and she also claims freedom from the strictures of romantic or marital commitment" (223). Cavanagh, *Wanton Eyes and Chaste Desires*, 118, sees the connections between Mirabella's social class and sexuality and notes the narrator's approval of her punishments.

37. Kenneth Borris, "'Diuelish Ceremonies': Allegorical Satire of Protestant Extremism in *The Faerie Queene* VI.viii.31–51," *Spenser Studies* 8 (1990): 175–211, offers detailed evidence that this episode is a complex and subtle satire of Puritan extremism, particularly of Puritan ecclesiology and

liturgy. Borris industriously details how the episode minutely satirizes contemporary doctrines of radical nonconforming Protestants. By this reckoning, Serena corresponds to the English church, allowing Spenser to "condemn radical Protestantism as a sectarian, socially disruptive threat to the existence of the English Church" (184). Calepine then becomes "the representative of cultivated, enlightened civility" of the "Anglicans" (191). Although I find Borris's allegorical correspondences often too ingenious (his term is "exceptionally subtle" [200]) to be altogether convincing, his conclusion rings quite true: Spenser presents courtesy as a "semi-theological" virtue, opposed to pride, and "relating to Christian charity, humility, pity, mercy, and salvation" (197). Borris sees Puritan liturgy and church organization as the targets of the satire. If Puritan theology—which centers, as does all Protestant theology, in the role of the will in the drama of salvation—is also satirized in the episode, that satire is subtle indeed.

38. One must strongly demur from the view of Tonkin, *Spenser's Courteous Pastoral*, that Serena has offended against the "laws of love" by fleeing "Cupid's just punishment" of Mirabella (105–6). This seems a classic case of blaming the victim.

39. Krier, *Gazing on Secret Sights*, reads the episode as a critique of Petrarchan love language: "Calepine's rescue of Serena from the cannibals reflects Spenser's wish to rescue the beloved woman from the intense publicity of the Petrarchan sexual gaze, since this gaze risks the appropriation of the woman by the male imagination in a denial of her otherness" (115). In addition to its questionable certainty about "Spenser's wish," the idea strikes me as unprovably idealistic, though valuable for its recording of the effect upon Serena.

40. See Culp, "Courtesy and Fortune's Chance."

41. Kiefer claims that in the "stories of both Calepine and Calidore, it would seem that the change and contingency embodied in Fortune serve the ends of providence" but in other cases Fortune "malevolently singles out the innocent and vulnerable for the worst adversity" ("Fortune," *The Spenser Encyclopedia*, 312–13).

42. William Nelson, ed. *Selected Poetry of Edmund Spenser* (New York: Modern Library, 1964), xxvii; quoted in Hamilton's edition, 685, at st. 31.

43. See MacCaffrey, *Spenser's Allegory*, 365–70; Williams, *Spenser's World of Glass*, 207–8.

44. See Borris, "Fortune, Occasion, and the Allegory," 138–39.

45. See Judith Anderson, *Growth of a Personal Voice: "Piers Plowman" and "The Faerie Queene"* (New Haven: Yale University Press, 1976), 178–

84; Berger, *Revisionary Play*, 233; and Tonkin, *Spenser's Courteous Pastoral*, 116–18, 143.

46. See Nohrnberg, *The Analogy of "The Faerie Queene*,*"* 717–18. The analogy quickly breaks down if one recalls that Meliboe (unlike Despaire) expresses no views on the hero's pursuit of his quest. Anderson, *Growth of a Personal Voice*, offers a more moderate statement but one that still nearly blames Meliboe for Calidore's decision: "It is true that Calidore's response is primarily his responsibility, not Melibee's, . . . but it is also true that the words and rhythms of Melibee's speeches have the strange, lovely power of enchantment" (178).

47. William Nelson, ed., *Selected Poetry of Edmund Spenser*, xxvii.

48. MacCaffrey, *Spenser's Allegory*, 369.

49. Tonkin, *Spenser's Courteous Pastoral*, 254.

50. See Revelation 20–22. Borris, "Fortune, Occasion, and the Allegory," sees the allusions to Revelation as expressing the optimism of the book's ending: "Spenser's carefully developed analogy with Revelation implies that, just as the old serpent escapes only to usher in the institution of the final enduring order of virtue (Rev. 20–22), so the diverse difficulties for man that the Beast's activities express are, however painful or destructive, ultimately to be surmounted forever in a realm beyond the vagaries of Fortune's dominion" (135–36).

Conclusion

1. One successful example is Donna B. Hamilton and Richard Strier, eds., *Religion, Literature, and Politics in Post-Reformation England, 1540–1688* (New York: Cambridge University Press, 1996). In "Still Reading Spenser after All These Years?" *English Literary Renaissance* 25 (1995): 432–44, an essay on *Mother Hubberds Tale*, Annabel Patterson notes that "religion is back in the angle of vision in literary studies" and that the "emphasis has shifted . . . to theology as only one component of a social, political, legal and pedagogic struggle over what role religion ought to play in everyday life" (433).

2. Even so knowledgeable a commentator as Leah S. Marcus makes no mention of religion in "Renaissance/Early Modern Studies," the essay that contains her comprehensive survey of recent developments in the field; see *Redrawing the Boundaries: The Transformation of English and American Studies*, ed. Stephen Greenblatt and Giles Gunn (New York: Modern Language Association, 1992), 41–63.

3. See Richard C. Trexler, "Reverence and Profanity in the Study of Early Modern Religion," in *Religion and Society in Early Modern Europe 1500–*

1800, ed. Kaspar von Greyerz (London: George Allen & Unwin, 1984), 245–69. Trexler's essay seems to have had little impact on literary studies, but, like several essays in this volume, it greatly expands our understanding of religion as "an all-pervasive force in pre-industrial society, by far transcending the life of the church" (1).

4. Stephen J. Greenblatt, *Learning to Curse: Essays in Early Modern Culture* (New York: Routledge, 1990), 157.

5. See Richard Mallette, "From Gyves to Graces: *Hamlet* and Free Will," *JEGP* 93 (1994): 336–55.

6. See Kaufman, *Prayer, Despair, and Drama*, 1, 8–9, 160. See also Shuger, *The Renaissance Bible*, 112–13, on the differences between Calvinist and earlier "conceptualizations of ideal selfhood."

7. See Zim, "The Reformation." Zim's goal is to show how Reformation hermeneutics overlaps with "the assumptions and practices of contemporary writers" (66). She is especially provocative in detailing how methods of reading the Bible "testify to the regeneration of the religious bases of English culture" in the sixteenth century (97).

8. See John R. Knott, *Discourses of Martyrdom in English Literature, 1563–1694* (Cambridge: Cambridge University Press, 1993). Knott's investigation of martyrdom is especially fertile when he reevaluates Milton's conception of heroism (see 151–78).

9. A notable exception is John R. Knott, *The Sword of the Spirit: Puritan Responses to the Bible* (Chicago: University of Chicago Press, 1980); see esp. 42–61 for Puritan attitudes toward preaching in the early seventeenth century.

10. The best summaries remain those by Obermann in "Preaching and the Word," and the introductory essays by Bond in his edition of *The Book of Homilies*, 3–38.

11. See John D. Bernard, "Contemplation," in *The Spenser Encyclopedia*, 190–91. Bernard shows how the portrait of Contemplation "also receives support from medieval and Renaissance literary theory" that associated the contemplative life with various genres and conventions.

12. In "Mammon," Prescott assembles a collage of scriptural echoes that Mammon employs as well as glosses and commentary, some from Reformation sermon discourse, on those echoes.

13. Glauce's urging Britomart to practice sexual repression mimes the "Homilie of Whoredome and Unclennesse" in *The Book of Homilies*; her taking the heroine to church for a kind of projected nuptial forecasts the marriage service from *The Book of Common Prayer*. These homiletic dis-

courses direct other discourses in the episode, including that of its "source," the pseudo-Virgilian *Ciris*, and the convention of the classical and medieval nurse-confidant (neither notable for emphasizing chastity).

14. In the portrait of the Hermit converge a variety of conventions and discourses that his homily helps to color: the Roman rhetorical-philosophical ideal of early retirement, medieval contemplative asceticism, the chivalric romance figure of the retired knight and counselor, and the Ariostan and Elizabethan hermit. John D. Bernard, "hermits," in *The Spenser Encyclopedia*, sees the Hermit as combining "worldly wisdom with a genuine religiosity" (360), but it seems to me Spenser's text emphasizes worldly wisdom, a trait Bernard implicitly attributes to the new "secular-philosophical hermit" of Elizabethan lore.

15. Greene, *The Light in Troy*, 31.

16. Two examples will suffice. Richard Helgerson, *Self-Crowned Laureates: Spenser, Jonson, and the Literary System* (Berkeley and Los Angeles: University of California Press, 1983): "the optimistic faith that had animated the early books, the faith that history was going the right way, seems to have left Spenser in the 1590s" (91); and Gary Waller, *Edmund Spenser: A Literary Life* (London: Macmillan, 1994): "by 1596 . . . the original design for the poem had been seriously compromised. . . . Spenser himself is acutely aware that something has gone dreadfully awry" (137). But see Gless, *Theology and Interpretation*, for a response that relies less on speculating about the author's intentions: "in Books II–VI, interpreters inclined toward providential optimism must work harder to sustain their version of the poem and the world it claims to mirror" (177).

17. Gless, *Theology and Interpretation*, 197. But Gless later seems to undermine his argument: "Interpreters inclined to notice the frequent moments when theological ideas appear to be invoked but also to collide with material native to other genres and discourses, however, will need to perform their . . . tasks of selection and projection with great energy if they are to achieve comparably optimistic constructions" (199). It is exactly at the "collisions" that we can see the poem most characteristically at work, where it is the most challenging and where it articulates its most beguiling, unresolved contradictions.

18. C. John Sommerville, *The Secularization of Early Modern England: From Religious Culture to Religious Faith* (New York: Oxford University Press, 1992), 8; see also 3–17, 44–54. This process is traced in ecclesiology in Claire Cross, *Church and People 1450–1660: The Triumph of the Laity in the English Church* (Atlantic Highlands NJ: Humanities Press, 1976), esp. 153–74.

19. Collinson, *The Birthpangs of Protestant England*, 98. Collinson's point is confirmed by Paul Whitfield White in *Theatre and Reformation: Protestantism, Patronage, and Playing in Tudor England* (Cambridge: Cambridge University Press, 1993). White sees an end in 1580 to the alliance between the drama and "Protestant publicists" (163).

20. Sommerville, *The Secularization of Early Modern England*, 8.

21. Ernst Cassirer, "Some Remarks on the Question of the Originality of the Renaissance," *Journal of the History of Ideas* 4 (1943): 55; cited in Greene, *The Light in Troy*, 28.

Index

126–30, 132–34, 138, 139; and Scudamour, 139; and Serena, 191–93. *See also* revenge, discourses of

Whately, William, 131
Whore of Babylon: and apocalyptic discourses, 146, 148; defeated by preaching, 41, 48–49; in Ger-

yoneo's monster, 160; in Ireland, 166; and Mary, Queen of Scots, 156–57, 158; in Mercilla episode, 154
will. *See* free will, discourses of
Wilson, Thomas, 92
witch's son, 105–6
Wright, Leonard, 155
Womanhood, 139